Wrestling with an Angel

EHUD LUZ

Wrestling with an Angel

POWER, MORALITY, AND
JEWISH IDENTITY

Translated from the Hebrew by
Michael Swirsky

Yale University Press
New Haven &
London

Published with the assistance of
The Wolfson Chair in Jewish Thought, University of Haifa
The Amos Fund for the Encouragement of Scholars and Writers
Oranim Teacher's College, Kiryat Tiv'on
Research Authority of the University of Haifa
and with assistance from the Louis Stern Memorial Fund.

Set in Sabon type by Keystone Typesetting, Inc.
Printed in the United States of America by Sheridan Books, Ann Arbor, Michigan.

Library of Congress Cataloging-in-Publication Data
Luz, Ehud.
[Ma'avaòk be-naòhal Yaboòk. English]
Wrestling with an angel : power, morality, and Jewish identity / Ehud Luz ;
translated from the Hebrew by Michael Swirsky.
p. cm.
Includes bibliographical references (p.   ) and index.
ISBN 0-300-09293-8 (n/a : alk. paper)
1. Jews — Identity. 2. Zionism and Judaism. 3. Ethics, Jewish. 4. Power (Social
sciences) — Moral and ethical aspects. 5. Sovereignty — Moral and ethical aspects.
I. Title.
DS143.L8913 2003
296.3'6 — dc21

                                                                2003001708

A catalogue record for this book is available from the British Library.

The paper in this book meets the guidelines for permanence and durability of the
Committee on Production Guidelines for Book Longevity of the Council on
Library Resources.

10 9 8 7 6 5 4 3 2 1

That night he arose and . . . crossed the ford of the Jabbok. . . .
Jacob was left alone. And a man wrestled with him until the
break of dawn.
When he saw that he had not prevailed against him, he
wrenched Jacob's hip at its socket,
So that the socket of his hip was strained as he wrestled with
him.
Then he said, "Let me go, for dawn is breaking."
But he answered, "I will not let you go, unless you bless me."
Said the other, "What is your name?" He replied, "Jacob."
Said he, "Your name shall no longer be Jacob, but Israel,
For you have striven with beings divine and human and have
prevailed."
Genesis 32:23–30

"And a man wrestled with him" —
Rabbi Hama son of Rabbi Hanina said:
It was Esau's guardian angel.
Genesis Rabbah 77

Contents

Preface

After the Bar Kokhba revolt (132–135 CE) and the eradication of all trace of Jewish political independence in Palestine, Jews gave little thought to questions of war. Long exile freed them from the sharp moral dilemmas confronted by any polity that is compelled to use force to defend itself. Jews considered warfare to be the "craft of Esau," that is, a matter for the gentiles, at least until such time as the Messiah would come. The Jews — "Jacob" — took no interest in armed conflict except insofar as it might impinge upon their fate as a minority living under foreign rule. To be sure, Jewish literature contains more than a few ruminations about war and the morality of war, but with the exception of Maimonides' Laws of Kings, they do not coalesce into any systematic teaching, such as the doctrine of the "just war" that developed in the Christian world out of direct experience. (Ironically enough, this doctrine relied to a considerable degree on ancient Jewish sources dealing with warfare, especially the book of Deuteronomy, and then had an influence on the Jews, in turn, when they returned to Palestine.)

Zionism, the resettlement of Palestine, and political independence thus posed moral dilemmas for the Jews that for many generations they had not had to confront. They then devised new norms for the use of force, such as that of "purity of arms," but they did not begin with a clean slate. Zionist thought and literature were influenced, consciously or not, by the body of earlier Jew-

ish interpretation of the classical sources dealing with these issues. The influence of the prophetic literature on the first waves of resettlement is clear; less
clear is the influence of the halakhic (legal) tradition, which had its origins in
the world of the Sages (i.e., partly in Palestine) but developed mainly in the
Diaspora, a tradition that stressed the sanctity of human life and the strict
prohibition against the shedding of blood.

The establishment of Jewish sovereignty and a Jewish military force represented a revolution not only in the standing of the Jews among the nations, but
also in the Jews' own image of themselves, their identity. The aim of this book
is to examine the problematic of Jewish identity in the Land of Israel that has
resulted from the forging of an ethos of the use of force. I shall try to show how
the Zionists were affected by their Judaic heritage, how it shaped their attitudes toward sovereignty and their moral stance concerning the use of power.
The return to full political life and the use of military force for political ends
entailed new responsibilities and aroused deep and often painful misgivings.
Philosophically speaking, the moral problems faced by the Jewish nation were
not essentially different than those confronting other nations struggling for
their independence. But for the Jews these problems had a particular importance, the origin of which must be sought in their Jewish heritage. The moral
challenge entailed in the political life of a sovereign Jewish state appears to me
to be one of the most critical and troubling ones faced by Judaism in our time.

This book is not a strictly historical or philosophical one but rather an
interdisciplinary inquiry incorporating both history and ideas. Hence it entails
intersecting planes as well as repetitions that are needed to round out the
discussion. The sources upon which I have drawn likewise belong to different
genres: historiography, philosophy, *publicité* (social commentary and ideological tracts), and belles lettres. The latter played a central role in the creation of
a Zionist ethos; writers and poets saw themselves, and were widely viewed, as
"scouts for the House of Israel" (Ezek 3:17) charged with showing the way to
the hoped-for future. It is thus impossible to separate literature from ideology
in the formative period of the Zionist movement. Not only is much of the
poetry of this period political in character, the same is true of the fiction.
Literature gave ideology a mythic dimension and was even more influential
than ideology in the actual realization of Zionist goals. What is more, Zionist
publicité, a genre that developed at a time when Jewish culture was taking on a
more secular character, generally avoided theological questions in favor of
ideological ones, leaving to fiction and poetry the task of wrestling with the
theological questions.

Most of the chapters in this book deal with ideological polemics that raged
among the various Zionist camps and between the movement as a whole and
its adversaries. Because one of my main interests here is in the rhetoric of

Zionism, I have drawn heavily on citations from the original sources in an attempt to show the intellectual and spiritual wrangling that accompanied the forging of a Zionist ethos. My criteria of selection were not historical but literary and intellectual. Therefore I sometimes cite views that were not part of the mainstream but that shed a distinctive light on the subject.

Many of the arguments presented here have been widely discussed in earlier studies of Zionism. I am greatly indebted to the works of Yosef Gorny (*Zionism and the Arabs, 1882–1948: A Study of Ideology*) and Anita Shapira (*Herev hayona*). My point of departure — an attempt to highlight the interaction, so fraught with ambivalence, between Zionism and Judaism — differs from theirs. I believe that, despite secularization, Jewish tradition continues to influence the political and social structure and national ethos of the Jews. As Sam Lehman-Wilzig and Bernard Susser noted, "something distinctively Jewish is clearly expressed in the political behavior of the Jews in their institutions everywhere and at all times" (page 7). The Jewish religious tradition is a very important, sometimes even decisive factor in the way political and cultural issues are resolved. Because I see the main thrust of Zionism as inseparably linked with the age-old Jewish tradition and as a continuation of its concerns — without denying the role of external influences, to be sure — I have tried to present this interaction against the broad backdrop of historic Jewish attitudes to power. A stimulating initial attempt at such an analysis was made by David Biale in *Power and Powerlessness in Jewish History* (1987). But whereas Biale stresses the lack of continuity in Jewish history and tradition, my basic assumption is that despite the great changes that have taken place, there are in the tradition certain fixed normative structures that find expression in the Halakha or even outside it in what I call historical experience or meta-Halakha.

This book has three parts. The first part, "A Will to Power," examines in a historical context the intellectual and spiritual factors that led to the emergence of a new ethos and self-image around Jewish aspirations to power. Although the political and military connotations of the term "power" are decisive, it has, in modern Hebrew literature, a much wider resonance. It does not refer only to the capacity to deploy physical force but also symbolizes a new morality and a new Jewish identity, fundamentally different from the traditional ones. It expresses a collective yearning for dignity and universal human recognition, to be achieved by the Jews assuming responsibility for their own fate. The term also conveys a yearning for full self-expression, spontaneity, creativity, and "earthiness" — as opposed, or in addition, to the excessive "spirituality" of Diaspora existence. In this sense, "power" is plainly a Romantic notion, akin to life itself, with its abiding capacity for renewal.

Part 2, "The Moral Price of Sovereignty," deals with controversies within the Jewish community over the general question of sovereignty and the use of force. In this section I discuss mainly thinkers who were critical of the Zionist program for the reassertion of Jewish sovereignty and the recasting of Jewish identity.

The central concern of the last part, "Power, Morality, and Identity," is the political and moral discourse that has actually been conducted in the Zionist movement, and afterwards in Israel, over the use of force. The operative concept here, in the arguments over what constitutes permissible use of force, is that of "Jewish morality." I show through examples how the various Israeli views on how to deal with violent Arab opposition to Zionism reflect, to a large extent, different Jewish self-perceptions. That is, the political positions Jews take are largely a function of the kind of Jews they want to be, which, in turn, depends on how they interpret their past. This, to take up at the end of the book.

Most of this book was written before the 1995 assassination of Israeli Prime Minister Yitzhak Rabin by a Jewish religious zealot, an event that revealed the dangers inherent in linking nationalism with messianism and sharpened the moral and existential questions raised here.

I would like to thank a number of colleagues who helped bring this book to its final form. First and foremost is Dr. Menahem Lorberbaum of Tel Aviv University, who read the manuscript carefully and called my attention to various obscurities and inconsistencies. Our conversations helped me enormously in conceptualizing and shaping this work. Professor Ze'ev Gris of Ben-Gurion University in Beersheba, a great authority on Jewish literature throughout the ages, shared his copious bibliographical knowledge with me and deepened my understanding of various issues of Israeli security. From the beginning of this project, my good friend Hayim Goldgraber gave me useful advice and alerted me to many other things being written on the subject. I am grateful to all of them. Special thanks go to Nili Landsberger, the editor of the Hebrew edition, and to Michael Swirsky, the translator, who labored far beyond the call of duty to help give form to this book and prepare it for press.

In 1995–99, the Shalom Hartman Institute in Jerusalem gave me a stipend that made it possible to prepare this book. The book was published with the help of a generous grant from Cheri and Hayim Goldgraber, from Brenda and Sammy Gewurtz, and from the Isaac Wolfson Chair of Jewish Thought at Haifa University. I am grateful to Professor Menahem Kellner, the chair's incumbent. Assistance was also provided by the Amos Fund of the Office of the President of Israel, the Arts and Letters Fund of the City of Tel Aviv, Oranim Teacher's College, and the University of Haifa. To all of them, my thanks.

Introduction

Identity and National Ethos

Nations see themselves as differing from one another in their ways of thinking, feeling, and behaving. Each has its own ethos, which it imagines to be unique. While I do not believe there is such a thing as "national character" — peoples change so drastically in the course of their histories — the notion is nonetheless not an entirely arbitrary one insofar as a people's present code of behavior bears the earmarks of a long-established cultural heritage. To use Schelling's well-known formulation, a nation's mythology is its fate. In this sense, and not deterministically, the history of a people reveals its character in a dynamic way, in an interplay of stimulus and response. A national tradition is shaped in part by challenges from without, but the way they are met is also a function of the tradition within. We can never say exactly how much a given historical process is determined by external as opposed to internal forces, but it is fair to assume that if peoples differ from one another in the way they respond to similar historical circumstances, it is cultural differences that are largely responsible. I hope to clarify this point with reference to the concept of "national ethos" to which I return throughout the book.

In his book *The Philosophy of Right,* Hegel calls into question the Kantian notion of moral obligation. In Kant's view, what motivates moral behavior is respect for the universal law of reason. Hegel sees this idea of Kant's as based on what ought to be (*sollen*), without any connection to natural reality, to what is (*sein*). Kantian morality, which Hegel calls *Moralität*, is general, abstract, rational morality that applies only to the individual and does not take into account all those human relationships, such as the bonds of love, family, and community, that are not subject to universal laws. Hegel tries to fuse the "ought" and the "is" in a single conception, *Sittlichkeit,* which includes these natural human ties because he sees human feelings as an essential basis for the moral life. In each country, this basis of sentiment is given shape and rational expression by the law.

For Hegel, *Sittlichkeit* is superior to Kant's abstract *Moralität* because it is a concrete ethic, derived from the real world and given expression in the social and political institutions that make up that world. Hegel takes into account the concrete moral obligations of the individual to the community of which he is a member. These obligations are based on established norms and practices, which, if the community is to survive, the individual must regard as serving his own interests. Whereas *Sittlichkeit* in effect obligates us to realize that which already exists, *Moralität* obligates us to realize that which does not yet exist. In the latter case, it is not communal belonging but reason that produces in the individual a sense of obligation.[1] There is thus a connection between *Sittlichkeit* and national or cultural identity. The individual is what he is by virtue of his membership in the community. When individual and collective identity are the same, the individual derives the moral meaning of his life from that of the community, which by its very nature is shaped by a shared history and cultural tradition.

The importance of shared cultural traditions in shaping the moral life of communities was pointed out by the historian Alexis de Tocqueville (1800–1859). In *Democracy in America,* he refers to the role of "mores" in American life. This term, from which we get the words "morality" and "moral," refers "not only to '*moeurs*' in the strict sense, which might be called the habits of the heart, but also to the different notions possessed by men, the various opinions current among them, and the sum of ideas that shape their mental habits."[2] De Tocqueville maintains that these "habits of the heart" or "mores," grounded in both biblical and republican traditions, have played a decisive role in shaping the American democratic ethos, particularly as a counterweight to individualism. They educate the citizen to a view of the world that is broader than his own self-interest, or rather to a view that identifies the general good with his own. Hegel and de Tocqueville help us to understand the meaning of collective morality. All national cultures espouse similar basic human values. Cultures differ in how these values are ranked in importance, how they are interpreted in law and everyday life, how they are translated into specifics, and what symbolism is used to clothe them. In short, what divides them is the mores from which members of the community derive their moral awareness and sensitivity. It is not necessarily the norms themselves that distinguish one nation from another but rather the way that the norms are articulated and institutionalized. Thus, as I shall try to show, moral judgment in any given society is not based only on abstractions but also on a distinctive tradition that rationalizes morality in reference to particular collective memories.

Particularistic communities provide a necessary grounding for individual moral development in that the bonds of loyalty that these communities foster among their members are an important source of motivation for moral behavior.[3] For most people, universal morality is not sufficient for this purpose, nor is it capable of overriding narrower loyalties. For Niebuhr, "no rational moral idealism can [by itself] create moral conduct. It can provide principles of criticism and reasons; but such norms do not contain a dynamic for their realization. . . . Rationalism not only suppresses the emotional supports of moral action unduly, but it has failed dismally in encouraging men toward the realization of the ideals which it has projected."[4] Social morality thus needs the support of forces arising from religion, tradition, and history.

Loyalty alone is an insufficient gauge of moral behavior; it must be combined with other attributes. Hermann Cohen distinguishes between primary and secondary moral virtues. Primary virtues, such as justice, relate to the generality of mankind and consequently are absolute. Secondary virtues, on the other hand, have to do with more limited ties and are thus relative. What motivates primary virtues is thought, whereas what motivates secondary ones is love. Love of others is a clear example of secondary virtues, for it relates to particular people.[5] According to Cohen, the secondary virtues provide the underpinnings of the primary ones. "Love" promotes "thought." Loyalty is a secondary virtue, but it strengthens all relationships, be they between man and man or between man and God.[6] Social morality thus depends on loyalty. Loyalty gives rise to covenantal relationships and intimate partnerships, which in turn supply the motivation for self-sacrifice and reaching out to others. In this way, loyalty undergirds moral behavior in a way that goes beyond the Kantian notion of obligation without, however, contradicting it.

Narrative and Moral Discourse

A nation is, in Robert Bellah's words, "a community of memory," that is, a community that cherishes texts, stories, and "habits of the heart" that become the basis of its mores.[7] Philosophers such as Alasdair MacIntyre, Michael Walzer, and Paul Ricoeur have stressed the link between narrative and morality.[8] We understand our lives as stories being acted out. Every morally significant act is in a sense part of the story, be it the personal, autobiographical or the collective, historical one. The integrity of the self, or what is called personal identity, presumes the integrity and continuity of the narrative in the framework of which our moral acts gain meaning. Similarly, the question of what is good for the individual can be understood only in the context of the integrity and continuity of the narrative: what is the best way for him to live out and perfect his selfhood? The story that constitutes personal identity includes not only the past but also the future, one's purposes and expectations. In this sense, there is also a utopian element in our identities, and it too must fit into the story we tell.

Our personal narratives form part of the narrative of the community in which we live. We learn to function in society and to respond to the way others treat us as we come to understand them through the stories we have heard. We cannot understand any society, including our own, except through the stories that constitute its primary dramatic sources. The telling of these stories is a crucial part of our moral education as members of society. The narrative is what motivates us to support the social institutions and practices in which universal values are concretized.

There is thus a deep affinity between historical or mythical consciousness and the world of human values. Such consciousness expresses itself in the affirmation of values. By the same token, the *transmission* of values from one generation to the next is not accomplished by rational or scientific means but through narrative. Reason alone is not enough to mold the life of a people. "History understood as pure science," Nietzsche says, "history denuded of sentiment, will mean for humanity a rejection of life and a rendering of accounts."[9] Myth is a part of all notions of meaningful history.[10] The distinction historians draw between objective history and memory (or myth) is valid in scientific discourse but not in life. Myth, that is to say collective memory, continues to operate in the modern understanding of history, and it is this that makes a sense of historical time possible. Any moral critique of a community must rely on a new, creative interpretation of its cultural tradition if the critique is to relate to the day-to-day experience of the community. Tradition is an essential ingredient in the moral discourse of any historical community. Divisive moral questions can only be resolved amicably on the basis of a tradition shared by the society as a whole. A people's moral accounting must include, among other things, a response to the question of whether its actions and decisions are congruent with its historical tradition and consistent with its distinctive narrative. This test is crucial for the maintenance of group identity.

In this sense, prophecy is a model of moral social criticism. The Prophets did not pretend to have discovered the moral principles they preached but rather always based them on epic history and the moral teachings of the Torah. They grounded their claim to truth in the Covenant that had been made in history with this particular people. Their utopian social vision was addressed first and foremost to the historical people that had been charged with its realization. They did not merely refer to history but reinterpreted it in accord with what seemed to them the fundamental values of the tradition, and it was on this basis that they called on the people to repent.[11]

Liberal rationalism, of which Habermas is a leading spokesman, maintains that only universal standards, oblivious to particular traditions, can enable us to criticize our own communities objectively, but he admits that such standards are not sufficient or effective when it comes to influence on society. "The principles of democracy based on the rule of law can be realized only if they can strike root in accordance with the varied political cultures of the peoples striving for a post-national existence. . . . The universal content must undergo a process of integration linked to the distinct historical life of each people and to its cultural forms."[12] To be effective, a critique must deepen and purify the particular tradition, releasing the universal elements — of solidarity with humankind and the truth of human existence — that are buried within it. If society is understood in the accepted liberal fashion, as a provider of services to and protection of the individual, there is no room in the moral argument for a particularistic ethos or historical identity. Rather, the argument must be conducted on purely rational, instrumental grounds, i.e., in accordance with *Moralität*. Only in a society that does not regard itself as bound together merely by interests or mutual advantage but also by a common history and culture can moral claims relying on *Sittlichkeit* be made.

Criticism of tradition is itself part of tradition even when the immediate stimulus comes from without. The regnant norms in a given society are never static; they are always open to challenge by new moral situations. When the new situation and the old norms are in conflict, a need for fresh thinking about the tradition arises. Here an underlying principle of solidarity is assumed, making it possible to rationalize and justify traditional norms. The task of the new thinking is to resolve the incongruity by invoking the metaethical (or metahalakhic) dimension inherent in the tradition or by referring to a different tradition than the one currently dominant. Resolving the incongruity means extending the solidarity on which the tradition rests into relations between individuals within the society or in relation to other societies. In this way we can also solve the problem of choosing among the conflicting claims of the same tradition. Such choices are not just arbitrary or subjective but anchored in rational, intersubjective criteria.[13] In short, authentic social criticism draws its rationale from two sources between which it strives to create a balance: the

ahistorical principle of universal human solidarity and equality and the historical principle of the conservation and development of tradition.

The Postmodernist Critique

The notion of criticism presented here is largely opposed to that most
widely espoused today in the humanities and social sciences. Many sociologists, historians, and literary critics, influenced by the Frankfurt School, on
one hand, and poststructuralism and deconstructionism, on the other, take it
for granted that society, politics, and culture are all subject to a hidden mechanism of repression. In this view, all knowledge is "ideological" and is used by
ruling elites to dominate minorities or lower classes. The task of intellectuals
then becomes that of sowing suspicion by pointing to these "empirical facts."
Indeed, the social sciences are engaged today in what Nietzsche called "the art
of suspicion": drawing upon Nietzsche, Marx, and Freud, they are looking for
the historical, sociological, or psychological bases of all human ideas and
values. We are called upon to suspect any kind of expression except the axiom
that all expression is suspect. It is a reductionism that claims to be scientific
and to operate in the service of freedom and equality, particularly in regard to
oppressed minorities.

In effect, it was this phenomenon that Martin Buber characterized fifty
years ago as a "demonic" attempt, unique to our time, "to expose and dis-
credit the realm of humanistic expression as a combination of fraud and illusion, 'ideology' and 'sublimation,' " the result of which would be a complete
relativization of all values and ideas.[14] It is not merely a suspicion that "the
other" is deliberately dissembling, but a conviction that he cannot act otherwise, that the discrepancy between his heart and his mouth, his words and his
actions, is not voluntary but an ingrained, inescapable necessity. If a man
comes and tells me what he thinks about a particular matter, I pay no attention
to what he says, nor do I grant it any importance as contributing to my
knowledge of the subject; what I mainly hear is what prompts him to say what
he says, his unconscious motivation, his "complex."[15]

In Buber's view, this suspiciousness makes it impossible for people to listen
to one another; instead of heeding what the other person is saying and what
concerns him, we are mainly interested in "examining his heart and probing
his soul," in stripping the mask from his face. Buber did not mean to deny the
legitimacy of what was called "the criticism of ideology," but he thought
science had an obligation to recognize its own limits. As a "postmodern"
thinker — the term had not yet been invented — who no longer had an innocent
faith in the omnipotence of reason and science, Buber called for a "criticism of

criticism" that would set bounds to scientific analysis, for such analysis could never take in the whole human reality.

Undeniably, postmodern criticism has, in varying degrees, made us more sensitive to "the other," he whose voice is not heard in the dominant culture. But such sensitivity sometimes comes at the cost of a loss of identity on the part of the thinking, speaking subject. For according to this school of thought, subjective identity is always questionable; in fact, it is merely a linguistic fiction with no reality behind it. Not only is the self fragmented and unstable; every concept has a privileged meaning, which derives from ideology or serves as a focus around which other meanings must array themselves. Personal identity is defined in contradistinction to and by negation of "the other." (For example, men are defined as not being women, Israeli Jews as not being Palestinian Arabs.) "The other" is always perceived through the distorting lens of prejudices deeply rooted in our particular culture, and as Foucault, for one, maintains, his image reflects our will to power. "The other" is not just he who differs from me; I see him as the one I am not and thus as a constant reminder of who I am. Hence the dialectical relationship between us. I am in need of him, even as I negate him, exclude him, and subjugate him. "The other" is always the one oppressed. In short, we live in a society and a culture that are completely controlled by oppressive politics. The impression we get from Foucault is that "power" is not a neutral term; although it can serve positive ends, in itself it is something negative. Yet Foucault does not suggest any real alternative to the use of it.[16]

The theoretical basis of the negation of identity suggests a new understanding of the role of language and hermeneutics. According to this understanding, one of the functions of ideology is to make the social reality seem natural, innocent, and unchanging. Ideology turns culture into "nature," and one of its weapons is the "sign," the meaning of which is ostensibly fixed rather than subject to redefinition by one or another system of signification. This view helps bourgeois capitalism perpetuate itself. Thus do we arrive at the need to "deconstruct" both the notion of the "subject," which has been presented as something fixed, and the notion of personal identity, which flows from it. Identity, both personal and national, is an arbitrary construction, the result of ideology and a desire to either dominate "the other" or reject him. And since the identity of every self-aware human subject is signified by a narrative — every self lives out the story it spins, be it in word or deed — the end result is that the narrative is emptied of value.[17] It is, of course, not a great leap from this to the delegitimation of the nation and of collective historical and cultural residues. It is assumed that there is no room for the collective memory that shapes a particular community but only for a multiplicity of narratives with nothing in common but the fact that they are narratives, hence merely relative. It is argued that this view works to reduce conflict in human society and create more harmonious human relations.

Deconstructionism is the most radical outgrowth of modern historicism. It seeks to instill a thoroughgoing awareness of one's own historicity and the changeability of reality. But toward what goal, then, should one aspire, and what needs to change along the way? Here deconstructionism proves itself a double-edged sword, for if no ideal or slogan — freedom or equality, for example — is to be trusted, it is not clear what criteria are to be used to make choices. Consequently, we find ourselves mired in an unending debate about the oppressiveness of all human discourse with no clear guidelines for taking meaningful collective action. So no decisions are made, and the total negation of all ideas and meanings leads ultimately to a vacuum, to "discourse about discourse."[18]

Myth, Identity, and Interpretation

As I have said, collective memory constitutes an essential basis for national identity and the sense of commonality. Criticism of the national narrative, by pointing out its limits and exposing its subjective relativity, undermines trust in the narrative's integrity and thus also the nation's secure sense of itself. Eventually, memory can become individualized altogether, leading, as Pierre Nora has pointed out, to the complete disintegration of the collective: "When it shed its identification with the nation, it lost its subjective force as well as its pedagogic mission, the transmission of values."[19] A society that loses its collective memory can easily lose the sense of solidarity that binds its members together as well.

In his book *The Use and Abuse of History,* Nietzsche discusses the ambiguity of "critical history." For him, we must destroy the past from time to time if we are to live. This is the task of critical history: it passes judgment on the past and eventually convicts it. But this process is fraught with danger, for it is always hard to set limits to the negation of the past, and as a rule, the new identity that we seek for ourselves is weaker than the one we rejected. As opposed to those who favored exploding all myths without reservation, as a sign of society's maturity, Nietzsche saw the destruction of myth as impeding social maturation. Overscrutinized by historical research, a given epoch can begin to fancy itself "singularly favored with a greater sense of justice than any other era." In this way, the people's natural impulses are weakened and the maturation of both the individual and the collective is retarded. A dangerous spirit of ironical detachment and cynicism comes to pervade society, leading to "a selfishness and shrewd practicality that paralyze its positive forces" and in the end destroy them. "The young become deracinated and doubtful of every custom and notion." The reason is that to believe in perfection and rectitude, every "living person," in Nietzsche's phrase, needs to be enveloped in mystery. Historical inquiry into the events of the past shows them to be so filled with fraud, inhumanity, violence, and absurdity that the path of illusion, which alone can enable the will to live to flourish, is necessarily ground down to nothing. Historical judgments, however proper and sincere, can be destructive in the absence of constructive purpose. Only he who would build for the future is entitled to judge the past.[20]

The moral ambiguity of radical social criticism is discussed by Reinhold Niebuhr as well. For him, such ambiguity is inherent in the very existence of the nation. The claim made by the latter to unlimited moral value is what gives it a "demonic" character. But such a claim could not be made if the collectivity did not proffer such values as justice, peace, and order to begin with. The almost religious awe in which people everywhere hold the ruling power derives in part from the fact that the latter represents these values. There is a religious element in all patriotism and political loyalty, as we see in modern "civil religion." How a regime can be criticized without impairing its moral stature is not a simple question. Although cynical realism can serve as an antibody against uncritical acceptance of the established order, it is unfortunately easier to tear down than to build. Unbridled criticism can thus lead to anomie and anarchy.[21]

Criticism of the national narrative can play a constructive role to the extent that it exposes contradictions within the collective identity and places the latter on a subtler, more authentic footing.[22] But such criticism becomes excessive when it negates national identity altogether. In Amos Funkenstein's words, "identity is both given and created, pre-existing and still coming into existence."[23] Any attempt to deny the reality of such identity is, in his view, a deception, for it undermines the discussion and contradicts our most basic experience. "There is no escaping the subject, either in epistemology, in history or in life." And since the narrative embodies the identity of the subject, we cannot do without it.

The decisive importance of the way tradition and myth are interpreted by national movements has been elaborated by Uriel Tal. Interpretation becomes more and more central to such movements "when there is freedom to interpret basic assumptions in a variety of ways." Myth, which is the soul of the nation, is not unambiguous. Every one of its applications, especially in the social and political realm, is pregnant with both positive and negative possibilities. It can give rise to racism and dictatorship and take on a demonic, destructive character, but it can also be humane and liberal.[24] Indeed, there is a tremendous gulf between Buber's humane, ethical understanding of the Jewish messianic myth and the chauvinistic, nationalistic interpretation given it by the poet Uri Tzvi Greenberg.

Nationality and Liberalism

Sociologists and political scientists distinguish two main types of states in terms of the relations between state and nation and between state and individual: in the *liberal-universal* model the state gives rise to the nation, while in the *cultural-historical* model it is the other way around. In the liberal model, nationality is identical with citizenship. The state is understood primarily in functional terms, as a framework intended to protect the rights of individuals and provide them with certain services on an equal footing. The individual is regarded simply as a citizen, an autonomous person subject to universal laws that apply equally to all, rather than as a member of a particular cultural grouping. The state itself is absolutely indifferent to the ethnic or religious affiliations of its citizens and does not interfere in these realms. More-over, it intentionally avoids any public expression of cultural particularity. "Civic religion," in this model, is a purely political religion, stripped of any particularistic trappings.[25]

In the cultural-historical model, the state is understood primarily as a framework for the expression of the distinctive culture of the nation. Hence, this model has a mainly communal rather than civic character. The individual is understood not as a completely autonomous entity but as part of a collective with a particular cultural identity. The state is meant to protect the rights of individuals but, more than this, to symbolize in its institutions the shared cultural identity of the majority of its inhabitants.

Although a purely liberal or "neutral" state, stripped of all cultural identification, is theoretically possible, there are, in fact, no examples of such states in all of history. Virtually all democracies are a mixture of the two types, with the regime in each case reflecting the particular ethnic composition of the majority of the public. Such states have shared symbols and rituals in which it is hard to distinguish the civic from the ethnic or even religious elements. Nevertheless, these states are regarded as liberal and open.[26]

Israel is closer to the second, communal type. It came into being primarily to ensure the survival of the Jewish people and to give public, institutional expression to its historic cultural identity. Nevertheless, a struggle is being waged in this country between partisans of the two opposing conceptions of the state, a struggle that is among the liveliest in Israeli political life. Most of the Jewish public sees the state as playing an important role in its own Jewish identity. But there are other, relatively small circles for whom "Jewishness per se is secondary and marginal." While it is seen as having a symbolic value in the life of the state, "its influence on public policy must be neutralized."[27] This viewpoint, which has been dubbed "Post-Zionist," negates the Jewish and Zionist character of the state and seeks to give it a purely civil, inclusive character. It sees an insoluble contradiction between a democratic state, seeking peace with its neighbors and promising full equality to its citizens, and a Jewish and Zionist state, which cannot help but oppress its ethnic and religious minorities and can never extricate itself from the conflict with its Palestinian neighbors. Political liberalism and political nationalism, in this view, are incompatible. What is more, the two entail diametrically opposed moralities, the one humane, the other self-serving. That nationalism, too, can have its humane side is overlooked. What we have here is a narrow, simplistic view of both nationalism and liberalism and hence also of justice and the legitimate exercise of power.

In her book *Liberal Nationalism,* Yael Tamir argues that not only is there no necessary contradiction between national and universal human solidarity, but the moral character of the particular community to which we belong is a condition for the development of our sense of universal justice. Ethnicity fosters individual development, self-expression, and fulfillment. Without the social and cultural context in which we live, we could not achieve autonomy, the capacity to make choices, or the faculty of criticism. The sense of justice, which is at the heart of liberal nationalism, is not only no more selfish than its liberal counterpart; it is even more consistent and humane in that it recognizes the importance of the national framework for individual self-realization. Because voluntary social bonds entail mutual responsibilities and obligations, they can sharpen our moral sense and thus facilitate commitment to universal justice more readily than does a liberal individualism — provided these social bonds do not degenerate into racism or ethnocentrism.[28] To be sure, "the morality of community is not meant to replace liberal morality, and ties of membership are obviously not the exclusive source of moral duties. Rather, it is argued that both these approaches, in a puzzling entanglement, shape our thinking on moral issues."[29]

The right to belong to a nation and to give public expression to this belonging is essential to being human. It is not alongside the rights of the individual; it is one of those rights. The individual's happiness depends not only on his enjoyment of equality before the law but also on his belonging to a particular group with a shared way of life. Liberal nationalism fosters collective ideals without losing sight of other human values, which must be taken into consideration as well. Even as it recognizes the public expression of the particular, it ensures the universal.[30] The concept of justice that legitimates exercise of power is one that recognizes the moral claims of nationality and the human rights it entails.

Zionism and the Jewish Historical Myth

One encounters the notion among various critics, particularly the Marxists, that national movements invent traditions to be manipulated by elites seeking dominance over the masses.[31] Without getting into a general discussion of this sweeping charge, it can be said that, at least in the case of Zionism, it is not accurate. The latter did not invent a national tradition for the sake of manipulation but rather reinterpreted an existing tradition as a source of continuity in the collective life. This is not to say that the tradition was not, at times, used in a manipulative way by certain people and institutions under particular circumstances. But manipulation was never the main motive for the reinterpretation of tradition; rather it was the desire of the Jews themselves to remain faithful to their roots under changing conditions. In other words, the tradition had remained in some sense normative for them, and they only disagreed as to how best to carry it on. No community can enjoy continuity without an unbroken collective memory and sense of historical connectedness that is expressed in the faith of its members as they fulfill in one way or another the expectations of the preceding generations and of the tradition itself. By "historical connectedness" I mean a sense of past events as continuing into the present and future, with an attendant sense of shared responsibility for what has gone before and what is yet to come. Such awareness is, as I have said, the very basis of collective identity, which is defined primarily by a distinctive concept of time.

As Edward Shils maintains, a tradition can undergo considerable change without being perceived by its adherents as having changed at all. The sense of continuity does not require an objective lack of change from generation to generation. What is essential is a feeling of solidarity and fraternity among the generations, which is fostered by a store of common images and memories.[32] There is a difference between the objective perception of an outside observer and the perception from within that is based on deep identification with the chain of transmitters and recipients of the tradition. The perpetuation of a tradition, whatever changes it undergoes, depends primarily on the existence of a desire to perpetuate it as something of value. From this derives the importance of memory and loyalty as motivating factors.

Thus, however significant Herzl's well-known declaration may have been in the historical situation in which he made it, the Jews did not have to wait for

Herzl to tell them what the author of the Book of Esther had already known, that despite being "scattered and divided," they were "one people." They saw themselves as having been a people since the dawn of history, and so were they perceived by their neighbors in the lands of their dispersion, a people with a common memory nurtured by shared texts, symbols, images, laws, and juridical institutions. The statement "all Jews are guarantors for one another" was not just an aphorism but rather an imperative meant to be realized in day-to-day life. It would not be far-fetched to say that Jewish history, especially of the biblical period, served as a model for the other peoples of Europe at a time when their national identities were crystallizing. Thus the modern idea of nationality, which captured the hearts of Jews under the influence of European nationalism, was not just a foreign implant or sign of assimilation but the result of a dialectic of mutual influence and borrowing, as the historian Jacob Talmon has pointed out: "It is true that the Jews imitated the gentiles, but prior to this the gentiles had imitated the Jews. It was under the influence of Judaism that the peoples of Europe became, in the Middle Ages, confraternities of believers, and their transformation into nations in the modern era was also furthered by what they had learned from Judaism."[33] And although the idea of the sovereign state did not arise until the sixteenth century, there is no doubt that already in the biblical view the Torah was meant to be realized by an independent people living in its own homeland rather than by "a scattered and divided people" living in exile. To ignore this is to ignore one of the fundamentals of Jewish consciousness down through history to modern times, a belief that contributed to the Jewish national reawakening, whose main impetus was European nationalism.

Zionism was a revolutionary movement with a secular orientation. It was thus natural for it to draw upon concepts like sovereignty, national honor, and historic right that were an outgrowth of the secular spirit of the age. Indeed, the influence of non-Jewish literary and philosophical sources upon Zionist thinking is clear and well known. Less evident is the process by which traditional Jewish notions, such as "the remnant of Israel," redemption, election, and messianism, acquired a different meaning and a different place in the life of the people as a result of these external influences. The surrounding culture cast a new light on these ideas, giving them a new lease on life and allowing the collective consciousness to change without losing a sense of continuity with the past.

The incorporation of ideas, images, and symbols from without, particularly where there already exists a well-developed sense of self, is never merely a passive process. Cultural adaptation entails mutuality between the one doing the absorbing and that which is being absorbed. The Maskilim (proponents of the Jewish Enlightenment) approached non-Jewish (Russian, German, etc.) literature differently from the way non-Jews did, reading it through their distinctive Jewish perspective.[34]

The philosopher Hans Gadamer has referred to this process as the "fusing of horizons": the personal and historical horizons of the exegete merge with the horizon of the text he is interpreting. The text is not to be understood as an object independent of us but only in relation to our concrete present, that is, as it applies to the concrete situation of the exegete, which, in turn, is always a "historical" situation, the product of a specific tradition. Every such application implies mutual transformation. The consciousness of the exegete is changed by the way he understands the text, but the text, too, is changed in accordance with the way the exegete, following his own lights, applies it. Historical understanding means the creation of a horizon shared by the exegete and the text. This act does not stand outside tradition but is an integral part of it, for as a result of the text's application to the concrete situation, tradition is advanced and passed on to the next generation.[35]

For many generations, the Jewish people saw itself through the mythical imagery of scripture. The present was understood on the basis of a midrashic interpretation of this imagery. Martin Buber describes the Jewish people as a "community of memory," memory arising from scripture and "proceeding from generation to generation," "its scope ever widening." Buber characterizes this memory as "organic" because it is embedded in the totality of the people's experience and serves as the basis of a sense of solidarity encompassing all the generations: "With their bodies and souls, the children remember what happened to their parents and grandparents." Buber explains that this memory does not develop of its own accord but as the result of "a desire to transmit, which seizes all of us the moment we become parents."[36] Indeed, Jewish culture is characterized by, among other things, a conscious, unceasing effort to sustain a sense of continuity in the face of change. In this culture, turning to the past is not just a matter of nostalgia but, as Franz Rosenzweig put it, of vital necessity: "Gathering up those essentials that have been left behind is a constant life necessity and not merely an occasional historical need."[37] This is reflected in the character of the Hebrew language, which is made up of layers from all the historical periods. Ancient texts like the Bible and Talmud had, and still have, an importance for Jews that is unparalleled in other cultures.

Beginning with the Haskala, the midrashic approach to the scriptures was gradually abandoned and with it the traditional answers to the question of the meaning of Jewish existence. The place of Midrash was taken by scientific, historical understanding as the code by which Jewish thinkers unlocked the riddle of Jewish existence and laid out a future path for the Jewish people. As a result of this change, various elements that had been central to traditional Jewish self-understanding were expunged from awareness or pushed aside. Yet the ancient myth did not lose its influence entirely, and the appearance of Zionism provided a powerful stimulus to its revival because it gave present meaning to the primordial events. Although Zionism borrowed heavily from the other social and cultural movements of the age, its motive force came from the ancient biblical myth.

Zionist historical thinking relies upon the biblical language of destruction, exile, and redemption, which had been at the heart of Jewish thought all through the ages. This perhaps explains the ideological fervor with which the various factions in the Zionist movement employed traditional semantics to arouse their followers to action. All alike felt driven by the threat of demise and the burning desire for redemption, however divided they may have been in the operative conclusions they drew.

The revival of the Hebrew language released tremendous reservoirs of pent-up energy. As Gershom Scholem puts it, the "apocalyptic sting" of Hebrew words gave them an explosive force that no amount of secularization could eliminate, for they had a life of their own.[38] This vocabulary, so integral to the language, continues, with or without our being aware of it, to shape the self-image of Hebrew-speaking people even when they see themselves as rebelling against the tradition, which the language represents. The Hebrew language, laden with traditional symbols and images that could now be reinterpreted in the spirit of the age, provided a bridge between past and future. The language thus provided the pioneers, most of them from traditional homes, with a sense of historical continuity despite the radical turn their lives had taken. Yitzhak Elazari-Vulcani (Wilkansky), one of the famous publicists of the Second Al-iyah, wrote:"No man can choose the elements that make up his soul, nor does he rule over it; . . . we are a link in the chain of the generations. . . . We can inscribe new tablets, but they will always give off the sparkle of the old ones — always, however hard we may strive to extinguish it. We can create a new morality, . . . but we cannot free ourselves of the manner of creation, the mode of expression, or the pattern in which the material is shaped. The 'what' may differ from that of our forefathers, but as regards the 'how,' we shall always be subtly impelled to follow in their footsteps."[39] And, indeed, the new ethos "created" by Zionism did show a pattern of influence by the legacy of ages past. The main concern of this book is to examine that pattern, with particular regard to the Zionist ethos of power.

PART I

The Will to Power

Power, Freedom, and Political Independence in Jewish Thought

"The Kingdom of Heaven" and "the Kingdom of Flesh and Blood"

Orthodox and non-Orthodox scholars disagree about Judaism's attitude toward the creation of a Jewish state. There are those who minimize the importance of political independence in the Judaic scheme of values, while others see it as central, indeed, as a prerequisite for the fulfillment of the Torah.[1] The historian Simon Dubnow regarded the ancient Jewish commonwealth as merely a passing phase in the historical development of the Jewish people.[2] Heinrich Graetz, on the other hand, in his early work *The Structure of Jewish History*, maintains that "the religious and the political are twin axes on which Jewish life turns," and "Judaism without the solid ground of a state under its feet is like a hollow, half-uprooted tree, sprouting leaves at the top but no longer able to produce branches."[3] Martin Buber shows that the idea of the "kingdom of heaven," central to biblical literature, is based on the belief that religion and politics are inseparable: "The absolute claims of God's kingdom are recognized when the people itself declares the Lord to be its king . . . and the Lord accepts kingship. It is not enough for Him to be 'God' only in the conventional religious sense; He is unwilling to yield to man all that is 'not God,'[4] the domain of secular life: it is precisely this domain that He demands and takes."[5] The "kingdom of heaven" is a theocratic idea establishing God as the Jewish people's sole ruler (sovereign), and it is He who from time to time designates representatives to carry out His will among the people. Although this idea requires the people's independence, it rules out sovereignty in the secular, modern sense.[6]

The stand taken by the sacred texts themselves on this question is ambiguous. In any event, they offer no proof that Judaism ever gave up the idea of statehood. The Torah addresses the Jews as a nation, not as individuals, and although it is possible to fulfill the Commandments under conditions of subjection to foreign rule, independence is the preferred condition. During the First Temple period and at certain times during the late Second Temple period (that of the Hasmoneans and that of the Roman conquest), the dominant view was that political independence was important as a matter of principle. As early as the end of the first century BCE, the Zealots, under Greek and Roman influence, took up "liberty" as a religio-political ideal, and the followers of Bar Kokhba later espoused it as well. But since the Jews were a subject people, the idea was somewhat different from its Greco-Roman antecedent: not a consciousness natural to a free people or a thing to be defended against attack, but a matter of liberation. The Jews were "chronologically, the first people who, politically subjugated, developed an ideology of liberation." This ideology was to have great influence upon Western history in medieval and modern times.[7]

The primary meaning of "liberty" for late-first-century Jews was, then, a political one. Josephus describes the Zealots as loving freedom and regarding God alone as their ruler.[8] Tannaitic literature is pervaded by the view that the Jewish people cannot be subject to the kingdom of heaven and a kingdom of flesh and blood at one and the same time. Subjection to human rule is seen as a consequence of throwing off divine rule.[9] The Zealots and the followers of Bar Kokhba drew activist political conclusions from this view, but following the failure of the great revolts the idea took on a more personal, existential meaning.[10] " 'The writing inscribed on the tablets was God's writing' [Ex 32:16] — read it not as 'inscribed' (*harut*) but as 'freedom' (*herut*), for there is no free man but he who engages in the study of Torah" (Mishna, Avot 6:2). As in the Stoic philosophy of the time, freedom has to do with man's inner state: he who studies Torah and keeps the Commandments is free. Hence, accepting the rule of heaven, unlike accepting human rule, does not mean subjugation but an exodus "from slavery to freedom," as we learn from the Passover Haggada and other sources.[11] This idea is well expressed in Yehuda Halevi's poem "Servant of the Lord": "Those who serve temporal powers are the slaves of slaves. / The servant of the Lord alone is free."[12] Indeed, it is clear from the discussion in the Halakha of the principle that "the law of the state is the law" that medieval Jewry did not see itself as being totally subject to the states in which it lived.[13] This notion, of freedom within slavery, was the regnant one among Jews up until the Emancipation, and it was compatible both with the prohibition against re-establishing an independent state until the coming of the Messiah and with the Jews' attitude toward the use of force.

Ambivalence Toward the Use of Force

Jewish tradition takes two different approaches to war and the use of force. This duality is already evident in the Bible. The Patriarchal narratives in Genesis and the Former Prophets see the people of Israel as destined to be "a great nation." There is the promise here of territorial aggrandizement, and greatness and honor are bound up with the defeat and expulsion of Israel's enemies, i.e., the realization of earthly political objectives. But in Deuteronomy and the Latter Prophets there appears the ideal of the "holy people," which entails the imperative to preserve the rights of the other peoples and gauges Israel's superiority, not in numbers or power but in its spiritual destiny.[14]

At various points, scripture alludes to a necessary connection between the fulfillment of Israel's historical destiny and the wielding of military force. The Torah not only commands the destruction of the Canaanites as a precondition of the establishment of the Hebrew commonwealth, but God Himself often appears as the champion of Israel's military cause, and the conquest of Canaan and the widening of its boundaries are described as "the wars of the Lord." Furthermore, the right to use force is not only regarded as necessary for the achievement of national and religious objectives; it is sometimes even described as a reward for having achieved them.

Yet the Bible warns in various ways against turning force from a means to an end. Unlike the pagan glorification of human might, the biblical attitude toward the latter is skeptical and critical. He who uses force — especially military authorities — must always be aware of its pitfalls. Biblical monotheism, which sees God as the absolute ruler of nature and history, served to restrain human aggressiveness. Biblical law limits the cruelty that may be inflicted in wartime and the moral corruption that can result (Deut 20–21). Real pacifism is also not alien to the biblical literature and found its way from there into the Christian tradition.[15] Unlike the Greeks, who regarded warfare as something natural and in some ways even positive, the Prophets envisaged universal peace and the abolition of war — the first thinkers in history to do so. In the Bible there is thus a tension between the Jewish people's political and spiritual values, but they certainly cannot be separated from each other.[16]

There is an even greater ambivalence toward military power in Rabbinic literature. Talmudic law is not pacifistic, but it tends to impose severe limitations on the use of force, to ensure humane treatment of the enemy in wartime and prevent the moral corruption of soldiers. Thus Nachmanides interprets Deut 23:10 — "When you go out as a troop against your enemies, be on your guard against anything untoward" — as follows: "Scripture warns [us] concerning situations where there is a danger of sin. And among the well-known practices of warriors is that they eat all sorts of abominable things, steal, plunder, and are not even ashamed to commit adultery or any kind of villainy. The most upright of men dons a cloak of cruelty and rage when setting out with his fellow-soldiers to make war against their foes. Therefore, scripture warns us, 'Be on your guard against anything untoward.' "[17] Similarly, there is a notable tendency in the Halakha to limit to a particular historical period the Commandments of making war against the seven Canaanite nations and Amalek on the premise that they have "vanished." There is also a tendency to restrict the legitimate waging of "optional wars" (*milhemot reshut*),[18] i.e., those aimed at extending the boundaries of Israel or glorifying its king (Maimonides, *Mishne Torah,* Laws of Kings 5:1). In general, it is fair to say that the Sages saw warfare as a necessary evil and peace as divine.

Such ambivalence toward warfare is no less pronounced, and perhaps more so, in Christianity. On one hand, its attitudes are based on the Gospel doctrine of unqualified opposition to violence. On the other hand, Christianity came to terms with the existing political structures and was more realistic than Judaism about the need to use force. Medieval Catholic theologians were quite concerned with the legitimacy of warfare and distinguished in principle between "just" and "unjust" wars. This distinction, grounded to some extent in the Deuteronomic laws of warfare, was eventually given a legal formulation by the well-known jurist Hugo Grotius at the beginning of the seventeenth century and incorporated into the United Nations charter. At the same time, there continued to be a strong Christian tradition of radical opposition to the use of force, particularly among sects that broke with the Catholic Church.[19]

The legal tradition in Islam sees all wars waged by Muslims against non-believers, or even against breakaway Muslim groups, as *jihad,* holy wars. The Muslim community as a whole is obliged to widen the territorial domain of Islam, eventually extending the rule of Muslim law throughout the world. There is thus, at least theoretically, a state of perpetual war between the Muslim state and the surrounding non-Muslim world. Nevertheless, there are, in practice, ways of putting off the obligation to extend Muslim rule, according to circumstances and the character of the infidel population in question.[20]

In Jewish culture, unlike that of Christian Europe, there was no admiration of the military hero or the weapons of war, nor was there ever a festival commemorating a military conquest.[21] The Temple is a symbol of the abhorrence of war and the weapons of war (see Ex 20:22). The Messiah is to arrive riding on a donkey, not a mighty horse. Characteristically, the Mishna forbids carrying weapons on the Sabbath on the grounds that they are repugnant to people, not ornamental (Shabbat 6:7). The Sages' concept of heroism is far from being a military one; it refers mainly to the moral attributes of restraint and devotion to God. "Our Sages taught: Those who are offended but do not offend, who are subjected to calumny but do not respond, who act out of love and rejoice in their tribulations — concerning them, scripture says, 'May His friends be as the rising sun in might' [Jud 5:31]" (T.B. Shabbat 88b). "Ben Zoma says: Who is the hero? He who subdues his lusts" (Mishna, Avot 4:1). "Who is the greatest of heroes? He who turns his enemy into a friend" (Avot de-Rabbi Natan [Schechter, Recension A] 23). The Sages turned many scriptural heroes into fighters of the "wars of the Torah."[22]

At the same time, the Sages taught that God's valor too was not to be seen only in His triumph over the wicked but also in His merciful restraint toward them in hopes of their repenting. The heroism of human self-restraint is thus an imitation of divine heroism. The study of Torah is considered a way of bringing peace, as it is said: "Scholars [of the Torah] increase peace in the world" (T.B. Berakhot 64a).

According to Franz Rosenzweig, "To understand Jewish ethics we must recognize how many [norms] which for other peoples belong to the military [realm] are, in this case, part of the ethic of the study of Torah."[23] To use William James' well-known phrase, the Sages succeeded to an amazing degree in making Torah study "the moral equivalent of war." James maintains that there are moral values vital for society, such as daring, courage, self-sacrifice, and self-denial, that develop primarily in wartime. War has the advantage of being "the only school that as yet is universally available" since it is "in the line of aboriginal instinct"[24] But, in fact, the heroic and quasi-ascetic ethos of Torah study incorporates most of the virtues James sees as rooted in the war experience.

We thus see in the Sages a tendency to transform or sublimate the martial ethos of the Bible. This is clear from the Rabbinic notion of *mahloket* (legal controversy); the characterization of it by the Sages as "the war of the Torah" alludes to its origins. The Sages themselves are referred to as "shield-bearers" (T.B. Bekhorot 36a), i.e., defenders, who wrangle with one another over points of law. " 'Engage in struggle'[25] — as in the phrase 'A man struggled with him,' which refers to military struggle, for war is a commandment, and we are permitted to fight with words and resolve questions and not show favoritism to anyone but only love truth."

This was the dominant tendency in Jewish religious thought until quite recently. Jews had internalized the value of military valor and given it a psychological and cosmic meaning: the real war is taking place in man's own heart, in the struggle with the evil impulse with the weapon God provided us. Faithfulness to the Torah and the Commandments is a kind of military service that demands suffering and heroic sacrifice, the epitome of which is martyrdom. In the story "Whither?" by Mordekhai Ze'ev Feierberg (1873–99), the hero's father gives a long sermon about the role of the people of Israel in the world. The sermon's main theme is a comparison of Israel to the army of the Lord: "More than three thousand years ago God gave us His Torah and made us His soldiers. We are the army of God and of all that is holy in this world."[26]

The legacy of the Prophets and the Rabbis gave rise, in Jewish tradition, to repulsion toward bloodshed and toward the glorification of political and military power. The Jews see warfare, which has played such an essential role in world history, as "the craft of Esau."[27] In Jewish history, its only significance is in the mythical past or the messianic future, not in the present. Two generations ago, Rav Kook voiced the view that the people of Israel had abandoned the sphere of world politics "under duress that was partly also a matter of inner will, until the happy time when a polity could be governed without wickedness or barbarism."[28] He thus saw exile as a crucible, necessary to prepare the people for renewed independence.

Acceptance of Exile

It has been claimed that the Jews did not engage in warfare and were willing to accept exile and subjugation because they had no alternative. This claim was challenged early on by the medieval philosopher Yehuda Halevi, according to whom their attitude toward exile was actually somewhere "between necessity and choice." Had they wished to do so, he said, they could have joined forces with their oppressors.[29] It was not a matter of mere passivity or lack of opposition but of a kind of nonviolent, spiritual resistance, the highest expression of which was martyrdom. Even if we accept Nietzsche's thesis that the transvaluation of values was a kind of "spiritual revenge" by the Jews against their oppressors or a rationalization of their own impotence, it cannot be denied that their faith was sustained by tremendous inner strength, which Nietzsche regarded as the dominant ethical attribute of the superman.[30] For him, transcending suffering was the surest way to achieve power, and thus exile was the ideal school for acquiring the fortitude that made the Jews the strongest race in Europe.[31] Kant, for his part, had distinguished between "might" and "dominion," defining might (*Macht*) as the ability to overcome "great hindrances." "[Might] is called dominion," he said, "if it is superior to the resistance of that which itself possesses might."[32] Employing this distinction, we could say that the Jewish people in exile was mighty but did not dominate its situation.

The religious interpretation the Jews gave their sufferings in exile had important political consequences, for it was this interpretation — and the well-known Three Oaths God had demanded of them, one of which was "not to rebel against the nations of the world" (T.B. Ketubot 111a) — that led them to rule out forcefully any thought of real change in their political situation.[33] Rabbi Joshua Joseph Preil (1858–96) claimed that the sages intentionally blunted the Jews' national pride as a means to guarantee their continued existence because they were confronted by a harsh dilemma that "could hardly be solved." On one hand, national pride would lead the broken and down-trodden nation to spiritual crisis and eventual annihilation; on the other hand, submission and abasement also inevitably lead to national extinction. The national leadership found the solution in a simple yet lofty idea: "They left the concern for Israel's honor and political sovereignty to God," while the people, for their part, were given the task of observing the Torah and mitzvot, which are "our breath of life and national pride, which distinguish us as a nation that need have no fear."[34] According to this view, the very survival of the Jewish people in exile depended both on keeping the Commandments and on refraining from provoking the gentiles and using violence. The strategy Jacob employed in his reunion with Esau (Gen 33) was taken as a model. Thus, Rabbi Yishayahu Horowitz (the Shela) writes: "As [the Patriarch Jacob] did in regard to gifts, prayers, and [the avoidance of] armed conflict, so do we conduct ourselves now toward the children of Esau, having no power but that which is in our mouths, to pray to the Lord, be He blessed, in times of trouble. To wage war against the gentiles is not our way, but rather we do battle through our advocates at court, who must be bold and forceful in appealing to the king and his ministers on Israel's behalf . . . until the Messiah comes."[35]

Self-defense, rather than active combat, was the essence of the Jewish strategy of survival. As the Midrash states, "He who stands up to a wave will be drenched by it, but he who does not stand up to it will not be drenched" (Genesis Rabba 44:15). This outlook should not, however, be identified with what Zionist ideologues called "the passivity of the exilic Jews." This myth, which was very important in shaping the Zionist ethos, encompasses a number of different ideas that are not inherently related to one another. To begin with, the medieval Jews generally did take whatever measures they could to defend themselves. When they had access to weapons, they preferred to use them to fend off their enemies, rather than surrender or commit apostasy.

Martyrdom was a last resort, when all possible means of self-defense had been exhausted. The Halakha, too, prefers self-defense over martyrdom.[36] Secondly, though theoretically "politics was [considered] for the gentiles,"[37] the Jews were certainly not indifferent to it. As the gentiles well understood, the Jews constituted a "state within a state," a fact which became a liability at the time of the Emancipation. Their survival in exile was due not only to their faith but also to their ability to create semi-independent political frameworks of their own that facilitated religious observance and to their skill at maneuvering in the political circumstances imposed upon them.[38]

In any case, there is a tension, if not an opposition, between the Rabbinic ethos of exile, which is mainly a personal one, calling for fidelity to the Torah and the Commandments, and the modern activist ethos that calls for boldness, physical heroism, and rational planning on a political-collective level. The historian Yitzhak Baer believed it was not only prolonged exile that had distanced the Jews from worldly life but also tendencies inherent in their tradition, at least from the time of the Second Temple on. Exile was not only imposed upon them but was also "one of the decisive political consequences of our ancestors' religious mode of thought." [39] Thus, according to Baer, it was factors inherent in the Jewish tradition that prevented practical redemption from taking place.

The first modern thinker to take note of this tension was Spinoza. In a well-known passage at the end of chapter 3 of his *Theological-Political Treatise* (1670), he considers the possibility of the re-establishment of a Jewish state. Such a thing could only come to pass, he says, if there is a change in certain aspects of the Jewish faith that "soften" the Jews' temperament and block the development of an assertive martial ethos. If Spinoza's negativity toward Judaism makes us suspicious of these observations, let us keep in mind the words of Moses Mendelssohn, a Jewish thinker who was faithful to his religion and his people. In 1770, a German nobleman approached him with a plan for the establishment of a Jewish state in Palestine. In his reply, Mendelssohn praises the originator of the idea for its boldness and grandeur but rejects it out of hand. Pointing out the difficulties the plan would entail, he writes: "The greatest difficulty which seems to me to stand in the way of the project is the character of my people [*Nation*]. It is not adequately equipped to undertake anything great. The pressure under which we have lived for so many centuries has deprived our spirit of all *vigueur*. It is not our fault; but we cannot deny that the natural urge to freedom has completely ceased to be active in us. It has transformed itself into a monkish virtue and expresses itself in prayer and patience, not in action."[40]

Unlike Spinoza, Mendelssohn blames the Jews' timidity on political circumstances, not on the Jewish religion: "It is not our fault." But elsewhere, when he is trying to dispel widespread gentile doubts as to the Jews' loyalty to the state, he cites the Jewish tradition, with its Three Oaths and its ban on hastening the End of Days, as proof that the Jews have no motive for taking political action themselves that could redeem them from exile.[41] These disagreements are a harbinger of the later polemic within the Zionist movement over the degree to which Judaism is to blame for the Jewish condition.

In any event, the "freedom" to which Mendelssohn refers is national and political in the modern sense rather than personal. In the Middle Ages, the Jews as individuals actually enjoyed greater freedom than most gentiles. As we shall see, one of the aims of the Haskala literature was to cultivate among the Jews the "urge" to freedom in the former sense, along with the moral qualities needed to achieve it. But in pursuing this goal, the writers posed a dilemma for the Jewish people: how far could it go in cultivating these qualities without losing is distinctive spiritual character, shaped as it was by the conditions of life in exile. This dilemma, which goes to the heart of modern Jewish identity, has concerned Zionist thinking and writing from the beginnings of the movement until the present day.

Earlier, the dilemma had been trenchantly posed for the Christian world by Niccolò Machiavelli (1469–1527), the first thinker to ask whether Christian ethics were compatible with the qualities need for effective political rule. He himself was convinced that the main Christian virtues, such as humility, mercy, and forgiveness, were an insuperable obstacle in the way of building a normal, healthy polity. One of his goals was to arouse the patriotism of the Italian people, which was divided and subjugated, and get them to unite and bring back the heroic greatness of the ancient Roman Empire. The only way to accomplish this, in his view, was to adopt pagan virtues. In a famous passage in his *Discourses,* he maintains that it was under the influence of Christian doctrine that people's civic spirit was dampened, that they were "weakened" and fell "easy prey to wicked men," for they were more concerned with bearing their suffering than with taking revenge upon their tormentors. He blamed Christians for being willing to bear humiliation without complaint, thus allowing hereditary rulers to wield power over them unopposed. It was thus necessary to abandon traditional Christian education in favor of education better suited to the needs of the polity. For him, there could be no mixing of the Christian ethos and the republican one.[42]

The clash between these two systems of values makes its first appearance in Jewish history two hundred years after Machiavelli, in the teachings of Ya'akov Frank (1721–96), the greatest of the false messiahs and the father of Jewish militarism. His vision of the rebirth of the Jewish people, which included dominion over the gentiles, flags, horses and chariots, was predicated on the Jews becoming warriors: "If you were really of the seed of David," he claimed, "you would not be sitting and studying doctrines and laws but trying to get hold of weapons." Instead of studying Torah, the Jews need to learn military tactics from a very early age. In order to do so, they must enter "Edom," i.e., convert to Christianity (as Frank himself did). If they do not do this willingly, they should be compelled to do so! Once they have learned to be warriors, they can organize themselves into legions, numbering ten million soldiers, to take part in a struggle against the heathen Turks and capture the Holy Land from them.[43] In Frank's teachings, we see for the first time the theme that is later to preoccupy Hebrew literature: the Jews must first be alienated from themselves — turning away from Torah, learning gentile ways, adopting their persecutors' ethos of military valor — if they are once again to be themselves.

As we shall see, there are a number of similarities between Machiavelli's thesis and certain themes in modern Hebrew literature — particularly the writings of Berdyczewski, Tchernichowsky, and Hazaz. These writers, too, saw the traditional Jewish ethos as an obstacle to be overcome if a life of dignity and freedom, both personal and collective, was to be achieved.

2

Shame, Guilt, and Suffering in Jewish Culture until Modern Times

Shame and guilt are two feelings that have a considerable effect on our moral decision-making, that predispose us to moral action. Their psychological effect is evident in that vague realm we refer to as "moral sensitivity," the cultivation of which is seen by society as one of the central purposes of education. These two feelings, which are among the underpinnings of every culture, play an important role in socialization: the internalization of social norms that promote self-restraint, obedience to the law, and identification with particular codes of behavior.[1] Psychology and sociology disagree as to whether there is any empirical basis for drawing a sharp distinction between "shame cultures" and "guilt cultures." But even those who refuse to make this distinction in a categorical way are ready to admit that cultures differ in the relative importance they attribute to shame and guilt. In some cultures, the former is the main motivating force behind moral behavior; in others the latter. Still, the two are closely related, and the distinction between them is not a simple one. In the words of the anthropologist Clifford Geertz: "Shame is the feeling of disgrace and humiliation which follows upon a transgression found out; guilt is the feeling of secret badness attendant upon one not, or not yet, found out. Thus, though shame and guilt are not precisely the same thing in our ethical and psychological vocabulary, they are of the same family; the one is a surfacing of the other, the other a concealment of the one."[2]

Shame relates primarily to the sense of one's own worth in the eyes of significant others. It is a feeling that arises when one fails to achieve one's goals or to project the ideal image one has of oneself. Hence it entails a sense of lack, defect, or failure. Weakness and loss of self-control can also provoke feelings of shame, accompanied by a fear of ridicule by the other members of one's group.

Psychologically speaking, the opposite of shame is honor.[3] At root, honor is a quintessentially social thing. It depends, at least in its origin, on some sort of social inequality or ranking and on the approval of the others. Achievement-oriented societies tend to offer honor as a goad to what they regard as achievement. One who does not compete successfully is ashamed of his failure. This is the source of the moral ambiguity of honor. On one hand, all that is noble in human nature is bolstered and reinvigorated by it. But on the other, honor can also go hand in hand with such negative attributes as selfishness.

Honor is connected with power, the ability to dominate one's natural or social environment. Power gives a person greater social weight and a greater claim to respect. Herein lies the connection between honor and freedom: subjugation means being deprived of honor because it means being deprived of power, of control over one's own fate. One who would be honored must be free. The slave has no personal identity and only acquires one insofar as he struggles for his freedom.

The achievement of honor may be accompanied by a desire for retribution. Self-respect entails the ability to repay both good and evil.[4] Psychologically, revenge is essential if shame is to be wiped away and dignity restored. Retribution is not just a matter of paying back but a direct expression of the principle of justice.

Whereas shame and honor are both primarily social in nature, guilt is an internal, private matter and therefore more closely related to morality. We experience guilt most directly as the pangs of conscience. There is the sense that we must pay for the harm we have caused others. In the context of religious morality there is the additional sense of personal accountability to God. A corollary is the imperative of examining one's deeds and motives honestly and without illusion.

The Ethos of Ancient Greece: Honor and Nobility of Spirit

There are vast differences between the Greco-Roman and so-called Judeo-Christian cultures — the twin pillars of Western civilization — in the meanings they give to shame and guilt. Feelings of guilt in the Judeo-Christian sense, i.e., pangs of conscience (internal) or moral responsibility toward a divine judge (external), were practically unknown to the Greeks.[5]

In the Homeric literature and Greek tragedy, which reflect the ancient Greek ethos, guilt (*ate*) is something nonrational, tragic, and mythic in origin that one inherits from one's forebears. It has nothing to do with individual responsibility to others or to the gods but is imposed by a demonic fate. Shame, in contrast, plays a powerful role in this culture. The sense of shame (*aidos*) is what distinguishes the noble individual and is synonymous with the sense of duty. Homeric man judged himself entirely by the criteria of the society to which he belonged. Praise and blame were thus a function of objective social standards, which, in fact, served as the basis of the moral life in its entirety.[6] Protagoras maintained that the senses of shame and justice were the underpinnings of political society and human solidarity, and therefore they should be inculcated in all men.[7]

Greek culture inherited from the heroic ethos of the Homeric age the notion that a human being should live for honor and praise. It is no wonder, then, that this culture should have had a distinctly masculine character. The heroic worldview seeks opportunities to win honor by one's deeds. In Nietzsche's view, what characterized the Greeks was their utter dedication to individual excellence and distinction, what they called *arete*.[8] Honor was the center of life, and any infringement upon it required immediate redress. The pursuit of honor was thus a great spur of initiative, daring, and risk-taking of all kinds, in both war and peace. Military victory was the most praiseworthy achievement of all. However bound up it was with human suffering, it was also the best way to demonstrate noble character. Heraclitus taught that "war is the father of all and the king over all," and "all things come into being and pass away through struggle." If the struggle between the forces of nature were to cease, nothing could exist. This "heroic" view dominated Greek history right down to the time of Alexander the Great and was espoused even by the philosophers of the age.[9]

In the philosophies of Plato and Aristotle, shame and honor become the inner imperatives that man, as a rational being, must obey. This development was very important in the history of moral consciousness. For Aristotle, true honor is the completion of virtue, or it encompasses all the virtues. That is why it is only to be found among the truly noble, those who excel in what he calls "nobility of spirit" (*megalopsychia*). For them, honor is the supreme goal. Nobility of spirit presumes a person's belief in his own worth, just as it presumes that one can be elevated by his own efforts. The person of noble spirit is entitled to respect, and he demands it. He who demands more respect than he deserves is arrogant, while he who demands less is lowly and self-effacing. For Aristotle, humility is worse than arrogance. A certain modesty, such as that of Socrates, is becoming, but to negate one's worth altogether, when what one deserves is esteem, is disgraceful. Thus, shame is only appropriate for the young, whose emotions are still strong and liable to lead them astray, but not for adults. Nor should the man of excellence feel guilt. As we have pointed out, guilt is the central motif in tragedy, but the tragic hero, in Aristotle's definition, is not an excellent but an average man. What is more, tragedy is meant for the improvement of the masses.[10]

The ideal of nobility of spirit does not allow for feelings of either guilt or the pity that results from it. A person of noble spirit will show generosity toward others, not out of sympathy for weakness or suffering but out of the self-respect that impels him to do the right thing.

The notion of "conscience," which implies self-scrutiny and purity of heart, has no place in Greek ethics. The famous rule "know thyself" does not mean "search thy heart" but "know thy true station" and "examine thy beliefs." This absence of personal and moral depth goes hand in hand with the assumption that the gods are not interested in human morality, that morality is a purely human affair.[11]

The Jewish Ethos: Penitence and Humility

In contrast with the ancient Greek ethos, which saw little moral value in guilt but viewed shame and honor as morally decisive,[12] the normative Judaic ethos has, since tannaitic times, been one of penitence. In this system it is humility rather than the sense of honor that is the condition for moral behavior.[13] The notion of "conscience," as understood today, does not appear in early Jewish literature, but the underlying idea of accountability before a higher authority is clearly already to be found in the Bible.

Guilt may be accompanied by shame and regret, but being directed first and foremost toward God, these feelings have a religious and existential rather than a social meaning. They prompt one to atonement, placation, and self-correction ("penitence") rather than revenge. The sense of guilt is not sufficient motivation for change in oneself or in the world around us. Guilt must be combined with shame, which embodies our ideal self-image. Shame and regret are essential for purity of heart: "One who commits a transgression and is ashamed of it is to be forgiven all" (Berakhot 12b), and "He who admits [his evil ways] and forsakes [them] is to be shown compassion (Prov 28:31). Unlike Aristotle, for whom shame is unworthy of the man of noble spirit, Jewish law views shame as a sign of precisely such a spirit. Maimonides includes shame as an element in the act of confession, which, in turn, is the beginning of penitence (Laws of Penitence 1:1).

Penetrating moral self-criticism is the root of humility, in the Jewish view. Opposed as humility is to anything that makes for arrogance — power, glory, dominion, worldly success — it is the hallmark of piety.[14] Humility, however, does not imply a feeling of inferiority. The proud are afraid to admit their weaknesses lest they impair their sense of superiority, while the humble admit their moral failings readily. At the same time, they recall that man is made in the image of God, making him morally responsible to the world and especially to his fellowmen. Thus, humility neither paralyzes them nor makes them morally passive in relation to their surroundings.[15]

The pursuit of honor, which Aristotle saw as characterizing the man of noble spirit, is not only alien to the spirit of Judaism but, like pride, is considered by Judaism to be a grave sin. One should not seek greatness for himself but leave it to others to attribute it to him. This does not mean that honor is unimportant or that it should not be taken into consideration as a source of human motivation, but only that it must not be the main motive behind moral action. Furthermore, one should not take credit for whatever honor comes his way, for it comes to him from God and not only from his own achievements. Thus the acquisition of wealth and power, which carry honor with them, is considered dangerous, for it can easily lead to arrogance, and this, in turn, is tantamount to idolatry. "Hate rulership" (Mishna Avot 1:10), for it "buries those who exercise it" (Avot de-Rabbi Natan, ed. Schechter, version B, ch. 22). Rulership deserves honor only when it promotes the service of God, and physical power merits honor only when used to protect the weak from attack. In general, no virtue is as opposed to the aristocratic Greek ideals of honor, pride, and nobility of spirit as the virtue of humility. One might say this constitutes the most fundamental difference between Greek and Jewish morality.[16] It is no accident that Hermann Cohen saw humility as the signal contribution of monotheism to ethics.[17]

The Honor of Jewish Suffering in Exile

Until modern times, the Jews cultivated assiduously the sense of guilt, as well, of course, as the associated sense of shame. But these feelings had nothing to do with the values of the gentiles or their estimation of the Jews. Rather, they sprang from the special position of the people Israel before God.[18] When Jews experienced shame and guilt, they interpreted them in terms of their own autonomous values and not those of their oppressors. This made it possible for the Jews to claim victory even when they had ostensibly been defeated, for it was not they who were humiliated but their persecutors. In the words of the poet, " The disgrace is not yours but your tormentors."[19] Seeing themselves this way enabled the Jews to disregard the world of the gentiles, with all its glory and supposed honor, and to feel absolutely superior to their social and cultural surroundings. Thanks to this self-image, they were able to retain their self-respect and dignity despite being an oppressed and humiliated minority.[20]

Although the Jewish ethos and that of medieval Christianity have much in common — in both humility was considered a virtue essential to holiness — the two societies differed profoundly as to the honor associated with rulership. In Christendom the chivalric code played an important political and social role until the end of the Middle Ages. According to the cultural historian Johan Huizinga, chivalry was, after religion, the most influential idea of that era.[21] Although the lower classes acted primarily out of self-interest, the upper classes were motivated principally by pride and honor. In its concern with honor, chivalry was a quintessentially aristocratic ethos. But as Burkhardt shows, beginning with the Renaissance and under the influence of Classical civilization, the concern for honor began to spread throughout European society until, in modern times, it became a significant motivating factor in all human behavior.[22] The revolutionary, modern spirit brought about the democratization of values originally confined to the aristocracy; the knightly ideal was transmuted into patriotism, which combines the spirit of sacrifice with a thirst for justice and zeal in the defense of the weak and oppressed. This phenomenon first came to the fore during the French Revolution.[23]

The Jews, an oppressed, humiliated minority, had no ethic comparable to chivalry except in some isolated instances in Muslim and Christian Spain. Both Muslim and Christian law forbade them to exercise any form of domination. The Jews did not see their honor as based on political or military power, in which all the other nations took pride, but upon a kind of heroic service on behalf of humanity as a whole. As Hermann Cohen put it, the sufferings of the people of Israel down through the ages have earned it the honor of taking part in the divine education of mankind. "Suffering willingly endured proclaims the historical honor of the sufferer."[24]

In his book *Jewish Self-Hatred,* Theodore Lessing (1872–1933) posits two principal ways in which human beings rationalize their suffering, which otherwise would appear meaningless: blaming others and blaming oneself. The first way leads to hatred of "the other," the enemy, while the second leads to destructive self-hatred. In his view, the Jews are the first and perhaps the only people who have tended to blame themselves for all that they have suffered, and each individual Jew, too, has a strong tendency to see whatever misfortune befalls him as punishment for his own sins. In this approach lies the key to the "pathology" of the Jewish soul.[25]

Lessing's statement should be qualified: until modern times the Jews were spared self-hatred by the fact that the guilt they felt was in relation to God rather than the other nations. Ernst Simon maintains that this feeling served as a spur to repentance and a moral elevation that had universal significance: "The normal behavior of normal nations leads to the well-known attitude of giving credit to ourselves for all our victories — and of ascribing to the evil enemies all our defeats. Israel's ritual has chosen almost the reverse. When remembering our national victories — on Purim and Hannuka — we add a prayer, 'for the miracles,' attributing to God the rescue from Haman's persecution and the victory over the Syrians. On the other hand, on the days of national mourning, when recalling the destruction of both Temples and the expulsion from Palestine or Spain, we say: 'Because of our sins were we exiled from our land.' This calculated change saves us from two opposite but complementary dangers: from resentment and from despair."[26]

Traditionally, Jews interpreted their suffering and degradation in exile not only as atonement for their sins but also as their destiny and mission in the world. In an almost paradoxical way, they saw their political and military weakness as a sign of divine election and of their moral and religious stature. Their very survival in exile confirmed them in their conviction that it was faith rather than political or military power that was decisive in history.

The Change in Self-Esteem in Modern Times

The modern period saw a radical change in the way Jews regarded themselves. Most of them, first in Western Europe and later in the east, rejected the traditional interpretation of the Jewish fate, the ethos that had always dictated the way Jews reacted to suffering and humiliation. Two factors were responsible for this change: secularization, beginning in Europe early in the nineteenth century, in the wake of the Enlightenment and the French Revolution; and the worldwide waves of anti-Jewish hatred and violence, of a previously unknown scale and ferocity, that occurred during this period.

The secular spirit of the Enlightenment gave rise to a new scale of values to be espoused universally by all men. A central concept of the Enlightenment, "human dignity," is part of the philosophical infrastructure of Kantian ethics. For Kant, this is a secular, universal idea, not of divine origin, as religion claims, but anchored in humans. The idea applies equally to all people without exception and serves as a common basis for the moral life. Dignity does not depend on any external social criterion or on a person's own achievements — as Aristotle, for example, held — but is a function of the inestimable inner worth of every individual.[27] In Kant's view, this idea is a "postulate of morality," the ultimate explanation for our moral experience, and in this sense it represents an act of faith. "Human dignity" became a synonym for the basic nature of humans and in particular for their moral freedom. At the same time, it conveyed the very value of life, for life without dignity would also be without meaning. A person stripped of his dignity has lost his humanity, which is tantamount to spiritual death.

Peter Berger has shown that in the modern world the term "dignity," in the sense in which we have used it here, is gradually replacing the traditional term "honor." This change in terminology reflects a profound change in the understanding of identity. "The concept of honor implies that identity is essentially, or least importantly, linked to institutional roles." On the other hand, the modern notion of dignity is based on a concept of identity in which the self takes precedence over any social role definitions. "This democratized self, which has no necessary social content and no necessary social identity, can then be anything, can assume any role or take any point of view, because it *is*, in and for itself, nothing."[28] Dignity is universal and egalitarian, since every human being shares in it.

One who is convinced that dignity is essential to man will defend it zealously against all who would take it away. In Croce's words, "The sole practical guarantee that the liberty and dignity of men will be treated with the respect and the regard which are its due is the readiness of men to fight for it. . . . There is no escape from the duty to struggle."[29]

Since self-respect requires that one insist on his selfhood and independence, there is an inner connection between dignity and freedom, on one hand, and power on the other. Power means the ability to defend freedom and dignity. It is the tool that can be used to compel recognition of oneself as an equal. The use of force by the oppressed against the oppressor not only serves as an outlet for rage and indignation; it also places them on an equal footing, asserting their common humanity and mutual responsibility. It forces the oppressor to acknowledge the wrong he has done to the oppressed and engenders in him a moral sensitivity that is the basis of human solidarity.

In any society, one of the purposes of the judicial system, with its system of punishments, is to instill in the criminal this sense of human solidarity. All forms of government take the right of retaliation away from the injured party and place it in the hands of the judiciary, which is supposed to treat everyone equally and put an end to the endless chain of retaliatory violence. When people tire of being victims and lose faith in the capacity of the courts to redress their situation, they are likely to take the law in their own hands.[30] It was in such a situation that the Jews found themselves in modern times, according to the Zionist interpretation. When Emancipation failed, they lost faith in the system of justice and as a result felt justified in taking power and using it to defend their freedom and dignity.

As we have said, secularization and increased anti-Jewish violence were among the factors that caused a change in the Jews' self-esteem and in their mode of response to suffering and humiliation. Possibly the earliest evidence we have of this decisive change is the harsh sentiment expressed in his diary by a fourteen-year-old German-Jewish boy who had been disappointed by the Jews' reactions to the Damascus blood libel of 1840. The boy was Ferdinand Lassalle, who later became one of the leaders of German socialism.

> One's hair rises, and every emotion is turned to fury! It is dreadful that a people should endure these things, whether they patiently bear their treatment or revenge themselves. True, fearfully true, is the following sentence from the report: "The Jews in this city endure cruelties which none but these pariahs of the earth would bear without making dreadful reprisals." Thus, even the Christians are surprised at our apathy and wonder that we do not revolt and that we prefer death by torture to death in battle. . . . Could any revolution be more righteous than that which the Jews in Damascus would cause if they were to revolt, to set every corner of the town on fire, blow up the powder magazine, and perish with their tormentors? Nation of cowards, you deserve no better fate. The trampled worm will turn, yet do you but bow the head more deeply.[31]

There is no clearer evidence of the change in Jewish self-esteem than this spontaneous outburst of rage, shame, and vengefulness aimed at rescuing lost Jewish honor. There is no trace here of a metaphysical interpretation of the Jews' suffering. Exile and its tribulations no longer have an expiatory or redemptive significance, and suffering is considered as a great wrong that requires "rebellion" and "justifiable revenge." Here we have a hint at the negation of martyrdom that was to take hold in the second half of the nineteenth century and the beginning of the twentieth.[32]

The words of the youthful Lassalle, who grew up in a semitraditional home and received a liberal, modern education, convey a strong sense of shame before the gentiles, accompanied by a stern rebuke of the Jewish people for its weakness and impotence. These feelings led him to question his own identity and break with his past. As a young man, however, Lassalle dreamed of becoming another Judah Maccabee for his suffering people until, discovering communism, he turned his back on them. Ironically, he died in a duel defending his honor as a Jew.

The Jewish Stigma and Ways of Coping with It

As long as they did not share values with the gentiles, Jews could not feel shame before their oppressors. But with their emergence from the ghetto, many of them lost the immunity to humiliation that had been instilled in them by traditional Judaism. Under the influence of the Enlightenment, their faith in the cultural superiority of Judaism collapsed, and, in effect, they began to see themselves through gentile eyes. Having internalized some of the ideas about Jews that were most common in gentile society, they felt shame. This psychological shift is well described by Ahad Ha-am:

> In past generations, when our forefathers took "You have chosen us" [a recurrent phrase in the Jewish liturgy] at face value, the contumely of the gentiles could not affect the purity of their inmost souls. They knew their own worth and were not upset by the "general consensus" of others, seeing all the parties to that consensus as an alien species, utterly different from them in every way. The Jew could then listen to the moral failings and sinful deeds heaped upon him by the gentiles without feeling shame or degradation. For what did he care what these "strangers" thought of him? If they would only leave him alone! But in our generation it is different. Now "our world" is much wider, and the European consensus affects us strongly in all "branches of life."[33]

"The new Jew," says Ahad Ha-am, "who enters into a pact with the general culture, no long sees himself as a superior breed, 'a species and substance apart from other men' (Halevy, *Kuzari* I:103); on the contrary, he does everything he can not to stand out and is grateful to others when they do not differ from him."[34]

As a result of this change in self-perception, many Jews began to see their Jewishness as a stigma, one of the main sources of the sense of shame.[35] This stigma then became the main factor prompting the Jews to try to change their image in the eyes of the gentiles. In their peculiar situation as a hated minority, humiliated and oppressed for many generations, many Jews felt inferior and blemished as human beings and thus unworthy of belonging to the larger society as long as they had not shed their distinguishing traits. Henceforth, self-hatred became rampant among them.

Isaiah Berlin used a parable about a hunchback to illustrate four degrees of discomfort typically felt by the modern Jew vis-à-vis his situation in a non-Jewish society.[36] He almost certainly had in mind the hunchbacked philosopher Moses Mendelssohn, the archetypal modern Jew. The first class consisted of those who maintained that they had no hump. If challenged, "they were prepared to produce a document signed and countersigned by all the nations . . . solemnly declaring that the bearers were normal . . . persons. . . . If, nevertheless, someone persisted in staring at their backs, the hunchbacks maintained that this was due either to an optical illusion or to a violent form of prejudice. . . . They quoted enlightened nineteenth-century liberal intellectuals, or learned anthropologists, or socialist theorists . . . who explained [that] the very notion of hunchbacks was due to a confusion, since no such beings existed." This is the reaction characteristic of assimilated Jews, who insist that their Jewishness is not a sign of inferiority and that Jews should be treated like everyone else.

The second attitude was the opposite of this. The hunchback did not conceal the fact that he wore a hump and declared openly that he was happy to do so, that to own a hump was a privilege and an honor, that it set him apart as a member of a superior group, and that those who persecuted and threw stones at him did so out of concealed envy. These persons said, in effect, "I am not ashamed of being a hunchback, very far from it; certainly I am a hunchback and proud of it." In a sense, this response fits the pattern characteristic of the traditional Jew who has turned his degradation from a liability to an asset. It is a response commonly found among the Orthodox, especially those influenced by Habad Hasidism, which is more sensitive than other forms of ultra-Orthodoxy to the attitudes of the gentiles.[37] We also find this response among secularized Jews, where it developed as a reaction to extreme distress and humiliation. Thus, among part of the Polish-Jewish intelligentsia, both before and during the Holocaust, there was an about-face in relation to the larger European society and a negation of European culture.[38] Yet paradoxically, we also find this response among Jews who aspired to integration in the gentile elite but presented their origin as a badge of honor and privilege. Typical of this group was the Jewish-born British statesman Benjamin Disraeli (1804–81), of whom Berlin writes elsewhere that despite his conversion to Christianity he continued "almost too insistently" to take pride in his Jewish ancestry. "No doubt the fact that he was born a Jew offered an obstacle to his career; he overcame it by inflating it into a tremendous claim to noble birth. He needed to do this in order to feel that he was dealing on equal terms with the leaders of his family's adopted country, which he so profoundly venerated."[39]

The third type consisted of those timid and respectful cripples who believed that by never mentioning humps at all and by inducing others to regard the very use of the terms as virtually implying an unworthy discrimination or, at the very best, lack of taste, they could reduce discussion of the topic to manageable and ever-diminishing dimensions and move among the straight-backed with almost no sense of embarrassment, at any rate to themselves. They tended to wear voluminous cloaks, which concealed their precise contours. Among themselves they did occasionally mention the forbidden topic and even recommended to one another various kinds of ointment which, it was rumored, if rubbed in nightly and for many hundreds of years, would very gradually lessen the size of the hump or — who knows? — might even remove it altogether. Such Jews, having lost all traditional religious belief, internalized the prevailing antisemitic stereotypes wholesale and, as a result, developed a virulent self-hatred, such as we see in the philosopher Otto Weininger.[40] Although they tried to efface their identity through extreme assimilation, they realized that their efforts were futile, for being Jewish was a matter of fate, an inescapable guilt that clung to a person with no rhyme or reason, much like the *ate* of the Greek tragedies. At the same time, there was always the possibility that such Jews would resolve their psychological dilemma by renewed identification with their people and with the honor of belonging to a downtrodden group.[41]

Finally there came those who said that a hump was a hump, an appendage which was neither desirable nor capable of being disguised nor yet of being slowly diminished by application of mild palliatives and, in the meanwhile, a cause of grave distress to those afflicted with it. They recommended — and this was considered audacious to the point of lunacy — that it be cut off by means of a surgical operation. This approach, which could entail apostasy (Herzl before writing *The Jewish State*) or "normalization," i.e., the creation of a new framework of national life that would be acceptable to the other nations (Herzl the Zionist), radically transforms the Jew's situation and identity.

These four approaches reflect the enormous change in the consciousness of the Jew that resulted from the transformation of his relations with his non-Jewish neighbors in the modern period. What they all share is the assumption that if the Jew is to integrate himself into gentile society, he must do so in a way that restores his dignity. The approaches naturally differ in the ways they recommend pursuing this objective. The first three are apologetic ones, characteristic of the emancipated Jews; the last is mainly to be found in Zionism. To be sure, the approaches are merely ideal types in the Weberian sense and not to be found in pure form in the real world.

How could the Jew rid himself of the stigma? If he believed it was his own fault, he would have to reform. But if it was merely a baseless prejudice, he might try to persuade others of his worth by demonstrating his abilities. Post-Emancipation Jewry took both these tacks. Many believed that by changing their values and behavior, effacing their ethnic identity, and energetically adopting the majority culture they could regain the respect of the gentiles. Others took the route of apologetics, which highlighted those aspects of the Jewish heritage that seemed most compatible with modernity rather than trying to shed this heritage altogether. As opposed to the Christian claim that since Jesus Jewish history had been inconsequential, the Jews pointed to their great contributions to civilization on the basis of which they were surely entitled to a place of honor among the nations. Not only had Jewish history not come to an end; it continued to be of universal significance. And on this basis, the Jews felt entitled to equal rights.

Both these approaches met with criticism and misunderstanding. The Jews' desire to free themselves of the image of an oppressed people and to integrate themselves into the larger society aroused powerful opposition in the Christian countries. The Jews were accused of arrogance and of seeking by devious means to take over the societies in which they lived. But within the Jewish world, too, particularly in Eastern Europe, there was bitter criticism of the way the emancipated Jews related to gentile society. Ahad Ha-am (1856–1927) saw this relationship as "slavery in freedom," whereas others condemned the self-denial and the pandering as two sides of the same coin, the coin of lost Jewish self-respect. Max Nordau (1849–1923), too, maintained that the assimilated Jew, who tried to rid himself of his outward blemish, became "a cripple within and a counterfeit person without, so that, like everything unreal, he is ridiculous and hateful."[42] A moral and an esthetic critique are here combined, the latter strengthening the former immeasurably. This combination, which we first encounter in the Haskala's attack on the traditional Jew, is now turned by nationalist Jews against the assimilated: the latter are seen as repulsive in both senses, "fake" but also "ugly" and "revolting."

The Shame of Exile and the Zionist Recovery of Jewish Dignity

The Critique of the Exilic Ethos

The image of the Jew as a weakling, unable to resist the violence that was his lot in exile, had long been a standard antisemitic stereotype. Jewish nationalist thinkers, both Zionist and non-Zionist, maintained that a passive acceptance of violence not only brought more violence but also distorted the moral image of the Jew because his impotence was tantamount to a renunciation of the freedom in which all human dignity is grounded. For the novelist Yosef Hayim Brenner (1881–1921), Jewish life in the Diaspora was repulsive and "pathological": "We are disgraced and ridiculed because we are weak, and as a result we are also ugly, and as a result immoral as well."[1]

All Jewish nationalist ideologies toward the end of the nineteenth century rejected the notion that the Jews could recover their self-respect by either suppressing or apologizing for their ethnic identity. They all claimed that the Jews could attain this goal only by fully identifying with the fate of their people and its unique history and culture. The isolated Jew could not hope to attain self-respect without a restoration of the dignity of the group.

The Zionists maintained that only by acquiring political and military power in a framework of sovereignty could the stereotype of the submissive, cowardly Jew be rooted out and gentile attitudes toward him changed. This was, of course, the position taken by Judah Leib (Leon) Pinsker in his work *Auto-Emancipation* (1982), perhaps the most important manifesto to call for the recovery of Jewish national honor. Pinsker believed the Jews lacked self-respect and dignity. Prolonged oppression and economic struggle had compelled them to put such considerations aside: "We fell victim to humiliating indignity, to the transient existence of migratory birds, which eventually became a legacy of irremediable calamity." But Pinsker did not exempt the Jews from responsibility for the loss of their honor. His standard for gauging the latter was the one common to all men, and it was this standard that made it imperative for them to recover their independence. Because the Jews considered themselves, and were considered by others, to be a nation, their relations with the other nations had to be based on the principle of sovereignty they all shared. The creation of a sovereign framework would enable the Jews to express their distinctive identity and culture freely, without having to look over their shoulders at the gentiles, and thus would their dignity be restored.[2]

The notion that the Jews have to acquire political and military power is one of the most important new developments in modern Jewish history, for it entails a radical transformation of the status of the Jews among the nations, a revolutionary change in their self-image and traditional ethos. The emergence of this idea was accompanied by bitter disputes among the Zionists over the question of the true source of Jewish weakness and degradation: is blame to be placed on the people and its culture or on unavoidable circumstances? If the former, then the new ethos of sovereignty will have to work an inner transformation entailing a radical break with the past and the creation of a new identity; but if the blame lies with the Jews' environment, it will be the creation of a new, "natural" environment that makes it possible to renew Jewish culture and recover Jewish self-respect without negating the past.

The new Hebrew literature devoted much attention to the responsibility of the Jews themselves for their own fate, particularly in connection with the destruction of the Second Temple and the weakness of the Jews in exile. The first to raise this issue was the poet Judah Leib Gordon (1830–92). In his poems "Between Lions' Teeth" and "Zedekiah in Prison," he makes the harsh judgment that it is neither exile nor gentile animosity that are responsible for the image of the Jew but their own prophets and sages, who, in their preaching and hairsplitting, have distanced the people from real life and brought destruction and exile upon them.[3]

This line of thinking was also taken up by Berdyczewski (1865–1921), who gave an extreme interpretation to the line from the liturgy "For our sins were we exiled from our land." In his view, the sin that led to exile was to be found in the Jewish religion and its proponents. Exile, with all its negative connotations, was the result not only of a political disaster that befell the people from without but also of the religious ethos, untrue to Judaism's original spirit, that had been imposed upon the people by their leaders within.[4] Gordon and Berdyczewski thus paved the way for a thoroughgoing re-evaluation of the Jewish cultural heritage.

It was from this reassessment that the extreme activists in the Zionist movement drew their deepest psychological impetus. There was apparently no difference in this regard between the radical left and the radical right. With some variations, they continued to maintain, with Berdyczewski, that it was the Jewish religious ethos that was to blame for the Destruction and the disgrace of exile.

In Brenner, too, we find penetrating self-condemnation. For him, it is the Jews alone who are responsible for their situation: "Enough, enough . . . [with] accusing everyone [else]; enough with blaming the whole world." Despite their treatment of the Jews, the European peoples "are worthy of respect," whereas the Jewish character is merely contemptible, rotten from the start. Thus exile "is not just sorrow and calamity but also, and mainly, the wrongdoing of our forefathers and descendants, . . . punishment and guilt all rolled into one."[5] This self-condemnation led Brenner to a certain understanding of antisemitism.

Brenner's well-known article "Self-Esteem in Three Volumes" is the most extreme example in Hebrew literature of the deep metamorphosis that had taken place in the self-image of the Jews. Brenner's point of departure, influenced to no small extent by Nietzsche, was that Jewish self-esteem had, up until the emergence of modern Hebrew literature, been based upon falsehood or self-delusion. There could be no genius within while degradation and ugliness reigned without. Hence the Jews' repudiation of the gentile world, which was incomparably richer and more beautiful than their own, arose not, as they thought, out of moral or spiritual superiority but rather out of a dreadful inferiority. "Jewishness is invariably a bloody plague. . . . You lie helpless and don't lift a finger. For Brenner, Weininger had been right: "The Jewish character is a feminine one. . . . There is no virility, no creativity. . . . There is [only] unending frivolity, vanity, submissiveness, timidity, and squawking."[6] Brenner calls upon the Jews to accept the harsh judgment of the gentiles, for they (the Jews) really are "base and lowly." Indeed, modern Hebrew literature, in Brenner's view, not only acknowledges the invalidity and lowliness of the Jewish character but also sees this acknowledgment as a necessary precondition for the Jews' elevation and redemption. Taking self-negation to an extreme, he asks, "How shall we be not-we?"[7]

Brenner's blunt accusations are to be seen in light of the main psychological problem with which Zionism sought to come to terms, the lack of a "national will." In his view, the passivity of the Diaspora Jews, their unwillingness to take any collective action to change their situation, is a function of their traditional mentality. The Jews' faith in "their messiah" is both the result and the cause of their weakness.[8] They must be persuaded that salvation depends on them, on their will alone. To this end, there must be a radical transformation in their thinking. They must own up to their "original sin," which was reconciling themselves to the degradation of exile. This confession, which means taking responsibility for their past, also means a willingness to take responsibility for their future.

An insightful discussion of the question of guilt appears in the writings of the poet Ya'akov Cahan. He demands a "fundamental solution" to "the question of [our] weakness": " 'I was too weak' — this phrase could serve as a motto for [all of] Jewish history (Heine). . . . Who and what, then, are to blame? Should we take comfort in the parable of 'the innocent lamb among seventy wolves,'[9] or should we rather examine our own actions to see whether we ourselves are really blameless? And what is the relation between our philosophy of life [*torat hayim*] and our weakness? Which came first? Has there not been a consistent reciprocal relationship between these two things?"[10]

Thus, true self-criticism, according to Cahan, should lead to the conclusion that our "philosophy of life" has been all wrong, that the time has come to correct it and change ourselves. But, how can the people consciously change its identity (in Brenner's words, "How can we be not-we?"); where shall it get the motivation (the "will," as Berdyczewski puts it) to make such a change? These questions are raised by A. D. Gordon (1856–1922) in his polemic against Brenner's "Self Evaluation." He agrees with the notion that the Jewish people at present lacks a strong national will but denies that the source of this weakness lies in the Jewish "character" or culture. For him, it is exile, not tradition, that has destroyed the Jews' will power. Our situation is a tragic one, and in tragic situations there can be no blame. Gordon sees in Berdyczewski's and Brenner's self-negation the "hypnotic," destructive influence of the Enlightenment on the Jews.[11] The most penetrating criticism of the distortion inherent in the Zionist "negation of the Diaspora" is to be found in the work of Yehezkel Kaufmann (1889–1963). He sees this interpretation as demeaning the Diaspora Jews and their culture. In its critique of Jewish culture, the Haskala, he maintains, internalized certain aspects of antisemitism: "The Haskala subscribed to antisemitism's indictment and began demanding that the Jews do penance so as to find favor in the eyes of the nations." The Haskala's moral ideal was that of the gentile, whereas the Jews were "a corrupt, dehumanized people." Zionism inherited this stereotype from the Haskala and based its negation of the Diaspora upon it, innocently assuming that the distorted anti-semitic image would make life in the Diaspora hateful to the younger generation. But, Kaufmann maintains, exile is not a moral sin or a product of any distortion in the character of Jewish culture itself; rather, it is a catastrophe, "an alienated state in which the Jewish collectivity finds itself as a result of certain factors which are no one's fault." Hence, no redemption can come from hating the Diaspora Jew. Kaufmann warns against fostering such hatred, for it can easily lead to a hatred of the Jewish people and of Judaism in general, and then Zionism will achieve the opposite of what it intended: it will instill in the younger generation the kind of self-hatred that has afflicted the Jews of the West: "The redemption of Israel does not mean the redemption of slaves, of wormlike creatures sunk in mire, filth, and depravity, but a people's hope of freeing itself from the cruel fate imposed upon it by its life circumstances.[12]

Appreciation of Martyrdom

Another aspect of the debate over the Jewish people's responsibility for its exiled condition is the question of martyrdom in Jewish history: does it represent inner strength, from which the "new Jew" can derive pride and inspiration, or is it merely passivity, "heroism that is weakness," in Hazaz's phrase, that is worthy of derision and contempt? This question is raised by the non-Zionist historian Simon Dubnow, responding angrily to Max Nordau's disgust with Diaspora Jewish life, which the latter refers to in one of his speeches as "a life of slaves and dogs":

> Can a wandering people that endure so much suffering in God's name, fighting for its eternal ideals and the honor of its flag with a moral heroism unparalleled in human history, be accused of lacking ideals or dignity? Or perhaps Nordau is only prepared to recognize dignity and spirituality in peoples that have conquered vast lands and set up mighty states, armed from head to toe? Glory, then, to the victors and woe to the vanquished! . . . It is he who loses his sense of moral freedom who shall be called a slave, not he who suffers persecution and depredation for the sake of such freedom, that is, he who resists his oppressors, albeit passively. Certainly resistance through action is better than resistance through suffering; but when one has no choice, when one confronts superior force, passive resistance, too, becomes an expression of supreme daring, and suffering becomes a kind of heroism, for they prepare the way for the active struggle of the generations to come.[13]

Though Dubnow does admit the superiority of "resistance through action," he denies that the Jews should feel any moral inferiority, for their passive resistance has been dictated by circumstances. He sees the legacy of passive resistance as a vital asset for future struggle. This raises the question of whether the active rebellion of his own generation represents a complete break from the Diaspora tradition of martyrdom and a return to the kind of heroism the Jews exhibited when they were still living on their own soil or whether it is a new manifestation of their age-old steadfastness. The Zionist movement has been wrestling with this question all along, with particular intensity at the time of the Holocaust.

Brenner, true to his negative assessment of all Diaspora Jewish existence, has no use for Jewish martyrdom, for in his view it does not represent real strength but merely a knack for accommodation.[14] The attitude of the writer Hayim Hazaz (1897–1973) toward martyrdom was more ambivalent. Yudka, the central character of his story "The Sermon," knows there is heroism in being martyred, but he doesn't approve of it because "when there is no choice, anyone can be a hero." Such heroism is "worse than weakness, a special gift of perversity" because it prompts the hero to take pride in what he has done: "See what awful depredations I am enduring! See what contumely and shame I am suffering! Who can compare with me?"[15] On the other hand, in the story "The Muddy Barrel," Moroshka claims that Jewish heroism in the Diaspora is the highest attainment of "completely free men," an attainment unmatched by any other people. The heroism of the latter brings only the spurious honor of "fist-fighters and strongmen who twirl their mustaches and wave their swords."[16] Shaul Tchernichowsky, too, in his early poetry, openly rejects martyrdom, but in poems written in later years his attitude toward martyrdom is much more favorable. Here, the poet depicts the spiritual strength and inner greatness of the martyrs of days gone by. This ambivalence indicates a painful wrestling with the tradition and a wish to invest it with new meaning. Thus, the poet Uri Tzvi Greenberg rejects the very notion of *kiddush hashem* (sanctification of the Name [of God], the customary Hebrew term for martyrdom), preferring instead the revolutionary slogan *haganat hashem* (defense of the Name), which expresses a transition from passivity to activism.[17]

The most complete, complex picture we have of the tendency to bridge the gap between the old and the new may well be in the poetry of Hayim Nahman Bialik (1873–1934). In his earliest poems, "On the Threshold of the House of Study" (1894), while still under the charismatic influence of Ahad Ha'am, he announces:

> My voice shall not be lost in the trumpeting of lies,
> From being a lion among lions I shall perish with lambs.
> I have not been granted fangs or claws —
> All my strength is for God, and God of life!

Bialik takes pride in the fact that Israel is the "nazirite of the nations," not to be redeemed through bloodshed or violence, that has "purified the spirits" and "exorcised the demons" of the "evildoers" among whom it has wandered. He identifies fully with the traditional image of the lamb, symbol of the martyrological ideal, and rejects the lion, symbol of assimilation. In his poem "If You Wish to Know Your Own Soul" (1898), Bialik calls upon the Jew who denies his origins, to recognize the well from which his holy ancestors drew the "strength of soul" that enabled them to "go forth joyfully to their deaths, to present their throats to every polished knife." In his poem "Nay, Verily, You Have Oppressed Us — From the Songs of Bar-Kokhba" (1899), we can already discern the change in his attitude toward the use of force: here he no longer rejects it but sees it as a realistic necessity. At the same time, there is in the poem a clear element of apology for the fact that the people of Israel must resort to force; it is not they who are to be blamed but rather the gentile nations who persecute them and stir up in the them the desire to take vengeance: you have "raised an evil animal, and kept it alive with our blood."

The final stage of the transition can be seen in the poem "The City of Slaughter" (1903), the key concepts of which are *busha* (shame) and *ashma* (guilt). But unlike in the earlier poems, the gentiles themselves do not appear, only the results of their actions, for what Bialik is doing here is calling his people and its God to account. He would seem to be following the pattern of the traditional liturgy, which sees the guilt and shame as a matter not between Jews and gentiles but between Jews and themselves, or, more precisely, between them and their God. By transferring the people's shame to the Divinity, Bialik gives a subtle new theological interpretation to the notion of guilt. The poet, who is the sole witness to God's disgrace, is sent, as it were, to bring the lesson of this disgrace to the Jews. He thus gives the new ethos he is proclaiming a theological dimension: the Jews take their guilt to be of a religious character, stemming from misplaced faith, a profanation rather than sanctification of God's name. They beat their breasts and pronounce themselves guilty. But they do not grasp where their real fault lies. There can only be true guilt where human beings take responsibility for their actions. Instead of taking charge of their destiny, the Jews await "the kindness of the other nations." This is why God abandoned His people. The theological and moral message the poet has been sent to bring the people is meant to awaken them to their true shame and guilt. The Jews today fail to conduct themselves in a way appropriate not only for the "heirs of the Maccabees" but even for the "great-grandchildren of lions [referred to] in [the prayer] 'Merciful Father,' the seed of saints" martyred during the Crusades in whose memory this prayer was composed. Bialik's sarcasm reaches a crescendo when he has God say of the Jews' cowardly, submissive behavior, "they increased My honor in the world, publicly sanctifying My name." The Jews betray the heritage of their past. Traditional martyrdom has become meaningless because the old world of faith has collapsed. Adherence to it is anachronistic and absurd. In the poet's view, the true imperative of the hour is for the Jews to defend themselves and avenge "the indignity of all the generations, from first to last."

It is thus not Jewish martyrology per se that Bialik rejects but only its liturgical use to evade responsibility and cover up failure. He seeks a revolution in Jewish behavior while retaining the positive values of the past. A pattern of conduct that may have been appropriate for other times is no longer appropriate for our own.[18] The traditional idea has lost its old meaning and acquired a revolutionary new meaning better suited to the "transvaluation of values" that has taken place in Judaism.

Following Bialik, Berl Katznelson (introduction to *The Book of Heroism*, 1941) and Zalman Rubashov Shazar (1889–1974) seek in the tradition of martyrdom the roots of present-day Jewish heroism, as demonstrated in the struggle of the Yishuv. In an article published in 1940, before the scope of the Holocaust became known, Shazar heaps praise on the Diaspora tradition of martyrdom. He rejects the view of martyrdom as mere passivity, seeing it rather as an act of conscious choice. The Jew chose death, not out of a love of death, "but out of a hatred of disgrace and a clear sense of where disgrace ended and honor began. There was a clear sense that one could incur disgrace and survive or take the path of honor and pay with one's life." He draws the conclusion that martyrdom is "a manifestation of the highest heroism and entails an activism that is in no way inferior to that of blocking the gate with rifle in hand."[19]

Such an approach was then quite exceptional among the younger generation of the Yishuv, who tended to reject with contempt the idea of martyrdom, particularly after news of the conduct of the Diaspora's Jews during the Holocaust reached Palestine. Even more interesting is the fact that, by contrast, young Diaspora Zionists sought inspiration for their revolt in that very tradition. In summer 1940, the Dror youth movement in Poland published an anthology entitled *Pein un gevuro: ennut ugevura ba'avar hayehudi leor hametziut shel yameinu* (Suffering and Heroism in the Jewish Past in Light of Present-Day Reality). Its introduction states: "We have uncovered the obduracy of men struggling for a great truth and for the right. Our history teaches us that we are a great people, great in its inhuman suffering and in its passion for life. Such a people can be oppressed but never destroyed." Mention is made of the Crusades, the anti-Jewish violence of 1648, and the pogroms in Ukraine during the First World War. "These are three epochs in the history of Jewish martyrology. . . . We can learn from them about our vitality and love of life. The facts we have cited should strengthen our desire to live and to survive this difficult time. . . . Our forebears were martyred and, in the name of the highest idea and truth, withstood the harshest sufferings without succumbing. In the vicissitudes of our life we are like the proverbial phoenix, arising from its ashes to new life."[20]

Ze'ev Ivianski cites these words in contrast to Tzvia Lubetkin, one of the leaders of the Warsaw ghetto uprising, who said that she and her comrades in the underground were rebelling against the whole of Jewish history and "beginning a new Jewish history." For him, "it was not a rebellion against Jewish history as a whole but a stand that represented one of its climaxes, the climax of an ancient tradition, a climax of resistance," which Jewish tradition crowned with the name of *kiddush hashem* (martyrdom). Of course this was not simply a continuation; the emphasis was not on the "glorification of weakness" or even on "attachment to the victim" but rather on the wresting of strength from weakness and suffering.[21] This is also how Abba Kovner (a poet and leader of the Vilna ghetto uprising) interprets the way the ghetto fighters viewed the relevance of past martyrdom to their situation, however different their own struggle may have been: "I tried to explain to my comrades in the ghetto that, while what was happening there was not martyrdom, it was inspired by real martyrdom. In martyrdom there is a choice, but Hitler had not left us any choice."[22]

Thus the metamorphosis of the symbol would seem to be complete: martyrdom represents the steadfastness of the Jewish people throughout the generations, but it takes on different forms in accordance with historical circumstances. "The proverbial phoenix, that rises from its ashes," is the symbol that comes closest to the "living dead," one of the central symbols of Nathan Alterman's poetry (1910–70). It reflects the mysterious, dialectical fate of the Jew, whose ability to survive derives from his awareness of imminent death and who defeats all those who would destroy him.[23] The ancient symbol could thus take on new meaning and serve as one of the main sources of support for the present generation in its real-life struggle.

But this attempt to bridge past and present was not taken up by the younger generation in Palestine, which was completely cut off from the Diaspora heritage. Despite Bialik's original intention of putting new content into old garb, his poem "In the City of Slaughter" was interpreted quite simplistically in Zionist ideology and used to bolster the typically negative attitude toward the Diaspora Jew, an attitude that reached an extreme during the Holocaust.

Sovereignty and Dignity: Between Right and Left

The new Zionist self-image, with its concept of dignity, was based on a negation of "the other." In this view, "the other" is a strange, complicated composite of two negative stereotypes: the enemy Arab and the Diaspora Jew. The Arab represents the constant threat to Jewish existence and arouses dread. The Diaspora Jew, on the other hand, stands for impotence in dealing with this threat, an impotence that derives from certain moral qualities.

According to the scholar and thinker Simon Rawidowicz, who severely criticizes the Zionist negation of the Diaspora, there is not a flaw in our makeup, which Zionism does not attribute to living in exile. The concept of exile *(galut)* plays the same role for Zionist ideology that "the Jew" plays for the gentiles, especially the antisemites.[24] "The exilic mentality" (*galutiut*) is a metaphor for everything that is negative about the Jews. This term has been widely used as a weapon by all sides in the ideological argument in Israel. All are in agreement that the main attribute of the Diaspora Jew is his lack of self-respect. Diaspora existence is shameful because it lacks the most essential ingredient of national honor, political sovereignty. The dream of sovereignty, the most widely shared of Zionist aspirations, cannot be understood in purely instrumental terms ("creating a safe refuge for the Jewish people," as the Basel Platform puts it). It is, first and foremost, the expression of a deep psychological need to restore the dignity of a people that has long suffered humiliation. It was surely Herzl's stress on the quest for political sovereignty, as a means of achieving dignity, that was responsible for the further development of the Zionist myth of auto-emancipation and his own meteoric rise. In this, he seems to have understood the needs of the Jewish masses better than did his opponent Ahad Ha'am.[25]

While the aspiration to political sovereignty was common to all factions in the Zionist movement, the right and left gave it different interpretations. The right was always more sensitive to symbolism. Thus it tended, in its ideology, to place more stress on the elements of degradation and honor. "The Diaspora is ashamed of you, O land," wrote Uri Tzvi Greenberg in the 1930s, at the height of the debate over *havlaga* (self-restraint in response to Arab attacks).[26] Similarly, Abba Ahimeir wrote, "When I read in the daily press about the murder of Jews going unpunished, I despise myself and am ashamed of being Jewish."[27] Palestine was, for Ahimeir, primarily "a rescue station for the people's honor."[28] The honor of Israel came first. The true meaning of honor the Jews would have to learn from the gentiles, for it was not something indigenous to them. The main thing was to change the exilic mentality by promoting identification with the Jewish heroes of old — the Zealots of Jerusalem, the fighters of Massada, and the warriors of Beitar — even though their struggle ended in defeat, and by espousing vengeance as a psychological means of purging the exilic mentality.

The left did not differ from the right in its negativity toward the Diaspora but only in the way it sought to achieve dignity: labor and creativity would accomplish the needed transformation of the Jewish character, rather than struggle against any external enemy. The Jew would regain his honor, first and foremost, by creating with his own hands the social, economic, and cultural basis for his existence. That which a person creates with his own hands is the most authentic expression of his freedom and dignity. The latter is not a matter of any outward attainment but of inward victory in an ongoing struggle between one's good and evil impulses. Man's main enemy is not his environment but himself, his own weakness and despair. Heroism is not expressed in a one-time act of sacrifice or victory in battle but in persistence and endurance in the face of a continuing challenge.[29]

"Jerusalem" and "Yavne"

In 1894, Theodor Herzl published his play "The New Ghetto." Four years later his friend and assistant Max Nordau published a play entitled "Doctor Cohen." In both plays, the Jewish hero feels obliged to challenge his rival, who has offended him, to a duel in defense of the national honor. Although the Jew is killed, he does rescue his people's good name, showing the gentiles that Jews are not just "cowards who can hear themselves defamed without taking up the sword in response." Herzl and Nordau, both of whom came from assimilated backgrounds, expressed in their plays a new concept of Jewish self-respect, which, in turn reflected a change in self-image. It was this new concept that provoked Ahad Ha'am, Herzl's and Nordau's great rival, to attack their literary work. He rejects contemptuously their efforts to glorify their heroes' readiness to die for their injured honor. There is no special moral virtue in such behavior, he maintains; rather, it is a ridiculous imitation of gentile norms: "I need not spell out how opposed such deeds are to the fundamentals of our national morality, that is, not only to the tenets of religion but to the moral sense that lives within us. None of the peoples of Europe, other than a few scholars and writers, has until now been able to liberate itself from this crude idea, that disgrace heaped upon us by others must be erased with our blood. But the true Jew, animated by our national morality, knows in his heart that a culture thousands of years old elevates him high above such heinous acts, which are a vestige of the ignorance and cruelty of old. His 'sense of honor' is secure and cannot be injured in the slightest by the insults of some boor. He responds to them with a single glance of contempt and goes about his business."

In Ahad Ha'am's view, Jewish notions of "the value of life and the essence of honor" are incompatible with the thinking of the heroes of Herzl's and Nordau's plays. For Jews, the useless sacrifice of life is not an act of honor but of infamy, and whoever commits it "betrays his people and sullies its true honor," which is that of its character and morality. This is far more precious and holy to them than their imaginary honor in the eyes of the gentiles."[30] Thus Ahad Ha'am distinguishes between "true honor," which goes along with authentic Jewishness, the fruit of a millennial tradition, and "imaginary honor," which is the fruit of imitating gentile ways.

Ahad Ha'am's critique of Herzl reflects his solid belief in a connection between the way Jews understood the value of life and honor, on one hand, and their ability to survive down through the ages, on the other. The secret of the Jews' survival, he maintains, is that "the Prophets, already in ancient times, taught them to respect only spiritual power and not stand in fear of superior physical force." The people's existence is assured as long as it clings to this belief. Herzl's insistence on a state as the sole solution only endangers the people's existence because it is likely to undermine the moral qualities that have enabled them to remain true to themselves; it may well lead them to seek their "honor" in the attainment of "physical power." Thus the thread connecting the people's present with its past will be severed and its historic base pulled out from under it.[31]

True to this viewpoint, Ahad Ha'am thought it was the Sages of Yavne and not the Zealots of Jerusalem who had saved the people from destruction, "for they concerned themselves with the eternal and not the temporal."[32] Although he follows a traditional Jewish line of thought, he casts it in secular terms: it is not the political framework as such that is decisive for Jewish survival but the spiritual and moral content of the Jewish people's life. This view came to characterize an entire school of Zionist thought. We find it, for example, in Brit Shalom.[33] The opponents of this school would later claim that it was typically "exilic" in its outlook.

Ahad Ha'am reflects the change that took place in the way Jews understood their historical fate: as long as they relied on divine providence, it was obvious to them that they did not need to worry about their political fortunes but only to fulfill the precepts of the eternal Torah, which protected them. Jewish survival was assured by God, for "the Eternal One of Israel shall not prove false."[34] There is an irrational optimism here regarding the ability of the Jewish people to survive in exile, in the face of the ever-present threat of extinction. But once it loses its belief in the "Eternal One of Israel" and the Torah as its protector and begins to see itself as master of its own historical and political fate, it is faced with the question of what will, in fact, keep it alive.

Zionism was notably pessimistic about the Jewish situation in the Diaspora. It was obsessed with the question of survival and debated this question with great vigor, along with the question of what ethos would be most conducive to survival. The new national values were understood not only as ends in themselves, but also as means of ensuring survival. This new turn is most evident in the writings of Ahad Ha'am, and it is responsible for the vehemence of the reactions they elicited.

Ahad Ha'am's severest critic was, of course, Berdyczewski. He raises two objections to the "national morality" Ahad Ha'am posited as a necessary condition for continued Jewish existence. The first objection is historical: if we look at Jewish history with an impartial eye, we shall see that there were periods when the ethic of scorn for brute force did not hold sway, for example, the Maccabean era or that of Bar Kokhba. What is more, even the conquest of the Land in the time of Joshua, which made possible "the creation of a spiritual and material refuge for the people" — an allusion to Ahad Ha'am's concept of the aims of Zionism — runs counter to his "national morality" in that it entailed displacement of the original inhabitants. Berdyczewski remarks ironically that if Ahad Ha'am had been the editor-in-chief of our ancient scriptures, he would have condemned such acts as barbaric and ordered the scriptures locked up in a *geniza*.

Berdyczewski's second argument is ideological: the Jewish people cannot go on living without regaining its self-respect. But in order to do this it must first undergo an inner transformation based on a re-evaluation of its historical heritage. The Jewish past must undergo a massive re-assessment, negating what needs to be negated and keeping what needs to be kept. Without such a re-assessment there is no chance of a Jewish revival.[35] Berdyczewski represents that school of thought that was trying to lay the groundwork for a "counter-history," i.e., to create "a counter-identity by distorting the other's self-image and identity and destroying his collective memory." His main weapon was the revision and reinterpretation of the source-texts.

Berdyczewski had no use for the Jews' traditional view of themselves as "a lamb among wolves," an image that up to that point had been considered a form of praise. Can it be, he asks, that an entire people will go on living only by virtue of the pity it arouses without being at all ashamed? It is not the Holy One, blessed be He, who is responsible for the exile of Israel from its land but the people itself, for the latter was not prepared to make any sacrifices for its land and began to flee even before the land vomited it out. Only a people like the Greeks, that is willing to fight for its land, deserves to stay on it. Berdyczewski thinks a determined "national will" could have changed Jewish history and prevented destruction and dispersion. Who is at fault for the weakening and decline of that "will"? The answer is the spirit of Yavne, which has taken over the people and instilled in it the ethic of softness and submission. In his attack on Ahad Ha'am, Berdyczewski declares that what we need now is a new Yohanan ben-Zakkai who will flee from Yavne back to Jerusalem. "Yavne and Jerusalem are antagonistic," and Jerusalem is to be preferred. "[The Zealots] who fell upon their swords . . . were superior to those who escaped the walls hidden in coffins."[36]

The polemic being conducted to this very day in the Zionist movement between Yavne and Jerusalem, or between Yavne and Massada, reflects not only opposing versions of Jewish honor and morality but also opposing spiritual strategies, each with different political implications for Jewish existence. The controversy over "metaphors" of Jewish identity and the factors making for Jewish survival has reached the public realm and becomes highly emotional in times of political struggle.[37] This debate finds expression, not only in *publicité* but also in belles lettres and, needless to say, historiography. Since the debate is about how the Jewish people has survived in the past, it is bound to be of highest importance for deciding the people's future course: will survival best be guaranteed by compromise with superior force or by uncompromising struggle?

"Which kept the Jewish people alive, Yavne or Massada?" asked Abba Ahimeir in the early forties and then answered definitively: all those peoples that made their peace with Roman rule have vanished from the face of the earth, whereas the Jews, who did not submit — either in Jerusalem or at Massada or at Beitar — still live, full of vigor and potency. For him, a people that does not give in will in the end be victorious, even after the most dreadful reverses, but a people that surrenders is destined to perish.[38] Yohanan ben-Zakkai is seen by Ahimeir as a traitor; not only did he collaborate with the enemy and contribute to the loss of the homeland, but he prepared the way for Diaspora Judaism.[39] The poet Yonatan Ratosh calls ben-Zakkai "the Jewish Petain" and a quisling.[40] Yitzhak Tabenkin, too, denies that Yohanan ben-Zakkai saved the Jewish spirit: "Our national existence was preserved by the military valor of the Jewish zealots and its memory, [the valor of] those who fought and did not give in, who clung until the last minute to the hope of victory. Thanks to them, the name of Yohanan ben-Zakkai, too, was kept alive, as were the Torah, the Hebrew language and culture, and the humane spirit our people has manifested."[41]

The advocates of "Jerusalem" maintained that their point of view was compatible with the Torah of Israel, which rules out any compromise when it comes to the fundamental issues of the people's survival. The advocates of "Yavne" naturally make the opposite claim. For them, Yavne symbolizes the eternity of the Jewish spirit, its superiority to physical strength, and thus a willingness to compromise on the political plane in order to ensure spiritual freedom, which is of the essence.

Yehezkel Kaufmann disputes Berdyczewski's claim that Yavne and Jerusalem were antagonistic. For him, Jerusalem would not have been possible without Yavne. Rabban Yohanan ben-Zakkai was an authority not only for Rabbi Akiva but also for the "ruffians." At Yavne, the strength the nation needed from time to time for war, rebellion, and messianic ferment accumulated. Hence it was by virtue of the ethos of Yavne, on one hand, and the memory of and hope for Jerusalem, on the other, that the Jewish people was able to survive in exile.[42]

Massada and the Warsaw Ghetto Uprising

Among the Zionist myths of power, that of Massada arouses the sharpest controversy, both in Israel and abroad. This myth, which has been a cornerstone of Zionist education for fifty years, has also been condemned in the harshest terms as symbolizing Zionism's distorted attitude toward power.[43] As in every argument over the use of myths, this argument, too, is at bottom politically motivated, yet at the same time it reflects a larger question that has concerned Zionism from the outset: how to ensure Jewish survival? Two main objections, the psychological and the historical or theological, have been raised to the use of the Massada symbol for educational purposes.

According to the psychological argument, the Massada myth expresses despair and a willingness to commit national suicide, in imitation of the besieged Jews of that ancient fortress. In other words, it implies a preference for death with honor over survival. The slogans "Massada shall not fall again" and "Never again" do not inspire courage or a will to fight to victory but rather a conviction that defeat is inevitable. Thus they become, in effect, a prophecy bound to fulfill itself through rash and extreme acts, blind to any alternatives. Stubborn adherence to a single-minded strategy can breed disaster.

Psychologists and historians both speak of a "Massada complex" (or "Massada syndrome") that is precipitated by prolonged psychological pressure. The reference is to any group of people that mistakenly feels isolated and permanently threatened by hostile forces and, as a result, develops a complex of persecution or anxiety not based on reality. In the present context, this analysis assumes that Israel, as a strong military power, is no longer under any threat of destruction and therefore that its anxiety is the result of a fixation on the past. The event — or symbol — from the past dictates political action in the present and blurs the vision of the political future.

This psychological interpretation seems to me exaggerated. The myth is not meant to reconstruct a past event but only to extract from it the elements that are needed as paradigmatic symbols. The mass suicide at Massada has never been an integral part of the present-day interpretation of the myth. It has either been left out or covered over, and, instead, two other elements, more essential to the Zionist mentality, have been stressed: the sense, always deeply rooted in the pioneer ethos, of being the last remnant; and the readiness to wage an unrelenting struggle for a new Jewish life in a situation of extreme isolation.

Originally, Massada symbolized the last refuge from a life of exile that had become intolerable. It was not the collective suicide that was taken as exemplary but the desperate struggle to create a new form of Jewish life based on freedom. It was, first and foremost, a personal struggle of each person with himself, out of an awareness that "there is nowhere else to turn" (Brenner) and "this is the final shore" (Katznelson). But it was also a collective struggle: the Zionist enterprise as a whole represented a kind of Massada, seen as a symbol not of despair but of a refusal to accept the demise of the Jewish people and a last chance for it to go on living. The readiness to give one's all to this struggle was a kind of wager against a fate that seemed sealed but that might yet be averted.[44] The slogan "Massada shall not fall again" was not an expression of confidence in the future but a desperate summons to muster all available inner strength in defense of this new beginning. For only when one finds himself in a situation from which there is no escape does he discover his full powers, enabling him to turn the inevitable to the avoidable. In the incisive formulation of Shlomo Lavi, "one hears among us an expression, 'Not Massada,' meaning no last stand, no suicide for the sake of redemption from slavery. And I say to you, we must be prepared for Massada too, prepared for the worst. And if we are really ready for this, too, we shall never again find ourselves at Massada but rather achieve complete freedom and the redemption of Israel from its black exile."[45]

The message of Massada is that we must be strong, so that we need never again be forced to choose between death and the humiliation of flight or submission. The slogan "Never again," that became popular after the Holocaust, is also less an expression of confidence in the future, confidence that we shall never again face destruction, than a firm decision that as Jews we must never again allow ourselves to fall into the kind of degradation and oppression that the Diaspora Jews came to against their will. And the surest, if not the only way of preventing this is to acquire political and military power. True, aspiring to power can blind us to the limits of power and the existence of alternatives. But this danger does not negate the importance in principle of the reality of power in the kinds of extreme situations in which the Jewish people has found itself, situations symbolized by Massada.

The other criticism of the educational use of the Massada symbol is the historical and theological one. Religious and nonreligious Jews alike have maintained that the deed committed at Massada runs counter to both the letter and spirit of Judaism and should not be held up as an example. Thus the sociologist Nahman Ben-Yehuda, in his detailed research into this myth, reveals the way historians and archaeologists like Yosef Klausner and Shmaryahu Gutman have adapted the story of Yosef Ben-Matityahu to the Zionist program. He says, "the cult of Massada is a cult of death, a cult of suicide, opposed to the principles of the Jewish religion, which values life and survival."[46] It has been pointed out that Jewish historiography glides over Massada almost completely; there is no mention of it in the traditional Jewish sources. The main stream of Judaism passes through Yavne, and it, not Massada, is what has kept the Jewish people alive. Judaism prizes life over death ("the sanctity of life"), and suicide is absolutely forbidden by Halakha. In only three cases does Halakha oblige us to "be killed rather than transgress": when forced, on pain of death, to commit "idolatry, fornication, and bloodshed." In other words, when the physical survival of the collectivity is weighed against its independence, it is survival that takes precedence, even though that may mean submission and humiliation; life may not be endangered for the sake of freedom. Massada is "an example of the highest heroism on the part of people who had no alternative, no option but the highest heroism, the supreme sacrifice." But "we are the children of those who refused to take their own lives, preferring to go into exile and choosing a life of degradation over heroism and greatness."[47]

As we have said, the accusation of suicide is irrelevant. Thus there remains the question to what degree the halakhic norms of martyrdom fit the modern Jewish situation. The inner difficulty in this will become clear if we substitute for Massada the Warsaw ghetto uprising, an action that has no justification in Halakha either. It is no accident that a figure like Rabbi Moshe Blau, a leader of Agudat Yisrael in the 1940s, could maintain that the Warsaw uprising "is not a Jewish phenomenon." In contrast to him, Tabenkin's view was that there was an analogy between a war of honor and a war of survival. The fighters of the Warsaw Ghetto were fighting for "the existence of Israel, for its honor." Regarding the ultra-Orthodox, who saw this uprising as "un-Jewish," he is harshly critical: "The Torah of Israel will not survive without the honor of Israel. Those who fought for its honor also saved its Torah."[48]

If we look at Jewish history with an impartial eye, we shall observe an instructive dialectic between the survival of the people and the survival of Judaism. On one hand, it is assumed that the people exists for the sake of fulfilling the Torah, hence the obligation to submit to martyrdom (in Hebrew, "sanctify the Divine Name") in certain circumstances. On the other hand, since the fulfillment of the Torah depends on the existence of the people, there are situations where the people's survival takes precedence over fulfilling the commandments, according to the principle that "You shall live by them" (Lev 18:5). The obligation to submit to martyrdom applies to each individual Jew, according to Maimonides (Laws of the Principles of the Torah 5:1–2); but it is doubtful that this obligation applies to the people as a whole. The tradition of martyrdom assumes that the martyrs will leave behind survivors, who will be inspired by their example to adhere all the more strongly to their faith. But if the self-sacrifice results in the annihilation of the entire people, it will have been a meaningless act. In other words, it is the physical existence of the people that makes martyrdom possible, and in certain circumstances this existence takes precedence over the fulfillment of the Torah. From a halakhic point of view it would be absurd to defend the observance of the commandments at the risk of the people's very life.[49]

Faced with the Nazi program of the total subjugation, humiliation, and annihilation of the Jews, the ghetto fighters decided they had to depart from the traditional norm and take up arms. Even if by this act they did not save themselves, it would serve as an example of martyrdom to the survivors. It is quite clear that this taking up of arms was not an act of collective suicide — Samson's "Let me perish with the Philistines" — but of faith in the continued existence, both physical and spiritual, of the Jewish people, an act from which the survivors would be able to draw the inner strength needed to hold fast to their Jewishness.

In short, it was the extreme nature of the situation, unprecedented in Jewish history, that forced the Jews to incorporate the uprising, the risking of life for the sake of life, into their scheme of "Jewish" values, something which had never before occurred to halakhic scholars to do. This resulted in the need to change the norms of martyrdom itself. And indeed, one of the leading halakhists in the Warsaw ghetto, Rabbi Menahem Zamba, concluded that under the circumstances it would be halakhically forbidden to undergo martyrdom in the way it had been done in the past. Because the enemy aims to destroy everything, we may not deliver ourselves into his hands: "If today Jews were being forced into apostasy, and we could be saved by agreeing to it, as was done in Spain or after the decrees of 1096 [the First Crusade], our death would in itself be a kind of martyrdom, but today [when apostasy would do no good, and there is no possibility of living as a non-Jew], the only way of sanctifying God's name is by actually taking up arms."[50]

This view reflects a sharp awareness of the difference between one historical situation and another and the need to adapt the Halakha accordingly. Of course, there is a difference between the situation of Massada and that of the

Warsaw ghetto, and it is this that explains why it was the former and not the latter that was chosen as the principal symbol of the Zionist struggle. Massada represents a choice between the certain death that would follow surrender and exile and the chance of a new life in the Land of Israel, whereas the Warsaw ghetto uprising symbolizes a choice between death in surrender and death in defiance. Nevertheless, the spiritual and moral basis of these two situations is the same: in both cases, resistance grew out of a sense of humiliation at the prospect of surrender and death; both represent situations of extreme isolation, together with a desire to break out of this isolation through resistance and achieve equality and solidarity with humanity as a whole.

The slogan "honor or death," common to many modern national liberation movements, seems to posit honor as a higher value than life itself. The Jewish philosopher Hannah Arendt attacked the Zionist movement, at the time of its struggle to establish a state (1946–49), for having adopted this slogan. A former activist in the World Zionist Organization, she was bitterly critical of its readiness to "die with honor, weapon in hand." This stance seemed to her to signify a negative change in the Jewish people's strategy of survival. Instead of "survival at all costs," which had been their chief concern for many generations, there now appeared something quite new among them, "honor at all costs." After two thousand years of exilic thinking, the Jews had suddenly stopped believing in survival as an absolute good and gone to the opposite extreme. Like the critics of the Massada myth, Arendt saw this stance as a danger to Zionism, for it seemed to reflect desperation and a readiness to commit suicide. This was behind her condemnation of the armed struggle of the Yishuv in general and the War of Independence in particular.[51]

In fact, the Jewish people had never seen survival as an absolute good; there was also the imperative "to be killed rather than transgress." One might even say it was precisely *because* they did not see survival as an end in itself that the Jews managed to survive. Furthermore, Zionism did not regard honor or dignity as opposed to survival but as an integral part of it. If dignity is understood as a whole cluster of values that make up identity, the choice between dignity and survival becomes less than absolute, for dignity is then a necessary condition for survival. To lose self-respect means to lose the meaning of life. Primo Levi, the Italian-Jewish writer and Holocaust survivor, speaks of the dilemma faced by his friend, the philosopher Jean Améry (also a Holocaust survivor), who had been assimilated as a Jew before the war. He did not feel capable of assuming an identity he did not have, for it seemed to him false and dissembling; tradition was, by definition, something one could only inherit. But "one needs an identity, or rather dignity, in order to live. In [Améry's] view, the two concepts overlapped; losing the one meant losing the other and dying spiritually; and once one's defenses are down he is also exposed to physical extinction."[52]

When the price of survival is renunciation of the last vestige of freedom and independence, giving one's life for them can come to seem preferable. The Jewish psychologist Bruno Bettelheim, who had had humiliating experiences in a Nazi concentration camp, wrote: "To survive as a man, not a walking corpse, as a debased and degraded but still human being, one had, first and foremost, to remain informed and aware of what made up one's personal point of no return, the point beyond which one would never, under any circumstances, give in to the oppressor, even if it meant risking and losing one's life."[53]

Clearly there is always the question to what extent self-respect can be forfeited. The oppressed, if they want to live, must draw lines in their relations with their oppressors. (It is this that is meant by "[being] killed rather than transgress"). The literature of the Holocaust supplies numerous examples of wrestling with the terrible moral price of survival: loss of self-respect so extreme that it raises the question of whether life is still worth living. In any event, those who struggle for dignity in a conscious way do not see their struggle as opposed to life but as a necessary condition for it. Viktor Frankl, the psychologist and Holocaust survivor, believed that "the search for meaning has 'survival value.' . . . Survival depends on 'for what' and 'for whom.' Existence is thus a matter of man's ability to 'transcend himself.' "[54]

Never has this truth been so clearly demonstrated as in the extreme situation faced by the ghetto insurgents. Precisely because, in their case, the national collective was confronted so brutally with the dilemma of the moral price of survival, the value of honor emerges, not as opposed to survival but as a condition of it. The decision to struggle in the face of certain death is an affirmation of the value of life, not in the physical but in the moral sense. It is an expression of loyalty to human values that gives meaning to existence, as we see in the words of Szymon Draenger, commander of the Jewish underground in the Cracow ghetto: "We have not prostrated ourselves in the least before the fatalism of death. . . . In its tactics and its propaganda, the enemy has forced our people to deal with problems of survival. To survive and to enjoy life, come what may, have become our people's watchword. The price of survival depends on the flexibility of each person's conscience or the possibilities opened up by money. But we affirm that we mean to survive only as free men and, if that is not possible, to die as free men. We want to live, and we know what for, but for that very reason we must fight."[55]

To go knowingly to one's death is to proclaim uncompromising loyalty to the entire cluster of values signified by the word "honor." In this basic sense, the ghetto uprising does not differ from traditional martyrdom. In both there is a metaphysical revolt in which the individual, to quote Viktor Frankl, "transcends himself." They differ in the address to which the revolt is directed. Martyrdom is a form of witness that breaks out of the circle of Jewish loneliness in a religiously hostile world in order to get directly to the Heavenly Throne. The ghetto revolt is a form of witness that tries to overcome Jewish loneliness within a world alienated from its human roots in order to achieve a new human solidarity. The struggle of the insurgents to "save Jewish honor" and their willingness to die for it do not seem to them matters of despair but of faith in the future of mankind in general and consequently of the Jewish people, which is to survive and renew its life in its own homeland. The uprising is a humane act meant to affirm the equal right of the Jews to survive as free people. For the insurgents, the sacrifice of their lives was to have meaning for those who would live on after them and carry on their way of life, realizing the human and national values for which they, the insurgents, were struggling. It was thus an exalted expression of national and human solidarity. Even the motto of the fighters, "We are fighting for three lines in history," cannot be understood merely as a desire for praise. Who would remember them or speak of their heroism? The people that would survive would draw the strength to rebuild its life from this memory: "Our death would be meaningless did we not feel that after we were gone there would be those [Jews in Palestine] who would mention our names with true emotion. Therefore, in the face of certain death, we are united with them in a battle for the future, and we wish to die in such a way that the disgrace of dying as slaves will not bring shame on the Jewish people in the future. We must lift up the banner of the dying folk, purge from its flesh the stain of slavery, and place it in the ranks of those peoples whose spirit is free."[56]

As Arendt notes, one of the hallmarks of modern totalitarian regimes is that they are not content with killing their enemies but insist on obliterating all trace of them as well. The main purpose of the German concentration camps was not just to eliminate their inmates from the face of the earth but to do so in such a way that no one would remember these people had ever existed. They perished anonymously, leaving no tracks, like nameless slaves who die and are forgotten: "Into darkness he departs, and in darkness is his name covered up" (Eccles 6:4). A free man rails against anonymous death; through his actions he leaves behind testimony to his existence. The ghetto uprising thus expressed not only a desire to die with honor but also a powerful will to live, to triumph against both physical and spiritual extinction. As they went to their deaths, the fighters saw their lives being carried on by the national and human collective to which they belonged. Their death had a larger historical meaning, which transcended the ending of their individual lives.

This motif, the close connection between the meaning of life and the meaning of death, has recurred frequently in Hebrew literature since Bialik first expressed it in his poem "The City of Slaughter." Bialik's lament for the slaughtered Jews of Kishinev was, "Your deaths are as meaningless as your lives." His words echo in the contrasting eulogy given by Ya'akov Zerubavel for the fallen members of Hashomer, written in 1912: "They lived beautifully and died beautifully; there was meaning to their lives, and there is meaning to their deaths." The victims did not, he explains, give their lives for a collective ideal external to them: "They themselves lived on the land and worked it, they themselves poured out their spirit and energy in this place, and the heroism of their death grew directly out of their life's activity."[57] There is hence a decisive difference between death that befalls a person as his inescapable fate, that he accepts or tries to evade, and death toward which one marches with open eyes, in the midst of struggle. As soon as one becomes the master of his own death he gives meaning to both his life and his death, a meaning contained in the word "dignity." But here this word means being not only true to one's conscience but also connected to a national or human collectivity before which the individual, in his fight, is seeking to bear witness. For those who remain behind and who remember him as they carry on their struggle for honor — for these, too, his death has a meaning. Avraham Sharon (Schwadron) compares the death of Jews in a pogrom in the Diaspora to the death of Jews in the Land of Israel:

> The difference between offering one's neck to the knife and [a death of defiance, signified by the cry of Samson,] "Let me perish with [my killers]" has to do, not with the part of the people condemned to destruction, but rather the part that survives, the people as a whole, which today lives in the wake of the annihilation of the Six Million and which will go on living after we are gone. . . . The difference is in the sensitivity that terrible catastrophe has instilled in the people's soul as it continues to struggle for life, redemption and freedom. . . . When our casualties occur on foreign soil, as a result of rioting and depredation anywhere in the world, it depresses our people and breaks their spirit, it causes their hands to go slack. But self-sacrifice, a heroic death in the homeland, sets an example, lifting our spirits, strengthening us and making us more productive.[58]

What Sharon's analysis implies is that the great value of Zionism lies not in providing the Jews with a safe haven, but in making it possible for them to live dignified, meaningful lives and die purposeful deaths.

The "Guilt" of the Holocaust Victims

Sharon's favorable comparison of death while fighting in the homeland with the passive death of the Diaspora Jews was written after the Holocaust, as part of a debate that raged in Israel over the behavior of those who had been the Holocaust's victims. The debate exposed a particularly raw nerve in the society in its complex relation, torn between shame and guilt, to what happened in Europe. The course of the debate was subsequently affected to no small degree by a changing climate of thinking and by the widening scope of historical scholarship, which gradually made for a less one-sided perspective. The Holocaust greatly exacerbated feelings of shame, for the Diaspora Jews had "preferred to die like beaten dogs rather than with dignity." This arrogant, distorted statement of Yitzhak Grynboim, a Zionist functionary who at one time had been one of the leaders of Polish Jewry, is not unusual in Zionist writing of that period. It is the product of a simplistic ideology that presented the Diaspora and its Jews as utterly lacking in a sense of honor, i.e., positive human values. The pain and indignity caused by Jewish weakness turned to a violent hatred of exile and a hunger for power. Implied in this view was the notion that the Jews, in their shortsightedness, passivity, and lack of self-respect, were essentially responsible for their fate. It was only because of the ghetto fighters that the honor of the Jewish people was saved.[59] From here it was not a great leap to the accusation, made by respected philosophers, historians, and psychologists like Hannah Arendt, Raul Hilberg, and Bruno Bettelheim, that the Jews had essentially collaborated with their exterminators. This distorted view of history, categorically distinguishing the heroism of those who rebelled from the cowardice and apparent treason of those who did not, was attacked by Alterman as early as in the fifties. He maintained that it was unfair to compare the life of the people in its own land with that in exile. Under exilic conditions, submission was not a sign of cowardice or lack of self-respect. It was not necessary to impugn the self-respect of the Diaspora Jews, the poet wrote, in order to justify the Zionist vision, nor do we have the right to deny Jewish history its dignity and heroism, "even when there is no gun in its hand and it is not on the firing line."[60]

In his very important eyewitness account, written not long before the final liquidation of the Cracow ghetto in 1943, Szymon Draenger examines unsparingly the reactions of the ghetto Jews to the extermination process. In a few sentences, he rejects all the antisemitic stereotypes concerning Jewish cowardice and submissiveness: "Of all the possible reactions of which they were capable," the one most congenial to them was "scornful superiority or unfeeling apathy — and, in any case, not active retaliation." For him, it was not cowardice that prevented the ghetto Jews from fighting but their exilic mentality. "Since time immemorial the Jewish people has recoiled from the law of the fist and from all physical violence. . . . The sanctity of the human creature and of his life do not allow us to take up arms and spill human blood, however many millions of victims this attitude has cost us." This, in his view, is a "pathological phenomenon," and it has put down such deep roots that it would be hard, well-nigh impossible, to root it out. Draenger tries to persuade his fellow Jews that the truest, healthiest, most natural response of free human beings to extreme evil is "fist against fist." But unlike the Palestinian Jews, whose reaction to Jewish behavior in the ghettos was one of profound shame, Draenger is ready to admit that "in the calm, hopeless gaze of [the ghetto Jews] into the eyes of death there was a greater measure of courage than could be found in any physical struggle with the enemy."[61]

But there was another, less obvious side to the bitter critique of the exilic Jews: it served to assuage the Yishuv's own guilt feelings for having stood by helplessly while they were being murdered. These feelings, which the psychologists call "survivor guilt," occur in those spared in life-threatening situations.[62] Stressing the disgrace of those who perished, as opposed to the dignity of the insurgents, helped relieve the distress occasioned by the failure of the Zionist movement to live up to its own watchword of taking responsibility for the Jewish people and saving it from destruction: when the crunch came, it had been unable to do so. There was, to be sure, some comfort in the fact that objective circumstances had limited its capacity to act, but this was not enough to wipe away the guilt entirely. Even as the Holocaust was taking place, the historian Ben-Tzion Dinur had called upon the Jewish people in general and the Zionist movement in particular to take stock and to ask itself: "Whose fault is it that the Holocaust has caught us so unprepared . . . ? In this, we have sinned, transgressed, committed iniquity against our people, against mankind, and against God. The first and most sacred duty of the living is to give an accounting. Why did the evil overtake us so suddenly, leaving no escape?"[63] For his part, Abba Kovner, a generation later, maintained that it was guilt that characterized our attitude toward the victims: "As we fortify our future, we are reeling from a heavy blow of guilt. The desire to preserve one of the most basic Jewish traits has led us to this difficult and terrible pass, which shows no sign of ever easing up."[64]

The ongoing argument over the extent of the Yishuv's rescue efforts during the Holocaust is thus the other side of the coin of the argument over the behavior of the victims: the guilt of the latter is juxtaposed with that of the former. The responses of the Yishuv have oscillated between shame and guilt. Over the years, the sense of guilt felt by Israelis has grown stronger. This guilt has displaced, or at least balanced out, the feeling of shame so prevalent in the Yishuv in the immediate aftermath of the catastrophe.

4

"The Remnant of Israel"

> To be a Zionist, you must first be one who understands the sorrow of the
> nation and the tragedy of the nation, one of pure heart and clear mind,
> and at the same time believe in the possibility of impossibility and have
> limitless strength to work for it and follow an untrodden path.
>
> Yosef Hayim Brenner, Me'ever lagvulin (Beyond the bounds)

The Wager as a Form of Faith

In the previous chapter, I discussed one of the most powerful motives for
the radical change in the self-image of the modern Jew and for the emergence
of the Zionist ethos of power: the feeling of shame and the passionate desire to
recover Jewish dignity. In this chapter, I shall discuss another motive, which I
call "the sense of ending." In Jewish tradition, the word *ketz* (end) has a
double meaning: it can be an ending, a final destruction, but also a new beginning, a redemption. This double meaning played an important role in the
discourse of the pioneers who came to the Land of Israel in the first decades of
the twentieth century.

Even the cynic will concede that the history of Zionism provides impressive
evidence for the power of a minority possessed by ideas and dreams drawn
from the depths of the spirit of an ancient people to alter the face of reality. The

course of Jewish history in the last hundred years has been decisively changed by a small group of people whose main characteristic was enthusiastic belief in the power of ideas and a passionate commitment to their realization.[1] Most of the opponents of Zionism at the time of its inception thought it was a kind of madness, an utterly unrealistic utopian daydream. Truly, had it not been for certain objective conditions favorable to the realization of its vision, Zionism would have failed, like many other abortive political movements in the modern age. Yet, essentially, it was conviction that wrought this decisive turn in the course of Jewish history.

To explain the motivation of this minority, I shall use the concept of "wager." I believe this idea is the Zionism's Archimedean point, the psychological power that drives it and shapes its ethos. The wager is a form of faith that Zionism inherited from Judaism but filled with new meaning: the resolve to ensure the survival of the Jewish people in an apparently hopeless situation. In such a situation, ambivalence and hesitation — waiting to act until there is a better chance of success or no risk at all — is out of the question since it can bring catastrophe and certain destruction; if there is any chance at all of rescue, it depends on bold, decisive action. If we decide to act, it is as though we made the following deliberation: if we choose inaction we shall certainly lose out, but if we have faith and act on it, we have a chance of winning; acting (having faith) cannot bring worse results than not acting (not having faith), but it has the potential of achieving better results. There is no certainty, only hope.[2]

The wager is a call to believe in ourselves, in our fellow human beings, or in God. If, for instance, we come to the realization that society is declining and will disintegrate if we do not act to change its course, and the goodwill of all of us and a shared belief in the possibility of change are required if we are to do so. The more who share this belief, the greater our chances of success. The fate of the world, or of society, depends on whether at least some individuals are willing to exert themselves to the utmost, knowing that others will stand on the sidelines and that the effort may not succeed. Whether or not to act is up to the individual. The decision is not a matter of logic, but there is also nothing absurd about it. Belief in the good is every bit as rational as its opposite. In any event, the individual determines her own fate. Yet it is only by virtue of her confidence, as expressed in her decision to act, that the world can be improved.[3] The individual cannot guarantee success, but she can determine whether the necessary conditions for success will be created. In Buber's words, "Each person determines the fate of the world with his whole being and all his acts to a degree that neither he nor anyone else knows; for whatever causality we perceive is only a tiny part of the totality of invisible, infinitely varied action of all upon all." Behind every human act, Buber continues, there is infinite responsibility. But there are those who feel this responsibility particularly keenly.[4]

The wager is based on practical, not theoretical, belief, i.e., on belief that can be confirmed or disproved by its results, which are unforeseeable. Gambling is thus a kind of self-fulfilling prophecy. If the outcome is positive, it will have been a true prophecy; if it is negative, the prophecy will have been false. Faith is a kind of active psychological power that permanently rejects and challenges the "factuality" of reality. The wager is not meant to validate the underlying faith but rather to motivate faith to begin with. In a situation that calls for taking a wager, the question of what we should do ceases to be a theoretical one and becomes practical. It makes a claim upon our will after having disposed of the stumbling blocks placed in our way by the skeptical, theoretical intellect, with its presumption of supremacy over our lives. The call to believe can only be addressed to one who has already been convinced intellectually but who claims she cannot bring herself to real faith; it will never be possible to convince someone who does not see the situation as offering a live, compelling option.

The Wager in Jewish History

The roots of the wager as a feature of Jewish faith can already be discerned in the prophetic view of history, which combines the divine decree with human freedom of choice. In *The Prophetic Faith,* Buber shows the Prophets assuming a dialectical relationship, not accessible to rational understanding, between the divine decree and human responsibility. From God's point of view, the future is already determined; but human beings must make decisions afresh every day as if the future were in their hands, knowing that, in the last analysis, they are subject to transcendent forces.[5] "The true prophet does not announce an immutable decree. He speaks into the power of decision lying in the moment, in such a way that his message of disaster just touches this power."[6]

In the face of seemingly unavoidable catastrophe, human beings tend to adopt two opposed positions: on one hand, succumbing to complete pessimism and despair on the assumption that the larger forces of reality are uncontrollable, so that there is nothing to be done; on the other hand, fully marshalling their inner powers to take practical action in order to change reality. In this situation a person is faced with the question of whether he should dare to undertake the impossible or simply make his peace with the inevitable. This decision can be made only on the basis of faith and trust, for "what is possible in a certain hour and what is impossible cannot be adequately ascertained by any foreknowledge. It goes without saying that, in the one sphere as in the other, one must start at any given time from the nature of the situation insofar as it is at all recognizable. But one does not learn the measure and limit of what is attainable in a desired direction otherwise than through going in this direction."[7] For Buber, this was the lesson God taught the prophet Jonah, who had thought the course of history was predetermined and could not be diverted. The Book of Jonah sets out to destroy the belief in historical determinism and assert that anything is possible, both complete destruction and redemption. It is on this assumption that the prophetic notion of *teshuva* (repentance, turning, or return) is predicated. If we do not repent, we shall certainly be lost; if we do repent, "perhaps God will have pity on us and we shall not perish," but "who knows whether God will change His mind?" (Jonah 1:6, 3:9). "Perhaps" and "who knows" are key terms in this tale of repentance.[8] Buber put this well: "Human turning and divine turning correspond the one to the other; not as if it were in the power of the first to bring about the second, such ethical magic being far removed from biblical thought—but 'who knows?'" Similarly, "It is not, as formerly, to all the people that the prophet holds out life, because he no longer expects the people to turn; but if a 'remnant' returns, perhaps *it* will find mercy."[9] This is a perspective that avoids all dogmatism in regard to the dialogical relationship between man and God. Since man cannot know the boundaries between divine determinism and human freedom, there can be no certainty that personal penitence will bring redemption here and now; but it is the only way to achieve it. The Sages put the matter incisively: "Since the world is judged according to most [of its behavior], and the individual is judged according to most [of his behavior], a person is fortunate if he can fulfill even one commandment, for [by doing so] he may tilt the balance for himself and for the entire world to the side of merit. But woe to him if he commits even a single transgression, for [by doing so] he may tilt the balance for himself and for the entire world to the side of blame" (Kiddushin 40b).

The wager, with its attendant hope, manifests itself in history as a power enabling the Jews to survive as a people *in extremis,* remaining faithful to their spiritual heritage however much it might seem to be contradicted by reality. Shlomo Ibn Verga, who was among the Jews expelled from Spain, relates the following:

> I have heard from the elders who left Spain that a ship was stricken with plague, and the master of the vessel headed for the nearest land and left the passengers on an unpopulated shore, and there many died of hunger. A few made an effort to go on foot to find some human settlement, amongst them a Jew, his wife and two sons. They made a mighty effort, but the woman, unable to lift a foot any longer, collapsed and died. The man carried his two sons until

he fell down in a faint, and the children also collapsed with hunger. When the man revived, he found his two sons dead beside him. In great sorrow he rose to his feet and said: "Lord of the Universe! You are doing a lot to make me abandon my religion. Know, then, truly, that despite the dwellers in Heaven, I am a Jew, and a Jew I shall remain, and nothing that You have brought upon me or will bring upon me shall avail."[10]

We have here an expression of faith that is clearly contradicted by reality and thus has in it an element of gambling. When faith appears to be vindicated, it becomes redundant.[11] In the face of absurdity and the implausibility of its aims, faith demands heroism, a trust that in the end the good will win out.[12] The ability to stand fast and never shrug off responsibility came, in Buber's view, from the Prophets, who taught the Jews that the real history of the world was not the one evident to the naked eye, the one that honors external achievement, but rather the hidden history, in which the spirit is secretly victorious. The very survival of the exiled Jews as a people was, for them, proof of the validity of their faith and their hope, and from their historical experience they drew the strength to "wager," that is, to stand fast and remain faithful to their Covenant with God.[13] Hence the return of the Jewish people to its homeland, the realization of "the two-thousand-year-old hope" (in the words of the Zionist anthem) is evidence to many gentiles of the power of collective hope in history.[14] Jewish historical consciousness has thus been stretched between two poles: the threat of destruction and the expectation of redemption. It was this polarity that determined the pattern of the Zionist wager.

The "Ever-Dying" People

One of the main factors motivating the Zionist wager was the concept of "the remnant of Israel," and this idea was of the highest importance in the shaping of the Zionist ethic of power. For Franz Rosenzweig, the idea dominated the "inner history" of the Jewish people: "In Judaism there is no group, no tendency, nay barely an individual who does not regard his manner of sacrificing incidentals in order to hold on to the remnant as the only true way, and himself therefore as the true 'remnant of Israel.' And so he is. In Judaism, man is always somehow a remnant. He is always somehow a survivor."[15] It is the mentality of the surviving remnant that, in Rosenzweig's view, distinguishes the history of the Jewish people. In world history, the basic ideas are those of expansion and domination, while the Jews alone keep themselves alive "by subtraction, by contraction, by the formation of ever-new remnants."[16] There is a close connection between the idea of a chosen remnant and Jewish stubbornness, zeal, and loyalty to truth.

The thinker and scholar Simon Rawidowicz showed that the Jews had always seen themselves as threatened with extinction. The Prophets had spoken of "the remnant of Israel" that would be left after the Destruction, and throughout the long centuries of exile there was hardly a generation that did not see itself as the last link in the chain. The Jews' fear of dying out was mixed with grief at the splendid past that was about to vanish from the world. Such fear can be paralyzing for both the conscious and the unconscious life, but in Jewish history it had the opposite effect, helping the Jews to surmount crisis and survive as a living people, however wounded and beaten down. It was something akin to Hegel's "cunning of reason": by anticipating their end, the Jews gained control over it, so that no catastrophe could take them by surprise, upsetting their equilibrium and overcoming them. By preparing unceasingly for their doom, they made it impossible: "There is no people more dying than Israel, yet none better equipped to resist disaster, to fight alone, always alone."[17]

Living in a constant state of crisis and risk made it imperative to marshal all spiritual resources, be they in the form of unique theologies or strategies of survival.[18] At the same time, it never occurred to the Jews that it was in their power to ensure their survival unaided. To think so would, as the Prophets had taught them, be prideful and sacrilegious and lead to disaster. The people believed its survival was assured by the special Covenant it, as a Chosen People, had with its God. God guaranteed the people's survival, and the people undertook to observe the Torah, all the Jews' spiritual, political, and social efforts being harnessed to this end.

The character of the Covenant was thus dialectical: from an ethical point of view, the behavior of the people would determine its fate. From a metaphysical point of view, God would assure the Jews' survival in any case.[19] There is something almost paradoxical in this notion of a "remnant," mixing, as it does, pessimism with optimism, the threat of destruction with the promise of redemption. As Maimonides put it: "God assured our father Jacob that, although his children would be humbled and overcome by the nations, they and not the nations would survive and would endure. . . . The Lord has given us assurance through His prophets that we are indestructible and imperishable, and we will always continue to be a pre-eminent community. As it is impossible for God to cease to exist, so is our destruction and disappearance from the world unthinkable."[20]

As a result of modern-day secularization, many Jews have lost their unquestioning faith in "the Eternal One of Israel," but the traditional self-image of the remnant remains an integral part of their historical consciousness. Concern for Jewish survival has played a decisive role in shaping the Jewish awareness of those who themselves experienced spiritual degeneration. And indeed, by the beginning of the twentieth century, Jewish sociologists, historians, and intellectuals had already begun to foresee the end of Jewish life in the Diaspora.[21] Others foresaw the possibility that the very success of the Zionist enterprise in Palestine might lead to the end of the Jewish people and Judaism as such because they doubted that the attendant secular revolution could bring about a spiritual renaissance.[22] This pessimistic vision has been shared, to one degree or another, by some of the most important Hebrew writers, including Berdyczewski, Bialik, Hazaz, and Alterman.

At any rate, a deep anxiety concerning the continuation of Diaspora Jewish life, nourished by rampant assimilation and growing antisemitism in Europe, was a steady refrain in the Zionist movement. Turn-of-the-century Hebrew literature bears powerful witness to this feeling. It foresaw an end of the Diaspora resulting from both inward and outward enslavement, humiliation, and political oppression. The message was that preventing a cataclysm would take a supreme effort, with only slight chance of success.

The same anxiety is echoed in the biographies of many of the settlers in Palestine, from the Second Aliyah, at the beginning of the twentieth century, to the Second World War. They saw their immigration as the only way, if not a particularly attractive way, of staving off disaster. Thus, Gershom Scholem explains what motivated him to immigrate to Palestine in 1920: "I immigrated because I thought there was no hope but here. I did not think we could be sure this enterprise would succeed. . . . I was always pessimistic about this, very pessimistic. I was pessimistic about everything Jewish, though I wanted to see it succeed . . . and I thought it was my duty to live in Palestine, or at least that one ought to try. There is no other way. . . . I always said. I am not so sure, but I am sure that if we do not make this attempt we are surely lost."[23]

Here we see pessimism about the Jewish fate but also a deep conviction that if there is any chance of salvation, it is in Palestine. On the other hand, the Jewish psychologist Erich Neumann, a well-known disciple of Jung, was convinced that, even if he himself was not to be among the rescued, the people as a whole would not disappear, that is, a remnant would be redeemed. In December 1938, Neumann wrote his teacher from Palestine: "In my opinion, what is happening to the Jews will be the salvation of the Jewish people, though it is not certain that I shall be among those rescued from this catastrophe. Our fate, which has brought us to this terrible pass, will force us Jews to mobilize our original inner reserves of strength or be wiped out. At the same time, it is very clear to me that we shall not be wiped out, though I am sure we will lose important parts of ourselves. To see this about to happen is an unbearable torment."[24] In another letter, in 1939, Neumann writes about the inner difficulty for him of realizing that he belongs to a dying people and, at the same time feeling there is something new being created in Palestine for which he bears responsibility. "The fact that this new thing must have the most unlikely object imaginable, the Jews, seems paradoxical to me, and I experience it as the hand of divine providence, that is, something typically Jewish."[25] A Jew deeply rooted in German culture, Neumann expresses here a typically Jewish faith, a faith so absurd that it can only be explained in religious terms ("the hand of divine providence"): out of catastrophe something new shall be born. Pessimism concerning the future of Diaspora Jewry did not, then, lead to passivity but rather to an active rebellion against what seemed like inexorable fate. This rebellion had the character of a wager.[26]

Brenner's "Nevertheless"

We find in Brenner's thinking the most typical example of the Zionist wager. He expresses it in a play called "Across the Borders." Yohanan, the hero, ruminates, in a poem concerning the remnant (a central concept for Brenner), about "a Jew, both visionary and sensible, and his situation, caught between two fires: either to lie to himself and dream, along with a handful of others, about national revival and immigration to the ancestral homeland, which have no basis in reality or in the character of the Jewish masses; or to show complete understanding for the eternal non-return to the safety of home, for the absolute end, unadorned."[27]

The question is an existential one of the highest importance, a question of life and death from which there is no escape. The hero faces two equally cogent alternatives. The first, however, is detached from reality, and the second represents certain destruction. This is the source of his despair and sense of being trapped. Why, in the end, does Brenner prefer the first alternative? His reply is, "the yearning for life" (*kosef hahayim*), an idea beyond reason but not opposed to it. Being fully cognizant of its incongruity with present reality, it cannot be rooted in logic but in moral fervor, a desire that prompts one to believe and act despite reality. It is faith "nevertheless." In the words of Menahem Brinker, " 'Reason' is what an awareness of reality requires. . . . [But] by the rules of such 'reason,' 'the Jewish people has no future.' The 'yearning for life,' on the other hand, repeatedly evokes faith in the ability to change human destiny out of free choice and fidelity to moral ideals. 'Rationally' speaking, such faith is a mere illusion. But from the viewpoint of the 'yearning for life,' it is unquestionable, for, from this perspective, reason encompasses only a part of human life."[28]

It is important to understand that Brenner's "passionate will to live" is not the same as the simple animal instinct that prompts every living creature to struggle for survival. The spiritual element that is the essence of the former has a moral and metaphysical significance, and in this sense it is indistinguishable from religious faith. For Brenner, "this idea, in all its depth, is not subject to logical or experimental demonstration, but is apprehended by the inner moral, religious, and poetic sensibility: the world is important, life is important — and the work of the world, the work of life, are important."[29] Brenner invested this idea with "messianic fervor in the exact sense of the word."[30] "The entrance of the ideal, the suprarational, into modern Jewish history is like the penetration of the supernatural into nature in religious mystery; it has a miraculous quality."[31]

Brenner's agnostic, skeptical view of history, so sharply opposed to Marxist thinking, was influenced considerably by pre-Marxist Russian socialism but was also closely akin to prophetic thinking. The latter, too, was also based on the assumption that we can never know where human freedom ends and historical necessity begins, so that "all is possible" (in Brenner's words). This is the old biblical way of thinking, oscillating between the two poles of destruction and redemption, which acquired a new meaning in Zionism. Rational analysis of the Jewish reality in the Diaspora leads to the conclusion that complete destruction is inevitable. But this deterministic conclusion leads not to passivity but to activity, which draws its strength from a basic moral loyalty to the Jewish people, to values and moral convictions rooted in cultural tradition and shared memories. Referring to Shatov, the enlightened, penitent hero of Dostoevsky's novel *The Devils,* Brenner writes: "For the true son of his people, the son of his people who has inner accounts with himself, with the nature of his people and the fate of his people, it is not possible to live a real life without a strong faith in that people, in its truth, its holiness, its great strengths. Such faith can also lead to faith in God, the people's God, the people's spirituality — even though it may not always satisfy the need for faith in God in general. . . . In the last analysis, every person of true feeling comes into the world through his people, sees humanity from the perspective of his people and in relation to it, and is touched most deeply only by his own people's fate, his own fate, this son of his people."[32]

Herein lies the meaning of the oxymoron Brenner uses to describe the behavior of those driven by the Zionist idea: they act both "willingly and reluctantly," for they are "forced to choose the only option that does not carry with it moral degradation."[33] The "yearning for life" that pulses within them is synonymous with faith in something greater than reason, something that touches the roots of the Jew's identity and self-respect and does not allow him to submit to the humiliation of a sealed fate.

The Brennerian "nevertheless" is a kind of wager, a summoning up of spiritual resources in a situation from which there is no escape, in order to stand the test of unquestioning loyalty to one's people and its legacy.[34] It is the "nevertheless" that "must always come at the end of a negative accounting," for in Eastern Europe "there is nothing to lose! . . . And only the pioneer whose 'nevertheless' is a part of who he is, the pioneer who is ready for anything — and not only here — is entitled to come."[35]

It is Brenner's spirit that we hear in the diary of the poet Yitzhak Lamdan, of the Third Aliyah, who wrote in 1923, after canceling a trip to Berlin in order to stay in Palestine: "Here, here is the only place — there is no other. The last journey, the last stop. . . . Here at last we shall have to find a solution, be it negative or positive, but here it is possible. Here we shall make the last, great attempt. You, too, be present when that attempt is made."[36]

The Zionist idea is thus based on a paradox: it presents itself as the "last attempt," the only chance of salvation, even though this chance seems utterly negated by a historical process leading inexorably toward destruction. "Is any of us capable of settling the wilderness?" Brenner asks. And he answers: "Our history until now tells us no. But who knows? . . . It happens in life that things which are impossible become necessary. . . . In any event, the attempt [we are making] is a great and earth-shaking one. It will be our last try."[37]

The skeptical, ambiguous expression "who knows?" evokes associations with prophetic patterns of thinking, where repentance figures as the last chance, however uncertain ("perhaps"), of rescue from certain destruction. The two are identical, not in content but in noetic structure. There is, of course, a great difference between the faith of the Prophets in the transcendent meaning of history — that is, in its being ruled by an omnipotent moral power that guides humankind through various twists and turns to full redemption — and Brenner's faith in the power of ideas to repair a flawed reality, accompanied by an absolute rejection of the possibility of full redemption. Needless to say, Brenner's virulent attack on "our historical identity" and his extreme negation of "the greatness of our heritage" go far beyond the reproofs of the Prophets. Yet, as Uri Shoham points out, "It must be recognized that only he who sees himself playing a role in the drama of the end-time and redemption can achieve as destructive an ecstasy as is reflected in these words."[38] Since for the Prophets, too, full redemption is not possible within history but only outside it, the gap between Brenner and them is not so great, particularly when we recall another of his key concepts, that of the remnant, which appears in the same context and has a distinctly prophetic ring to it. This idea, which appears in numerous variations throughout Brenner's fiction and *publicité* is integral to the prophetic pattern of his thinking. The source of Brenner's great influence on his generation was, among other things, the almost seductive charm this traditional image had for them. The poet David Shimoni (Shimo-novitch), a member of that generation, calls the feeling Brenner gave his associates the "brotherliness of Massada," which is "the tragic, exalted brotherliness of individual survivors."[39]

The Pioneering Impetus: Despair and Faith

The sense of being a remnant is one of the main sources of the Zionist pioneering ethos and, in particular, of the demand for personal *hagshama* (realization) — contributing through one's own actions and example to the achievement of the Zionist goals. Looking back at the youth movement to which he once belonged, Eliezer Livneh writes: "What was called in the Zionist movement *halutziut* [pioneering, particularly the physical work entailed in settling the Land of Israel] has deep roots in the ideas of historical Judaism and has been tested in the latter's historical experience. In earlier periods, one spoke of 'the remnant of Israel' and 'a remnant shall return' (Isa 20:20–21). The number of Jews was not considered an indication of Israel's stature. In the long history of the nation, large parts of it have been lost, cut off, and even assimilated among the gentiles. What remained in the end was a minority. But this minority was, by itself, of great value from a Jewish point of view."[40] Livneh points to the strong connection between *halutziut* and the concept of the "remnant," but he also notes that few have grasped the dialectical contradictions under the surface here. On one hand, the pioneering ethos has prompted a certain select group, which sees itself as the vanguard of the Jewish people, to summon up all its strength and act with unparalleled daring; on the other hand, this ethos implied an acceptance of the loss of the masses of Jews in the Diaspora.

The importance of loyalty to tradition, nurtured by the mentality of the "last survivors," is a recurrent theme throughout the history of Jewish thought. What is new in Zionist thinking is the idea that this loyalty dictates a historical activism, that is, bold action to rescue the Jewish people that only a select few, prepared to serve as a living example for the people as a whole, can make. The first literary manifesto to express the pioneer ideal clearly and fully was the 1904 essay "A Voice Calls Out" by Yosef Vitkin, who took part in the First Aliyah. Here we see most of the hallmarks of the pioneer ethos, based on the consciousness of being a remnant. Reflecting on the history of movements of national liberation, Vitkin advocates the use of the slogan "victory or death." "We must," he believes, "keep before our eyes the abyss into which we are falling." The people of Israel is standing at the mouth of a volcano, with nowhere to escape. What conclusion should we draw? We must "fight desperately, like bears whose young have been slain! All the pain, the protestation, the terrible sighs that have accumulated in our throats, held in by terrible fear, must now be given vent in a huge, superhuman national effort to save and resuscitate ourselves." Vitkin likes to use military terminology. And, indeed, such terms came to play a prominent role in the pioneer ideology. The term *halutz* (pioneer) itself originated in the military terminology of the Bible. The *halutz* is the soldier who marches into battle ahead of the rest of the army.

Vitkin was aware that there was something "superhuman" about this rescue effort and that the doubts of the experts as to its feasibility could not easily be put to rest except by acting and experimenting. He was also aware that scorn and despair would be the lot of all those who undertook the project. Who could withstand such a test? Only the chosen remnant that took responsibility for the people's fate. "Our people pays attention to quality, not quantity; our Torah also commands us to expel from the camp whoever is suspected of valuing his private life more than that of the people as a whole, whoever is faint of heart." Salvation is envisioned as the work of a favored few, "embittered heroes, who will fight desperately for their cause without the least thought of eventual retreat." These few, "the people's true soldiers," must organize themselves into brigades for the inevitable, harsh, prolonged battle — "a peaceful war" — with their enemies and with themselves.[41] All revolutionary movements think of themselves as vanguards, and thus what Vitkin proposes is nothing new. What set the Jewish pioneer ethos apart was the consciousness and the rhetoric of the small remnant of a people doomed to destruction in exile.

Like Vitkin, Moshe Beilinson claimed that every revolutionary cadre that aspires to become a mass movement must begin with a select few, for the idea alone will not suffice to influence the masses. It needs "practical" validation, which only this select group, committed to living by the idea, can provide: "The moral idea alone, however clear and solid, cannot have a decisive effect on human will . . . , but deeds and example do have the power to take hold of the masses, to sweep them away and ignite in them the fire of pure idealism. The willing, loving sacrifice of the few, sometimes very few, gives strength to all the movements."[42] The fact that the masses are in no hurry to join the movement is not just a matter of "indifference." "There is wisdom in the conservatism of the masses" that does not permit them to follow the minority because it is too risky: "The minority can and must stake its whole existence on one card, that of the change for which it is calling. And the 'masses' ensure the survival of the people as a whole and can take only a safe direction, already well paved by the minority."[43] For Beilinson, the differences in viewpoint between minorities and the masses should not be seen as being merely between idealism and selfishness. History will vindicate both.

The imagery Vitkin uses to describe the Jewish situation—"abyss," "volcano," "conflagration"—is common in the writings of the proponents of "catastrophic Zionism," the most prominent of whom were Yitzhak Tabenkin, on the left, and Vladimir Ze'ev Jabotinsky, on the right. But such imagery can be found, too, in thinkers like Nahman Syrkin and Berl Katznelson. Syrkin writes: "All of us, the entire people, stands at the edge of the abyss, which will soon swallow [us] up altogether."[44] Katznelson describes the immigrants of the Second Aliya as "a small, weak remnant that itself stood at the edge of an abyss," drawing its strength, not from any faith in the Zionist vision, but "from the thought that perhaps we are the last."[45] These images suggest the apocalyptic temper underlying the Zionist ethos, and particularly that of the pioneers.[46]

Where does this outlook come from? Buber distinguished between sheltered and unsheltered periods in history. In the sheltered periods, human beings feel the inner security of being at home in the world; in the unsheltered, the world becomes an alien place.[47] This latter was the situation of the "rootless" generation at the turn of the century. To be sure, alienation is the hallmark of modern consciousness in general, but Jews were particularly sensitive to it. The crisis of faith and destruction of traditional values suddenly left the Jew cut off from his community, culture, and homeland. The exile in which he found himself was twofold, both territorial and "cosmic" (as A. D. Gordon called it), that is, an alienation from the very roots of his being. It was a basic insecurity, not only physical but also existential in the deepest sense. These alienated Jews had lost the "shelter in the bosom of eternity" enjoyed by the pious.[48] If we add to this the loneliness they felt as the only ones who seemed to care about the disintegration of Jewish society, we can understand the despair of some of the Eastern European Jewish intelligentsia.

The Hebrew literature of the period evinces a profound skepticism about the possibility of a revival of the Jewish people and about the Zionist enterprise. This skepticism arose, in Aharon Appelfeld's view, from "a lack of faith that the improvement in outward circumstances could bring about a healing. For the core, the hidden core, is ill."[49] "Can the dead awaken? Will the dead be shocked?" cried Bialik. This is not merely a lack of a faith in the fortitude of the people but a deep fear that Zionism's tidings of "worldly" redemption would spell the end of Judaism itself.[50] "Sometimes I feel that I am taking my own life," confessed the great rebel Berdyczewski.[51] The prophetic proclamation of Bialik in his poem "Utterance" ("*Davar*") conveys a similar idea: "And with a trumpet blast of resurrection on our lips and shouts of joy, we are dragged to our graves."

How does the sight of the "abyss" become "a source of strength"? How does despair turn into an instrument of hope and determination? In a speech praising the pioneers, Bialik said that the readiness for self-sacrifice, which for him was on the "borderline of religiosity," was only to be found where there was felt to be no escape.[52] A. D. Gordon distinguished between "the despair of exhaustion" or "emptiness," found in those whom reality has beaten to the ground and deprived of any will to live, and "the despair of heroism" or "creative despair," which is "the despair of the person who still makes great demands of life and has great faith in his own worth, who is readier to rely on his own living spirit and demanding will than on the blackest [external] reality." It is precisely this person's deep despair and sense of disaster that remind him of the strength of the hidden creative powers within him that are seeking expression.[53] The great paradox of despair is that only through it do one's latent moral powers become evident, powers that bring one to do what thitherto had seemed impossible: "The hour of danger fills the one endangered, be he individual or nation, with life force, heroism, and vital depth in such measure as to enable him, at times, to perform wondrous deeds that he otherwise could not perform."[54] "Creative despair," or what Gordon calls "the greater disbelief," arises from the profound contradiction between faith and reality. Great faith cannot accept this contradiction and rails against it. Thus, while "the lesser disbelief" can bring one to suicide, "the greater disbelief" leads the believer to rebel against reality and act to change it out of a sense of responsibility for human life in general. Creative despair is an expression of faith and dedication so great, "even unto madness," that the common good comes to be identified as one's own.[55]

Forces of Repulsion and Attraction

Creative despair is thus an essential component of the Zionist wager. This is how Yitzhak Tabenkin summed it up retrospectively in 1938: "We saw the darkness before it came. . . . We marched knowingly toward the darkness. Was there even a moment in what we did here when we were not nourished by despair? Was anything created without seeing the dark, without seeing the abyss into which the House of Israel was slipping? It was seeing this that was the source of our strength. It was not only the dream of redemption that led the Jews to write books, erect cities, capture ports and build settlements. I believe none of this would have happened if there had not been deep within us a feeling of 'nevertheless,' meaning that in spite of the despair we would overcome."[56]

Tabenkin distinguishes two mutually complementary driving forces behind the pioneering ethos: the force of repulsion — the abyss, the negation of Diaspora existence — and the force of attraction — the dream of redemption. It is the force of repulsion that stirs and awakens, but it does not indicate a direction. The latter depends on the existence of a positive ideal, rooted in the historical consciousness of the nation. This accounts for the role of the Land of Israel in Zionist thinking: it serves as a positive ideal without which it would not have been possible to mobilize the energies needed to bring the chosen course to realization. External pressures must be supplemented by an ideal internal core that is embedded in the heritage of the past and conducive to historical continuity.

While Tabenkin stressed the negation of Diaspora existence, Ben-Gurion stressed the dream of redemption. His pioneering grandiloquence was decidedly messianic: "We are ourselves the result of very great forces at work within Jewish history." The strength of the pioneering movement is in "the full concretization of great historical forces, the gathering together of sparks that have shone in Jewish history in every generation and epoch, the sparks of messianic longing, the longing for redemption."[57]

On the other hand, for Katznelson, who did not take a messianic position, we find a much more skeptical note about the course of history: "It might be better if we kept our beliefs to ourselves and didn't make assertions about them, about the certain outcome of events, about historical necessity. . . . We live in an era when certainties have diminished and promises proven false, but . . . the negation of that which should be negated is as trenchant as ever."[58] In Katznelson's view, the main motif in Zionism is "the negation of that which should be negated." He was referring to rebellion, refusal to accept the exilic Jewish fate. He stressed the difference between Marxian socialism, which "nourished its followers on faith in the historical process that was their agent," and *halutziut,* which had no such objective certainty. "What we have is the recognition of our great misfortune [and] faith in the strength of our people, which refuses to accept destruction." We cannot console our camp with the certainty of victory.[59] It was not messianic belief that brought such figures as Brenner and Katznelson to Palestine, but only the shame of submission, of accommodation of the Jews to their own disintegration in the Diaspora. It was a flight from the decadent reality of life in exile, a desperate attempt to create a purer way of life, having come to a sober rejection of all the alternatives. As Katznelson writes: "The rebellion did not happen because people had a good program or knew how to save the nation, how to save Zionism. It was a rebellion of isolated individuals who themselves did not know the way and had no confidence in any particular course of action."[60]

A Final Card: The Sole Solution

In 1930, Enzo Sereni wrote: "Fate has dealt us this final card, our last and only hope. And it, too, is time-bound, such that tomorrow we shall no

longer be able to take advantage of it, as in the ancient adage [Mishna Avot
1:14], now sung by the pioneers, 'If not now, when?' "61 For its proponents,
Zionism was a final card, and if the people did not have the wisdom to use it,
there was no hope. The people's situation was an urgent one, requiring the
concentration of resources at a single, decisive front or "standing fast at the
narrow forward position."62 Thus Zionism was not only the one option for
salvation, displacing all other strategies of Jewish survival, but it demanded
"the forcing of the end," a daring action here and now, lest the moment be lost
forever. In the traditional concept of redemption we already find the idea that
proper timing is critical.63 But in this view, while failure to seize the appropriate moment can lead to destruction, the latter is not absolute, for the eternal
existence of the people of Israel is guaranteed by God. Here, however, failure
to take advantage of the opportunity means absolute destruction. The fear of
missing the historic moment haunted Herzl, for example, at every step of the
way: "[We must act] now or never get the Land of Israel." In 1919, shortly
after the Balfour Declaration and the British conquest of Palestine, David Ben-
Gurion expressed a similar sentiment: "This is a fateful hour for us: either we
shall go back to being a healthy, normal people, or we shall see that our
national hope is lost forever. . . . Many generations were able to wait. . . . Now
we can wait no longer. . . . This hour of destiny will never recur. If not now,
when?"64

Ben-Gurion, more than any other Zionist politician, was motivated by messianic aspirations. It is therefore not surprising that he wrote in the thirties, "I
believe we stand on the verge of the end of days, from both a Jewish and a
universal human point of view. The great redemption that our prophets foresaw, the redemption of the [Jewish] people and of mankind, is approaching.
Our generation has been called upon to hasten the coming of redemption. Our
destiny is not to put off (*lidhot*) but to force (*lidhok*) the end, the end of Jewish
and human suffering alike."65

The pathos of the end-time, the final battle, can be found in every nation's
dreams of liberation and every political and religious uprising. In Zionism it
was nourished by the extended experience of exile and associated messianic
longings. Zionism saw itself as the only full-fledged solution to the question of
Jewish survival. It was, as Gershom Scholem put it in the 1930s, supposed to
assure, "through an exceptional historical effort, not the miserable perpetuation of our existence from one generation to the next, but our permanent
ongoing existence, once and for all. The Land of Israel is the medium of a
historic leap (!) meant to establish national immortality."66 As we shall see,
there was no essential difference in basic attitudes between the Zionist right
and left. Even when the left refrained from using the explicitly messianic

terminology employed by the right, its reticence was a matter of strategy and not a denial of the underlying myth.

Zionism was fed by a sense of destiny on the part of a minority that believed that it alone held the key to the riddle of history, giving it the right to lead the masses, even against their will, to redemption. Belief that the Zionist idea promised the one complete solution to the Jewish problem inspired great zeal. Without this enthusiasm, it is doubtful that Zionism could have succeeded in its bold undertaking. But the other side of the coin was intolerance, hostility, and even violence toward competing ideologies and political factions, both within and without. Vestiges of this zealotry are still to be found in Israeli political discourse, especially that between left and right. Each side is convinced that its way is the only one that will assure the continued existence of the state and that the other's is a path to certain destruction. No wonder the various advocates of Diaspora life have attacked Zionism for its pessimism and fanaticism, which to them seem narrow-minded.

Is It Really the Last Card? Pro-Diaspora Reservations

Advocates of Diaspora life rejected the basic premise of the Zionist wager, that the Diaspora was doomed and the establishment of a sovereign Jewish state in the homeland was the only chance of saving the Jewish people, the last card. By the turn of the century, David Frishman had begun to speak out against such exclusivist thinking. He maintained that the Greeks and Romans had disappeared because they staked everything on one card, that of land. When the land was taken from them, there was no possibility of their surviving. "[Jews] no longer really believe that the Jewish people is eternal," he wrote bitterly. Many were, indeed, haunted by the feeling that it had reached the end of its journey. Jews had lost "the art of waiting," becoming impatient and intolerant. With an optimism typical of what the Zionists called "exilic thinking," Frishman wrote that if he was worried at all, it was for his son, that is, for the next generation or two. But as for the Jewish people in general, he had never been and was not concerned: it would find a way to save itself. Judaism was an idea and thus eternal. Like Simon Rawidowicz in "An Ever-Dying People," Frishman wrote: "In every generation it was believed that the end had come, and there was always good reason to think such bleak thoughts," yet the Jewish idea always won out. Whenever the Jewish people in one place seemed on the point of vanishing, a new center of Jewish life appeared elsewhere. Frishman, a Hebrew writer who from the time of the Hibbat Tzion movement had been consistently anti-Zionist, declared that he felt more Jewish than any of those scurrying about in their attempts to rescue the

Jews, for he still had the ancient Jewish belief in the future and thus did not feel the urgency of finding cure-alls for the present.[67]

This was also the approach of Franz Rosenzweig. He called the Zionists *kleine Juden* (little Jews), seeing himself as an *Alljude* (all-embracing Jew) in that he could give credence to all the options for securing Jewish survival, both in the Diaspora and in the Land of Israel.[68] He saw great danger in the attempt to hinge Jewish survival on a tie to the soil. The latter was a source of sustenance, but it could also hamstring the nation and betray it. A people bound to its land and loving that land more than its own life was always in danger of being wiped out. Unlike Nathan Alterman, who would write in the 1940s that "[a] nation defeated on its own soil shall seven times arise," Rosenzweig, at the beginning of the twenties, wrote: "Though this love might save the soil of the homeland nine times from the clutches of the enemy, and the life of the nation with it, the tenth time only that which is more beloved, the land, shall remain, and the nation itself shall perish." He saw the guarantee of Jewish survival, not in the outward means relied on by other peoples, but in inward ones: ties of blood and ancestry. "We ourselves put our trust in kinship and abandoned the land."[69] Thus Rosenzweig could view Zionism as, at best, only one of the ways of "prolonging the life" of the Jewish people from one day to the next but not as the only way and certainly not as a "complete solution" to the problem of the Jews.

Rosenzweig was writing before the Holocaust, but Rawidowicz, who lived in the United States, took his negative stance toward Zionism at the very height of the Holocaust and in its aftermath. He was harshly critical of the view that Zionism was the last card, the only guarantee of the Jewish people's survival.[70] At the root of Zionism, he maintained, was a "longing for the End." Such longing "is both a continuation of the old messianic utopianism of the *galut* and also a protest against that passive hope, and this combination is naturally charged with dialectical tension. The new vision entails a "hastening the End" that is nourished by a deep belief in a particular solution to the Jewish question. The hope for redemption is one thing, and the adoption of a particular final course of action is something else. Rawidowicz called for a renewed appreciation of "the ideology of survival." He negated the alternatives that Zionism was proposing: either the Land of Israel or the end of the Jewish people. The people of Israel, he maintained, had in its history been able to combine a yearning for the End with a yearning for the Endless. A utopia of the End of Days can be quite reassuring, stirring hearts and healing broken ones, at least temporarily. But the illusion that the End has come is a dangerous one. It could bring the Jews living in the Land of Israel to desperation, which in turn could lead to the disaster of another Massada, another cry of "Let my soul perish with the Philistines" (Jud 16:30). The traditional faith in "heaven" must not be replaced with a faith in "earth." Zionism must not be seen as a complete solution, nor must a state be seen as essential for Jewish survival, for such views weaken the will of the Diaspora to survive and they hasten its demise. The Jewish people must "continue to join the End to the Endless, while refusing to be misled by the End and not allowing its own yearning for the End to induce it to contempt for the Endless and all that it entails in the daily life of the nation."[71]

The American Jewish historian Jacob Neusner describes the pessimism of the second- generation Jews of Eastern European origin in the United States. In the twenties and thirties, he maintains, "they had a strong feeling that all was lost, that the Jews had lost their identity as a group. . . . We were afflicted with the 'last-Jew-on-earth' syndrome, and we assumed that, whatever the future of the Jewish people was, it would not be in America. . . . There was a deep feeling among the Jews of that generation that we could not survive in a free country. It was as though, to remain Jews for another thousand years, you needed external pressure."[72] Neusner himself is an avowed optimist concerning the future of the Jews in the United States, which he believes is "the promised land," because of the enormous success the Jews have had in becoming a part of American society and at the same time retaining their Jewish identity.

Diaspora intellectuals question the Zionist anxiety that Diaspora Jewry will disappear, claiming that Diaspora Jewish life is legitimate and viable. In the view of Baruch Kurzweil (1907–72), "the hesitation of the Diaspora is two-fold, religious and existential, regarding the invitation to make the bold leap into the secular political adventure, limited in time and space, of the State of Israel. The Diaspora hesitates to stake its life upon, and cast all its being into, the crucible of the state. It hesitates, for the sake of its own survival and that of the [Jewish] people, to trade eternal hope based on an idea that is beyond time and space for the limited, concrete here and now of Israel. States arise and disappear in the course of time; ideas and hopes do not depend on them."[73]

This, then, is the basis of the ideological argument between Zionism and the Diaspora: Zionism claims that the "Jewish situation" requires a wager, a "bold leap into the secular political adventure." From this point of view, the hesitation of the Diaspora means losing the opportunity given the Jewish people to put an end to exile before exile puts an end to the Jews. But the Diaspora rejects this program "for the sake of its own survival and that of the [Jewish] people." It claims that the negation of Jewish existence in the Diaspora is not only contrary to historical experience but likely to be a self-fulfilling prophecy.

The Wager on Establishing a State

In the 1930s, as the situation of the Jews in the Diaspora worsened and the conflict between Zionism and Arab nationalism deepened, the feeling of being a remnant, with all its catastrophic overtones, grew stronger. Given the powerlessness of the Jews, now shown to be weaker politically than ever before, this mentality became one of the main sources of the Zionist "will to power." It gave a small, lonely minority a feeling of heavy moral responsibility and the determination to struggle. "We are orphans in the world," wrote Berl Katznelson in 1940. "On the weak shoulders of the remnant of Israel here falls a huge burden that we are not strong enough to bear. The whole of future Jewish history may depend on what happens to us, on the way little David now reappears here to face the great Goliath." He called upon his comrades to instill the feeling of being a remnant deep in the hearts of the Jews living in the Land of Israel. "For us, the remnant of Israel confronting its fate in this country, there is no other way but the way of loyalty, which is also the way of valor, of responsibility for the collective, for the individual, for every Jew."[74]

The choking of the Yishuv decreed by the British government in its 1939 White Paper and the destruction that befell European Jewry, which under certain circumstances could have engulfed the small Jewish community in Palestine as well, gave a terrifying relevance to the fear expressed in the old words. It was this fear that nourished the ethos of power out of weakness, the heroic defiance of a small, abandoned, isolated minority struggling against mighty forces. Powerful literary testimony to the mood of the Yishuv at the time of the struggle for independence is to be found in the lyric and public poetry of Nathan Alterman, the main theme of which is "life on the verge of the apocalypse" and the central image of which is the "living dead." This poetry reflects the sense of weakness turning into strength, the mysterious dialectical fate of the Jew who seeks the strength to survive out of an awareness of approaching death and then defeats all those who would destroy him.[75]

In the decade preceding the establishment of the state, myths of desperate heroism began to play a central role in the consciousness of that generation. "There began to appear," Anita Shapira writes, "ideas of taking a desperate stand, of a hopeless 'final battle' intended to ensure that the memory of the valor of the Yishuv, annihilated in the heat of battle, would shore up the spirits of future generations of Jews, serving them as a source of pride and national vitality."[76] At a meeting of the Zionist Executive on April 18, 1940, David Ben-Gurion said: "Do you ask what the chances are that our own struggle will succeed? No one can guarantee anything. . . . Let us assume the worst that our struggle does not succeed. Is [it] not worthwhile for its own sake? Shall we not lose even more if we bow our heads and accept and submit? Do we have no other moral or educational or human reckoning than that of material gain and loss? Must we not concern ourselves with the soul of the younger generation in the Land of Israel and in the Diaspora, the soul of the people, the generations to come?"[77] Four months before the war broke out, Katznelson announced at a rally: "We shall not lose faith or forsake our efforts for redemption because the whole world is sunk in darkness and wickedness. We are being tested more than at any other time in our history. . . . It may be that this test will be too much for us, but if we endure it we shall save not only the existing Yishuv but the [Jewish] people [as a whole]."[78]

Acts that had until then seemed mad and unthinkable began to seem possible, logical, and even natural. Even so cautious a personality as Moshe Shertok (Sharett) spoke of the need for a strategy of wager, going so far as to see it as distinguishing a Zionist from a Diaspora stance. Given the sense of an impending calamity for Zionism—"the destruction of the Third Temple," in his words—he asked himself what lesson the Yishuv could draw from the destruction of the Second Temple. What would have happened to the Jewish people had it not revolted against Rome? Would it have been saved, or would this "salvation" have led to complete absorption into the Roman Empire, as had happened to other peoples? Such ruminations led Shertok to the conclusion that, in the last analysis, if the Jewish state was doomed to be destroyed by Rome, it was better for it to have been destroyed after the revolt because this revolt gave us the dignity, pride, and courage not to surrender without a struggle.[79]

Buber's disciple Ernst Simon sharply condemned the "Zionist doctrine of desperation" at this time, paraphrasing it as follows: "This[, they say,] is the decisive last hour of Jewish history. Now, just now, the fate of the entire people shall be decided, whether it is to continue or cease to exist. The possibility of continued existence depends on a single condition: the building up of the Land of Israel as a Hebrew state in our own generation. If we do not succeed in this, we shall lose, not just one battle, but the entire war for our survival. Thus we stand 'on the last wall.' Thus, 'the whole country is our Massada.' Thus all means that seem appropriate to achieving this exalted end—the rescue of a great and ancient people from a destruction decreed for it in its true eleventh hour—are justified and hallowed."[80]

But Simon, in his criticism, was expressing the views of a small minority in the Zionist camp. An all-or-nothing spirit at that time swept most of the movement, as Ilan Amitzur has written: "The Zionist movement's demands became maximal in every area. Its behavior had come to resemble that of a gambler who trusts his luck blindly. What had formerly been 'extremism' was now 'moderation.' " While Shertok was still saying that "we have something to lose," Abba Hillel Silver announced at a giant rally in New York that "the Jewish people no longer has anything to lose but its illusions" but much to gain if it stands tall and directs its energies to aggressive political action. Everyone was saying this was "the right time, not to be let slip by."

But the movement's president Chaim Weizmann warned of disaster if it should take an extreme path. The success of the wager depended not only on the Zionists' subjective "spirit of combat and non-surrender" but also on an objective international situation: "In the past, it has happened that national movements took similar wagers and won, because a favorable international climate developed; . . . but there were also national movements the lot of which was not improved, which wagered away all that they had . . . [, not to be regained] for many decades." It was only the combination of Zionist activism and a favorable international situation that made the wager successful, and Weizmann himself played an important role in making that situation favorable: it was his diplomatic strategy that created the conditions for the breakthrough achieved by Zionist activism. The wager was thus a necessary but not sufficient condition for political success in certain situations.[81]

"There Is No Choice": The Slogan of the Survivors

The remnant struggling for the survival of the Jewish people expressed its sense of moral justification in the well-known slogan *"Ein breira"* (There is no choice). Beginning in the late 1930s, this slogan was widely used in the rhetoric of the labor movement, and it was decisive in shaping the ideology and military ethos of the Yishuv. British policy in Palestine, the Arab refusal to recognize the Jewish people's right to the country, and, above all, the destruction of European Jewry gave rise to the feeling that the Jews had no alternative but to fight to the death.[82] In retrospect, the slogan was an admission that Jabotinsky had been right in predicting that Zionism would not be able to escape the use of force to attain its goals, but at the same time it implied that the war had been forced upon the Jews. The poet Nathan Alterman expressed this feeling well when he wrote, concerning the Jewish state, in the early fifties:

> Among kingdoms in the course of time,
> You alone — those who fall in your name attest —
> Sought to the end to arise by the ploughshare
> And not by the sword. But in you arose as one
> Redemption and destruction.[83]

There is something apologetic in Alterman — as there is in the name "Israel Defense Forces" — that derives from the psychological difficulty Jews have had adjusting to the rules of international political struggle. Those on the extreme right (Uri Tzvi Greenberg, Yisrael Eldad) have seen this self-justification as the vestige of an abject exilic mentality and rejected it contemptuously. In their view, Israel's wars are not the result of having no choice but an expression of the sovereign will of the nation, which has come to take possession of its land on the base of a divine promise and destiny.

The sense of having no choice was very important for morally justifying the Zionist movement and for sustaining the morale needed for the Yishuv's struggle in the period before independence and in the years that followed.[84] Up to the Lebanon war (1982), all Israel's wars were seen by those in power (leaders of the labor movement) as having been forced upon the country by a hostile environment. The slogan also served to dampen hatred for the enemy. If the principal motivation for the struggle was necessity and not hostility, and if necessity cannot be gainsaid, there is no place for the idealization of war or the creation of a cult around it.

But the slogan "There is no choice" also had a destructive moral potential. Martin Buber, alone among the Zionist leaders, rejected this slogan, sensing the dangers it carried. In his view, justifying all wars in advance could encourage insensitivity to the means employed and in this way lead to an increase in the level of violence and the perpetuation of the conflict. Indeed, the assumption that all of Israel's wars were matters of no choice enabled politicians to evade with relative ease the responsibility for any given war and its consequences, placing the blame entirely on the other side. This assumption also naturally prompted the leadership to seek security on the basis of military power and avoid looking for other kinds of solutions to the conflict: compromise, political agreements, and so on.[85] The slogan "no choice" is thus morally ambiguous: on one hand, it can provide motivation for making the best use of force and for softening feelings of hatred and vengefulness toward the enemy; on the other hand, it can also be used to justify the use of force without restraint.

"The New Jew" and the Remnant Mentality

In his speech accepting the Jerusalem Prize, the Czech writer Milan Kundera suggested a definition for a "small nation." It is not a quantitative definition but a situational one: a small nation is one that cannot take its own existence for granted. It can disappear completely, and it knows this. Unlike "big nations," which need not concern themselves with the question of their own survival, the small nation sees its existence as being under permanent threat.[86] Kundera's definition is marvelously apt for the "Israeli situation," as it is referred to.

Zionism hoped that the establishment of a Jewish state (a "safe refuge") would give the Jews a sense of security, a feeling that their survival as a people was assured and the black cloud of "the remnant of Israel" that hovered over their history had lifted. And that, indeed, is how matters looked to Israelis until the 1960s. But this feeling of normalization proved ill-founded. Even in their own country, Jews today continue to feel like survivors. It seems to me there are two reasons for this: first, the traumatic memory of the Holocaust has been compounded by fear that the country would be destroyed militarily from without, particularly after the Six-Day War of 1967 and the Yom Kippur War of 1973. "Historical memory resisted all ideological attempts to wipe it away."[87] Second, there is uncertainty that Israeli culture, which has its origins in a break with traditional religious culture, can serve as an adequate platform for Jewish existence. In times of fear and distress, the "old Jew" turned to the holy books and found strength and protection there, whereas the "new Jew" is left without the support of tradition. Israel is still in search of its Jewish identity, a situation that inspires insecurity and doubts about the future.

According to the sociologist Simon Herman, the Jews see themselves as a people that has escaped destruction, and no study of Israel, Jewish identity, or the relations between Jews and other groups can ignore this factor.[88] Herman's thesis is borne out in various ways in Israeli literature, for example in Yoram Kaniuk's novel *The Last Jew*. Kaniuk is a writer of the "Canaanite" school, which sees the whole history and culture of the Jews in exile as an unfortunate digression, but the novel's hero, Evenezer, is clearly a product of that history. Believing that he will be the last Jew left alive after all the others have been annihilated, he tries to commit all of Jewish history to memory. Through memory, he tries, as it were, to avert the evil decree. There is something insane or at least morbidly melancholy about this effort. Evenezer symbolizes the perennial Jewish existential situation: "Every generation has its last Jew — [who embodies] the misery of living at the edge of extinction. But this work in particular . . . teaches that madness, bereavement and suffering are what guarantee survival, and it is precisely the fact that [members of] a race or people see [themselves] as the last that ensures that it will go on living."[89]

In Kaniuk, the survivor mentality leads to madness, which, in turn, leads to an obsession with the past, and this, paradoxically, ensures survival. But for the writer Hanokh Bartov, this mentality is a fruitful one, inspiring love for a rich tradition. In an interview, Bartov declared that the responsibility of re-membering devolves upon the few who are left, and this is the moral meaning of life in Israel: "The fact that I was born a Jew is meaningless. I embrace Judaism both because I am the heir of a great and rich heritage that I love and because I feel that I am the surviving remnant, that I cannot do otherwise, for we are the last."[90]

Finally, in Aharon Megged, the survivor mentality produces unrelenting fear of a genetically determined fate. For him, living in Israel has brought no change in the Jew's basic existential situation. "The Jew is someone who lives under a death sentence." Here in Israel, too, he is filled with fear, though it is repressed. The Zionist thinkers dreamed that in the Land of Israel a "new Jew," bold, heroic, and free of fear, would arise. But this was an illusion. When our security is even slightly threatened, the fear returns and with it the "old Jew." For here too, the Jews are an alien minority, an interloper with no rights. Jewishness has not changed since the time of Abraham. The old paradigms of all of Jewish history that are found in the Book of Books embody the unchanging genetic code of the Jewish people, and its determinism is inescapable.[91] For these writers, the Land of Israel is no longer a safe refuge or a final solution to the Jewish problem. The image of the remnant, which had been repressed for a time in Zionist ideology and Hebrew literature, returned in the consciousness of those born in the land in the wake of the Holocaust, bringing renewed questioning about the meaning of loyalty to the past.

5

The Wager in Greenberg's The Ways of the River

The Betrayed Covenant

The Holocaust confirmed the Zionists' prediction of destruction for the Diaspora and gave a new relevance to the notion of the "remnant of Israel" that had figured so prominently in their wager. The Holocaust also greatly reinforced, for Zionists, the ethos of power and its corollary, the aspiration to political sovereignty. An authentic reflection of such thinking is to be found in the poetic cycle *The Ways of the River,* by Uri Tzvi Greenberg, most of which was written during and immediately after the Holocaust.[1] This work is one of the most profound, important expressions of Zionist "theology." Indeed, it presents itself as a latter-day version of traditional Jewish theology, giving religious significance to current events; renewing the meaning and power of traditional faith in the face of the yawning contradictions posed for it by present reality; calling for a new moral stance; and charting a future course and destiny for the Jewish people. It is no accident that *The Ways of the River* placed Greenberg briefly in the center of the national consensus after a long period of being shunned by the public. The main reason for this prominence, as Dan Miron has pointed out, was that Greenberg "gave expression to the experience of bereavement and catastrophic destruction that united the Yishuv and the Jewish people as a whole, spanning all divisions and disagreements."[2] The work lays bare the deepest spiritual impulses behind the Zionist wager; hence its significance for the present discussion. The poet draws up a harsh indictment of exile, messianism, martyrdom, and the gentile world (symbolized by Europe). The main concern of the book is the problem of loyalty to the Covenant.

God's absolute silence during the Holocaust presented the Jew with a challenge: to remake his faith in complete freedom, choosing between absurdity and meaning, between negation and defiant affirmation. Renewal of faith thus meant, in André Neher's words, "gambling on life":

> The heart of the theological problem of silence in the Holocaust [is] in the fact that [during it] both God and man, the two partners bound together in a spoken dialogue through the covenant, withdrew into silence simultaneously. In their mutual silence there appeared a void into which a third force, evil, introduced itself. This radical evil, symbolized in the Book of Job by Satan, found its historical incarnation in the Holocaust. It constitutes a challenge to the word of man, and the response to that challenge can only take the form of a wager. . . . Man, faced with the silence of the Holocaust, is obliged to decide between . . . two polar responses to divine silence. This choice is a wager between the historical actuality of silence and the metahistorical potential of the word. Indeed, the Jewish attitude to silence is characterized by recurring attempts to create the word anew by means of a wager upon life. The creation of the State of Israel soon after the Holocaust is an expression of this phenomenon in the form of a wager upon the renewal of the life of the Jewish people in the biblical land of the word. The termination of the historical exile through *shivat tzion* (the return to Zion) means the end of the exile of the word and the metaphysical return from the actuality of silence toward the potentiality of the word.[3]

God's silence has put Jewish faith, which is predicated on the Covenant between the people Israel and its God, to the supreme test. The future of Jewish faith will be determined by the way the people react to this utter hiddenness on God's part. The response will have to be in the form of actions, not words: the Jews are being called upon to wager on their belief in revolutionary action, for only such action can repair the rift between the people and its God. The Holocaust represents the end of exile, but more than this, the end of the exilic mentality, the epitome of which is martyrdom. Because this ethos did not stand the test of the modern Jewish situation, it must be rejected wholeheartedly in favor of a new ethos of political and military power. Greenberg's poetry gives this power a religious meaning for the first time, seeing in it a new source of hope, a way for the Jews to renew the Covenant that had been breached in the Holocaust and to go on affirming their faith in a God who redeems His people despite His silence.

Greenberg sees the Holocaust as the severest test in the history of Jewish faith. It calls the continued existence of the Covenant into question. The possibility that the people will rebel against God and abandon the Sinai Covenant is, for the poet, quite real:

> Israel proclaims from Sinai that there is no Supreme Being! And without Him
> Tablets fall and sink . . . and nakedness and fornication ensue, wild men with
>   their weapons,
> Each one, even the Jew, doing his body's bidding in this world! (267)

God becomes "the former God of Israel" (250). In a sense, the Covenant has been broken, or at least seriously disrupted, by God's silence in the face of the Destruction but also by the people's sin of "forgetfulness," "negligence," and "naiveté" (160). Greenberg does not attempt a theological or metaphysical explanation for the catastrophe, which would contradict his sharp attack here on God. He goes so far as to reject all the traditional paradigms of theodicy, such as the Akeda (the Binding of Isaac) and the prophecies concerning the Servant of the Lord. "God did not choose them for an Akeda, for a test to expiate a minor collective sin" (268).[4] The Holocaust is not a punishment for sin, for even if we admit "that it is indeed our fault," "we are no more at fault than any of the other nations" (263). The Holocaust also has no educational significance, either as a great test or as a crucible, nor does it, in any sense, represent martyrdom. Finally, no eschatology can justify it. In short, there is no metaphor capable of describing or explaining this terrible event.

> For even mortals' inner eyes are impotent:
> They, too, burst asunder
> At the sight of that place where words are silenced,
> The silence preceding the coming of words into the world,
> And similes fail before the power of the thing described. . . .
> For the sights are of primordial fear and sorrow — in all their rawness. (148)

Since no metaphor can capture the reality, the status of language ("words") as representing reality is compromised. The disaster that was beyond words showed that "the time had come to dismantle all words and combinations of letters written down and return them to being unjoined letters, as it was before the Torah of religion was given at Sinai" (239). We must remember that "Sinai," for Greenberg, is the source of poetic language. Its words are hewn from the scriptural revelation. Hence doubt about the standing of language also leads to a wavering of commitment to the Sinai Covenant. It is the savage, chaotic situation of "the silence preceding the coming of words into the world." In such a situation there are only two legitimate responses: holding one's peace or venting one's rage.

> [It is] the end of the value of words not born of thunder,
> Not escorted by guards with swords drawn;
>
> .   .   .   .
>
> Only speechlessness, or mighty roaring, is fitting,
> The speech of God to Moses, the prince of his people,
> That precedes the splitting of the sea. (336)

In his *Book of Accusation and Belief,* Greenberg writes that tears without anger or action are an exilic response that insults victims and mourners alike (130).[5] The theme is even stronger in *The Ways of the River:* "Weeping and rending are in vain if they do not wrest the iron ox to the ground by its horns" (207). Words are only of value if they bring about deeds that transform reality for the better: "Former glory restored — that is the end of the dirge" (61). Thus faith in words cannot be recovered without giving faith a new meaning. The chance of renewing the dialogue between the people and its God, in the face of such deep hiddenness on His part, depends on the creation of a new reality, which can provide a basis for hearing the words. It is for the poet to pound the wall of the people's obtuseness so that it can overcome its "negligence" and forgetfulness and take its fate in its own hands. As against the sin of negligence, which brings destruction in its wake, there is the faith of the poet that "through poetry we shall bring ourselves back to a living awareness" (336).

"Beyond Despair . . . There Is No More Despair"

There is no logical basis for trying to renew the dialogue in the midst of the Destruction, for in the present situation there is not the least sign of hope. The attempt to do so is thus purely a wager on the part of those who have reached "the end of the road," i.e., utter despair.

> We have drunk all the poisons to the dregs,
> And come to the end of fear,
> To the end of all roads — and life!
> There is something beyond this, halleluya!
> It is beyond despair, halleluya!
> And there, there is no more despair . . . halleluya!
> For beyond the night there is no night. (340–41)

What utter despair produces is not nihilism but a vigorous appreciation of life, a stubborn decision to perpetuate Jewish existence, out of faithfulness to the Covenant and a desire to rebuild the basis for dialogue. This faithfulness is an inner existential need to revalidate one's selfhood, to say yes to fate, which is also destiny.

See, the tall ladder of pain is set on the ground, and behind it
There is no wall or window, only a cave and sealing stones all around;
Snow and more snow, or grass and more grass, without end — and streams.

  . . .

Climb it and descend, climb it and descend.
You are a remnant, a bodily witness.
Beyond pain, there is no more pain!
Beyond despair, there is no more despair!
You are a remnant, a physical witness.
Beyond pain, there is no more pain!
Beyond despair, there is no more despair! (113)

The phrase "beyond despair, there is no more despair!" appears again and again in the development of Greenberg's poetry. (The first instance is in the cycle "Virility Ascendant" [32]). Greenberg sees in it the essence of post-Holocaust Jewish experience, as we see in his speech accepting the Talpir Prize:

> Allow me to quote something I once declared in a poem during my first years in Palestine: "Beyond despair, there is no more despair." . . . With the decline of Christianity in Europe, the Existentialist thinkers and poets saw no way out; and when there is no way out, all is permitted, and man lives by lust. There is no sovereign, either above or below. But we Jews, whose faith is intact, and whose heart, *having been broken,* is utterly whole,[6] have, even after Hitler's destruction, leaped over the abyss of despair and overcome it. Despite ourselves, we have affirmed our existence, body and soul. And together, despite ourselves, we have fulfilled our destiny — contrary to every reckoning of "rational despair"; together with those Jews who were caught up in the craze of the various "isms," we have all embarked wholeheartedly upon a war of liberation, with the feeling that we must win, that there is no alternative, for, in fact, we have no desire whatsoever for an alternative. As we all know, disbelief, with a nihilistic tinge, is widespread among our people. Yet for all this nihilistic disbelief, how many have actually been brought to abandon their faith in the Covenant of the Jews by the red-black light of the Hitler-night that has come over the world?[7]

For those who saw themselves as survivors with a responsibility to bear witness, the Destruction did not weaken but only strengthened the imperative they felt to carry on the Jewish heritage. "In this we follow them as heirs. / All that was good and precious we must, by their blood, carry on / To all eternity, by the light of the [Burning] Bush" (200), "that their eternal connection not slip from the hands of the living" (237), "for there is none but us to proclaim, from the mountain of myrrh, the tidings of the future to the nations and the world, / To give mankind the blood of fresh longing and lasting expression, as we have" (165). Thus, we must not let the gentiles see us despair: "Better that the nations should see us as a people taken from fire to fire, / That knows well the abyss of affliction but in the abyss does not despair" (126). Those who have survived must live with the knowledge that "the imperative is to live: in order to carry on the legacy" (379), to pass on the tradition to the next generation. It is an imperative "to survive come what may, the imperative to suffer the life of the covenant" (195) by which Jews lived and raised their children throughout the generations (237). It is this "miracle of suffering," not physical strength, that keeps the people alive (130). This explains the paradoxical connection between the bitter indictment of God and the desperate clinging to faith. It is not an innocent faith but one that is well aware of the alternative: the abyss of utter extinction. In "The Song of My People the Sea, My People the Forest," Greenberg expresses the difference between this faith and the innocent faith of the "simpleton" and the "fool." He who walks upon the sea, knowing full well that it is a sea and not a field and that this sea could swallow him up at any moment, has no assurance of a miracle, but out of inner necessity he hopes for one. "The hoped-for miracle" is what gives the walker on water the strength to plow and plant, even though he knows that what he is dealing with is a sea and not a field (38–39).

Yearning and Imagination

Yearning (*kosef*) is one of the key terms in Greenberg's poetry, playing a role analogous to that of will (*ratzon*) in secular Zionism: that which supplies the main impetus to realization ("If you will it, it is no dream"). But for Greenberg the concept takes on a metaphysical meaning: yearning makes man human in the full sense of the word, for it is the manifestation in him of the divine, the active spiritual force that aspires to break the bounds of man's finitude in order to reach the infinite. "For in yearning is God to be found, the omnipotent one who gives wisdom / To man when clouds block his path."[8] The source of yearning is mythical memory, the recollection of past revelation that is still present.[9] He who remembers deeply also yearns deeply. Forgetfulness and the repression of memory, in contrast, lead to the repression of yearning. Yearning also has a very strong emotional component: pain, nostalgia for long-lost places. Hence, it is only when man reaches the "earthly shore" that "his yearnings cease to hurt" (238). Yearning can be so strong as to become part of his physical makeup. The power of yearning "in the flesh" is enormous for Greenberg, and no obstacle can stand in its way.

For there is a power of longing to which no other power compares,
Which none other can stop;
For there is a power of prayer in the tissues of the body,
Concentrated, like rays through the clouds;
For there is imagination, the longed-for, which bridges and links
The possible with the impossible,
And good sense accompanies it in all its leaps,
Traversing the distances with it, lest it stumble,
Guiding it around pitfalls and dead ends;
This it is that checks its footing and firms its foundation. (138)

Two spiritual forces help yearning to reach its goal: imagination and sense. Imagination has a "prophetic" quality, in that it can anticipate possibilities where they do not seem to exist. It cuts through ordinary, superficial reality to that which is latent within (138). When yearning joins imagination, it becomes an active force capable of achieving the seemingly impossible. But to reach its goal, imagination requires the guidance of common sense. What appears to be irrational can, in fact, draw upon a higher rationality. Indeed, Greenberg makes frequent use of expressions like "the logic of vision," "the sense of the soul," "the miracle of reason," and "the wisdom of the heart," all of which point to a combination of two apparently contradictory things: intellect and imagination, sense and feeling, miracle and law. "The intellect grasps what the imagination grasps" (*The Book of Accusation and Belief,* 65, 94), but in regard to the future, imagination takes precedence: "It is not the intellectuals who are right, but, always, the wise of heart." "Wisdom of the heart" is the wisdom of reality. It is the same as "insight into the times," that is, it has a true perspective on the past that allows it to see into the future.[10]

What is meant here by imagination is thus not something shadowy or mysterious but rather something grounded in the higher laws of reality that can be grasped only by prophecy, in the logic of its vision. The fact that, for Greenberg, intellect and imagination are not opposed but complementary is highly significant for understanding the wager as self-fulfilling prophecy. It is a unique combination of painful yearning, prophetic imagination, and common sense.

The Revolutionary Renewal of the Covenant

Zionism, in Greenberg's view, is the Jewish people's great wager on survival, and the Holocaust only sharpened the need for this wager. Only a total revolution that puts an end to exile and its attendant humiliation and reestablishes Jewish sovereignty can prepare the ground for a renewal of the people's faith in its God. For only a sovereign people, "that glorifies its sword and spares its flag victims, / Stands tall before God and man, its vision shining," its prayers heard, its deeds blessed (270). The Jews cannot remain faithful to the Covenant without a new historical revelation, which, in its redeeming power, outweighs the terrible destruction. This is the basis of Greenberg's obsessive, passionate messianism. Not only is it the only way of shaking the foundations of exilic life but, paradoxically, it is also the only idea that can give meaning to the suffering, martyrdom, humiliation, and destruction the Jews have suffered in exile. "Here is the prelude to the Messiah, here the gateway to the end of long-suffered shame" (*The Book of Accusation and Belief*, 61).

The revolution for which Greenberg calls will require a change in the way certain basic Judaic values are understood, above all, exile and redemption.[11] The traditional belief in redemption, clung to by the Jews throughout their long years of dispersion, has proven false. Diaspora Jewish life was "deceived by a spurious belief" (245, 154) and "a fruitless longing for the skies" (88). "The good yearning was in vain, / In vain the exalted prayer" (245). God's silence has persisted through two thousand years of exile, since Titus ripped down the Temple curtain (72), and in the end the "God of Israel" became "the God of the gentiles" (102). Greenberg sees exilic Jewish faith as having two fatal flaws:

1. A disproportion between the heavenly and the earthly (293). The people of Israel, out of a "desire for all of heaven," "beyond the laws of kingdoms, climates, and tongues" (235), has gone too far. The Jews have become "experts on heaven," "engineers of lofty highways," but they are not "experts on earth" (344). Their life line has thus become crooked (230). Here, Greenberg joins in the Zionist critique of the excessive spirituality of the Diaspora Jews.

2. An enfeebled capacity for dreaming. The Jews' longing for redemption is weak. "Not enough did we long. This is not the way a people's flesh longs! / Not enough did we feel the desire for real sovereignty, the carnal desire for a commanding, pressing redemption" (293). This weakness is demonstrated by the fact that the Jews join "nonvision to vision, one species to another that is unrelated," "revolution and nonrevolution, . . . neither here nor there" (295). In other words, while yearning for the Messiah they cling to the pleasures of exilic life. This analysis of the defects of Jewish faith points to the required remedies: first, a new orientation, revealing a new (yet old!) dimension within the Covenant that demands activism and greater responsibility for our own fate. This is what is implied in the turn from "heaven" to "earth," which entails a sanctification of the everyday. "O spirit of the race, stop your wandering from heaven to

heaven! / Come down and dwell within borders! The soil upon which you stand / Is holy, for it has bread and water for both body and spirit" (235). "There is nothing more for us in heaven, . . . only the Hidden Face / . . . Here, here below is all that is precious, all that is holy, all that is desirable" (88). In addition, the "fleshly" yearning for redemption must be cultivated, until it is strong enough to overcome the obstacles that block its path (138).

Given the failure of the old faith in the Covenant, it is no wonder that Greenberg looks forward to the making of a new Covenant. In his manifesto "Towards Ninety-nine" (1928), he writes that the "Hebrew revolution" has, all at once, taken on the character of another Sinaitic revelation (42). The Holocaust, which brought things back, as it were, to their primeval state, has added impetus to the demand for a new Covenant and a new Sinai (334, 305). In like fashion, the poet calls upon God to renew the Covenant He made with Abraham, only this time it is a sacrifice, not of animal flesh, but of the flesh of the Jewish people that is to seal the pact (166). To renew the Covenant there must be some sign, such as the one given to Abraham (167, cf. 234), and it can only be the restored kingdom itself. Yet the poet feels that "the air of my generation, pregnant with miracles, is like that preceding a theophany" (114). There is the strong expectation of a new revelation, the signs of which he sees in a growth of both yearning and anger:

> This generation's veins run with potent anguish,
> And the air is pregnant with miracles and expectation, tense with longing
>   and rage:
> It is like before the giving of the primeval words, both desired and
>   commanded;
> Like an utterance: Let it be! Let it appear in the light of gracious deeds;
> Like the template of exalted freedom for which we yearned.
> This generation shall bring it about by itself; it will not happen of its own
>   accord (116).

In fascinating, dialectical fashion, Greenberg returns to the traditional Jewish pattern of dealing with suffering, though he gives it a revolutionary meaning. In this pattern, suffering requires — in Joseph Dov Soloveitchik's terms — a practical, halakhic response rather than a philosophical, metaphysical one, for man cannot explain the source of the evil that has befallen him. In the face of suffering, faith is not maintained by intellectual (theological) means, but by a life program. The question of why I suffer is replaced by the question of what I must do so as not to be crushed under the weight of my suffering and so as to remain faithful to the Covenant. The practical answer is: "Turning fate into destiny and elevating oneself from an object to a subject."[12] This is what

Greenberg means in his call for "a great act of penitence:" the Jewish people must "take hold of the cursed wheel of suffering and still it," must "grasp the wheel of exilic fate" in order to turn it "toward the primordial, but also most recent, destination" (1999). The image of the wheel, which recurs frequently in *The Ways of the River*, suggests the fixed cyclicality of Jewish history, of destruction followed by apparent redemption, with everything seeming to revert to what it was previously. Diverting the wheel means putting an end to this process by uprooting the Jews from exile.

The Need for Decision "At the End of the Road"

Among the poems making up *The Ways of the River* is one that, in my opinion, sums up the Jewish existential situation requiring a wager for the renewal of faith. It is the poem beginning "At the end of the road stands Rabbi Levi Yitzhak of Berditchev, demanding an answer from on high" (271–75). Woven together in this poem are many motifs scattered throughout the book. In terms of its theological import, this is the book's central poem, a thesis confirmed by Greenberg himself.[13]

Greenberg sees Jewish history, particularly during the period of exile, as a history of fence sitting: the Jews wish for redemption, but when the opportunity presents itself they hang back from achieving it. They mix "vision" with "nonvision." Thus, after each destruction that might have sent them packing, they cling once more to exile, as though in the midst of a pleasant dream (294). But after the total destruction of our time we cannot go back to the old approach that said, "Take hold of this, but do not let go of that." We have reached a moment of truth, requiring an unequivocal response. The call for decision appears in a number of the poems in *The Ways of the River* (268, 295), but nowhere does it have such power and clarity as in this one, which presents the two possibilities, loyalty and desertion, as utterly polar, with no possibility of compromise between them.

Greenberg's aim in his poetry is to confront us with inescapable truth. The Holocaust, the destruction of the exiles, was for him a radical turning point in the relations between the Jewish people and its God, for it put an end, at last, to the legitimacy of exile. The Destruction requires a fresh interpretation of the Covenant, which, for Greenberg, entails a return to the original core of faith that had been distorted in exile. This basic intuition gives a profound theological dimension to the Zionist vision "prophesying" the decimation of the European Diaspora. While one may have reservations about many of the practical implications of Greenberg's interpretation, the power of its demand for decision-making must be recognized.[14]

Greenberg and Brenner:
Two Approaches to the Zionist Wager

The left and right wings of the Zionist movement, despite their ideological differences, also had much in common. There was a particular commonality of outlook between the radical right and the activist left of the labor movement, the most prominent representatives of which belonged to Hakibbutz Hameuhad (the United Kibbutz movement). This phenomenon is not in itself remarkable if we recall that the spiritual fathers of the radical right (Greenberg and his circle) started out in the labor movement. To exemplify this affinity despite difference, let us compare two figures who left a deep impress on the thinking of their respective camps, Uri Tzvi Greenberg and Yosef Hayim Brenner. Such a comparison is, in a way, audacious—some might even say far-fetched—but the fact is that of all the Hebrew writers, Greenberg felt himself closest to Brenner in personality and literary direction. Both these writers had something of the status of prophets in their respective circles, although Brenner, unlike Greenberg, lacked any prophetic ambition. Both were harsh critics of their generation and saw their literary activity as a sacred mission. Hence the ascetic life both led. A certain rhetorical tone, of appeal and alarm, is also characteristic of both writers; and both employ this tone to express a sense of inexorable fate as well as the necessity of rebelling against it. There are certain common elements in the biographies of the two figures as well: both came to Zionism after despairing of "Europe" and all the other ideologies current in the Jewish world. That is, they came to the Land of Israel not so much out of positive Zionist conviction as out of a rejection of Diaspora life, which, because of the Jews' own blindness, obtuseness, impotence, and lack of interest in being redeemed, was threatened with extinction.[15] Both "prophesied" the end of the Diaspora and condemned the Jewish propensity to martyrdom.

It is probably not accidental that the key word throughout Greenberg's writing, "yearning" (*kosef* or *kissuf*), is virtually the same as that in Brenner's, "the yearning for life" (*kosef hahayim*). It is true that the terms have very different meanings for the two writers: for Brenner, yearning is something existential and irrational, the roots of which are hidden from view; for Greenberg it is metaphysical and grounded overtly in mythic memory. Nonetheless, there is a common spiritual ground to the uses made of this term by the two writers: the faithfulness of the remnant. For Brenner, it is loyalty to the Jewish people and its languages and literature; for Greenberg, it is faithfulness to God and the spiritual message of the Jews. Hence, for Greenberg, the Zionist wager has a theological meaning related directly to biblical historiography and myth, whereas for Brenner it is primarily an act of existential heroism only indirectly inspired by biblical prophecy. Greenberg's wager is a much more passionate one, which sees no alternative solution to the crisis of Jewish faith but Zionist maximalism.

Furthermore, although both Greenberg and Brenner speak of "the Jewish situation," they differ greatly in the ends and means they advocate Zionism employ for addressing it. Greenberg wants Zionism to fulfill the myth of redemption in its entirety. To accept only partial fulfillment would represent failure in his eyes, for it would connote insufficient determination to reach for the whole. His motto would be "all or nothing," either complete redemption as promised in the ancient myth or complete destruction. Greenberg hated the middle way, what he called "the golden mean." This view stemmed from identification with myth so complete that the latter was seen not merely as a source of inspiration but as an exclusive guidepost. If reality did not fit the mythic ideal, that was reality's loss. Such absolutism not only sanctions the use of extreme means, such as unrestricted violence, but also carries the danger of utter defeat and destruction; no ideal is ever fully realized. Brenner's motto, on the other hand, would be just the opposite: "nevertheless" — though we may not achieve everything, we must press on. He did not expect Zionism to work for complete redemption at any cost but held that even partial fulfillment was worth striving for. As Menahem Brinker has said, Brenner's "nevertheless" "was grounded in the possibility of retreating from the grand Zionist program to a more modest one," i.e., making do with "the lesser, but perhaps achievable ideal, one which also demands enormous effort and heroism, while foregoing the more ambitious ideal, which, when held up against reality, could only breed despair and inaction."[16] Brenner's wager, then, demanded no less effort, sacrifice, or heroism than Greenberg's, but seeing no possibility of complete redemption in this world, it took its stand on more limited ground. Herein lies the essential difference between the left- and right-wing approaches to the wager. While drawing inspiration from the historical myth, the left only partly identified with the latter and did not see it as its sole standard of fulfillment.

Messianism and Realism

Utopia and Messianism

It is often said that Zionism represented a "return to history." Generally, what is meant is that it rejected the religious conception of history that had been regnant until the beginning of the modern era and adopted a secular one: Jewish history was now to be understood as a product of "natural" forces, like the history of other nations, and not, uniquely, as the working of divine providence. This was one of the implications of the idea of "normalization," at which Zionism aimed. Yet the latter retained an umbilical connection to the messianic, otherworldly strand in traditional Judaism. And because the proponents of Zionism had a rather optimistic belief in progress and the ability of science to solve most human problems, they also believed that what had been too difficult for earlier generations would not be so for theirs. Hence, there is a utopian dimension to much Zionist thinking, particularly that of the labor movement. A combination of Jewish messianic myth and Enlightenment rationalism gave rise to the Zionist utopia.

Zionism's relation to messianism was complex and controversial.[1] Was it a continuation of the old faith in a new form or a rejection of that faith? Jacob Katz claimed that the principal motive force of Zionism was not "Jewish distress," i.e., antisemitism, but, in fact, the messianic idea, the old dream of independence that the Jewish people had never relinquished. Basing his ideas on a

sociological analysis, he highlighted the irrational factor in Zionism in comparison with other Jewish movements and those among other peoples. True,
messianism was not, in his view, the only factor, and several others, such as the
disintegration of traditional society and the rise of antisemitism, did play a role.
Yet this irrational element was of crucial importance, so that the attainment of
mere territory or statehood would not be enough. Evidence of this can be seen,
first of all, in the very insistence on the Land of Israel as the goal of immigration
in spite of the special difficulties settlement there entailed. Were it not for the
messianic factor, the Jews would never have made their state here; the country
had an attraction for them that outweighed all rational considerations.

The utopian dimension of Zionist thought, too, reflects a messianic propensity. This utopianism was not a mere afterthought but a vital inner force that
proved essential in recruiting support for the movement. Zionism had a distinct advantage over other utopian movements in its ability to point to a
particular *topos,* an actual place that would provide the ideal setting for realizing its vision. Its utopia could not be realized anywhere else. There was an
irrational conviction that the ancient homeland would have a revolutionary
effect on the Jewish people. It would not only heal them of all the pathologies
of exile; it would awaken their latent powers, and this would ensure the
utopia's realization. The other utopias current among the Jews themselves did
not have a similar source of energy. Katz thus objected to the efforts made by
other Zionists (like Gershom Scholem) to minimize the importance of messianism for Zionism.[2] These efforts, he believed, did not reflect the sentiments of
the people, as the Orthodox opponents of Zionism well understood.[3]

Generally, I accept Katz's opinion but with some qualification. Messianic
imagery did play an important role in shaping the historical consciousness of
many Zionist thinkers and activists. This imagery found expression mainly in
the belles lettres of the period. Messianic imagery and motivation were vital to
the success of the movement, which used them to give a new meaning to the
idea of redemption. We see here the complex, dialectical connection of Zionist
thought with traditional Jewish thought. Zionist messianism symbolizes both
continuity and rebellion: rebellion against the traditional quietism that was
prepared to wait indefinitely for redemption, believing that a miracle would
come from on high, and against belief in the power of magical mysticism to
bring redemption. But at the same time, Zionism identified with the old Jewish
longing for ultimate redemption.

Will as a Wonder-Working Power

There is a deep gap between utopian thinking and the scientific view of
reality. Science, in its presumption of empiricism, seeks to moderate, if not

entirely suppress, the kinds of imaginary visions that are essential to revolutionary politics, whether of the right or the left. Science domesticates historical thinking by purging it of all that is magical and lofty in order to make it more "realistic," which means antiutopian. "Principally," wrote Max Weber, "there are no mysterious, incalculable forces that come into play, but rather one can, in principle, master all things by calculation."[4] When the facts are denuded of mystery, they can never serve as the basis of a visionary politics that seeks to give meaning to the life of society. Thus, oppressed, enslaved groups, striving for freedom and dignity, reject the advice of scientific scholars to look at history objectively, "realistically," and "responsibly."[5]

Zionist historical thinking was marked by the duality of necessity and will, determinism and personal freedom. The messianic vision of the End of Days gave the Zionist view of history a deterministic cast. Yet along with this there was a stress on personal choice. The two seemingly contradictory thrusts were combined in Zionist theory, and their combination gave a powerful impetus to Zionist utopianism.

The belief in will as the decisive factor in the fate of the nation was the antithesis not only of Orthodox quietism but also of the optimistic faith of those emancipated Jews who entrusted their fate to foreign rulers. Early on, Moses Mendelssohn noted that the constant oppression and persecution of the Jews in exile had taken away their desire for freedom and that what was needed if they were to be redeemed was willpower on their part. To this, Herzl added: if the will be strong enough, the legend, the dream, will become reality. This is a dominant motif in the poetry of Uri Tzvi Greenberg. For him, the "yearning" of the Jews in exile has not been strong enough; it is a "yearning of the spirit" but not a "yearning of the flesh," and therefore they have not been redeemed. Thus what is needed, first of all, is to change the mentality of the people from a dependence on external powers (God or foreign regimes) to a readiness for free choice. As Ben Zion Dinur puts it: "Zionism stressed the idea that if human beings really wanted to they could accomplish great things. . . . There was great faith here in the inherent powers of the Jews, their latent talent for action. This belief in the nation and renewed estimation of its will became one of the pillars of Zionist ideology."[6] Belief in the power of the popular will took the place of belief in God. It was a profound change of orientation, a "re-orientation to ourselves," resulting from a secularization of Jewish thinking.

Paradoxically enough, this faith in the people's own powers was reinforced by the old belief in miracles. The national movement's attitude toward the concept of miracle, like its attitude toward messianism, was quite ambivalent. On one hand, there was a total rejection of faith in "divine" intervention, a faith that was blamed for the people's lack of desire to be redeemed; on the other hand, there was a new faith in "human" miracles that was a product of that very desire. It was a desire to achieve miracles with our own hands, without God, as expressed by Ze'ev (Aharon Ze'ev, b. 1900) in his popular poem "We Bear Torches:" "No miracle befell us, / No vial of oil did we find, . . . / We dug into the rock till blood flowed . . . / And there was light." These words were incorporated into a children's song meant to strengthen belief in human action while warning against the traditional concept of miracle, as expressed in the story of the Maccabees' discovery of the vial of oil when they went to cleanse the reclaimed Temple. In the formative years of the movement, Hannuka was made the Zionist holiday par excellence, and the Hasmoneans became the most popular symbol of auto-emancipation.

But it was precisely the Hasmoneans who now came to be seen as symbolizing the belief that, if the will were strong enough, the miracle that occurred in olden times would happen again. According to Klausner, the leading historian of the Second Temple period, the Hasmoneans acted against reason and cold calculation. They believed that spirit would win out over matter, that "psychological power" would defeat "terrible practical power."[7] A. D. Gordon, like Berdyczewski, maintained that there were situations in the life of a people where practical calculations, based on "scientific" or rational considerations, should not be made. "If our forefathers in Hasmonean times had made their plans on the basis of exact calculations, if they had adhered to the most logical and realistic political path, they would undoubtedly have been weaker, and the Hebrew people would have been doomed to extinction."[8] In emergencies, the will of the nation rises up against science and common sense and enables things to be done that afterwards seem unbelievable even to those who did them. For him, Zionism is not a practical movement in the accepted sense, but a matter of optimism, "an impossibility," the success of which depends on miracles: "We all admit that our situation is dangerous, that our fate hangs by a hair between life and death, but we do not want to admit to ourselves that our salvation will come only by a gigantic, almost miraculous effort of will, so that, in this sense, we can say, with the masses, that we shall be redeemed and rescued forever by miracles alone. In any event, this 'miraculous' way is much more natural and much nearer at hand than any of the practical approaches."[9] But it is our misfortune, says Gordon, that "we are too realistic" and "afraid to tackle any impossibility. . . . We like to enter the game only when it is clear that we will win."[10] Here we clearly see the gulf, pointed out earlier, between utopian and empirical thinking.

How strongly this notion influenced the practical politics of Zionism can be seen from some of the responses to the events at Tel-Hai.[11] As David Remez remarked about the Jewish armed stand there: "In every strategy, it is easy to demonstrate defeat in hindsight and hard to predict victory. . . . Apparently we now find ourselves embroiled in an old dispute, one not to be decided by argumentation or reasoning. There is a practicality that reckons retrospectively that we should have left and another practicality that insists on standing firm until the last possible moment. And then it happens that the impossible becomes possible."[12] In a similar vein, Brenner writes, "Calculation clearly indicated [that they could not hold out against the Arabs,] but the heart, the dedicated heart, believed in miracles, believed the order of creation would be changed in our favor, because dedication is omnipotent, because the love of our soil can move mountains; and the desire to believe made its own calculations — calculations, dreams."[13]

Chaim Weizmann, that shrewd, cautious statesman, is quoted as having said, "You don't have to be *meshuga* [crazy] to be a Zionist, but it helps." And Ben-Gurion, the great rationalist among the Zionist statesmen, is quoted as saying, "In the Land of Israel, he who does not believe in miracles is not a realist." In defense of his support for the British partition proposal of 1937, Ben-Gurion fulminated against the nay-sayers: "I do not have the certainty of those who know in advance that this is the greatest disaster that can befall the people of Israel at this time. I still believe in miracles." He was astonished by Britain's suggestion that "it [had] the power to work this great and awesome miracle" and deeply stirred by "the splendor of the vision treasured in our souls these hundreds and thousands of years."[14] Ben-Gurion's passionate belief in "miracles" was grounded in the ancient dream, both historical and mythical, of restoring Jewish independence. It was Jewish-history-turned-myth that nourished faith in the power of the will to work wonders.

Thus a movement, which criticized faith in miracles, remained itself bound to this faith, though giving it a new interpretation. The vanguard of the Jewish people had bestirred itself to accomplish the impossible with its own hands. For, as we know from scholars of religion, miracles occur when they are wanted and worked for with full devotion. So measured a historian as Ben Zion Dinur had the audacity to publish a historical essay with the title "The Miracle of the Rise of Israel and Its Historical Foundations."[15] He opens with an explanation of his strange mixture of the purely religious with the historical and scientific: "The political rise of Israel, given its historical circumstances, is undoubtedly one of those great phenomena . . . which at the time seem inexplicable on the basis of the natural course of things and, indeed, utterly contrary to it. Hence, people tend to see [these phenomena] as caused by the intervention of powerful, incomprehensible forces . . . and to assign these events to the class known as 'miracles.'" But "even miracles do not occur of their own accord, and man helps them along." Thus, Dinur probes for the "laws" underlying the miracle, the inner strengths of the Jews in recent generations that "brought them to this point." He concludes that what happened here was not a one-time miracle but the result of a long-term struggle, particularly in the last three generations. For him, the miracle laid in "the great resolution of those generations," which had invested their lives, their vision, and their energy in the work of building, out of "confidence . . . and faith in what was to come."[16]

This way of thinking was shared by both right and left: the freely chosen human act, product of a determined will, is what makes "miracles" happen. No wonder, then, that a movement like Gush Emunim,[17] which sees itself as the heir of a way of thinking that existed in Zionism from the very beginning, has adopted the slogan "messianic realism."[18]

"Mysticism" and "Realism": The Left-Right Polemic

The success of any national movement depends largely on whether it can strike a balance between the nonrational, mythic element in its ideology and the rational, pragmatic one. This balance is also expressed in the formulation of goals, political strategies, and expectations of what can be achieved at any given time. On the face of it, the issue is one of a rational assessment of reality and the forces at work within it, but the degree to which success hinges on such psychological factors as fervor and determination, i.e., on willpower, is hard to gauge and therefore a matter of ongoing controversy. In Zionist politics, the question of balance between the visionary and the pragmatic was debated from the very outset.

At the end of the 1920s, following the emergence of the radical right as a political force in Jewish Palestine, a polemic raged between the right and the left over how Zionist goals should be realized. The debate turned on the appropriate balance to be struck between the two components of Zionism referred to in the terminology of that time as "mysticism" — a nonrational vision that was oblivious to concrete realities — and "realism" — a pragmatic outlook that gave the greatest weight to tangible factors. The polemic was primarily concerned with the question of strategy, the left advocating an evolutionary approach — going stage by stage and setting intermediate goals, making do with a minimum in the present and expecting complete realization only in the distant future — the right favoring bold steps toward an immediate achievement of the final goal, without too much consideration of reality factors, on the assumption that only such action could change reality enough to achieve the desired ends.

Because politics is anchored in historical awareness, this strategic debate took on a wider meaning, turning into a historiosophical polemic over the relative weight of rational and nonrational factors in Jewish, and especially Zionist, history. The ferocity of the debate arose from the unusual conditions in which it developed — unusual in comparison with those of other national-liberation movements. Since the Jews had no territory or common language, there was a yawning gap between reality and the radical goals Zionism set for itself: the revival of a language no longer spoken and the uprooting and transfer of living communities to a country from which they had been absent for two thousand years. This polemic continues to be relevant today in the light it sheds on the character of Israeli politics.[19]

The difference between right and left was in the relative weight they gave to the visionary element as a guide for action. The right saw the psychological, subjective factor as decisive because it "preceded all material reality" and overcame it.[20] The main thing, then, was to stir the fires of belief and imagination, thereby inspiring the masses to great, revolutionary deeds. Seeing adherence to the vision as decisive in the process of realization, the right saw no need to set forth a clear program translating that vision into concrete reality. It saw itself as the true heir of Herzlian political Zionism, and its publicists were always quoting what Herzl had said to Baron de Hirsch in 1895, when turning to him for help:

> Believe me, the policy of an entire people — especially one that is scattered all over the world — can only be made out of imponderables that float high in the thin air. Do you know out of what the German empire sprang? Out of reveries, songs, fantasies, and black-red-and-gold ribbons — and in short order. Bismarck merely had to shake the tree, which the visionaries had planted. What, you do not understand an imponderable? What then is religion? Consider, if you will, what the Jews have withstood throughout two thousand years for the sake of a vision. Visions alone grip the souls of men. And whoever does not know how to deal in visions may be an excellent, worthy, practical-minded person and even a benefactor in a big way; but he will never be a leader of men, and no trace of him will remain.[21]

The key sentence is, "Visions alone grip the souls of men." Of course, he does not mean to negate entirely the value of action, but it is the vision, the myth, that takes precedence. And indeed, this was one of Herzl's greatest achievements: firing the Jewish imagination and will with the myth of a Jewish state. But it was not clear how the vision was to be realized.

In Uri Tzvi Greenberg's view, historical reality is only a pale, distorted reflection of myth. Consequently, he does not assess political action by its contribution to actual redemption but by its psychological effect, that is, the extent to which it shapes and enhances the mythic, visionary experience:

True was the doctrine of Bar Kokhba, even when Beitar fell,
And true the Gush-Halav doctrine until the last days of Yohanan.[22]

In 1951, Yehoshua Heschel Yeivin published an article entitled "The Concreteness of the Non-Concrete as a Fundamental Principle of the Israeli Liberation Movement." Yeivin had joined Abba Ahimeir and Uri Tzvi Greenberg in
the "Ruffians' Compact" (*brit ha-biryonim*), which laid the foundation for the
extreme right wing of the Zionist movement. Although the article was written
after the establishment of the state, it summarizes well the spirit of the extreme
right from the early 1930s on. Yeivin set out to demonstrate that symbols and
ideas are the only true reality: "In our own generation, only he who is blind
from birth can be such a 'naive realist' as to believe that what is real is what we
see before our eyes and feel with our fingers. . . . The only true reality is the flag,
the idea." And though it cannot be weighed on a scale, there can be no doubt
that it is the decisive factor in the present; if we did not postulate this we could
not explain why the pioneers went to sacrifice their lives for the Land of Israel
in particular. For Yeivin, there is "nothing mystical, nothing beyond the grasp
of common sense" about it.[23]

Here myth, under the influence of Greenberg, becomes the supreme reality.
It is the source of what he calls the human "power of longing," which, when
linked with the imagination, is activated and becomes a self-fulfilling prophecy. This imagination is not something mystical but a power that grasps reality
according to its higher laws, which are only evident to poets and prophets. For
Yeivin, the fact that Zionism "prophesied" both the Jewish catastrophe in
exile and the re-establishment of the Jewish people in its homeland is the most
conclusive proof that ideas and symbols are "the most real realities."

Acclaim that is heard repeatedly in right-wing *publicité* is that in the history
of Zionism those who were considered the least practical-minded, the visionaries and believers, were vindicated, while the realists, those with minimal
expectations, proved completely wrong. Zionism was never rational but,
rather, the most absurd thing imaginable, with no reasonable chance of success.[24] It succeeded by taking a venturesome path, "betting the whole kitty,"
without considering objective factors or the constraints of reality. In his article
"Varieties of Adventurism," Yisrael Eldad exalts the latter as a value connecting the human tendency "to risk one's life, as a primal testing experience," on
one hand, with pioneering in service of an ideal, on the other. Without this
tendency to adventurism, "there would be no revolutions or martyrdom."
Accordingly, Herzl was an adventurist. What is more, all Zionism was a wondrous adventure, led by all kinds of " bold forces": "influential teachers, visionary leaders, and, above all, pioneers and fighters who did the actual work

of realization." In this adventure there was something of the "cunning of history," which uses human beings' natural risk-taking tendency in order to achieve a purpose that transcends them.[25]

Eldad was greatly influenced by Nietzsche's notion of the importance of "monumental history," historiography that glorifies outstanding personalities and heroes. Such readings of history, Nietzsche maintained, are of great value wherever the people are in need of fresh inspiration to accomplish great things or to rebel against the gray, oppressive pettiness of the present. But alongside this positive value, he stressed the accompanying danger: "monumental" historiography, knowingly or not, distorts the past, thereby endangering the present. The poetic imagination upon which it relies tends to ignore distinctions between present and past, i.e., between historical situations. It does not recognize the fact that history never quite repeats itself.[26]

The left, for its part, sought to integrate the mystical with the empirical in the process of realizing its goals and stressed the fruitlessness of imagination not accompanied by practicality. This integration became its hallmark, distinguishing not only its political strategy but its entire worldview. Its ideology, which was to be the main spiritual force in the realization of Zionism, drew upon two different sources: historical romanticism, which stressed the nonrational elements in national life; and humanistic, universalistic European socialism, which favored rational planning in the political and social spheres. In 1933, in a eulogy of Hayim Arlosoroff, Katznelson sketched a profile of the ideal Zionist man of action. He would be favored with high intelligence and partial to the intellectually exoteric yet employ all the means at his disposal to help realize something beyond intellect. His rational efforts would have a nonrational background, and behind his hard-nosed practical calculations there would be an idea drawn from the depths of history.[27] This combination of idealism and empiricism may be observed among many of the pioneers of the Second and Third Aliyot. Their belief in utopia was nourished in no small measure by a belief in the power of science to realize the ancient ideals. Thus the leftist utopia was, from the outset, anchored in concreteness and "small beginnings" (Zech 4:10).

Recognition of the need to combine the mystical and the concrete is evident in statesmen such as David Ben-Gurion. Like Yisrael Eldad, Ben-Gurion defined Zionism as "the greatest adventure in the history of the Jewish people since the destruction of the Temple," and he maintained that without adventurism the goals of Zionism could never be realized. He acknowledged that the doubts of the "clever ones," the "Diaspora realists," were well grounded.[28] But he did not admit any contradiction in principle between mysticism and realism. He believed Zionism would have to embrace both, without blurring the difference between the two. He assigned a distinct realm to each of the two forces, insisting that we take a realistic, critical approach to the outside world —the English, the Arabs—while remaining mystics among ourselves. Realism was appropriate for all concrete actions we might take in the immediate future; mysticism—i.e., deep faith and strong, unflinching will—was needed for the long haul.[29] The practical process leading from insubstantial dream to fully fleshed-out reality would require both a concentration on deeds and a gradualist approach to the work of construction.[30] Such moderation offers a greater chance of reaching the goal than do visionary pronouncements. Modest actions will be nourished by the vision, the irrational faith, the hope of complete redemption, not only of Israel, but also of humanity as a whole. Hidden spiritual forces are at work in us that will help us overcome external obstacles and even the fear of death. "Call it mysticism. . . . We all draw succor from these depths." But when it comes to the concrete question of what to do next, there can only be cool, hard calculation, like that of an engineer setting out to build a house.[31]

The upshot was that we would have to live in constant tension between the desire to hasten redemption and the need to take given realities into account. It was a kind of positive opportunism. While the right viewed any acceptance of partial solutions as failure, and making-do the sign of a lack of daring and weakness of will, the left saw the impossibility of full realization under the given human circumstances. This camp was willing to settle for partial achievement in the short run without giving up hope that eventually the goal would be reached. Since such a stand did not demand everything at once, it did not have to resort continually to extreme measures (like violence) to achieve its goals. There was an a priori immunity to exaggerated expectations that could lead to disappointment or even despair. The ability of the labor movement to combine the rational and nonrational in its view of history was one of the key ingredients in the success of its political strategy. But the balance between utopianism and realism that characterized the central, labor stream of the Zionist movement was gradually lost after the establishment of the State of Israel in 1948. In the 1950s, the utopian element began to wane, at least in secular circles, and Israeli society found itself in crisis over the question of realization, which, in turn, meant a crisis of identity as well. This turn of events, the reasons for which I shall explore later on, was bound up with a profound change in the historical outlook of the Israelis, involving a dilution of the myths that had given rise to utopianism.

PART **II**

The Moral Price of Sovereignty

7

Criticism of the Idea of Sovereignty in Non-Zionist Thought

Secularism, like everything destructive, is both liberating and risky. But Zionism was a calculated risk, in that it brought about the destruction of the reality of exile. The enemies of Zionism certainly saw the risk more clearly than we Zionists did.

Gershom Scholem, *Devarim bego* (For good reason)

The Modern Concept of Sovereignty

The role of sovereignty in the Jewish scheme of values became a live question only in the modern period, in response to the challenges of emancipation and Zionism. Along with the issue of Halakha, this has been the main question dividing Jews in the twentieth century. It has been a debate not merely over strategies of Jewish survival, but over the very meaning of Judaism. To understand the issue, we must look at the notion of sovereignty in modern thought in general.

The aspiration to autonomy as expressed in sovereignty is one of the hallmarks of modern secularism. The philosopher Jean Bodin (1520–91) saw sovereignty as the antithesis of the medieval notion of rule, according to which the ruler was subject to no law but that of God. Bodin defines the sovereign, by contrast, as "the supreme [body] of subjects and citizens, not limited by law," this body being itself the source of the law and its sole legitimate interpreter and executor. Although he tries to limit the sovereign's exercise of power, for example by subjecting it to "natural law" or a kind of constitution, he is unclear on this subject.[1]

The term "sovereignty" as it is used today has two distinct meanings. Outwardly, it consists in the recognition by other nations of the independence of a particular political community in relation to other such communities, i.e., of its right to conduct its internal affairs without external interference and to defend itself, when necessary, from external threat.[2] Inwardly, sovereignty is what characterizes the supreme source of legislation, law enforcement, and governance within the community. Together these two concepts of the legitimate exercise of power, outward and inward, provide the basis of the idea of the modern secular state.

In the nineteenth century, the idea of sovereignty was connected with that of nationhood, that is, with the right of national self-definition or self-determination. A common view, though not the only one, identified the two, thus making the idea of the nation one of the main sources of violent conflict in the modern era. Jacob Talmon has shown that a certain trend in modern political thought, beginning with Machiavelli and extending through Hobbes and Hegel, has seen the sovereign state as an all-powerful, autonomous entity, limited only by those obligations it chooses to undertake. This notion represents, according to Talmon, "a rebellion against a two-thousand-year-old tradition and a return to a pre-Christian way of thinking. . . . [It is thus], indirectly, a shaking off of the influence of Judaism."[3] It is no wonder that the idea of sovereignty, which found its way into Jewish thinking under the influence of the European national-liberation movements, aroused strong opposition from both liberal and Orthodox Jews. The negative attitudes of both to the idea of Jewish nationalism in general and Jewish sovereignty in particular also had a good deal to do with the violence — especially toward Jews — that had accompanied the growth of nationalism in Europe and the traditional Jewish abhorrence of the use of force. Thus it is clear that the debate within the Jewish community on this issue was a debate on the meaning of Jewish identity in the modern world and in relation to certain moral ideas.

Doctrines opposed to the idea of Jewish nationhood in its modern sense began to be disseminated in liberal and neo-Orthodox circles during the struggle for emancipation, long before the Zionist movement appeared on the scene (in 1882). Those advocating such doctrines were bent on easing the integration of the Jews into European society by obscuring the national character of Jewish tradition. The appearance of Jewish nationalism toward the end of the nineteenth century spurred fresh criticism of the joining of Jewish nationhood with Jewish sovereignty. Some opposed the aspiration to independence in the Jewish homeland because it would require Jews to shed blood or oppress other peoples. Others opposed it because of its distinctly secular character, turning as it did on modern man's determination to make his own laws and be his own master. These critics were concerned to preserve Jewish uniqueness and saw the notion of sovereignty as an alien, assimilationist graft. In their view, the rise of modern nationalism, accompanied as it had been by outbreaks of unrestrained violence, made it imperative for Jews, with their heritage, to provide a model of humane living by the very fact of not having a sovereign political framework of their own, or by establishing a theocratic community the sovereign ruler of which was God Himself.

The Zionists, who were in favor of the re-establishment of Jewish autonomy in the Jewish homeland, were also sharply divided over the meaning of sovereignty for Jewish nationhood. Some saw it as a springboard for the fulfillment of the messianic dream of restoring the Jewish commonwealth to its biblical borders, primarily by military means. Another faction saw the Zionist endeavor as the cornerstone of a new humanity and a new world order. For them, the return of the Jewish people to its homeland would inaugurate a new chapter in the history of the world, marked by a gradual reduction in the use of force in international relations. Their attitude toward sovereignty was thus reserved. Between these two extremes was a large group who saw sovereignty and even the use of force as a necessity dictated by the circumstances of the Jewish people in the modern world. Sovereignty was needed to defend Jewish dignity, liberty, and security in the face of the violence Jews were experiencing in the various countries where they lived.

In the following chapters I shall not give a full accounting of these controversies but only of the key issues that engaged the disputants. I shall begin with the ideological positions of those who opposed sovereignty in principle, seeing it as contrary to the mission of the Jewish people and of Judaism, and then discuss the question of how the Holocaust changed the debate over the use of military force among Jewish thinkers in the Diaspora. Finally, I shall present the main positions toward sovereignty and military power taken by those Jews who came to live in the Land of Israel before the establishment of the state.

The Neo-Orthodox Critique: Yitzhak Breuer's Torah State

Neo-Orthodoxy has attacked the basis of the modern concept of sovereignty — the secular, humanistic notions of freedom and sovereignty — maintaining that these notions, which promised to redeem humanity from oppression, had, in fact, led to chaos, tyranny, and bloodshed. Neo-Orthodoxy saw war as the idolatry of our era, the result of modern man's revolt against the absolute sovereignty of God. Man's freedom is guaranteed only when he accepts divine rule and conducts his life according to divine law. The biblical idea of theocracy, "the kingdom of heaven," provides the only assurance of justice and peace among nations and within them. Unlike ultra-Orthodoxy, which rejected the quest for renewed Jewish sovereignty on theological grounds, the tradition of the Three Oaths,[4] as well as because of the secular character of the national movement, neo-Orthodoxy questioned the independence movement out of a fear that it would have bloody consequences.

Yitzhak Breuer (1883–1946) was one of the guiding spirits of Agudat Israel in Germany during the interwar period. Although influenced by the thinking of his grandfather Samson Raphael Hirsch, who had laid the foundations for neo-Orthodoxy in Germany during the Emancipation, he had an entirely different political and historical outlook. Hirsch's philosophy of Jewish history took shape during the time when German Jewry was struggling for equality. As an Orthodox Jew, he could not deny Jewish nationhood entirely, as did the Reformers of his day, but he gave it an extremely narrow interpretation: it consisted in collective faithfulness to the Torah and the way of life based upon it, and nothing more. It was a purely theological concept with no political or cultural significance. The exile of the Jews was part of the divine plan for the education of the human race. Historical experience would bring humanity to the desired end: recognition of God. To attain this end, he wrote: "it became necessary that one people be introduced into the ranks of the nations which, through its history and life, should declare that God is the only creative cause of existence and that the fulfillment of His will is the only goal of life. . . . This mission required for its execution a nation poor in everything upon which the rest of mankind reared the edifice of its greatness and power; externally subordinate to the nations armed with proud self-sufficiency but fortified inwardly by direct reliance upon God, so that, by the suppression of every enemy force, God might reveal Himself directly as the sole Creator, Judge, and Master of nature and history."[5]

Hirsch stressed the positive significance of exile: lacking the implements of statehood, the people of Israel demonstrates that the Lord alone is the true master of history. Exile is neither punishment nor catastrophe but a mission. Furthermore, in exile the Jews carry out their task more successfully than they could in their homeland, for it was living in the Land of Israel that caused them to sin, that brought them to succumb to acquisitiveness and material pleasures and forget their destiny. That is why their land was taken from them, and in its place the Torah was made "[their] soil, [their] basis, and [their] purpose." Their "existence as a nation" is not in need of "transitory things."[6] Hirsch saw life in exile, without a state, as proof of the supremacy of the "feminine principle" of home and family over the "masculine principle" of the citizen and the state. In the life of other nations, the masculine principle holds sway, whereas the history of Israel since the destruction of Jerusalem reflects the victory of the feminine principle.[7]

In Hirsch's thought, the lack of a state is connected with Judaism's mission to fight "Amalekism," which is Judaism's antithesis. Amalek lives by the sword and worships power, for which he is willing to sacrifice all divine and human values;[8] whereas Abraham, the father of the Jewish people, was willing to give up homeland, fortune, fame, and status—all those things that people obtain by force or its attendant machinations—to ensure, in a peaceable way, that the world would be governed by justice. The destiny of Abraham's descendants is to proclaim the victory of unarmed moral force over armed physical force. Hence a bitter war of ideas rages between Amalek and Israel. Amalek hates Abraham's descendants with an uncompromising hatred and seeks to destroy them, while Israel is commanded to erase the memory of Amalek. Hirsch gives this commandment a daring interpretation, referring to it as an inward struggle. Israel is to root out from within itself all traces of Amalek, especially the cult of the hero in all its forms, the laurels that the nations, in their blind enthusiasm, bestow upon murderers. "The memory of Amalek is what makes the deeds of Amalek the curse of mankind." Instead of holding violence up to contempt, each new generation among the gentiles is drawn into an admiration of it, and its dominance is thus perpetuated. Only when the very name of Amalek is erased from human memory will the ground be ready for the establishment of a moral order, in which human history will reach its culmination.[9]

Unlike Hirsch, who downplays the element of nationhood in Judaism out of a belief in emancipation and integration, Breuer stresses this element, calls for aliya—he himself came to live in Palestine in 1936—and sees the establishment of a "state [ruled by] the Torah" as the most important challenge facing contemporary religious Jews.[10]

In Breuer's view, the historical essence of the Jewish people can be grasped only against the tragic background of world history. The root of the tragedy lies in the pagan quest for sovereignty, which is the cause of all wars, civil and international. World history is the history of persecutors and persecuted, of national ambitions, of wars that grow crueler as material civilization develops.[11]

The issue of sovereignty is central for Breuer. He tries to prove that basing it on secular grounds has been a failure because the state is incapable of realizing the ideals of justice that it proclaims. Secular sovereignty means "both inwardly and outwardly, the will of the state is supreme, limited only by territorial boundaries. Within those boundaries it rules without restriction."[12] The state is arbitrary, adhering to moral laws only when it is expedient to do so.[13]

The modern state is an institutionalization of the "bestial will," i.e., a will that knows none of the moral constraints to which ordinary individuals are subject.[14] One reason for this, according to Breuer, is the failure of Western, Christian civilization to come to terms with the human body. Jewish culture regards the body as something holy and thus tries to restrain its powers. European civilization, in contrast, is alienated from the body, recognizing its value for sport or art but never relating to on its own terms. Thus European culture, in all its manifestations, is unable to tame the "blond beast" in man or to redeem humanity from the scourge of war.[15]

As long as the bestial will holds the reins of power, as long as states insist on sovereignty and each takes the law into its own hands in matters both foreign and domestic, there will never be true peace among nations or within societies. Indeed, with the development of technology, cruelty and violence will only grow. The anarchy that has characterized human history will continue to precipitate one catastrophe after another, just as the Prophets foresaw.[16] Man's unending entanglement in war and revolution is a sign that he is in exile and that the Divine Presence has exiled itself from history.

Only the subjugation of the state to divine law can heal the human malady. God is the only true sovereign and the source of all law: that of nature, that governing individuals, and that governing nations. Only a society that recognizes God's sovereignty can be truly just. The Jews are the only people in the world who have foregone the rebellious assertion of sovereignty that denies divine law and instead have sought to create a visionary state in which that law prevails. Hence the only power that can redeem humanity from its tragic predicament lies in the metahistory of Israel.

There can be no greater opposition than that between Judaism and the sovereign state. In fact, "the gulf between the visionary Jewish state and the rebellious, bestial state is so deep that it would be better [in the context of the Torah] not to apply the term 'state' to the former at all."[17] The Jewish state is an institutionalization, not of the "bestial will" but of the "visionary will." "The visionary state," says Breuer, "has no lust for power, for it is not a human being, and it is remote from all impurity, for it is untainted by death. Strength and power have no value for it. . . . The vision of justice is its highest, most absolute value, and it received the law of justice from the Creator, be He blessed, who is Himself justice. . . . This is legitimate sovereignty, and this is true freedom."[18]

It was not for nought that this people was educated in Egyptian exile, where it learned in its very flesh about the cruelty of rebellious self-rule. This experience created a deep divide between it and the rest of humanity. The Exodus from Egypt was an exodus from the common, natural history of the human race and an entry into metahistory.[19]

Exile saved the Jews in the period of the Second Temple. They were forced into exile just as the Jewish concept of sovereignty began to be corrupted, and there was a danger that the sovereignty of the state over its subjects would displace the true sovereignty of God. Exile was thus not merely a punishment, but also a kind of rescue: it saved the Jews from the extinction that would have resulted from substituting human for divine rule.[20]

Jewish nationhood is "conditional"; it denies the people any inherent value and demands that it stand fast in the service of the ideal. Breuer attacks secular Zionism for calling "conditional nationhood" a merely exilic idea, born in the Diaspora and perhaps necessary there but, now that we are on the way to national revival, exchangeable for nationhood of the unconditional variety. He maintains that the notion of conditional nationhood was born when God made the Jews. Such nationhood is stronger than the unconditional kind and provides greater assurance of national survival, as Jewish history shows.[21] For Breuer, the Torah and the very existence of the Jewish people are "a protest against might": "Not the might of armies and not the cleverness of diplomacy, but the 'escutcheon of God' alone can protect state and land from decline and fall. Judaism has not rejected might only as a consequence of dispersion, . . . [has not merely made] a virtue out of necessity. Every line of Holy Scripture is a protest against might. Indeed, the genesis of the Jewish people itself is a divine demonstration against might."[22]

It is no accident that, during the Second World War, which was also a war against the Jews, the latter had no allies. "A people that denies its own sovereignty stands alone in history."[23] For Breuer, this war had a messianic significance, for it demonstrated the failure of secular humanism, the failure of humanity to redeem itself. In this war, history came to a messianic end. The return of the Jewish people to its land and the establishment there of a "Torah state" would be harbingers of the redemption of mankind as a whole from its tragic dilemma. But precisely when the idea of secular sovereignty has demonstrably failed, in Breuer's view, Zionism is trying to establish a "rebellious state" instead of a "Torah state," which would have been a first step in the messianic process of establishing world peace. Thus it is in the Land of Israel itself that a universally significant confrontation between history and metahistory is taking place: "Our era is characterized by a clash between history and metahistory. And we shall not find any place where this clash is as direct and vigorous as in the Land of Israel. For it is precisely in this era, in which the mortal illness of history as a whole has become so clear, that secular Zionism has arisen. . . . Secular Zionism has built the national home, too, on the model of non-Jewish history. . . . It thinks such a national home can bring an end to the Jewish exile. And it does not see, or does not want to see, that such a national home only replaces one exile with another: Jewish exile with that of the gentiles. . . . Only on the basis of metahistory can the Jewish people build its national home in the Land of Israel, and only the rule of divine justice can protect it."[24] Whereas the accepted Zionist position was that the Jews must re-enter history, Breuer's position was just the opposite: it is the gentile nations that must free themselves of the shackles of ordinary history so as to enter that history of which God is the ruler.[25]

Breuer's critique of unconditional nationhood, which in some respects anticipates the later views of Yeshayahu Leibowitz, warns against the dangers of deifying the nation or the state. The state that demands absolute sovereignty, that sees itself as an end in itself, is foreign to the spirit of the Torah, which views the state merely as an instrument for achieving justice. But Breuer has nothing to say about how the Torah's theocratic ideal is to be realized in our day. The state he envisions is a utopia with no relation to political realities, and it is doubtful that it could serve as a basis for achieving justice in concrete terms. When we look more closely at his views about the role of religion in the proposed state, it emerges that the latter would be a clerical polity in every respect.[26] In such a state there would be no tolerance, freedom, or equality for nonreligious Jews, not to mention non-Jews. On another level, Breuer foresaw that, unless the Jewish nation was governed by the Torah, it would quickly become embroiled in endless wars and bloodshed, like all the other nations.[27] But it is doubtful that a regime of Torah would be capable of preventing violent conflict with the Arabs. Unlike Buber, for example, Breuer had no practical proposals for settling this conflict. The Arab-Jewish problem was quite remote for him. He also failed to foresee the possibility, now materializing before our eyes, that religious Jews would treat the state itself as something holy, as an instrument for furthering the messianic process by violent means.

Orthodoxy and Pacifism in Eastern Europe

A small but important group of Eastern European Orthodox Zionists stands out. These thinkers tried to change the traditional Jewish world from within, primarily by emphasizing the moral dimension of religious observance. Personalities like Nathan Birnbaum, Hillel Zeitlin, and Avraham Kook were especially sensitive to the deepening rift between religion and morality in traditional Jewish society, a rift that they saw as the main reason for the declining influence of the Torah. They tried to broaden the scope of the spiritual Jewish world by showing that the universal moral ideals of the day were to be found within the Torah, and they saw in it the means of realizing the universal utopia of justice and peace. Except for Rabbi Kook, each in his own way had strong misgivings concerning the idea of Jewish sovereignty. In their criticism of the traditional society of their time for not pursuing this goal, they evinced a burst of moral passion unprecedented in the Jewish religious world since the end of classical prophecy.[28] All these thinkers, without exception, preached *teshuva* (lit. return, i.e., penitence) in its original, deep sense: a radical change in the way people thought and lived their lives. They saw this inner change as a precondition for outward change of a political and social nature. In this, they were close to the ideas of such non-Orthodox religious thinkers as Gordon and Buber.

Although we do not yet have a complete picture of this prophetic school of thought, it can be seen against the background of a dramatic encounter between two worlds, that of Eastern European Jewish Orthodoxy, which was in decline, and that of the Russian revolutionaries. All the prophetic thinkers were to some degree peace oriented, but they were radical to different degrees. The most radical among them was the little-known Aharon Shmuel Tamares, who wrote under the pen name "One of the Concerned Rabbis."

HILLEL ZEITLIN: THE TERRITORIALIST ALTERNATIVE

The prolific writer Hillel Zeitlin (1871–1942) abandoned religion as a young man but in later years returned to it and became a mystic. He was never a fully convinced Zionist, fearing the moral consequences of the actual realization of Zionist goals, i.e., the moral price the Jewish people would have to pay for renewing its political life in the ancient homeland. This fear, which we have also seen among the Orthodox and some non-Orthodox Zionists, shaped Zeitlin's attitude toward Zionism through all the twists and turns of his spiritual career. He was reluctant to bind the Jewish future to the Land of Israel, not only for practical reasons but also for religious and moral ones.

Being an advocate of nonviolence and not a devotee of Rav Kook's dialectical optimism, he sought a way out of the dilemma of seeking to build up the Land of Israel on purely moral foundations while knowing full well that it could not be done. His solution was original but not practical: he supported both Zionism and Territorialism (the idea that the Jewish question could be solved in a country other than Palestine). Whereas the latter aimed at saving the Jewish people from its physical predicament, the former should, as he saw it, aim for a purely spiritual rebirth.[29] This dichotomy had its origins in Ahad Ha'am's famous distinction between "the problem of the Jews" and "the problem of Judaism."

In Zeitlin's view, the Torah's position on the use of force was close to that of Tolstoy: we must not fight evil with invalid means but only with education, indoctrination, and the development of character. In effect, we must not use force under any circumstances.[30] In 1906, after the height of the first Russian revolution, Zeitlin wrote: "People get used to seeing the source of all evil, all that is despicable and unworthy, in one political arrangement or another, and they shirk the duties of the heart and all that is deep and historic in man. . . . They think that by following one social program or another they will redeem the world."[31] The Torah of Moses appeared as a spiritual force in a pagan world dominated by war and was meant to put an end to war by stressing the unity of the human race and the transformation of human nature. All the wars Moses fought were forced upon him. The commandment "You shall not let anyone live" (Deut 20:16) is based purely on necessity: the wild Canaanite peoples were preventing Israel from achieving its sacred mission, and that is why the Torah had to put aside its inherent compassion. But the true spirit of the Torah is found not in this verse, but in the verse "Do not provoke them to war" (Deut 2:9).[32]

Zeitlin wrote with a prophetic, messianic, peace-loving passion. His views took shape during the interwar period, when the modern totalitarian movements — communism, fascism, and Nazism — were in the ascendant and on the eve of the Holocaust that wiped out a large part of European Jewry, including Zeitlin himself (who perished in the Warsaw ghetto). He lived in the belief that his era was one of messianic travail and that he himself was its harbinger: "Go, call to your generation: Be prepared . . . [, for] the day is approaching which the prophets have always foretold." Zeitlin was referring to the prophetic vision of world peace. Before humanity can come together in a unity that allows each people to develop its uniqueness without impinging upon the others, the world will be taken over by blind, cruel forces that speak of "liberty, equality, and fraternity" but commit terrible acts. In "A Word to the Nations," published during the First World War, Zeitlin addresses his vision to all the world's peoples in the fashion of the prophets of old. He calls upon them to recognize the Jewish people's mission and to cease persecuting it, so that it can devote itself to its peaceable purpose: the building of a new human society on the basis of the Torah. "When the peoples recognize that there is no end to bloodshed, they will turn to the true revolution, the 'revolution of the spirit,' of which the Jewish people is the bearer." The world does not need a social revolution but a spiritual one. The people Israel is charged with the task of leading mankind toward universal peace.

The time is ripe, but if the Jewish people is to fulfill its destiny, "it must redeem itself, redeem the sanctity of its soul." In exile, it must do this by establishing small, elite communities of mystics, alongside outstanding individuals who will seek "inner elevation and . . . the improvement of [their] people and the world." They shall be the nucleus out of which the redeemed, redeeming people shall develop. In the Land of Israel, this will be done by setting up a model society. The Jewish population there must, in its entirety, be "a holy thing, untainted by the exploitation or expulsion of the Arabs in its midst." An act that has in it any element of theft is absolutely forbidden. The commandment to settle the Land is indeed of unsurpassed importance, but precisely for this reason it cannot be fulfilled by means of a transgression — i.e., by buying land from the wealthy Arab landlords and driving out the poor tenant farmers who have been living on it since time immemorial — but only by pure, sacred means.[33]

Like Buber, Zeitlin maintains that it would be a mistake to permit the nation what is forbidden to the individual. The whole Jewish ethos is directed against this concept of hallowed egotism. Only when the Jews are worthy will the land be restored to them, even if "they lack any power whatsoever." Their heroism and wisdom will not help them hold onto the land if their actions do not prove them worthy of it. Clearly, only a few will be able to measure up to this demand, and this is Zeitlin's intention: the Land of Israel is not meant to solve the physical problem of the Jewish masses but to serves as the basis of a universal movement of redemption. There shall arise in the Land of Israel a rarefied, model society, with no place for "acts of Cain, great or small, open or concealed." "This holy soil beneath your feet has been waiting for you for thousands of years, and now that you have come back to it, after unimaginable longing and innumerable tribulations, you have unsheathed your sword upon it and desecrated it."[34]

Zeitlin distinguishes between short-term and long-term goals. In terms of the former, a territorial solution must be found for the persecuted Jewish masses; in terms of the latter, small coteries of immigrants must be trained in the Diaspora to build a society in the Land of Israel that can serve as a model for all humankind. We thus see in Zeitlin the old Jewish fear of practical programs to bring about redemption. The demands he makes of those who would live in the Land of Israel are geared to an idealized community, which few would be capable of building. Thus, "the Land of Israel is removed from the realm of the real and relegated to the realm of the dream."[35] Zeitlin clung to this belief until he was put to death, along with the whole of Warsaw Jewry.

THE PACIFIC IDEAL IN THE DIASPORA:
THE TEACHINGS OF AHARON SHMUEL TAMARES

The teachings of Rabbi Aharon Shmuel Tamares (1869–1931) are an unusual phenomenon in Eastern European Orthodox thought. They are the only clear instance of Orthodox rabbinical pacifism.[36] Tamares rejected Zionism, not out of a pious aversion to "forcing the end," but because of his special view of the Jews as a nonpolitical nation whose very existence is the antithesis of modern nationalism.

Tamares was born in a small village in the Russian province of Grodno. After finishing his studies at the yeshiva of Volozhyn, where he absorbed some secular Hebrew culture, he served for forty years as the rabbi of another town in that province, Mileczyc, near Bialystok. He published a long series of articles in the Hebrew and Yiddish press, as well as books, dealing with the relation between religion and morality. Throughout his life he engaged in polemics, expressing himself on almost all the issues that were debated by Polish and Russian Jewry from the end of the nineteenth century on. He was best known for a series of articles criticizing Orthodox anti-Zionism, written in 1898–99, when the latter opposition was first crystallizing. There, he attacks Orthodoxy for its rigidity, its remoteness from the thinking of the younger generation and from the Haskala, its narrow-minded fanaticism, its resistance to any spiritual or social change, and its excessive concern for ritual law at the expense of the moral commandments.

As a young man, Tamares was attracted to Zionism, but after serving as a delegate to the Fourth Zionist Congress (1900), he became disillusioned with the movement over its estrangement from Jewish tradition and its enthusiasm for nationalistic slogans. He gradually came to despise all the ideological movements then current in the Jewish world and decided to devote his life to "purifying Judaism" and reorienting it to a pacific, messianic ideal. The Russo-Japanese War, the Russian revolution of 1905, and the First World War reinforced his pacifism. His book *The Assembly of Israel and the Wars of the Gentiles* (Warsaw, 1920) was written under the influence of the Great War and the pogroms that came in its wake. The thrust of this book, Tamares writes in a letter to Zvi Yehuda Kook, "is to stop the idolization of kingdoms and states. . . . As you know, this idolatry is considered by superficial thinkers to stem from the Bible, and pursuant to the law that 'he who uproots idolatry must plant something in its place,' I have found it necessary to show that in our Bible and our Talmud themselves kingship is reviled, and the heroes of the Bible are the Prophets, not the kings."[37] The sting of these words is directed at Zionism for basing its political aspirations on the Bible.

In the book, Tamares analyzes various theories as to what causes war. For him, war is not accidental, but neither is it foreordained; it is the consequence of modern culture and education. The persistence of warfare signifies a moral crisis: nationalism reflects a great emptiness in the soul of modern man, and the sword is the only way left to him to express himself.[38] This militarism is a new form of idolatry, which has survived among the nations and surfaced again on a large scale now that moral religion has been lost. Thus it is not mere political or social change that will rid humanity of war but only human renewal, the achievement of a higher level of moral consciousness and sensibility.[39] The Torah, "the essence of our national culture," in seeking to perfect the individual, provides the best instrument for combating tyranny and realizing the humanitarian, pacific ideal. This great power of the Torah is rooted in its special concept of freedom the Torah fosters (see below).

The culture of the Torah is not dependent on time or place; it is a portable culture, and its portability contains a solution to the riddle of why the Jewish people has never been demoralized by its wandering and suffering and why it has reached such a high level of intellectual and moral development: "The Jew invented a pocket Bible and Mishna to carry in his pack, so as to be armed with spiritual sustenance and secure in the perfection of his personality: a whole storehouse of exalted sentiments, acute ideas, wonderful sayings, and sage expressions."[40]

Exile and the study hall (*beit midrash*) were the twin pillars of the Jewish people's training for its mission, and they were interdependent. Between the fire of Torah and the fire of exile there was forged, over thousands of years, a unique culture, "soft as wax in worldly matters but hard as iron in matters of the soul." This culture made the Jew open to all noble ideas.[41] Despite the outward defects the Jews acquired in exile, their religious and moral sentiments found more fertile soil for their development in exile than in the land of their birth. For "prayer that springs from satiety and fullness is unlike that which springs from hunger and distress." Exile gave rise to the purest of national cultures as well as to the most elevated human type: "The lengthy training of the Jew by the spiritual nobility of the Torah, on one hand, and the lowliness of the distress of exile, on the other, cleansed him of crude selfishness, the pollution of the primordial serpent, and made him a rare creature, a superior human being, with a tender, clear, attentive soul that could respond to all things good and efficacious."[42]

Exile brought the Jew closer to God, purified his soul, and moderated his temperament.[43] Witness the deep revulsion Jews have felt toward bloodshed right down to modern times. It was only when they began to despise exile that there arose "political" Jews who could shed blood the way others did. Hence exile should not be understood as the Zionists understand it, as a purely secular manifestation of "the mauling of a lowly creature in the jaws of one stronger than it," with "none of the benefit or exaltation of a weighty, soul-wrenching tragedy."[44] As Zeitlin correctly noted, Tamares did not actually attribute positive value to exile in any simple sense, but he romanticized of it.[45] And indeed, among those modern Jewish thinkers who view exile in a positive

light, such as Hirsch and Hermann Cohen, Tamares stands out as the romantic. The positive attitude of the others stems from their affirmative view of
emancipation and their hope of integrating the Jews into non-Jewish society
and culture, whereas Tamares's is based on a radical pacifism and a fervent
admiration for the noble human type that exile has produced.

Tamares is critical of all the pacifistic movements for concentrating their
efforts on the relations between states without attacking the evil at its source,
namely, the fact that rulers were coercing their subjects to shed their blood for
the fatherland. All the high-flown rhetoric about progress and culture is empty
as long as man has not obtained the elementary freedom "to keep his head
intact."[46] Tamares therefore calls for what today is known as "conscientious
objection" and for cultivating a hatred of all violence, "for no exploitation or
violent crime would be possible anywhere if the hatred of the wicked by those
around them — eyewitnesses to their murderous acts — were not dulled."[47] At
the same time, he cautions against the natural tendency to fall into the mentality of the victim, for it is the victim's fear that goads him to indiscriminate
violence. Hence all individuals, and the nation as a whole, must live by the rule
that "one should be more careful not to harm others than to avoid being
harmed oneself" (Tosefta, Baba Kama 23a).

If Judaism is to be renewed, it must be by the creation of an original Hebrew
culture that will present a living protest against the world's madness. The basic
feature of such a culture is "ceasing to do the work of Cain" (murder). We
must "work out for ourselves a distinctive style such that everything created in
our world will be free of the pollution of the primal serpent." Poetry, art,
psychology, and morality — all must be purified of "ruddy stains," i.e., the cult
of blood.[48]

This messianic passion is rooted in a feeling that the First World War represented a great crisis in European culture, a feeling to be found in Kook and
Zeitlin as well. The crisis presents a historic opportunity for Jewish culture,
the hallmark of which is a protest against idolatry. The Jews must take up
wholeheartedly the task of realizing in exile the vision of the Prophets and lay
the groundwork for a realization of the messianic ideal. "But if Isaiah's grandchildren themselves deny their ancestor's heritage in favor of that of Esau,
humanity is lost, lost for all eternity."[49]

Needless to say, Tamares's positive attitude toward exile and his notion of
the Torah as embodying a pacifist national culture led him to a harsh critique
of political Zionism.[50] The Jewish people should, in his view, direct its hopes
toward Zion as its spiritual homeland, "the land where our prophets walked
before us," and as "a physical refuge for its national life, though only as an
extra margin of safety."[51] Zion cannot be built by negating Diaspora life but

only by recognizing the latter's worth and complementing it. Zionism should supplement and develop in us the things we have learned in exile. It is not a sick, degenerate people that is seeking to recover and restore its homeland but "a living, breathing nation, healthy and sound of spirit in exile, that longs to return to the land of its fathers with all [the] vigor and tremendous spiritual baggage acquired during its wanderings in foreign lands."[52] Indeed, there must thus be ongoing interdependence and mutuality between the Diaspora and the Land of Israel: "The raw material of the 'special Jewish qualities' shall be brought from exile and reworked in Zion, polished shall this material be; for the soil of exile is the best soil for [these] special Jewish qualities to grow in, a factory for developing and refining this material, better than can be found in the Land of Israel."[53]

The Liberal Critique

Most of the liberal Jewish ideologies that reject the need for sovereignty share the idea that exile is neither pathological nor abnormal for the nation but, in fact, a sign of the highest level of national existence, to which all nations should aspire. It is, if you will, a supernormal way of being. According to these views, the Jewish people's survival is not dependent on merely external, objective factors, like a state or a land, but rather on the sum total of its inner, spiritual qualities. The Jews are thus not in decline or fallen from some primeval ideal condition, as Zionist thought would have it, but, in fact, on the rise toward a peak of spiritual existence that has no need for a political framework. Such existence has a universal human meaning because it is free of the moral flaws from which every normal nation suffers. Unlike the Zionists, who believed that only with a homeland of its own could the Jewish people combine ethnic particularism and moral universalism, these thinkers maintained that nationhood based on holding onto territory and acquiring political power led inevitably to bloodshed, oppression, and fanaticism. By contrast, exile provided the ideal platform for achieving a synthesis between particularism and universalism, protecting cultural distinctiveness while showing genuine solidarity with humanity as a whole.[54] The Zionist counterargument touches not only on the existential question of where the best chance of assuring Jewish survival is to be found, but also on the moral one of where the demands of Judaism can be fulfilled most completely, in exile or the homeland.

HERMANN COHEN: THE IDEALIZATION OF SUFFERING IN EXILE

The thought of Hermann Cohen (1842–1918) is the most profound expression of turn-of-the-twentieth-century Jewish liberalism.[55] Cohen's concept of Judaism is grounded in his neo-Kantian moral philosophy. Jewish religion, which he sees as the purest and most complete embodiment of Kantian morality, is, in his view, based on two key ideas: *teshuva* (repentance, turning, return), which is concerned with individual moral perfection and reconciliation with God; and messianism, which seeks the moral perfection and unification of humanity as a whole. Messianism is the main contribution of Judaism, or, more precisely, of biblical prophecy, to the philosophy of history. Messianism depends upon monotheism; the oneness and uniqueness of God are a precondition for the moral unity of mankind. Cohen follows the Reformers in giving messianism an idealized, symbolic interpretation. Messianic fulfillment does not mean the return of the Jewish people to its homeland but its infinite quest, while in exile, for the perfection of the world. Messianism and progress are equivalent.

Messianism imposes on the Jewish people a heavy yoke of suffering, for it requires them to give up the protection of statehood, the only people in the world already called upon to do so. In this they symbolize the goal of history. The Jewish people has sacrificed worldly happiness in order to merit a spiritual vocation: "Of what use is all the happiness in the world, all linguistic [efflorescence], all the world's glory, as compared with this national privilege, rooted in faith?"[56] For Cohen, unlike other liberal thinkers, this sacrifice is the secret of Jewish survival and essential to Jewish destiny. The messianic idea is epitomized by the biblical image of the Suffering Servant of the Lord (Isa 53).

Initially, Jewish particularism stands in contradiction to the universal Jewish mission. The contradiction is resolved, in Cohen's view, when one regards Jewish history as a necessary development. Universalism can only be achieved through an initial setting apart of the people of Israel, but in their history there is a gradual enlargement of the universal element at the expense of the particular. The first breakthrough comes with the Prophets, who concern themselves with world politics in a thoroughly cosmopolitan manner. Yet they remain patriotic Jews because the time is not yet ripe for their message in all its purity. They are compelled to speak in particularistic terms to avoid being seen as detached from their own people. In any event, the idea of sacrificing statehood in favor of universal unity is to be found here, at the very beginning of Jewish history. "Israel launched its career only when it gave up the trappings of this-worldly nationhood and began a new existence . . . [one] with a universal mission."[57] Thus, from the outset, the state was of no real importance in Jewish thinking. The survival of the Jews in exile is the clearest proof that Judaism is not tied to any narrow political framework. Today, if the ethnic or national element has any justification, it is as a factor that will preserve the Jewish religion until the messianic vision is fully realized. Cohen stresses the

importance of the prophesied future as opposed to the past. He sees no concrete task for the Jewish people in the present except that it serve as a symbol
of the fact that the world has not yet been redeemed.

Cohen rules out nationality as the basis for a state. While the folk is a
natural given, the state is a mere legal construct. He distinguishes between the
political concept of the nation (*Nation*) and the cultural and religious concept
of nationality (*Nationalität*), a distinction reminiscent of Steinheim. Ideally,
the "nation," i.e., the state, comprises "a multiplicity of nationalities." In the
optimistic spirit of the day, which envisioned unending progress, Cohen sees
this as the political goal of humanity as a whole: a confederation of states, each
of which is a confederation of peoples. In this sense, Zionism is obviously a
regression and, as such, is doomed to be a mere episode in Jewish history.[58] It is
antithetical to the real messianic thrust of Judaism, seeking as it does to take
Judaism back to the earlier stage of political separateness. It prefers the
worldly happiness of statehood to the suffering of a spiritual mission.

The main innovation in Cohen's thinking is not the idealization of suffering
in itself; the latter is rooted in the Jewish tradition, which fairly early on
invented the exalted symbol of "the Suffering Servant of the Lord." His originality lies in using this idealization to strip the concept of national redemption
— an inseparable part of the messianic vision — of all concrete meaning. To do
so, he makes use of a dubious reinterpretation of the sacred texts, in particular
a tendentious, selective reading of the Prophets. The aim is to substantiate his
political philosophy, which is based on the idea of progress. His faith in human
goodness is boundless; history leads toward a messianic era in which war and
violence will have been eliminated and humanity united around the idea of one
God. It is what Gershom Scholem calls an accommodation to the era of bourgeois self-delusion.[59]

Cohen was writing before the First World War, which explains his exaggerated optimism concerning the ability of modern Western culture to shape
human fate. The worst disasters to befall the Jews in his time were the Dreyfus
trial and the pogroms in czarist Russia. He did not foresee the horrors of
modern totalitarianism. It is thus no surprise that Cohen had no inkling of the
volcano on which German Jewry was sitting and which would erupt shortly
after his death. It is worth pointing out in this context that the notion that the
multinational state would eliminate international conflict had considerable
influence over Zionist thinkers as well, men like Martin Buber and Shmuel
Hugo Bergman, who advocated a binational state in Palestine.

Cohen's ideas about the meaning of Jewish suffering in exile found dramatic
expression in a pacifist play, "Jeremiah," by the Jewish writer Stefan Zweig.
Published in 1917 while the First World War was still raging, the play enjoyed

great popularity. In it Zweig calls upon the Jews to love suffering, regarding it
as a divine test. He puts the following words into the mouth of the prophet
Jeremiah, who stayed behind in Jerusalem with the remnant of the Jewish
population after the destruction of the Temple, then accompanied them into
exile: "He chooses those only whom He has tried, and to none but the suffering does He give His love. Let us therefore rejoice at our trials, brothers, and
let us love the suffering that God sends. . . . Happy are we to be vanquished,
and happy to be driven from home, by God's will, . . . happy is our hard lot,
gladsome our trial. . . . Give praise to affliction, ye afflicted; give praise to trial,
ye sorely tried; praise the name of God who, through tribulation, has chosen
us for all eternity."[60]

The play ends with a paean to the wandering, suffering people:

> Scatter your seeds, scatter your seeds,
> In unknown lands,
> Through numberless years.
> Wander your wanderings, watered with tears.
> On, people of God; for wherever you roam,
> Your roads leads through the world to eternity, home. . . .
> For through the ages our path leads unerringly,
> To the goal of our desire,
> Jerusalem![61]

But in Zweig's "Jeremiah," the "return to Zion" loses all concrete meaning
and becomes something altogether spiritual, a symbol of the endless exile and
wandering of the Jews among the peoples of the world. It is a great paradox.
Zweig regarded his play as "a prophetic tragedy and a hymn to the Jewish
people, which, from its perpetual defeat was able to turn its fate into the basis
from which the 'new Jerusalem' would spring: a life beyond nationality,
marked by a vision of brotherhood, mutual tolerance, and universal enlightenment." He had great reservations about "the dangerous dream of a Jewish
state, with cannons, flags, and military medals," admiring "the painful idea of
the Dispersion."[62]

MESSIANISM AS A WITHDRAWAL FROM HISTORY: ZIONISM IN THE THOUGHT OF FRANZ ROSENZWEIG

Unlike Hermann Cohen, who rejected Zionism outright, Franz Rosenzweig (1886–1929) was ambivalent about it. Having grown up in the midst of
a Jewish renaissance and seeing Jewish life in its fullness as something positive,
he was well aware of the affinity between his aspirations and those of the
Zionists. He saw the greatness of Zionism in its insistence on the wholeness

and integrity of Jewish man. But this spiritual affinity led him to dwell on the dangers facing Zionism as a political movement, dangers that could well lead to a narrowing of the spiritual horizons of Judaism.[63]

Rosenzweig's reserved attitude toward Zionism is a function of his overall view of the course of history, in particular his opinion that war and violence are essential to history.[64] In this he is close to such pessimistic thinkers as Schopenhauer, Burckhardt, and Spengler, who see history as dominated by irrationality rather than the unending progress of Hegel, Marx, and liberal Jewish thinkers like Hermann Cohen. Domination is basic to history, and thus "war and revolution [are] the only reality known to the state."[65] Because violence and suffering are essential to history, they can have no positive purpose, as Hegel thought they did. Challenging Hegel, who sees history as a kind of theodicy, Rosenzweig argues that every human deed is liable to become sinful, precisely after it has entered history and has become part of it, because through the interrelation of acts in history no act is merely personal but is caught up in the impersonal nexus of cause and effect beyond the control and the intention of the actor. Religion, not history, is the only true theodicy for him. For this reason God must redeem man, not through history but through religion.[66] Rosenzweig is convinced that European civilization is on the verge of collapse and that only extra-European, superhuman powers can save it.[67] In effect, he is alluding to the redemptive role of Judaism, which is "a piece of metahistory cast into history."[68] Although domination and expansion are characteristic of world history as a whole, "Judaism, and it alone in all the world, maintains itself by subtraction, by contraction, by the formation of ever new remnants."[69]

There is a great similarity between Rosenzweig's critical view of the modern nation-state and the position of Isaac Breuer. Both of them take as their point of departure a theological reading of history. Since history is filled with war and violence, it is of necessity a realm opposed to holiness and divine salvation. Both thinkers see modern nationalism primarily in terms of war and violence, and both see Judaism as being outside history yet cast into it. For Breuer, Judaism is a living protest against history; for Rosenzweig, it is a source of hope and a tangible symbol, in this world, of the End of Days. But Rosenzweig does not regard the idea of secular sovereignty as a positive challenge to Jewish faith, which he sees as fulfilling its role in history by completely withdrawing from it. Breuer, on the other hand, sees secular sovereignty as a challenge to faith of the first order because, in his view, it is only the Jewish people who can save humanity from its tragic fate by offering a model of statehood utterly opposed to the accepted one. Breuer's rejection of the modern notion of sovereignty thus has nothing to do with aspirations to national independence per se but rather with the idea that the nation itself is the ultimate source of all law and rightful authority.

Rosenzweig, we see, viewed history in a political perspective, and it was the latter that determined his positions regarding both Judaism and Zionism. Having fought in the First World War, a direct result of the rise of nationalism and imperialism, Rosenzweig came to the conclusion that nationalism was the greatest catastrophe ever to visit mankind in general and the Jews in particular. It could not, therefore, be used to define Jewishness. Indeed, the latter is not to be understood in ordinary sociological, historical, or philosophical categories at all, for unlike other nations, the Jews did not emerge as a people owing to particular historical circumstances; rather, it was a sense of purpose and mission that determined their character and constitution from the outset. But the philosophical approach that separates the spirit from its concrete bearer, the people, is also insufficient. In other words, no secular explanation can make sense of the phenomenon of Jewish nationhood, and only a concept that combines the historical and the metahistorical can come close to explaining it. Here Rosenzweig is continuing the line of thinking of Rabbi Nahman Krochmal, who tried to combine an empirical examination of Jewish history with a metaphysical perspective on it (the "absolute spirit").

Rosenzweig wanted to show that the Jewish people was not subject to historical time. Its existence had never depended on such objective factors as land, language, or man-made laws. From the first appearance of the Jews as a people, these factors had been transferred from the concrete, historical sphere to that of holiness, which released them from the constraints of time. Exile was there from the very beginning, and the Jewish people went from one exile to another. Its right to its land was not autochthonous but derived from its divine mission. In their wanderings in exile, the Jews retain "the freedom of a wanderer who is more faithful a knight to his country when he roams abroad, craving adventure and yearning for the land he has left behind, than when he lives in that land."[70] Even when the Jewish people dwells in its own land, it is a "resident alien." Unlike other peoples, it does not derive its security from external factors but from internal ones: the "community of blood" (*Blutgemeinschaft*) and the chain of the generations. Eternity is in its soul. Generational ties take the place of ties to the soil. "We were the only ones who trusted in blood and abandoned the land."[71] The land provides sustenance, but it also ties the people down and betrays them if they hinge their longevity upon it. A people dwelling on its own soil is always in danger of extinction.

The Hebrew language, too, ceased early on to be used as a vernacular and became a sacred tongue. The holiness of the people's language has an effect similar to that of the holiness of its land: it does not allow them to confine their focus to everyday life. Just as the holiness of the Land of Israel made the people in exile feel estranged from their surroundings and prevented them from putting down roots in time, so too did the Hebrew language.

This removal from dependence on time is even more noticeable in the case of a third factor that sets the Jewish people apart — its lack of secular law. It is by means of such law that a people tries to determine its future, to withstand the tide of cosmic time and carve out a time of its own. But the nature of law is such that it constantly changes, for it is only through change that it retains its validity. Rosenzweig maintains that law is changed by violence and revolution. Law is based on force, and renewed vitality brings counterforce to bear against it, pressing for change. Thus law, the purpose of which is to establish order, becomes itself a cause of disorder. The resolution of the conflict between old and new is always temporary and likely to be undone by the sword. The state's violence is directed not only inward but also at other states. This is why "war and revolution [are] the only reality known to the state."[72]

With the Jews it is different: the law, i.e., the commandment, is not based on violence but on love, the love of God for man and the love of human beings for one another. Hence the law cannot be changed. Among the Jews, law has been elevated to the status of holiness, releasing it from dependence on time. No change can be made in it without a belief that the new is rooted in the old, so that, in effect, it is not a change at all. Whereas the gentiles go through revolutions in which, from time to time, the law sheds its former garb, here there is rule by a law that no revolution seeks to nullify.

In Rosenzweig's view, the fact that the Jewish people does not depend on outward security shows that "it has reached the point to which the nations of the world still aspire."[73] In effect, the Jews are the only "true" people, while the others are still coming into being: "In the last analysis, there is only one true people, and it is a non-people. All the other peoples, which no one doubts are peoples, have only recently set out on their journey toward peoplehood; that is why they attribute excessive importance to outbreaks of war and the like, for only [in them] do they experience, briefly, what it means to be a people."[74]

This, then, is the root of the difference in principle between the Jews and the other nations with respect to war: the Jews are the only people who already have what the others, consciously or otherwise, are seeking, a "national myth" or "soul," i.e., an inner spiritual purpose that would give them respite from the press of worldly concerns. But what the other peoples do have is a shared, universal religious myth. Christianity has created an inner conflict for the peoples of Europe between their national distinctiveness and the larger common history, a conflict that keeps them from achieving unity of spirit. This is the hidden cause of all wars and other historical events. The gentiles have bad consciences, for as peoples their existence is merely physical and crude. The Jew is a magnet for their hatred and their hidden enthusiasm, for he has already overcome his restlessness.[75]

For the other peoples, war is not a problem because it seems to them simply a manifestation of natural vitality, a risking of life for the sake of life. "A nation that goes to war accepts the possibility of dying. This is not significant as long as nations regard themselves as mortal." But when a nation's mission is eternal, it cannot put its life in the balance, for if it did, "how is the world to recover if the essence of this people is eradicated from it?"[76] This is why the Jewish people has not engaged in warfare. All its wars belong to its mythical past.[77] The Jew is indeed the "only pacifist" in Christendom. It turns out, then, that the fact that the Jew is not ruled by history makes him the bearer of hope for mankind, of a message of redemption from historical time with all its tribulations. The Jewish people's position outside historical time means that it is already living in a redeemed state and has anticipated the eternal. In the cycle of the Jewish year, with its sabbaths and festivals, it creates its own time, an end-time, and lives its life as if the world had already been perfected. It has no need to take the long way of world history. In sum, its pacifism is the logical outcome of its having reached the destination and is not just starting out. "Though living in a state of eternal peace, [the Jewish people] is outside of time agitated by wars. . . . Its holiness hinders it from devoting its soul to a still-unhallowed world, no matter how much the body may be bound up with it. The people must deny itself active and full participation in the life of this world, with its daily, apparently conclusive, solving of all contradictions. It is not permitted to recognize this daily solving of contradictions, for that would render it disloyal to the hope of a final solution. In order to keep unharmed the vision of the ultimate community, it must deny itself the satisfaction the peoples of the world constantly enjoy in the functioning of their state."[78]

It is clear from this last sentence that Rosenzweig is close to Cohen, and the liberals in general, in their assessment of the place of a state in Jewish life. Like Cohen, he, too, believes that for the Jew to realize his messianic mission he will have to forego the false happiness a state gives its citizens. But whereas Cohen thinks the Jew's mission necessitates his full integration into the process of history, Rosenzweig is of the opposite view. For both, the Jew's home is no particular piece of land but rather eschatological time. Redemption comes in the present; living in eschatological time makes the Jew feel at home everywhere, though he may be outside his homeland. Both thinkers view the Diaspora as the most authentic form of Jewish existence. But while the liberals see the Jewish people as having reached the end-time, and the eschatological vision as having been fulfilled in whatever country the Jews find themselves, for

Rosenzweig, with his pessimistic view of history, the end-time is reached by a withdrawal from history.[79] The dynamic of messianic redemption, which has been so real and important in exilic Jewish consciousness, is given by Rosenzweig an almost Christian interpretation, quite different from the original one: the Jewish people has already redeemed itself by stepping out of historical into sacred time. In practice, the Jews of the Diaspora must refrain from taking any part in the cultural or political life of the countries in which they live. "We are enjoined to remain outsiders, strangers to the entire cultural legacy of the nations of the world, even when they permit us to take part in it."[80] Rosenzweig is thus critical of Jewish liberalism for the same reason that he is critical of Zionism: both movements are too political and too assimilationist.

Rosenzweig gives authentic expression here to the Jews' sense of chosenness, and it is no accident that his view of Jewish history closely resembles that of Orthodoxy in general and Yehuda Halevi in particular. For the latter enunciates, more clearly than any other medieval Jewish thinker, the notion that Jewish history does not obey the natural laws that control the fate of the other nations. Although this notion has the effect of justifying the exilic Jews' downtrodden condition and giving it meaning, it does not insist that the exile need last forever or that the Jews never engage in political activity. For Rosenzweig, in contrast, exile is eternally normative, an ideal condition, and Jewish involvement in the political affairs of the gentiles is ruled out.

In Rosenzweig's theological-historical view, there is a reversal of roles between Judaism and Christianity, which he presents as two paths to the same divine truth: Judaism is the eternity beyond time whereas Christianity is the eternity within time, eternity coming into being. It is paradoxical that Christianity, known from the outset for its otherworldliness, should be the one to have to deal with the contradictions and problems of the secular world — morality, politics, war — i.e., that it should bear active responsibility for the world. Judaism, meanwhile, is charged only with setting an example for the world to emulate. Judaism here almost takes on the character of a Protestant denomination, and, of course, this view is utterly contrary to that of Zionism, which sees Judaism as superior to Christianity by virtue of being active in history, seeking to shape the totality of man's this-worldly life, both individual and collective.

Rosenzweig's historiosophical view of Judaism explains the disagreement between him and the Zionists over the conclusions to be drawn about the two basic experiences of the Jewish people in modern times, assimilation and anti-semitism. Although he does not doubt the importance of these phenomena, he does not see them as necessitating a restructuring of Jewish existence. Assimilation is not a new development but a process evident throughout the history of Jewish exile.[81] It is therefore not a threat to Jewish survival. The inner logic of assimilation is that it is never complete; Judaism's strength has always lain in "holding its own while absorbing values from without." So, he maintains, the inner strength of Judaism will be tested in the coming decades, not, as Zionism would have it, in the Land of Israel but in the Diaspora. With this, he regards the Zionist form of "assimilation," its striving for normalization, as much more dangerous, for its goal is an attainable one.[82]

Antisemitism, too, in Rosenzweig view, is not limited to the modern era, as Zionism would have it, but a timeless phenomenon, the result of an envy of Judaism, in which eternity is realized, by Christianity, which is still "eternity coming into being." All other antisemitic claims are, in his view, merely a cover for this one metaphysical animus.[83] Rosenzweig ignores the fact that since the Emancipation, Jews had not had the option of living in the way he envisioned: "a quiet life that looks neither right nor left," against which "the power of world history breaks."[84] The tide of history was washing over the Jewish people and threatening to drown it. Undeniably, the great existential predicament of the masses of Eastern European Jews, deprived of any ground on which to stand, was foreign to Rosenzweig. All he has to offer the Diaspora Jews is a new, modern version of Torah study, a way of returning to Judaism. And, indeed, he remains the leading example of a modern *ba'al teshuva* (returnee to religion). But his path could not meet the burning needs of Europe's Jews.

LIBERAL SECULAR NATIONALISM: SIMON DUBNOW AND DAVID FRISCHMAN

Unlike Cohen and Rosenzweig, who represent a liberal religious view of the fate and destiny of the Jewish people, the historian Simon Dubnow (1860–1941) developed a comprehensive theory of nationhood that viewed life in exile as something positive in liberal, secular terms. His notion of Jewish nationhood was influenced by the thinking of late-nineteenth-century liberal circles in Eastern and Central Europe on the question of establishing multi-national states. What they had in mind was a polity organized so as to satisfy the need for autonomy, particularly of a cultural nature, of the various peoples living within it and at the same time preserve its own unity. Such ideas were particularly well suited to the multinational empires already in existence at the time, the Hapsburg and the Russian.

In his *Nationalism and History: Essays on Old and New Judaism,* Dubnow maintains that the Jewish people is the most historical of peoples, not only because it has been in existence so long, but also because of its great influence. The latter has been the result of a process that has raised the Jews to the highest plane of national existence. He distinguishes three stages in their development:

the racial, the political or territorial, and the cultural or spiritual. This, he claims, is the pattern in which all nations develop. The decisive element in the fate of a nation is not its outward vigor but its inner strength. The sign of the perfection of a nation is its ability to preserve its identity in the face of the loss of political freedom, which is usually seen as a necessary condition of national existence. A people that manages to go on developing even after such a loss and even after losing its land and language and being scattered and fragmented — "such a people has reached the highest stage of cultural-historical individuality."[85] There is only one example of this in all human history, the Jews, who have gradually lost those political characteristics that depend on having a country and augmented their spiritual characteristics. The Jews are "the People of the Spirit." Dubnow, a nonreligious Jew influenced in considerable measure by the ideas of Ahad Ha'am, does not mean only religion but culture in general, of which religion is one manifestation. This view goes hand in hand with another idea he expresses in his great work *The Chronicles of an Eternal People,* which highlights the shifting of the spiritual center of Jewish life from place to place. Jewish autonomy in the Diaspora is, for him, the clearest expression of the "instinct of self-preservation" of a people with a highly developed self-awareness. The Jewish people is "the highest type of cultural-historical or spiritual nation."[86] Its extraterritoriality is not an anomaly because there is no necessary connection between a people and its homeland. In this light, Zionism seems to Dubnow a misleading messianic venture.

Dubnow is well aware of the dangers inherent in the national idea. He shows understanding for the cosmopolitan tendencies of the Maskilim (advocates of the Haskala) of his day, tendencies he sees as the product of "revulsion and disgust" at the violence and other ugly effects of nationalism. At the same time, he does not see this evil as intrinsic to the idea of nationalism itself but, rather, due to the morally distorted way it has been interpreted. The claim of the "cosmopolitan" Jews that nationalism is antiprogressive is criticized by Dubnow as based on a confusion of concepts, a failure to distinguish two different kinds of nationalism, the particularistic and the egoistic. Particularistic nationalism aims only to assure a people freedom of cultural development by giving it a measure of self-rule, such as the autonomy Jews have sometimes enjoyed in the Diaspora. Such nationalism is entirely compatible with the great ideas of progress: liberty, equality, and fraternity. Egoistic nationalism, on the other hand, has a defiant, aggressive character. It tries to dominate other peoples, whether politically or culturally. Viewing the nation as a spiritual entity, there is no contradiction between particularism (the aspiration to distinctiveness) and universalism (the aspiration to human solidarity), as the Marxists and humanistic cosmopolitans charge. Universalism and cosmopoli-

tanism should not be confused. The idea of the spiritual nation is fundamentally a moral one; it does not entail attacking others but only at expressing and
defending oneself.

The Jews present a paragon of the particularistic variety of nationalism. The
Jewish people, "because of the special conditions of its existence in the Diaspora, is not able to aspire anywhere to primacy [or] dominance."[87] Its history
is one of struggle, "not by force of arms but by the spirit [cf. Zach 4:6]," a
struggle for exalted values that by their very nature cannot be obtained by
unworthy means.[88] Beginning at the time of the Prophets, Jewish national life
was transferred from the political to the spiritual realm, "for the state was
merely the shell placed around the kernel, which was the nation."[89] The objective traits of nationhood gradually gave way to more subjective ones.[90] In
Dubnow's view, spiritualization freed the Jewish people of any taint of "national egoism" and was thus "a manifestation of supreme civic rectitude."

> There is absolutely no doubt that Jewish nationalism, in essence, has nothing
> in common with any tendency toward violence. As a spiritual or historical-
> cultural nation, deprived of any possibility of aspiring to political triumphs,
> of seizing territory by force or of subjecting other nations to cultural domina-
> tion, . . . it is concerned with only one thing: protecting its national individu-
> ality and safeguarding its autonomous development in all states everywhere
> in the Diaspora. . . . A nationality of this kind manifests the highest sense of
> social justice, which demands that the equality of all nations be recognized as
> an equal right of all to defend themselves and their internal, autonomous
> life.[91]

Pursuing this line of thinking, Dubnow comes to the conclusion that "if the
national idea . . . [can] be combined with the ideal of humanity, the Jewish
national idea . . . will be in even closer harmony with it. . . . It is fitting and
proper for the descendants of the Prophets to raise aloft on their flag the
unsoiled national idea that combines the Prophetic visions of truth and justice
with the noble dream of the unity of mankind."[92]

The thinking of David Frischman (1859–1922), a committed Hebrew
writer who dreamed of a revival of Hebrew culture, was close to Dubnow's.
Frischman prefers to speak of the "people," not the state. A people is created
by God, whereas a state is man-made. Not only can a people exist without a
land; such existence is the very goal of humankind. "This people teaches
humanity as a whole how to do without the state." The Jewish people has a
special gift for intuiting what will come to pass in the End of Days. Two
thousand years ago, it already sensed that peoplehood without statehood was
possible, indeed that it was essential for all peoples. The Jews hope all other

peoples will come to recognize this principle in the end. Rabban Yohanan ben Zakkai, in the first century, taught the Jews that land was not all. He gave them a "portable homeland" (a reference to Heine's well-known phrase), a land that could be carried in one's hands or pockets and that could not be taken away, for "it is all spirit, and the spirit is eternal." For Frischman, the state is a transitory thing that cannot take the place of the eternal idea of Judaism. In the view of the latter, an existing state is nothing; the main thing is to strive for the ideal, not the ideal itself. Frischman sees the long tutelage the Jews have undergone in exile as having made them incapable of wronging others and developing in them "a habit of complete uprightness." Judaism represents a protest against the cruelty of the other nations, and it is precisely because of this that they all hate the Jews. The Jews themselves will never be able to treat another nation the way the antisemites have treated them.[93]

The Holocaust put an end to most of the anti-Zionist ideologies, but it did not remove the issue of Jewish power, embodied in the state, from the Jewish public agenda. What is the lesson that the Jews should learn from their disaster? What kind of commitment is required if they are to be loyal to themselves and to the memory of the slaughtered? These kinds of questions, which are of concern in both the Diaspora and Israel, will be the theme of the following chapter.

8

Sovereignty and Jewish Commitment after the Holocaust in the Thought of Emil Fackenheim, George Steiner, and Irving Greenberg

The Holocaust has strengthened among many Jews the sense of being the survivors, a "saving remnant," with all the responsibility that implies for remembering past generations, remaining loyal to them. Forgetfulness means betrayal and disloyalty: "If I forget thee, O Jerusalem, may my right hand forget its cunning" (Ps 137:5). In Jewish tradition, the demand to remember is at the heart of a covenant between the people and its God that carries moral and religious imperatives. Memory thus plays an active moral role of the highest order: to remember is to be aroused to do what we should be doing.

The first, most spontaneous expression of commitment toward those whose lives have been cut short is a resolve to go on living. This resolve, however, goes beyond mere biological survival; it has, particularly for Jews, a sacred dimension and specific value content. The survivors must ask themselves to what heritage or moral values they are expected to be loyal. Because all historical consciousness is selective, the interpretation given to past events determines which elements and aspects of the past will prove decisive in shaping the collective ethos. The historical memory of suffering is socially and morally ambiguous. On one hand, it can serve as an ideological tool of oppression and exploitation, where the past is used to justify mistreatment of others in the present. On the other hand, such memory can provide an unparalleled goad toward liberation and human solidarity (the Exodus from Egypt providing the prime example). The past, revived among us, can bring to light unsuspected strengths of spirit and resources for creativity, constructive action, and human brotherhood. From this perspective, the question how to remain loyal is the flashpoint of all theology.

Emil Fackenheim, George Steiner, and Irving Greenberg are three Diaspora Jewish thinkers who have grappled with the meaning of Jewish loyalty and commitment after the Holocaust. At the center of my discussion of their ideas stands the issue of Jewish sovereignty. These three perspectives reflect different assessments of the importance of the Jewish state and the power it embodies for the perpetuation of the Jewish people and its tradition. In this respect, this chapter continues the discussion in chapter 7.

Emil Fackenheim: Survival as a Religious Duty

Emil Fackenheim formed his views about the Holocaust after the Six-Day War. He gives all of Jewish history a theological interpretation, seeing it as a series of tests of faith. The Covenant between the Jewish people and its God is grounded in mutual faithfulness that is put to the test anew in every generation. Jewish historical thinking distinguishes two kinds of events that have a reciprocal relation to each other: "root experiences" and "epoch-making experiences." The former are public, mythic events that are engraved in the living memory of the nation, because they embody its understanding of the Covenant, i.e., God's redeeming presence (the Exodus) and His demand for absolute commitment (the revelation at Sinai). These are past events, but they also serve as archetypes in present-day awareness. Epoch-making events, on the other hand, belong to concrete experience in the present, and they make new claims upon Jewish faith. Such events "did not . . . produce a new faith. What occurred instead was a confrontation in which the old faith was tested in the light of contemporary experience." Jewish theology does not negate the root experiences. It overcomes the contradiction between present experience and past faith by the use of a midrashic methodology: epoch-making events are interpreted in light of root experiences, whereas root experiences are interpreted in light of present events. Consequently, the new demand does not bring with it a new faith but is interpreted as an expression of adherence to the old faith.[1] The Holocaust, too, is integrated into this series of trials; it is an epoch-making experience that makes new demands on the old faith, calling for a midrash that can bridge the gulf between the two. Fackenheim maintains that the Jewish resolve to carry on after Auschwitz, to cling wholeheartedly to life, is in itself testimony to the power of faith, of steadfast hope. He interprets this resolve as both a protest and a wager:

The ways of the religious Jew [today] are revolutionary, for there is no pre-vious Jewish protest against divine power like his protest. Continuing to hear the Voice of Sinai as he hears the Voice of Auschwitz, his citing of God against God may have to assume extremes which dwarf those of Abraham, Jeremiah, Job, [and] Rabbi Levi Yitzhak. (You have abandoned the covenant? We shall not abandon it! You no longer want Jews to survive? We shall survive, as better, more faithful, more pious Jews! You have destroyed all grounds for hope? We shall obey the commandment to hope which You Yourself have given!) Nor is there any previous Jewish compassion [for] divine powerless-ness like the compassion required by such . . . powerlessness [as Jews have now experienced]. (The fear of God is dead among the nations? We shall keep it alive and be its witnesses! The times are too late for the coming of the Messiah? We shall persist without hope and recreate hope — and, as it were, divine power — by our persistence!) For the religious Jew, who remains within the midrashic framework, the Voice of Auschwitz manifests a divine presence which, as it were, is shorn of all except commanding power. *This* power, however, is inescapable.[2]

It is the same pattern of faith we have already seen in Uri Tzvi Greenberg's poetry.

Fackenheim's theology is deeply rooted in *midrashic* thought, though there is a great innovation in the way he responds to the recent catastrophe. Facken-heim speaks here of the "Voice of Auschwitz," with its "commanding power." This commanding voice is the sole evidence of "a divine presence which, as it were, is shorn of all." Although he refrains from attributing to Auschwitz the status of a revelation parallel to that at Sinai — as Elie Wiesel, for example, does — he is even more concerned about our "not listening," our taking "false refuge in an endless agnosticism," in flight from "a voice speaking to us." What does the "Voice of Auschwitz" command us? "Jews are forbidden to hand Hitler posthumous victories. They are commanded to survive as Jews, lest the Jewish people perish. . . . A Jew may not respond to Hitler's attempt to destroy Judaism by himself co-operating in its destruction." The abandon-ment of Judaism is, today, the greatest sin, equivalent to that of idolatry in ancient times.[3]

The sacred duty to remember those who were murdered, to remain Jewish and thereby create new hope, is, for Fackenheim, the 614th commandment, added in our generation to the 613 that Jewish tradition finds in the Torah. The very decision to remain a Jew, whatever that might mean, is a supreme imperative. Fackenheim, who had at one time been quite critical of Jews who made survival an end in itself,[4] became, after the Holocaust and the Six-Day War, the principal spokesman of that point of view, seeing it as a fitting response to unprecedented new circumstances: "I am convinced that future historians will understand it, not, as our present detractors would have it, as the tribal response mechanism of a fossil, but rather as a profound, albeit as yet fragmentary act of faith, in an age of crisis to which the response might well have been either flight in total disarray or complete despair."[5]

Is there not something paradoxical in the fact that it is Hitler who, in the post-Auschwitz era, has made Judaism necessary?[6] Is there not something to Jewish survival beyond the demonstrative negation of negation, beyond defiance of the Jews' would-be destroyers? Is this the only reason for our existence as Jews, the new basis of the Covenant? Fackenheim is troubled by this question as he considers whether the Jew can still be said to bear witness to the world. Clearly, the tradition of martyrdom has come to an end. The medieval Jews who were martyred believed wholeheartedly that the world was in need of their sacrifice and that by studying Torah they were helping to sustain the world, "but what, in their final moments, the pious Jews of Auschwitz believed or did not believe is a mystery which can only be revered but which will never be fathomed."[7]

If, however, we have no evidence of the faith of the victims, how can we know what faithfulness to their memory entails? Here emerges the great embarrassment and uncertainty implicit in Fackenheim's thinking. The very attempt, after the Holocaust, to turn Jews into "witnesses" gives us pause, for it is likely to "stifle impulses for sheer survival and elementary normalcy with unnecessary or impossible burdens." That is, he is afraid that the desire to bear witness to the universal spiritual significance of Judaism will overwhelm the desire to be normal and simply survive, which is the supreme Jewish imperative after the Holocaust. He does not want to shirk the responsibility of giving some positive meaning to Jewish survival, for to do so would be to betray the Jewish past and the universal meaning of Jewish fate. Although it is clear to him that the age-old exilic tradition of martyrdom came to an end with the Holocaust, he seeks some way of connecting this tradition with present-day Jewish existence. He thus takes care not to make things too explicit. The Jew "bears witness that without endurance we shall all perish." By his steadfastness in a world of cynicism and despair, he gives humanity hope that after Auschwitz the crisis can be withstood; for he *must* withstand it and not "abandon the world to the forces of Auschwitz" but rather "work and hope with unyielding stubbornness for a . . . new . . . age." As it turns out, this work includes, among other things, identification with the universal values of Judaism, such as peace, justice, and brotherhood, as long as Jewish existence as such is not endangered by them.[8] Fackenheim does not make clear what moral demands are made of the contemporary Jew. He addresses both religious and irreligious, for in his view the Holocaust has broken down the barrier between them. Both bear witness "against Satan" by affirming their Jewishness. The only remaining distinction is "between inauthentic Jews who flee from their Jewishness and authentic Jews who affirm it."[9]

The one concrete conclusion Fackenheim draws is that the moral Jewish response to the antisemites of the world is "not to encourage them by [our] own powerlessness" but to amass strength.[10] The latter becomes a substitute for martyrdom, "for after Auschwitz a Jew's life is holier than his death, even if [that death] be for the sanctification of the divine Name." Fackenheim bestows upon the Jewish will to survive a kind of transcendent holiness: the Jews are commanded to survive precisely because the "Aryans" want to wipe them out. This is the close connection, then, between the Holocaust and the establishment of the State of Israel: "the commanding voice of Auschwitz" leads to the Jewish state. It is the state that ensures Jewish survival, first of all by virtue of its power and second because it is a symbol of hope, of "steadfastness." It brings Jewish impotence to an end.[11]

The crucial question that must be posed to Fackenheim — and all his critics do so — is whether the Holocaust may be used as the principal justification for Jewish existence in our time, so central that it eclipses all other events in Jewish history. His answer is unsatisfactory for both the religious and the nonreligious. The religious Jew cannot see the Holocaust as a central event from which the "commanding voice" of God issues forth, for to him the God of Israel is a redeeming God, and destruction and violence do not reflect His presence but rather His hiddenness. It is this redeeming God, not the punishing, chastising one, who commands. No positive theological meaning can be derived from the destruction, nor is it coincidental that Fackenheim's "negative theology" brings him not to belief in the existence of God, but to faith in the survival of Israel!

But it is doubtful that the nonreligious Jew could find in Fackenheim a satisfactory rationale for remaining Jewish. If he is a fervent nationalist, he can draw from Fackenheim a spurious legitimation of violent struggle that knows no moral bounds, for as soon as survival becomes an end in itself, all other values get shunted aside. If he is a sober rationalist, he cannot believe in the special fate of the Jewish people. He cannot see their sufferings in the Holocaust as being more significant historically than the sufferings of other peoples. It is only on a theological level that Jewish suffering has any meaning. But for the secular Jew this is a scandal that must be brought to an end by a joint struggle of all mankind against evil, oppression, and injustice. If his survival as a Jew has any meaning, it does not depend on the Holocaust, and there is no special reason why he should use the latter to justify his Jewishness. He may, indeed, not need any such justification. Whether we like it or not, simply identifying as a Jew may be enough for him.[12]

George Steiner: The Text as Jewish Homeland

George Steiner is a literary critic whose books and articles always attract the interest of European and American readers. Born in France in 1929 to a family that had lived in Vienna for many generations, he sees himself as heir to the Central European humanistic tradition in which such Jewish intellectuals as Heinrich Heine, Walter Benjamin, Karl Kraus, and Franz Kafka played an important role. Educated in the German *Bildung* tradition and knowledgeable in a number of languages, Steiner is a typical "marginal Jew" who, not belonging organically to any one place, can assume a critical stance toward a particular culture while being at home in the universal culture of Europe.

Hannah Arendt describes this type as a "pariah," an ostracized individual whose situation can lead him to great humanistic creativity of universal import. Prominent in the ranks of such people are writers and critics whose world is that of the text and whose existential situation as exilic Jews is connected to their literary pursuits. They do not feel they belong anywhere, but their detachment becomes a salient advantage and even a mission. The text, the book, serves them as a substitute "place," representing the realm of truth. Thus the Cairo-born, French-Jewish writer Edmond Jabès explains: "For me, the book is the Jew's true place, but it is also the writer's true place." For him, exile is "an utter inability to belong." "The Jew never had territory, a place of his own. . . . To me, Judaism is a text."[13] Although the meaning of "text" is vague here, it clearly does not refer to the world of the Torah in the traditional sense but to an abstract process of creativity with only a tenuous connection to the past.

Steiner differs from Cohen and Rosenzweig in having developed a critical attitude toward Zionism after the Holocaust and the establishment of the State of Israel. For him, the Holocaust provides a flashpoint not only for a penetrating critique of Zionism but also for a comprehensive moral critique of Western culture in general as seen through "Jewish" spectacles. The passion that fills this critique is drawn from biblical prophecy.[14]

At the root of Steiner's critique of Zionism is his negative view of nationalism, which contains motifs we have encountered in other Jewish thinkers, such as Hermann Cohen and Franz Rosenzweig. In this respect, Steiner and North American Jewish theologians like Richard Rubinstein, Emil Fackenheim, and Irving Greenberg are at opposite poles. For them, the Holocaust clearly carries a Zionist lesson, the need for Jewish sovereignty and power, whereas Steiner's

conclusion is the opposite: the task of the Jews after the Holocaust is a hermeneutic one, giving the classical texts a new ethical interpretation that will
purge the seeds of destruction from Europe's humane, universalistic heritage,
desecrated and falsified by contemporary chauvinistic nationalism. The Jews
are called to this task of cultural rescue not only because of their "prophetic"
mission, but because they are to some extent responsible, albeit unintentionally, for preparing the ground from which this nationalism sprang.[15]

Steiner first formulated his provocative views about Jewish nationalism and
Zionism in his 1965 article "A Kind of Survivor," which immediately elicited a
storm of responses both in Israel and elsewhere.[16] The article contains the
kernel of ideas he later developed in even more extreme form. An example is
his well-known concept of the dialectical relation between Zionism and Nazism. The pattern of his thinking is roughly this: It was Judaism that gave the
world the idea of the "chosen people." Although this idea was not necessarily
antihumanitarian in its origins, it inspired modern nationalism and particularly Nazi barbarism. The Nazis gave the idea a racial interpretation, on the
basis of which they set out to annihilate the Jewish people as the very antithesis
of totalitarian nationalism and symbol of the "bad conscience" of mankind.
The State of Israel arose as a response to the Nazi attempt at genocide, and in
this respect it was necessary; but like all states, it was drawn willy-nilly into the
unrestrained use of violence and other invalid means of asserting itself, so that,
more and more, its ethos came to resemble Nazi nationalism itself. For Steiner,
this is, from a Jewish point of view, an absurd and intolerable state of affairs.
"By one of the cruel, deep ironies of history, the concept of a chosen people, of
a nation exalted above others by particular destiny, was born in Israel. In the
vocabulary of Nazism there were elements of a vengeful parody on the Judaic
claim. . . . But if the poison is, in ancient part, Jewish, so perhaps is the
antidote, the radical humanism which sees man on his road to becoming
man."[17] Furthermore, "it may be that the Jew bears some part of the historical
responsibility for the crime against man that is tribalism, chauvinism, the
myth of racial election [which] almost annihilated the Jewish people [itself] in
this century, coming like a boomerang out of a travesty of the remote Judaic
past. . . . To be wanderers and scattered among the nations may, for some of us,
be a moral necessity."[18]

Feeling a deep sense of guilt for this Jewish "contribution" to modern nationalism, Steiner sees the role of the Jewish people as one of atoning for their
sin by living a life of detachment and alienation. "Nationalism is the venom of
our age. It has brought Europe to the edge of ruin. . . . When a Jew opposes the
parochial ferocity into which nationalism so easily (inevitably) degenerates, he
is paying an old debt."[19] Steiner thus fashions a modern midrash on the traditional Jewish view of exile as atonement for collective sin.

Steiner says he has "never been sure about houses." His ideal is that of the Wandering Jew, the guest. "The Jew has his anchorage, not in place but in time, in his highly developed sense of history as a personal context. Six thousand years of self-awareness are a homeland."[20] The nation-state is a dubious refuge for the Jew. "What have the kindred of Spinoza and Heine to do with flags or oaths of national fidelity?"[21] The Jews have a different role to play, "to show that, whereas trees have roots, men have legs and are each other's guests."[22] Although the ideal of the supranational society still seems ludicrously remote, humankind will, in the end, have no other way to avoid destroying itself. "If the potential of civilization is not to be destroyed, we shall have to develop more complex, more provisional loyalties" than those flowing from national belonging. Being a guest, the Jew can examine anew in each place the relation between conscience and political or intellectual commitment, combining national loyalty with skepticism and humanity. The motif of loyalty and betrayal, which is one of the central themes of the theology of the Holocaust, is an important motif for Steiner, too. They can persuade the Jews that their destiny is not faithfulness to any state, for no state is worthy of absolute loyalty, but rather loyalty to the truth in the texts. Hence there is a kind of treason that is actually loyalty and a kind of loyalty that is actually treason.

Steiner admits that Zionism is a well-nigh essential condition of Jewish life. "The strength of Israel reaches deep into the awareness of every Jew," and "the survival of the Jewish people may depend on it." He admits, further, that without the State of Israel his own Jewish identity will not survive and that he himself may need a refuge one day. But this state is a "sad miracle." "Sprung of inhumanity and the imminence of massacre, [it] has had to make itself a closed fist" in the face of the pack of wolves threatening to tear it apart. But "the nation-state bristling with arms is a bitter relic, an absurdity . . . alien to some of the most radical, most humane elements in the Jewish spirit."[23]

After the Six-Day War, Steiner became even more critical of the Jewish state. Instead of seeing it as a "sad miracle," upon which the people's survival might depend, he began to see it as a phenomenon that actually endangered their survival, even more than dispersion. He was convinced that Jewish survival could not be made to depend on the survival of the State of Israel or any other state. In 1970 he wrote: "The defeat of Israel would be a great disaster, a human tragedy which would affect the life of every Jew wherever he might be, however alien he might feel to the ideals of Zionism. But it could well be an even worse disaster if Israel grew into no more than a small fortified enclave among wretched and implacable enemies. The scattering of two million Jews, their wandering again among the nations, would be a hideous thing. But it would not, I believe, ultimately endanger the survival of Judaism as a vision of human conduct. That survival is the central mystery of our being as Jews. Without it, the somber singularity of our history would make little sense. There is that in Zionism and the nation-state, which does threaten the transcendental ethical presence of 'Israel' within the Jewish conscience."[24]

Twenty-five years after the Holocaust, he does a cost-benefit analysis of exile, a cold, cruel analysis, and finds that the benefit outweighs the cost:

> Through ill fortune and good fortune, the Jews of the Diaspora were saved from the corruptions and lies of national military power. The cost of this dialectical paradox was enormous — the near-total destruction of European Jewry. I am, I think, in no need of being reminded of that. But the gains were very great also. No Jew, in two millennia, had to deny that he was torturing prisoners. None had to walk armed amid the hatred of an occupied town, blowing up houses, holding hostages. Innocent of power, Judaism developed its genius for truth, its ability to survive among many languages and cultures, its refusal to trust facile national ideologies. Jews were compelled to be themselves and to be creative wanderers among men. Of this enforced condition came their formidable contribution to the whole genius of modern science, of modern feeling.[25]

Thus the price (the decimation of European Jewry) might have been worth paying and continues to be worth paying even now. Steiner is more and more skeptical about the cultural and spiritual achievements of the Jewish state. Israel, in his view, has locked Judaism in a prison and, in its ongoing fight for survival, is holding it hostage.[26] He enumerates many individual Jews, from Marx to Claude Lévi-Strauss, without whom modern life would be unrecognizable and is quite dubious of Israel's affinity for this creative vision.

Like other Jewish intellectuals, Steiner finds a substitute for an earthly Jewish homeland. It is not the Torah, which Heine defined as the "portable homeland" of the Jews, for Steiner is not religious and he reads the Torah critically. The alienated Jew has another, more abstract spiritual homeland to which he clings. This homeland is "the truth," "the text." In an article published in the mid-eighties, "Our Homeland, the Text," Steiner uses his astonishing verbal skill to suggest, through wordplay and free adaptation of traditional imagery, that what he is offering is a modern Jew's legitimate midrash on the ancient scriptures.[27] He wants to create the impression that his interpretation of Jewish history is the direct continuation of the traditional Jewish reading of it. Although the biblical Covenant places the Jewish people on a particular piece of land, the "promised land," history has uprooted them, chastening and purifying them and making them into a spiritual entity that has left the world, with all its impurity, to the gentiles. (In this, Steiner is very close to Rosenzweig.) Steiner bases his thinking on Hegel's notion of Judaism as a religion alienated from the world and humankind, but he converts this judgment from blame to praise. "In post-exilic Judaism, . . . active reading, answerability to the text on both the meditative-interpretative and the behavioral levels, is the central motion of personal and national homecoming. . . . The dwelling assigned, ascribed to Israel is the House of the Book. . . . The . . . Solomonic Temple may have been an erratum, a misreading of the transcendent mobility of the text. . . . The centrality of the book does coincide with and enact the condition of exile." The text is the tool of exilic survival. "Reading [and] textual exegesis are an exile from action, from the existential innocence of praxis, even where the text is aiming at practical or political consequences."[28] The wanderer bears the world on his shoulders, as it were, by means of the text.

The text is not only the Jews' means of survival; it has, in effect, taken over their fate for better or worse. No other nation's fate has been so decisively determined, so prescribed by its literature; and no other nation has read and reread the scriptures responsible for its fate as have the Jews. "The stronger the prophecy, the more often it is proclaimed, the greater its inertial thrust towards realization. In his dread history the Jew would seem to have been intent to certify the accuracy of the road mapped for him by the Prophets." The Jews have enacted the "script" that was dictated to them. "The price for the 'keeping of the books' (for this 'going by the books') has been, literally, monstrous." The Holocaust confirmed the books' message in the most dreadful way. Here again, Steiner is suggesting that it is not only the Nazis who were responsible for the Jewish fate; the Jews themselves bear a certain guilt, having rushed into their fate headlong. "The notion that the night-vision of the Jew has, somehow, in some secret measure, brought on itself the torments foreseen, is irrational, but haunting none the less."[29]

The question arises how the Jews nevertheless managed to hold on to their sanity and not commit suicide in the face of these scriptural prophecies of doom. For Steiner, this is "*the* Jewish question." One answer is that scripture includes not only such prophecies but also the idea of the remnant and of the redemption of the Jewish people through restoration to their homeland. But this vision need not be understood as referring to something imminent, something that will occur in our everyday world. Scripture is equivocal about this. The fact is that both camps, the Zionists and the anti-Zionists, can bring proof for their positions from the messianic hints in scripture. Until the meaning of these hints becomes clear, the gathering at Zion is merely a preview, something temporary and "pro-visional." In any event, without the metaphysics and psychology of the "pre-script," there is no way of making sense either of Jewish fortitude through all the suffering and persecution or of "the rationally, geopolitically absurd return of a modern ethnic group to a largely barren strip of earth in the Middle East, to a strip of earth long occupied by others."[30]

The Jews found in the text a substitute for the political and social activity that was denied them. In Judaism, unlike in Hellenism and Christianity, the letter vivifies rather than mortifies the spirit.[31] The Jew's true commitment is to preserving the text from being misread. "Each text rightly established and expounded is an *aliya,* a homecoming of Judaism to itself and to its keeping of the books." "A true thinker . . . must know that no nation, no body politic, no creed, no moral ideal [or] necessity, be it that of human survival, is worth a falsehood . . . or the manipulation of the text." Knowledge of the text and preservation of it in its pristine form *"are* [the Jew's] homeland. It is the false reading [of it] that make[s] him homeless."[32]

"Judaism defines itself as a visa to the messianic 'other land.'" Central European Judaism and its secular successor American Judaism made exile, dispersion, and powerlessness the heartland of modern intellectuality. Past persecution and suffering have been replaced by a powerful creative impulse that has shaped much of the politics, art, and intellectual activity of our generation. From this impulse arises the conflict between secular Jewish ideals — truth, justice, and conscience — and the demand of the nation-state, the expression of a revived "natural paganism," for absolute loyalty. The conflict finds expression in the Dreyfus Affair (1894): Jewish morality, secularized but still unyielding, and "the politics of truth" collide. It was the inevitable clash between nationalistic, territorial politics and a people that felt at home in exile.

This analysis brings Steiner to the conclusion of his article. The nation-state is based on myths and martial glory; it sustains itself by self-deception, lies, and half-truths, all incompatible with the quest for the truth of the text. Nationalism is a kind of madness that stifles thought and the unswerving pursuit of justice. The Jews, being at home with the text, must, by their essence, be strongly opposed to the vulgar mystique of flag and anthem, the soporific slogan "My country, right or wrong." "The locus of the truth is always extraterritorial." In a physical homeland the text can lose its vitality, and its truth can be betrayed.

The State of Israel is an entirely understandable effort to normalize the Jewish condition, an effort that is, in many respects, admirable and perhaps even historically inevitable. But "it is, at the same time, an attempt to eradicate the deeper truth of . . . at-homeness in the word, which [is] the legacy of the Prophets." "It is . . . difficult to believe that this unique phenomenon of unbroken life [Judaism], in the face of every destructive agency, is unconnected with the exilic circumstance." Furthermore, "the notion that the appalling road of Jewish life and the ever-renewed miracle of survival should have as their end, as their justification, the setting up of a small nation-state in the Middle East, crushed by military burdens, petty and even corrupt in its politics, shrill in its parochialism, is implausible."[33]

In sum, Steiner accepts the Jewish state as a necessity, understandable even to him and, as the Hebrew saying has it, "necessity cannot be dismissed." On the other hand, he is bitterly critical, not only of the state's behavior — which he is entitled to criticize — but also of the very idea of setting up a Jewish nation-state because it is a betrayal of Jewish history. What is left is thus "simultaneously [to] labor for Israel and against it."[34] It is not clear what concrete import this statement can have or whether it is logically consistent.

It cannot be denied that the Jews' relationship to "the text" and its role in their history is unique phenomena.[35] But Steiner's interpretation of the way the Jews see *themselves* is far-fetched. To present Judaism as something grounded entirely in time and indifferent to space ignores scripture's explicit demand that the Jews maintain a worldly existence. Their life has never been so abstract, nor have they ever seen it as merely symbolic. As Scholem puts it, Steiner is trying to live outside of history. Certainly the participation he envisions is restricted; he sees the Jews as involved in human history as a whole only through their "word," their ideas, their spiritual creativity, and not through any concrete activity. In effect, they are estranged from the world. The most creative Jews, in his view, have been the "marginal" ones with no living connection to the Jewish people, not Rabbi Akiva or Maimonides, for example, who were tied to their people with every fiber of their being. His vision is thus suited to an isolated, alienated intellectual elite, not to a people bearing responsibility for its own survival. To his credit, Steiner presents these arguments not as a response to the collective dilemmas of the Jewish people but rather as a personal response not necessarily relevant to the people as a whole.

Irving Greenberg: The Ethics of Jewish Power

Irving Greenberg stands out among Jewish thinkers of the last generation for having tried to formulate a systematic theological and ethical justification for the Jewish people acquiring and using power in the wake of the Holocaust. Although he never mentions Steiner in his writings, he grapples with arguments that Steiner has made. By training, Greenberg is an Orthodox rabbi as well as a secular scholar. He was influenced in no small measure by his teacher Rabbi Yosef Dov Soloveitchik but has gone much further in his views. For some years he taught at an American university but left it in order to devote himself to Jewish communal affairs. In addition to being a firmly committed Zionist, he is among those who have fought most consistently for Jewish unity as well as for pluralism and tolerance, a position that cuts him off almost entirely from Orthodox circles. He has, however, a significant following in the wider American Jewish community.[36]

Like Fackenheim, who developed his theology in the wake of the Six-Day War, Greenberg claims to take seriously the historical events that have been decisive for the Jewish people in our time. It is unthinkable that the Holocaust and the establishment of the Jewish state would not leave their mark on Jewish theology. History is not theologically neutral; it either strengthens the Covenant or poses a challenge to it. In effect, since history is the principal realm in which man and God meet, it is the testing ground of theology.[37] Thus one cannot evade, as the ultra-Orthodox do, the question of which approach to history the Jews, whether in the Land of Israel or in the Diaspora, should take in the face of these events. They cannot remain passive or mere outside observers.

Greenberg believes it is only now, some fifty years after the restoration of Jewish sovereignty and power, that we are "beginning to confront the profound challenge to religious understanding and ethical capacity implicit in this revolutionary change."[38] He bases his call to the Jewish people to seize power and be prepared to use it in time of need on a theology that distinguishes three stages in the history of the Covenant between God and Israel, a Covenant intended to lead to the redemption of the Jews and all mankind: the biblical stage, coinciding with the period of the First Temple; the Talmudic stage, coinciding with the period of the Second Temple and of the exile; and the Zionist stage, the pivotal points of which are the Holocaust and the establishment of the State of Israel. These three stages represent a process in which the perceptible intervention of God in history diminishes and the realm of human responsibility is enlarged. Psychologically speaking, it is a kind of growing up. Theologically, it is a process of secularization (not, however, a movement toward atheism!), of the withdrawal of God "behind the curtain" in order to leave more room for human action. Each stage is connected not only with the appearance of a new theology and ethos but also with structural changes in the life of the Jewish people (such as the transition from subjugation to independence, or the reverse) and the emergence of a new leadership (such as that of the Sages in place of the priests and kings, following the destruction of the Second Temple) that takes responsibility for adapting Jewish life to the new conditions and self-understanding.

It is not our concern here to provide a detailed description of the changes Greenberg associates with each stage. Suffice it to say that the changes that are theologically essential can only be understood dialectically. The matter can be summed up in the following paradox: the more God withdraws from the world, the more He is revealed within it. Extensive revelation is replaced by intensive. Instead of being revealed at well-defined points in time and space where His rulership of the world is evident, God is revealed indirectly, in a multiplicity of events and actions initiated by man. For example, the First Temple period is characterized by asymmetrical relations between God and His people: He is the initiator and senior partner who rewards and punishes, imposing His Torah upon the people and revealing Himself in dramatic historical events, in Jewish self-determination and in the concentration of worship in a single place (the Temple). In Second Temple times, and even more so after the destruction of the Temple, there is a greater balance between the covenantal parties: the Sages, who lead the people, take a more active role and greater responsibility, as real partners with the divine. Parallel to this, a process of diffusion takes place in the Diaspora: God reveals Himself to His people in conditions of dispersion and lack of sovereignty in every synagogue and wherever Jews study the Torah. His providential care of His people comes to be hidden (as in the Book of Esther, where God is not even mentioned), and miracles are concealed rather than out in the open. In the third stage, the present one, the diffusion becomes even more pronounced. God is everywhere: in political life, on the field of battle, in social activity, in business, in medicine and education. But there is a far-reaching process of secularization, in which religious responsibility is transferred almost entirely from God to man.

Greenberg here joins the distinguished company of such religious-Zionist thinkers as Kook, Buber, and Gordon, who tried to give secular existence in general, and the existence of an independent Jewish society in particular, a theological meaning. It is clear that the main issue concerning him as a theologian is the connection between religion and politics. In language quite reminiscent of Buber's, he states that the Jews of the third era will prove true to themselves if, while upholding Jewish sovereignty, they are able to fill it with Jewish content.[39] It is a double test: can Judaism survive in the framework of a sovereign state as it did in the Diaspora? Can the Jews remain faithful to Jewish values despite the radical change in their situation?

The Holocaust, on one hand, and the transition to sovereignty, on the other, require a change in Jewish self-understanding that implies fundamental theological and ethical changes as well. Theologically we have entered an era of silence on our part that parallels the profound hiddenness of the divine. Our faith in redemption and in the meaning of Jewish life cannot be confirmed by speech but only by deeds of love and the giving of life: "In an age when one is ashamed or embarrassed to talk about God in the presence of burning children, the creation of an image of God — viz., a human being of infinite value, equality and uniqueness — is an act that speaks even louder than words. This image points beyond itself to transcendence. The human vessel imprinted with the image of God testifies by its very existence to the source of that image. Perhaps this testimony is the only statement about God we can make."[40]

Like the poet Uri Tzvi Greenberg, Irving Greenberg maintains that, in the face of God's absolute silence during the Holocaust, a silence that can be interpreted as a violation or even abrogation of the Covenant, the only way for us to renew our faith is to create new life. Seen this way, the struggle for Jewish survival after the Holocaust, survival made possible by the religious and irreligious alike, is the strongest evidence of God's presence in the world and of the hope for redemption. The religious message implicit in the existence of the Jewish state is a call to secularity, to action within the world. This is the paradox of the third stage: "religious" activity must be primarily secular in nature. But secularization should not be confused with ideological secularism. The claims of the latter were called into question by the Holocaust, when man, wielding unrestrained power over life and death, made himself into a god. After this event, any departure from the yardstick of human worth, equality, and uniqueness is ipso facto a denial of God. The most exalted task, dwarfing all others, is to rescue the image of God by working for a more humane mankind. This is not a task for the Jewish people alone, but for all men: the elimination of all stereotypes and prejudices, equal treatment for all the disadvantaged. In this, the Jews have a central role to play by virtue of their special position in history.

Greenberg makes a bold claim: God's silence in the face of the annihilation of the Jews signifies the breaking of the old Covenant. In its place a new one has been created which derives from the Jews' free choice to continue their commitment to Him in spite of His failure, as it were, to stand by them. Now the tables are turned: whereas in the first stage it was God who took the initiative ("Go forth from your land, your birthplace, and your father's house"), now it is man. God's silence is understood as a call to mankind in general and the Jew in particular to assume greater responsibility, unprecedented in history, and to play a more active role in bringing about redemption. Henceforth we are responsible for our world as well as for God's good name. By demonstratively failing to save His people, the Holy One Himself has, in a manner of speaking, sent us a message: Do not rely on Me alone! Take responsibility for your own fate! Significantly, Greenberg sees this as a responsibility not only toward ourselves but also toward the other peoples with whom we come into contact.

The Jews' main response to this divine call has been to acquire the power to ensure Jewish freedom and prevent another holocaust.[41] This is the most decisive change that has taken place in the Jewish condition in the third stage, which is, as we have said, one in which the focus shifts from the sacred to the profane, is from powerlessness to power. This historical process has itself brought about the normalization of Jewish existence. But for a people whose existence was for so long abnormal, adjusting to normalcy is difficult because it entails a change in the Jews' self-image as well as their image in the eyes of others. Jewish ethics developed under conditions of powerlessness. The challenge from within that Judaism faced during the period of exile was to fashion a culture that could preserve the Jew's dignity and give meaning to his life despite his inferior political status. This approach made for a tendency to glorify martyrdom and passivity and encouraged the view that the mission of the Jewish people would be revealed in the next world or in the messianic era rather than in the here and now. The Holocaust put an end to this ethos and the theology that underlay it. Martyrdom in the traditional sense now signifies a "moral affront" and a risk of complete annihilation. The Jews' obligation to achieve power, on the other hand, is a "sacred principle."[42] Jews everywhere understand the summons to power as a call to serve God out of a position of strength rather than weakness. The prayer of the powerful is completely different from that of the powerless. The first is likely to focus more on self-scrutiny and self-judgment, for the powerful person does not turn to his God to save him from a crushing fate but rather to strengthen his conscience and good intentions, as a friend and as a partner in his wielding of power.[43]

Greenberg is well aware of the ambiguity and danger inherent in the call to power, but they do not deter him, for, in the overall moral calculus, the survival of the Jewish people after the Holocaust is, in his view, a necessary condition for our faith in the triumph of the good. Although power corrupts, there is no alternative that is any more moral. The only alternative is death. Hence his dialectical attitude to power: to forgo it out of fear of staining our hands with innocent blood means betraying the slain and shirking the responsibility imposed by their fate. Yet an unrestrained, uncritical use of power would be a violation of another imperative imposed by the Holocaust: to create a more humane life. The conclusion to be drawn is that there is a dual imperative and a dual obligation, dialectically related: to go on living, which entails acquiring power; and to make a better world, one more in the image of God, which entails restraining the use of power. These, then, are the two parameters of the new situation: powerlessness is incompatible with Jewish survival, but power is incompatible with absolute moral purity. "Moral maturity consists of grasping both these truths without evasion or illusion. Moral responsibility consists of the continuous struggle to contain both truths without letting them paralyze either the will to power or our moral faculties."[44]

This analysis makes for greater balance and sobriety when it comes to criticizing the way Israelis wield power. For Greenberg, such criticism can be justified as long as it does not call into question the very fact of power or deny the very legitimacy of the Jewish state. Any use of power, however well intentioned, inevitably has immoral consequences.[45] In the premessianic world, the good is often the result of ambiguous processes: moral acts with immoral side effects, mixed with immoral acts that yield legitimate fruit. Greenberg calls upon Diaspora Jews to be less innocent and delicate, more realistic and mature, in their attitude toward power. Prophetic standards do not apply in a premessianic reality. Instead, we should adopt the halakhic approach, which applies principles to the concrete world we live in to the extent that circumstances allow. In his view, the greatness of the Halakha lies in its striving for messianic perfection by means that are flawed and entail compromise. In this, Greenberg seems close to the principle of *quantum satis* (sufficient measure) in Buber's situational ethics, but his political conclusions are different. Buber was resolutely opposed to realpolitik whereas Greenberg is more ambivalent about it.[46] Prophecy is, in a sense, necessary to the proper exercise of political power, but this does not mean that the ruling authority can adopt a prophetic stance. Prophets, speaking in the name of the spirit, can demand absolute rectitude, but government is obligated to protect the people. At the same time, woe to the government that ignores prophetic demands: it will almost invariably sink to the level of exploiting the very people it is meant to protect. There is thus a moral conflict here that has no clear-cut resolution. "Show me a people whose hands are not dirty, and I will show you a people which has not been responsible. Show me a people which has stopped washing its hands and admitting its guilt, and I will show you a people which is arrogant and dying morally."[47]

For Greenberg, the normalization of the Jewish people is a necessary given, a price it must pay in order to survive, where survival is itself a moral and religious imperative and a test of Judaism's ability to contend with the moral dilemmas of power, to persist in "mending the world," if only on a small scale.[48] He does not delude himself that the Jews are any more moral than other people. He sees this assumption as a veiled form of racism, a distortion of the idea of chosenness. But precisely because they are like other people they should not be judged by different moral standards than others. There is no place for the double standard applied whenever Israel is criticized. Such judgments can be carried to extremes that are destructive and dangerous, for they undermine Israel's legitimacy. Its right to exist does not depend on its adherence to ideal moral standards any more than that of any other nation. To pose such a condition has an antisemitic ring, in that it discriminates between Jews and others. Making absolute moral demands leads to the destruction of the imperfect good that can be achieved.[49]

The ethics of Jewish power must be determined by the standards of normal politics. Partial failure and wrongdoing are inevitable. Instead of the extreme utopian vision of the Prophets, for which there is no room in this world, there must be a mechanism of limited self-criticism that allows for improvement and the minimization of evil: "Sin is inevitable; therefore, the ethical health of a society is judged not so much by its ideal procedures or potential ability to do good but by the excellence of its corrective mechanisms."[50]

Greenberg does not spell out sufficiently how he sees such mechanisms operating. One gets the impression he is more interested in the theological justification of power and less in how it is to be limited and restrained. In regard to the latter, he makes do with hope and faith that as they get used to exercising power, the Jews will once again become the moral vanguard of humanity. He is content to have them behave "ten percent more" morally than other peoples. How does Greenberg justify theologically his position that Israel is not to be judged by higher standards than other peoples? Is this not what the Prophets did on the assumption that such standards were, in fact, the meaning of the Covenant between the Chosen People and its God? ("You alone have I singled out of all the families of the earth; that is why I will call you to account for all your iniquities." Amos 3:2). Greenberg's answer is that the prophetic demand was valid in a different context, in another time. The Prophets could make such a demand because they had promised the people that God would save the righteous from destruction. When the Land was under God's continuous, watchful gaze, moral perfection could be expected of the people as a condition for their continuing to live there. But today we are living in the wake of the Holocaust, an event where God clearly did not intervene on behalf of the righteous. This fact signifies a change in the terms of the Covenant. God calls upon man to assume full responsibility for the Covenant's realization, but now God's moral right to expel the Jewish people from its land is no longer operative; after the Holocaust, no one, not even God, can expect the Jewish people to justify its existence by being perfectly moral.[51] Greenberg does not make clear whether he means this "right" is no longer operative under any circumstances or only if the people has failed to live up to the term of the Covenant. In other words, is there, theologically speaking, some minimal moral level that is a prerequisite for remaining on the land, even in the eyes of a God who kept silent during the Holocaust, or has the Jews' right to live and build their polity there become unconditional? Has the Torah's stipulation that Israel's independence in its own land depends on its moral conduct been nullified after the Holocaust? Greenberg does not make this clear, and as a result, the dialectic he posits between the imperatives of survival and of humane behavior becomes blurred.

There is much to be said for Greenberg's criticism of Diaspora Jews who speak scornfully of the "mere survival" of the State of Israel and are prepared to scrap it if it becomes, in their view, just another "Levantine" state. He sees this approach as ignoring the religious meaning of "mere normal existence," in defiance of the forces of hatred and destruction. Israel's physical survival indicates the legitimacy of the hope of redemption based on the Covenant and the power of transcendence. In its life, however secular, Israel provides believing Jews with living proof that their hope of redemption has not been in vain. And Greenberg is largely correct in his complaint about the Diaspora Jews' exaggerated criticism of Israel's behavior, criticism which is sometimes a function of the fact that they do not bear responsibility for fateful, life-and-death decisions. There is, however, a danger that he, like Fackenheim, will be misunderstood as granting absolute theological validity to the state and its military power, a position fraught with danger. Greenberg himself is aware of this danger when he writes that the reliance of a polity upon absolute authority to give legitimacy to morally imperfect acts can jeopardize the freedom of other polities and the pluralism needed domestically for democracy to work.[52] This leads him to the conclusion that the authority to lead the Jewish people should, at the present time, be given to nonreligious politicians. Would it not be more correct to say that prophetic religion must always be critical of political institutions if they are not to be become sanctified? Would it not be fitting, at a time when Jews are exercising power and, intentionally or otherwise, not always exercising it to the good, that a voice of religious conscience speak out for justice in the midst of "normalcy"?

Fackenheim and Greenberg see the Holocaust as the greatest watershed in Jewish history since the destruction of the Second Temple. For them it represents a fateful challenge necessitating radical change in the way Jewish faith and commitment are understood. Both seek a religious justification for the centrality of the Jewish state in Jewish life and see its establishment and exercise of power as the most authentic response to the Holocaust. Their thinking is thus political theology in the full sense of the term. This theology poses the question of whether Judaism can enter into a covenant with politics that does not endanger them both. That is, can religion combine its justification of the state with its critical, prophetic role vis-à-vis state power? This is a question of the greatest contemporary relevance. For Fackenheim, the Holocaust is a point of departure for a "theology of survival," elevating Jewish survival to a religious precept in its own right, a corollary of which is the affirmation of political power. But this theology does not pay sufficient attention to the moral problematic of the Jewish people's attainment of power. Making survival a moral commandment in and of itself can lead to a distortion of the Jewish heritage, which never saw survival as an end in itself, and it can undermine the rationale for the existence of the state.

Steiner's critique of Jewish nationalism, though not addressed directly to Fackenheim, is implicitly a critique of Fackenheim's absolutization of the Holocaust and the state. Steiner refuses to see the Holocaust as a watershed in the life of the Jewish people, requiring existential reorientation and new faithfulness and commitment. If anything, he sees the Holocaust imposing upon the Jews an obligation to deepen their universal, humanitarian mission in exile, precisely because of their indirect theological responsibility for the horrors of Nazism. The loyalty of the Jews to the Jewish state is bound to distort their true loyalty to the text, that is, to truth and moral conscience. Rather than seeing their suffering as a goad to broader human solidarity, the Jews are led by the state to focus solely on their own interests, and a power-oriented ideology arises which is alien to the humane heritage of Diaspora Jewry. But because Steiner nevertheless recognizes the need for a state, at least as a refuge for persecuted Jews, it is not clear how he envisions its survival being ensured without military power, which must sometimes employ inhumane means to achieve its ends.

Irving Greenberg is aware of this problematic, and his thinking tries to come to grips with it. He maintains that the Holocaust obliges the Jews to a dual faithfulness: to the imperative of physical survival as a people, of which the state is an expression, and to the humane imperative of creating a better world. The ethic of power must take into account both of these allegiances. Any attempt to foster one at the expense of the other is, in his view, a betrayal of the memory of the slain. The aggregation of power is an authentic response to the imperative of taking responsibility for our own fate. The message of the Holocaust for the Jews, immanent in their whole history, is the need to combine the two commitments: the particularistic commitment of an oppressed, humiliated people, newly rescued from total annihilation, to the establishment of a stronghold in its homeland, together with a constant effort to avoid the unrestrained use of force; and the universalistic commitment to solidarity with the oppressed of other nations, precisely because its own long history has been one of oppression.

PART III

*Power and Jewish Identity
in Israeli Public Discourse*

Sovereignty and Power in Zionist Debate
during the Mandate Period

It is right to obey justice; it is necessary to obey the strongest power.
Justice without power is powerless; power without justice is tyranny.
Justice without power is defied, for there are always wicked men; power
without justice is condemned. Justice and power should therefore be
combined; and so to this end the just should be made strong, or the
strong be made just.

Blaise Pascal, *Pensées*

Means and Ends

Until the 1930s, most Zionists in Palestine as well as in the Diaspora
believed that the Zionist vision of creating a Jewish majority in the country
could be realized without resorting to the wholesale use of military force and
without injuring the rights of the Arab population. They believed that the
purity of their movement's intentions would spare it the brutality and violence
that so often accompany nationalist struggles for independence. This belief
was nurtured both by the prophetic view of history that had had such a strong
influence upon Zionist thinking and by the humane ideals of European liberalism and socialism that had left their stamp upon the Jewish national idea. The
Zionist vision combined particularism and universalism, and there was as yet
no inkling of any contradiction between the two. Gradually, however, this

belief proved illusory, and there was a painful awakening, fraught with misgivings. The greater the distance between vision and reality and the more tenuous the link between national aspirations and humane ideals, the deeper the dilemma facing the Zionist movement: how could force be used without falling into the moral corruption it entailed?

The doctrine of "just war" as enshrined in international law distinguishes between two kinds of right: *jus ad bellum,* the rightful initiation of war, and *jus in bello,* the rightful conduct of war. The great difficulty of this doctrine lies in defining the relation between the two kinds of right. The issue is analogous to that of the relation between means and ends: if a war is just, does that justify the means by which it is waged as well? When survival is at stake this becomes a particularly thorny moral issue.[1] Its complexity is owing to the moral ambiguity of what Kant calls "the laws of necessity": when one is fighting for one's life, no law in the world can impose limits upon him.[2] The same holds true when the fate of a people is at stake, and it becomes necessary (i.e., justified) to violate rights enshrined in law (the law of war). This line of reasoning usually underlies what politicians and military people like to call "higher necessity" or an "emergency," in which means normally considered illegitimate must be used. But such a position can easily lead to justifying even the most selfish of nationalist claims. As long as the purpose of using force is defined as survival in the simplest sense of the term, it becomes unclear which means are permissible and which not.[3]

A court adjudicating cases of individual wrongdoing, which fall under criminal law, must distinguish between wrongful acts that are excusable and those that are not. The test is the proportion between the wrongs prevented and allowed. This principle also applies to the use of force in the political realm, especially when it is meant to ensure the survival of the political body in question. But here the application of the principle is not so clear-cut. All agree that the use of force in self-defense is justifiable when the danger to survival is clear and present. But where there is no such danger, the question of means becomes much more complicated. Since political processes are often lengthy and unpredictable, there is always a danger that the long-term outcome will be more harmful than beneficial. Then too, there is the risk that means will override ends and, rather than achieving the initial goals, will influence the way they are chosen.[4] Because power is seductive, there is a tendency to redefine objectives in proportion to the available means. From a moral point of view, this process is illegitimate, and the great question is how to prevent it.[5]

Inevitably, the relation between means and ends must be understood dialectically: they cannot be completely separated, even when sharply opposed; rather, mutuality between them must be sought. The means we choose must be subject to constant scrutiny both by those who employ them and by public opinion.[6] Rather than adapting our goals to the means at our disposal, we must adapt the means to the goals we have set: the means must be examined for their proportionality and relevance to the goals.[7]

The Zionist movement confronted two great moral questions once it became clear that the quest for Jewish sovereignty in the Land of Israel would require the use of force against its Arab inhabitants. The first question concerned Zionism's goals: what moral grounds did the Jews have to settle a land that was already partly populated by others and to establish sovereignty over it? The second question concerned the means Zionism would employ to achieve its ends: what are the limits of the legitimate use of force? There is, of course, a reciprocal relationship between these two questions. The way Jewish rights to the country were understood depended on how the status of the Arabs living there was understood, be it as equal partners or as aliens, and this determined the position one might take on the use of force. Other scholars, notably Yosef Gorny and Anita Shapira, have treated both these issues at length. My discussion of the issues will be from a viewpoint that has not yet received sufficient attention, namely, the role played by Jewish tradition in shaping the rhetoric of this argument and the relation between this rhetoric and the way the ends-means question was viewed.

The principal moral claims concerning the use of force began to be heard in Zionist circles as early as the turn of the twentieth century, but it was only during the period of the British Mandate over Palestine (1920–48) that the outlines of the argument in the Zionist camp over the place of Jewish sovereignty in the Land of Israel and the way to attain it became clear. The establishment of the state confronted its Jewish citizens with new political questions — the struggle of a body lacking sovereignty and that of one that has it cannot be compared — but the main moral arguments over the right to the Land, how to respond to Arab terror, and so on remained the same, although their importance in the public eye fluctuated with changing circumstances. I would like to stress once again that I am not concerned here with the vicissitudes of Zionist politics during this period but rather with the claims made by the three main ideological groupings within the movement: the religious humanists, led by Martin Buber and his friends; the Revisionists (Jabotinsky, and his followers in the radical right); and the centrists of the labor movement.

Religious Humanism: Martin Buber and His Circle

POLITICS AND FAITH

The religious-humanist position was represented, in the main, by academic intellectuals like Martin Buber, Ernst Simon, Gershom Scholem, Judah

Magnes and Samuel Hugo Bergman. Most belonged to the Brit Shalom (Covenant of Peace) organization (1925–33) and eventually to the Ihud (Union, founded 1942). This group did not carry great weight in the Zionist movement and had few supporters, but because it included prominent, articulate intellectuals, it posed a challenge to other ideological groupings within the movement. Its political and philosophical views, and even some of its practical proposals, were shared by left-wing, secular, socialist groups in Palestine, such as Hashomer Hatza'ir (the Young Guard).

The religious humanists saw themselves as carrying on the legacy of Ahad Ha'am and A. D. Gordon, who had understood Zionism primarily as a movement of cultural revival, embracing certain political and social ideals, a movement whose aim was to solve "the problem of Judaism" not "the problem of the Jews," to use Ahad Ha'am's distinction. They believed that the Jewish people had a moral mission that would be put to the test by the realization of Zionist goals. Achieving national aspirations without violence or harm to others was the great challenge posed for Judaism by the political rebirth of the Jewish people in its homeland, and this was Zionism's universal significance. If the latter were to achieve its goals in disregard for the harm or injustice it caused another people, it would fail, both on the spiritual and the practical levels. Hence, Buber maintained, the Arab question was, above all, an internal Jewish one.[8]

In its view of the political and social realms as the arena in which religion would have to prove itself, the group was close to the "political theology" later current in Protestant Christianity, particularly among the immediate post–Second-World-War generation. In Germany, political theology sought to bridge the gap between religion and politics so characteristic of modern secular society. In its view, the challenge posed for religion by modernity was that of taking responsibility for the political and social reality. But this presented a dilemma: religion must take a stand on political and social issues, but since the authority of theology is metaphysical and thus absolute, there is a danger that such a stand will sanctify politics. Religion may turn into politics and politics into religion.[9] This danger can be seen retrospectively in the political theology of Carl Schmitt, whose thinking provided a kingpin of Nazi ideology.

Buber avoided this danger by developing an undogmatic political theology (*teopolitika* is his term), which he believed was in the prophetic tradition: politics are to be judged by transcendent moral and religious criteria. Such judgment is a religious duty incumbent upon the conscience of each individual and not only upon the Establishment. Each person is responsible directly to God for his political decisions. Buber rejects the apocalyptic perspective of Jewish messianism, of which he sees latter-day incarnations in such secular messianic movements as Marxism. He views all kinds of apocalyptic thinking as an evasion of individual responsibility for the course of history. Redemption is to be concretized in the world by an ongoing process of repair, beginning with an inner transformation of the individual soul.[10]

Because politics is subject to constant change according to the circumstances, there can be no room for a theopolitical doctrine that is fixed for all time. We have no way of knowing which area of concern should come first, and thus we cannot say in advance which path leads to the goal. The process of perfecting the world extends to all areas of human life. In other words, there is no unambiguously messianic political course. But we can prepare the ground for the revelation of the "kingdom of heaven" in every area. Hence the urgent need to assess whether the direction we are taking at any given moment is appropriate for the goal. Buber refuses to believe that we can depend on some future "leap" while, in the meantime, doing the very opposite of what we seek to achieve. He believes we must create today, if possible, a place that can be filled tomorrow by that which we hope for.[11]

It is what Ernst Simon calls "critical messianism," or, using Paul Tillich's formulation, an attempt to mix history's transcendent and immanent dimensions without eliminating the tension between the two.[12] Phenomenologically speaking, this point of view lies somewhere between the traditional religious outlook and the purely secular one. Unlike secular messianisms, which rely on an exaggerated confidence in man's ability to redeem himself, critical messianism takes cognizance of man's limitations and his constant need for repentance and divine aid. But unlike traditional religious messianism, which rejects any active effort to bring about redemption in history, this approach still sees history as the stage on which redemption is to materialize.[13] It thus encourages firm faith and patient hope in the ultimate result without neglecting action in the here and now. Its optimism is hedged by skepticism about any false messianism that proclaims the world redeemed when it is not and about the power of any revolutionary act to root out evil completely.

In Buber's view, the believer may not separate the secular from the religious, for all concrete reality is God's abode. This is particularly true of Judaism, which calls for the application of divine principles to the totality of human life. The main concern of faith is man's moral responsibility before God for his political and social actions. As long as the Jews lived in exile, they could not meet this demand. But with their return to the homeland, they have taken upon themselves the fulfillment of the prophetic vision, so that henceforth they bear responsibility as a religious nation. That is, they may no longer divide life into two realms, one where the distinction between right and wrong has validity, and one where it doesn't.[14]

POLITICS AND MORALITY: THE "LINE OF DEMARCATION"

The question then became how to realize the prophetic, messianic ideal in the given political circumstances of the Jewish people. Buber, in his response, rejected both extreme views, the one making morality subservient to politics, the other subjecting politics to morality. On one hand, he did not agree with the politicians whose sole concern was the good of the state, as they defined it. They were deaf to the claims of morality, not because they did not recognize its legitimacy but because, for them, morality and politics (i.e., the good of the state) were one and the same. On the other hand, Buber disagreed with the moralists, with their abstract notions of right and wrong, by which they judged all situations one way or another without continually asking themselves what could be done in a given situation to prevent harm to the nation. He saw both points of view as deficient: the politicians lacked the suprapolitical perspective that, alone, transcending the petty concerns of the hour, could have guided them toward the nation's true purpose; the moralists lacked any sense of what could and could not be done under the given conditions. The result was that "between these two camps, any chance of doing that degree of right and correct action which reality permits to be done is lost."[15]

Between these two positions, Buber posited a third way that took into account both the good of the state or group and the principles of morality and that sought to implement the latter to the extent possible. The central notion in Buber's political philosophy is that of the "line of demarcation" between the degree of good achievable and the degree of harm unavoidable in a given situation: "It is indeed true that there can be no life without injustice. . . . But the *human* aspect of life begins the moment we say to ourselves: we shall do no more injustice to others than we are forced to do in order to exist. Only by saying that do we begin to be responsible for life. This responsibility is not a matter of principle and is never fixed; the extent of the injustice that cannot be determined beforehand but must be reassessed each time, must be recognized anew in the inner recesses of the mind, whence the lightning of recognition flashes forth. Only he who acknowledges it, as the result of serious examination which leaves no room for pricks of conscience, only he can live a human life; and a nation that does so-its life is that of a humanitarian nation."[16]

The "line of demarcation" is an individual compass indicating the right direction to take in every situation or, as Susser puts it, "the shifting meeting point in an ongoing clash of two total commitments": to absolute morality and to the group for which, as a statesman, one bears responsibility. Because every historical situation is new, one cannot rely on established precedent to set a more distinct boundary between the two conflicting obligations.[17] There can be no a priori position: the line must be redrawn anew in each situation. The critical choice for Buber is not between politics and morality but "how far to go" (*quantum satis*). To what extent, in a given situation, can we serve both God and our group?[18]

Buber admits that

> we are not able to live in perfect justice, and in order to preserve the community of man, we are often compelled to accept wrongs in decisions concerning the community. But what matters is that in every hour of decision we are aware of our responsibility and summon our conscience to weigh exactly how much is necessary to preserve the community and accept just so much and no more; that we do not interpret the demands of a will-to-power as a demand made by life itself; that we do not make a practice of setting aside a certain sphere in which God's command does not hold but regard those actions as against His command, forced on us by the exigencies of the hour as painful sacrifices; that we do not salve, or let others salve, our conscience when we make decisions concerning public life but struggle with destiny in fear and trembling lest it burden us with greater guilt than we are compelled to assume.[19]

What implications did this theory have for the burning issues facing Zionism? How were we to know "how much [was] necessary to preserve the community, . . . just so much and no more"? The answer depended on which goals Zionism saw as vital for the survival of the Jewish people, both in the Diaspora and in the Land of Israel. Hence, even if we were to accept Buber's principle of not doing "more injustice to others than we are forced to do in order to exist," we would still have to do determine what that minimum was.[20]

AUTHENTIC AND FALSE NATIONALISM

Buber sets forth two general criteria for drawing this moral line. The first is faithfulness to Jewish tradition, which he sees as a form of religious humanism. It is this faithfulness, of which he sees evidence in the Bible, that determined the Jewish people's fate in the past and will do so in the future. The decisive factor in this fate is not the commonly recognized laws of history, in which outward political success plays so great a role, but faith in the nation's humane universal mission. The Jewish people cannot deny its true essence, for this is its destiny. Hence Buber maintains again and again that a policy that is immoral is also politically unsound; it cannot succeed, for it contradicts the essence of the Jewish people. In other words, a moral politics is a matter of historical realism and not just of theology.[21] Needless to say, acceptance of this criterion depends on acceptance of Buber's reading of Jewish history and tradition.

The second criterion for Buber is that the way the line of demarcation is drawn is determined by an acknowledgment of the rights of "the other" and the limitations these impose upon us. For Buber, this acknowledgment is not something formal or expedient but the fruit of a dialogical relationship that grasps "the other" as a "thou" as it grasps the self as an "I." It is in this light that we can understand Buber's pronouncement, "the Arab question is a Jewish question." The Jews' understanding of themselves depends on their understanding of their Arab neighbors.

Buber distinguishes between two types of nationalism: that which is "authentic," "true" or "justifiable" as opposed to that which is "false" or "arbitrary." Justifiable nationalism is a kind of remedy: it arouses the people to struggle for what it lacks, but at the same time it recognizes the rights of "the other." This entails a continual redrawing of the line between one nation's rights and the rights of others nations, a line that cannot be fixed once and for all.[22] True nationalism does not view the nation as a supreme principle; it recognizes that, over and above the peoples of the world there is an authority, named or unnamed, to which all owe an accounting.[23] Arbitrary or false nationalism, on the other hand, exceeds the bounds of legitimate need and remedy and becomes itself a dangerous disease. Such nationalism is guilty of hubris, of tragic blindness: it sees nothing but itself and is motivated mainly by a desire for power.

The question of where the one type of nationalism ends and the other begins is everyone's concern, but it must weigh particularly on the nation's leaders. Buber stresses that this is not merely a moral demand but "a matter of life and death for the people." Periodically, the leaders must do a serious stocktaking, for it is upon this that the people's fate depends: shall it recover its strength or decline? Self-criticism is not a sign of weakness but of health. Morality becomes strength, but only to the degree that the nation views itself as a branch of the human family and a bearer of supranational responsibilities, not as an end in itself.

THE NEGATION OF SOVEREIGNTY

For Buber, Jewish sovereignty is not an ideal worthy of aspiration, and, in fact, he has principled reservations about the whole notion of the nation-state. The revitalization of the Jewish nation and the concretization of its tie to its homeland do not depend on the establishment of a sovereign Jewish state. Although in the past the Jews always hoped for renewed independence, this hope did not arise from the desire for power or glory, which motivates the patriotic nationalists of other peoples, but from their longing to realize in their state the ideals of the Prophets. The establishment of an organic Jewish society that fosters human relationships both within and without is far more important than the achievement of Jewish sovereignty per se. In Buber's view, "all sovereignty becomes false and vain when in the struggle for power it fails to remain subject to the Sovereign of the world, who is the Sovereign of my rival and my enemy's Sovereign as well as mine." He fears that making sovereignty a goal, as most Zionists have done, could encourage the narrower sort of nationalism that sees only as far as the visible horizon.[24]

During the period of the debate over partition (1936–37), Buber was utterly opposed to Jewish statehood, claiming that it would damage the spiritual character of the Jewish people. It was such ideas that animated his book *Königtum Gottes* (The Kingdom of Heaven), where he articulates his anarchistic political theology.[25]

Other leading figures in Brit Shalom also saw sovereignty as opposed to the spirit of Judaism. Ernst Simon, for example, thought it was a dangerous notion in that it offered a shoddy European-style remedy for the Jews' national inferiority complex. Simon shared the view of Hermann Cohen that the Prophets were harbingers of exile and the view of Simon Dubnow that in terms of spiritual development the Jewish people had reached a stage where it could maintain its national life without the framework of a state. "Out of motives the gentiles will not grasp, we must be a people without a state, serving as an educational model for both the Arabs and for the rest of the world."[26] The aspiration to statehood, which the Revisionists have demanded be expressed openly, reflects, in his view, an assimilationist tendency; rather, Zionism should proclaim that its aim is not to create a state.[27]

The importance of Jewish tradition for Brit Shalom is evident from the words of Samuel Hugo Bergman: "Our political outlook springs from the worldview of Judaism. We want the Land of Israel to be our country in the sense that the 'prevailing way of life [here]' will bear the impress of the moral and political attitudes of Judaism, that we shall realize here the Torah that has been alive in our hearts these two thousand years, though our opponents see things differently." For him, all the other Zionist factions based their views on the European notion that the state is the possession of one people. Such a notion can be used to justify the mistreatment of national minorities. The universal mission of Zionism is to undo the identification of nation with state. Bergman goes so far as to declare that "the Holy One, blessed be He, showed benevolence toward the people of Israel in making its national home the homeland of two peoples."[28] This accounts for the openness of Buber and his friends to the idea of establishing a binational state in Palestine, one in which sovereignty would be shared by Jews and Arabs. The binational idea was for them not merely the most practical solution to the conflict but an ideal alternative to a national state, an alternative that could immunize the Jewish people against the virus of nationalism.

There are echoes here of the views of Ahad Ha'am and A. D. Gordon, but the political consequences are much farther-reaching. Ahad Ha'am and Gordon never thought the Zionist ideal should be to *avoid* creating a Jewish majority in the Land of Israel. Furthermore, though they recognized the right of the Arabs to the country, they saw the historic right of the Jews as superior. Bergman and Simon, both of them products of German culture, were influenced considerably not only by the teachings of Buber but also by those of the two greatest philosophers produced by German Jewry before the rise of Nazism, Hermann Cohen and Franz Rosenzweig. It is from Cohen that Bergman borrows the idea that the European identification between nation and state should be broken, while in Simon we hear some of the criticism leveled by Rosenzweig against Zionism.[29]

FROM THEORY TO PRACTICE

Buber and the members of Brit Shalom were more sensitive and farsighted than most Zionists concerning the destructive influence prolonged military conflict could have upon the new Jewish society. They were preoccupied, philosophically and morally, with the connection between Zionism's goals and the means it employed to achieve them. In Buber's view, we must first consider the possibility that the means we choose will take us further than we wish to go. We must thus be extremely cautious in choosing the former, examining them again and again. Second, there is a danger that the means we employ will lead us to a different outcome than the one we desire.[30] Means incompatible with the desired ends will in the end subvert them.[31] Hence, the redrawing of the moral line is done "not in order to keep one's soul clean of blood" but in order to achieve our objective.[32] Redemption cannot be achieved through sin committed intentionally for its sake.[33] There is no place for a schematic distinction between earlier and later, between redemption and repentance, as is assumed by those who say we should first build "Zion," whatever means are called for, and then fill it with spiritual and moral content. "If we do not begin here and now, under the circumstances and constraints of this hour, we shall never do it,"[34] for "God will refuse to accept a sanctuary from the hands of Satan."[35]

The basic political assumption of the religious humanists was that Zionism could not be brought to fruition without first obtaining the consent of the Arabs.[36] Since the Arabs view the Zionist aspiration to sovereignty over the Land of Israel as an absolute wrong, the Zionist movement must recognize the equal rights of both peoples over the country, foregoing its claim to the greater part and establishing a binational state on the basis of complete political equality. According to Magnes, it is out of faith that the Jews must make their "great plunge," showing generosity to their neighbors and offering them a peace based on mutual trust.[37] While this trust must be mutual, the initiative must come from the Zionist side, not merely because the land is already inhabited by the Arabs, but because the Jews' mission obliges them to do so. For the same reason, the Jews and the Arabs cannot have a common moral yardstick; more is demanded of the Jews than of the Arabs.[38]

Magnes was not troubled by the question of whether it was always possible to adhere to moral principles in the process of settling a land whose inhabitants were hostile, a question that troubled quite a few people, among them Arthur Ruppin, one of the founders of Brit Shalom in 1925, who resigned from the group after the Arab attacks on the Jewish community four years later.[39] To the argument that Zionist aims could not realistically be attained by peaceful means in view of Arab opposition, Magnes had a ready reply: we would do better to wait until such time as it can be done. "If we cannot find ways of peace and understanding, if the only way of establishing the Jewish National Home is on the bayonets of some empire, our whole enterprise is not worthwhile, and it is better that the Eternal People, which has outlived many a mighty empire, should possess its soul in patience and plan and wait."[40]

Be patient! — thus did Magnes advise the Zionists four years before the rise of the Nazis to power in Germany. Neither he nor Buber was sufficiently sensitive to the steadily worsening situation of the Jews in Eastern Europe or to the tragic necessity that Zionism found itself confronting. Until the day he died, Buber rejected the notion of the Arab-Israeli conflict as a "tragedy," an unavoidable collision between two rights, just as he rejected the slogan *ein breira* ("we have no choice"), which began to be heard in the Yishuv in the late thirties.[41] For him, these two approaches served to evade a search for alternatives that could provide a true solution to the conflict. How were the Zionists supposed to act in the face of the Arabs' consistent opposition to the settlement of Holocaust refugees in Palestine? Should the former have renounced this objective only because the Arabs saw it as wrong, or should it have been forced upon the Arabs, as Magnes, too, was willing to assert after the war?[42] And if the latter, who should be the one to do this — the British, who were ruling the country, or the Jews?

Buber and Magnes were not true pacifists. In a 1939 letter to Gandhi, who had attacked Zionism for espousing violence, Buber came to the movement's defense, declaring, "I cannot help withstanding evil when I see that it is about to destroy the good. I am forced to withstand the evil in the world just as the evil within myself. I can only strive not to have to do so by force. I do not want force. But if there is no other way of preventing the evil destroying the good, I trust I shall use force and give myself up into God's hands."[43]

At the same time, both Buber and Magnes condemned any military action that was not strictly in self-defense. During the Arab Revolt (1936–39), they were opposed in principle not only to the Irgun's acts of blind retaliation, which were condemned by the governing bodies of the Yishuv as well as the Hagana; they also opposed any military initiative meant to thwart Arab attacks, maintaining that this was foreign to the spirit of Judaism. As to how one should act when the situation is not one of true self-defense, the reply is, "In this case, a person who seeks truth and justice must restrain himself." Buber and his circle preferred the Jews to be the victims. This would allow them to appeal to the conscience of the world or to the British police and demand protection — anything, as long as they are not compelled to exert military force that would sabotage all possibility of an agreement with the Arabs.[44]

Most of the Zionist leaders were unwilling to accept such martyrlike thinking, which smacked of the exilic mentality. They also rejected all the group's operative suggestions, not because these were impractical or because they themselves were oblivious to the moral problems entailed in realizing Zionist aims, but because they had a different view of the vital needs of the Jewish people. As they saw it, the focus on moral issues by Buber, Magnes, and others kept them from being sufficiently attuned to these needs. The latter were farsighted in regard to what Zionism could ultimately expect from a prolonged conflict with the Arabs, but they had no practical answer for the present, as even their proposals were not acceptable to the Arabs. They were unable to recommend a rational policy that would treat both Arab and Jewish national aspirations fairly. Even their most moderate programs drew no positive response from the Arab side. Like many who shared their liberal, humanistic outlook, they refused to recognize that there were human problems that could not be solved by peaceful means but only by force.[45] At the same time, the challenge these thinkers posed to Zionism pushed its leaders into a deeper moral stock-taking than they might otherwise have been ready to undertake. Buber saw clearly the dangers awaiting the Zionist undertaking, but these dangers did not deter him.[46] Despite all the disappointments he experienced in his life, he remained faithful to the Zionist undertaking when intellectuals like Hans Kohn and Hannah Arendt, whose political views were close to his, abandoned it as immoral.

The Ideal of Sovereignty and Jewish Militarism

VLADIMIR JABOTINSKY: THE MONISM OF THE GOAL

The views of Jabotinsky (1880–1940) and his supporters on the Israeli right are the polar opposite of Buber's. Buber saw Zionism primarily as a movement of spiritual revival that would have to be sensitive to the means it chose to achieve its objectives, for the means would affect the ends in a decisive way. Jabotinsky, in contrast, saw Zionism first and foremost as a political movement for the renewal of Jewish sovereignty in the historic territory of the Land of Israel, a goal that in his view justified the use of all necessary means.

Jabotinsky was a consistent, loyal devotee of Herzl's political Zionism. To use Ahad Ha'am's familiar dichotomy, his Zionism drew its strength primarily from "the problem of the Jews" rather than "the problem of Judaism." In his view, the Diaspora Jews lacked, above all, a sovereign political framework that could secure their position and restore their dignity. Like Herzl, Jabotinsky was far from traditional Jewish culture, the symbols of which were almost totally foreign to him, and, like Herzl, he sensed in an almost prophetic manner the approaching European-Jewish catastrophe. He saw Zionism mainly as an emergency rescue effort in a situation requiring a bold response. Because it was an emergency, a matter of saving lives, the accomplishment of all other Zionist goals, be they social or cultural, would have to wait. Thus although he was an extreme individualist, a liberal, and a democrat, he maintained that all these values would have to be put on the back burner until the primary objective of Zionism was achieved. He would say, "It is absurd to hold two ideals, just as it is absurd [to worship] two gods. A wholesome soul can only be monistic."[47] Only once the Jews achieve sovereignty can they nurture spiritual or social ideals to their heart's content. This monistic outlook underlay the bitter dispute between him and his rivals.

Long before most other Zionist leaders, Jabotinsky understood the Arabs' opposition to Zionism. He did not believe an agreement between Jews and Arabs was possible, and he opposed any appeasement or concession until such time as the Jews could establish an "iron wall," a military force that would protect them and persuade the Arabs that their ambition of blocking Jewish settlement in Palestine was futile.[48] Some who had come in the Second Aliya had reached this conclusion before him, but he was no doubt the first to make it the cornerstone of a political philosophy.

Jabotinsky's sharp perception of the seriousness of the clash between Jews and Arabs did not keep him from respecting Arab nationalism.[49] But he stood fast in his belief that historic justice was on the side of the Jews and they alone were entitled to sovereignty over the Land of Israel. The Arabs deserved the rights of a national minority, and the Jews would grant them such rights, but only once there was a Jewish majority, achieved by decisive military strength. He firmly rejected the claim that there was anything immoral about this approach; quite the contrary: "It must be one or the other: Zionism is either moral or immoral. We should have answered this question for ourselves, in the affirmative, before accepting the first shekel.[50] And if Zionism is moral, that is, justified, justice must be won without taking into account whether anyone gives consent or fails to do so. And if A, B, or C want to interfere by force in the attainment of justice because it is inconvenient for them, they must be prevented from doing so, again by force. This is [the moral course]; there is no other."[51]

Jabotinsky was of the opinion that granting a homeland to a homeless people was a matter of justice, particularly since the Arabs did not lack for land outside the Land of Israel in which to achieve political sovereignty of their own. And since Zionism's goal was justifiable, the use of violent means to achieve it was justifiable too. Hence the creation of a Jewish military force was, for him, a condition for the realization of Zionism, for the creation of a Jewish majority in the land.

This point of view became more sharply delineated as Jabotinsky grew more fearful for the fate of the Jews of Europe in the face of growing antisemitism and the rapid rise of the Arab nationalist movement in the late twenties and early thirties. He believed masses of Jews could be brought to the Land of Israel all at once, thereby achieving two objectives: relieving the plight of European Jewry and creating a Jewish majority in Palestine. Whether such an outlook was realistic in light of the objective circumstances of the time is still being debated. In any event, we see here an additional thread, clearly messianic, that connects Jabotinsky's thinking with Herzl's: the belief that the problem of the European Jews could be solved and a strong foundation for Zionism in Palestine laid by a bold act that would sweep the Jewish masses away and harness them to a collective effort that would change the situation overnight. From this derives one of the main motives behind Jabotinsky's demand that the "final objective" of Zionism, the establishment of a state based on a Jewish majority, should be openly proclaimed, for only by presenting such a grand vision could the masses be fired up and the resources found to settle the land.[52] The path of "one step at a time" espoused by the Zionist leadership and the labor movement seemed to him a dangerous one, not only because it abandoned the Jews to their fate but also because it detracted from the passion and enthusiasm of the masses.

Jabotinsky is rightly considered the father of modern Jewish militarism. The latter derived from his monistic view of the way Zionist ends were to be achieved. Regarding the renewal of sovereignty as the highest and most urgent goal and the setting up of a military force as a basic condition for attaining it, he saw a need to change the Jews' traditional attitudes toward political and military power. This, in turn, meant developing a sense of national honor that they completely lacked.

National honor expresses itself along two main parameters: dignified demeanor (*hadar*) and the exercise of power. As early as 1904, in an obituary of Herzl, Jabotinsky sketches a portrait of the "true Hebrew," contrasting the latter with the "ghetto Jew," which he refers to by the antisemitic Russian epithet *zhid*. He justifies this usage as follows: a nation living a healthy life on its own soil and shaping its own fate does not lack for ideal types that embody the national image in all its purity. But the Diaspora Jews, whose fate depends on others, have not had such ideal types since the days of Bar Kokhba. The common archetype of this nation, the *zhid,* is, in fact, the result of emasculation and distortion, for it did not develop freely but under external oppression. As a result, when we dream about the true Hebrew and try to imagine what he is like, we have no extant models to draw upon. There is no alternative, then, but to work backwards, taking the negative stereotype as our point of departure and constructing from it the exact opposite. "Let us strip this image completely of all the attributes typical of the *zhid* and fill it brim-full with the qualities it so characteristically lacks. Since the *zhid* is ugly and sickly and without outward charm, let us give the ideal image of the Hebrew manly beauty, stature, broad shoulders, grace of movement, and brilliantly colored [garb]. The *zhid* is fearful and downtrodden, so the other must be proud and independent. The *zhid* is roundly despised, so the other must be charming. The *zhid* [is] used to submission, so the other must know how to command. The *zhid* loves to hide, holding his breath, from the eyes of strangers, so the other must have the boldness and confidence to face the entire world, to look everyone straight in the eye and wave his flag before him, [proclaiming], 'I am a Hebrew!' "[53]

I know of no other passage in Zionist literature that expresses so clearly the contrast between the negative stereotype of the exilic Jew and the manly, heroic image of the new Hebrew. The psychological paradox inherent in the latter is that of the double negation: because no concrete, positive model of the pure Hebrew is currently available, one must turn to the image employed by antisemites and negate it in order to fashion a positive alternative. This means one must agree a priori with the antisemitic critique of the Jew. Like Herzl, Jabotinsky, with his romantic, lyrical sensibility, captured the charm the knightly ideal held for the modern Jew. I have mentioned Huizinga's observation about the importance of this ideal in the development of modern patriotism. "The conception of chivalry as a sublime form of secular life," the historian writes, "might be defined as an esthetic ideal assuming the appearance of an ethical ideal. . . . For the source of the chivalrous idea is pride aspiring to beauty, and formalized pride gives rise to a conception of honor, which is the pole of noble life. . . . The feudal knight is merging into the soldier of modern times; the universal and religious ideal is becoming national and military."[54] These observations apply to Jabotinsky's ambitions remarkably well, for he was well acquainted with other movements of national liberation and sensed in them something the Jews lacked that was essential for their revival.

It should thus not be surprising if, for Jabotinsky, it was the Hebrew soldier, the antithesis of the ghetto Jew, and not the farmer tilling the soil of the Land of Israel who epitomized the national rebirth. All the qualities Jabotinsky extolled in the model he thought worthy of emulation came together in the figure of the Hebrew soldier. He was the first writer in all of Jewish history to stress the positive side of military life. In the Talmudic tradition, as I have shown, the militaristic ethos was transformed, its values sublimated, so that religious observance came to be thought of as a kind of military service and the struggle against the evil within man as a kind of war. Jabotinsky sought a reverse transformation, at least as an educational objective for his own generation. Hence, of all the biblical heroes, he chose Samson as the central character of his novel and as an object of identification. Although he acknowledged that the term militarism had bad connotations and that war itself was something ugly, he saw military life as excelling in such Spartan virtues as simplicity, equality, self-discipline, cooperation, and, of course, dignified demeanor (*hadar*). Since the Jews lacked these important attributes, and there could be no national revival without them, he regarded imparting them to the younger generation as the greatest educational challenge and for this purpose established Beitar, the Revisionist youth movement. The latter was the only Zionist youth movement run in quasi-military fashion, as Jabotinsky himself pointed out in his article "The Idea of Beitar."[55] He thought the most important educational goal was to prepare young people for war. This way of thinking was based on his apocalyptic politics or perhaps on his intimate acquaintance with the psychological needs of the Eastern European Jewish masses in the interwar period. Knowing that "hatred of warfare is the spiritual legacy of our people," he saw a need for psychological transformation through military training.[56]

In his article "At the Fireplace," written in 1936, the year the Arab Revolt broke out in Palestine, Jabotinsky tried to alert Polish-Jewish youth to the importance of military preparedness and to forge a new mentality befitting a people that felt increasingly alone in the face of threats of violence. The Jews, he warned, could rely only on themselves and only on force, which would be their sole consolation. In the following decade, this impulse would grow stronger and more widespread. For Jabotinsky, the task of the present generation was simple: "Young people, learn to shoot!" Sad as it might be that Jews had to learn this, there was no arguing with necessity. "It is clear to all that, of all the conditions that will make it possible for us to achieve statehood, knowing how to shoot is unfortunately the most important." Precisely because the Jewish people had so long been taught to hate war, its highest duty now was to acquire a martial mentality, a "longing to shoot." Jabotinsky not only raised militarism to the level of a supreme imperative for the Jewish nation, but he heaped contempt on the other achievements and aspirations of the Zionist movement.[57] This way of thinking was certainly alien to most of the Zionist leadership. Unlike Jabotinsky, who had grown up in an assimilated environment and been captivated by the romantic fervor and liberal spirit of nineteenth-century nationalism, they came from the Jewish Pale of Settlement, where government and army symbolized oppression and were viewed with suspicion.[58] As Katznelson saw it, Revisionism in general, and Jabotinsky in particular, had no need for Jewish cultural continuity. The latter wanted something noble, of ancient Jewish stock, that could connect Zionism with the lineage of Joshua and Bar-Kokhba. But as for the rest of Jewish history and the enduring human type associated with it — for these he had no use. He even tried, on a theoretical level, to dismiss them. Katznelson claimed that this was the source of Jabotinsky's hatred toward the labor movement: the later, historically speaking, was, after all, continuous with Jewish history; its cultural world did not remain what it was at the time of the Second Temple but had absorbed elements of the Jewish exile. It was this history that had given rise to the contemporary socialist ideal type.[59]

Jabotinsky's monism enraged his Labor rivals not only because they had a different concept of power, but because they instinctively sensed great danger in his elevation of sovereignty to an absolute, opening the way to a glorification of military force. Nonetheless, they could not deny the element of truth in his insistence that the Jews would have to change their traditional self-image if they were to re-establish their sovereignty over the land.

Jabotinsky's Zionism represents an attempt to "force the End." He sees redemption as the result of a great political effort on the part of the Jewish people to liberate itself from exile by focusing its energies on one thing, at least for a certain period of time. But this way of thinking could easily lead to the conclusion that it was only by military force that Zionism would prepare the ground for the redemption.

A high-minded, avowed liberal, Jabotinsky never completely lost respect for the Arab adversary. We see this in his willingness to give the Palestinian Arabs the status of a national minority with full civil rights. Some of his followers drew more extreme conclusions from his consistently monistic worldview. When power becomes a supreme imperative to which all other values and aspirations are subject, they maintained, certain conditions might favor the unlimited use of force. The emergency that confronted the Jews in the 1930s and 1940s could well be seen as such a condition. Despite the essential differences, both ideological and tactical, between Jabotinsky and his followers, the latter's extreme conclusions did flow logically from his basic assumptions.

THE VISION OF THE DAVIDIC KINGDOM IN
THE POETRY OF URI TZVI GREENBERG

Historical and quasi-mythical symbols played a vital role in the poetry and code of behavior of the Second and Third Aliyot. They drew upon tradition in a largely emotional fashion, looking not for practical political guidance, but for the justification and inspiration needed to mobilize themselves for *hagshama*. In the poetry of Uri Tzvi Greenberg, which served as a major source of inspiration for the extreme Zionist right, mythical symbols helped establish the basis for a radical nationalist vision, that of the re-establishment of the ancient kingdom of Israel in its biblical boundaries. This vision was espoused by a small but important faction, especially once it was translated into an assertive political ideology with a strong attraction for young Jews, both in Palestine and in the Diaspora.

The ideology of the radical right — which developed as a result of disappointment with the slow progress of the Zionist undertaking, the deepening plight of Diaspora Jewry, and a crisis of values that followed the First World War — was largely free of moral misgivings regarding the Arabs or the use of force. For Greenberg, the Arab-Jewish conflict was just another instance of the eternal conflict between Jews and gentiles, in which there was only room for hatred and an uncompromising struggle for power. Unlike Jabotinsky, who saw the conflict as rooted in a clash between outside settlers and the native population, Greenberg and his circle believed the Jews had prior claim to the land and it was the Arabs who were interlopers trying to take it over.[60] Jabotinsky respected the Arabs and believed cooperation with them was possible once they reconciled themselves to Jewish settlement. The radical right took an extreme isolationist stance, scorned the Arabs, and thought what was going on was a clash between two cultures between which no compromise was possible. They thus viewed relations with the Arabs entirely in terms of a struggle for power.

> And I say a land is conquered by blood
> And only conquered by blood, consecrated to the people
> With the sanctity of blood . . . and it is blood that will decide who rules
>   here.[61]

Unlike Ahad Ha'am and Buber, who believed the Jews had survived in exile only because of their prophetic, humanitarian ideals, Greenberg maintains that it was the longing for dominion (*malkhut*) that kept them alive. For him, Zionism offers no solution to the problem of antisemitism, as it claims to do, because the conflict between the Jews and the gentiles is eternal and can be decided only by the sword. Zionism is an awakening of "Jewish blood" and "the Jewish race" in order to realize the ancient vision of re-establishing the Davidic monarchy in all its glory. Greenberg's messiah is thus a warlike one in the full sense of the word, and the sign of his coming is the blood flooding the earth. This messiah has been summoned to avenge the humiliation of all past generations of Jews at the hands of the gentiles:

> Twice the blood for blood!
> Manifold disgrace for spit.[62]

No poet has expressed more powerfully than Greenberg the humiliation felt by the Jewish people in exile: "The spit of the gentiles, which clung to the Jews' clothing and faces, polluted the . . . exiles' blood. The Jew's humiliation became a congenital trait, passed down from generation to generation."[63] The common image of the Diaspora Jews as "sheep" aroused in him a deep contempt: "My fathers' pronouncement disgusts me: We are like sheep."[64] The idealization of this image (the "lamb") only proved to him how terribly distorted the figure of Jewish man had become as a result of prolonged humiliation. The Jewish people must choose between a kingdom and disgrace: "We are sentenced to rulership, power, . . . or a hell of ignominy."[65] "Rulership" and "dominion" are key terms in his poetry, synonyms for sovereignty, and in Hebrew they reverberate with past glory. What the Jewish people most lack is a "lordly character."[66] Like Jabotinsky, Greenberg believes that lordliness is achieved primarily on the field of battle: "A people is only partly born to rule; it gains respect on the field of battle, growing [in stature] from the blood [shed there]."[67] There is thus a need for radical "psychotherapy" to purge the Jewish mind of the poison with which it has been contaminated. "The blood of all the ancient conquerors and avengers" must course joyfully through the Jews' veins.[68] Military struggle is the only way for them to overcome the heritage of exile and acquire this new identity.[69] The cruelty of the deeds they must commit in order to redeem themselves is in proportion to the indignity and fear they have suffered in the lands of their dispersion.

Greenberg's poetry bears witness to a revival of the Jewish myth, a powerful surfacing of archetypes that had lain dormant in the Jewish unconscious for many generations. On one hand, there is something about this recrudescence that is quite alien to Jewish tradition, at least since Talmudic times, a tradition that worked long and hard to rein in these archetypes with legal norms. On the other hand, their reappearance touched something deep in the Jewish soul, which in its oppression has longed for the return of past greatness so as to be able to exact retribution of its oppressors.

This poetry was a powerful inspiration to a small but influential group on the radical right wing of the Zionist movement during the 1930s and 1940s, a group that was one of the main components of the Lehi (Fighters for the Freedom of Israel) underground (1939–49). Greenberg gave poetic expression to ideas that then continued for decades to ferment under the surface until, after the Six-Day War, they burst forth in the form of two maximalist messianic movements, one secular, the other religious: the Whole Land of Israel Movement and Gush Emunim (the Bloc of the Faithful). His ideas had an outstanding interpreter, too, in Yisrael Eldad, who drew them together into a coherent body of thought and gave them some philosophical depth. There is thus good reason to examine Eldad's work here, even though most of it has only been published since independence.

ELDAD'S LADDER

Yisrael Eldad (Scheib) immigrated to Palestine from Poland in 1941 and immediately attained a prominent position in the intellectual leadership of Lehi, which he held until its dissolution shortly after independence. In 1949, he founded the journal *Sulam* (Ladder), which appeared until the mid-sixties and provided a mouthpiece for his ideas. In the years that followed, his views continued to echo in the very heart of religious Zionism, in Gush Emunim, and for this reason it is important to understand his way of thinking. His erudition and polished, often sarcastic, polemically effective writing style made Eldad the most brilliant intellectual on the Israeli right since Jabotinsky. His command of Hebrew and the Jewish sacred literature gave his writing a modern-day homiletical character. He makes extensive use of word plays, literary allusions, and marvelously free exegesis of the traditional sources.

Eldad was influenced not only by Greenberg but also by Berdyczewski and Nietzsche. He superimposed the latter's notion of the "superman" on Berdyczewski's idea of the ancient Hebrew myth, and Greenberg's concept of "dominion" (*malkhut*) provides the mucilage to hold them together. Political consolidation of the people in its own homeland is a precondition for fulfilling its spiritual mission. A worldly dominion is a precondition for a spiritual one, which it potentially includes. From this derives the moral justification for taking the path of war when returning to the land.[70]

Eldad finds the essence of his own Zionism in Greenberg's use of the idea of monarchy. For him, Zionism did not grow out of antisemitism, nor does it merely seek a "safe refuge for the Jewish people." Rather, it springs from the Jews' ancient messianic longing and their sovereign will to be a free people in their own homeland. He negates the notion of the state as alien to the Jewish spirit and overly materialistic in its concern, so characteristic of modern liberalism, for individual rights and security. Eldad admits that Jabotinsky's idea of the state was necessary in its time as a reaction or antithesis to both Diaspora life and the spiritual Zionism of Ahad Ha'am. But Zionism's true aim is the establishment of a Third Commonwealth for the Hebrew race. Eldad continues Jabotinsky's monism but takes it to an extreme. In his view, Jabotinsky was wrong in clinging to liberalism and Western democracy as ideals and not as means. This is the source of Eldad's attitude toward democracy: Zionism is a movement for the redemption of the Jewish people from exile, and until this objective is attained we must reject democracy as an ideal.[71] In any event, we must regard it only as a means to achieve Zionist aims. Eldad thus clearly advocates a totalitarian, revolutionary regime that subordinates all politics to the realization of the idea of dominion.[72] He does not see the Zionist revolution as bound in any way: "The sanctity of the goal knows no criterion except that of effectiveness in reaching [it]."[73] Zionism needs no justification for the means it uses to redeem the people.[74] It is almost superfluous to spell this out: it is a concretization of political messianism, nourished both by a sense of impending catastrophe and by a sense of destiny, of historical necessity, the alternative to which is destruction.[75] According to Halakha, the saving of life supersedes all the Torah's other commandments. "Our highest moral imperative is that of [staying] alive. The commandments and morality and justice were given to us so that we might live long upon the land, and there is nothing higher."[76] But the fulfillment of the messianic dream requires "establishing supreme national dominance with an eye to the supreme goal of [establishing] the kingdom of Israel."[77]

Viewing Zionism as a redemptive process in two senses — the rescue of people and land and the realization of the vision of the kingdom — led Eldad to the conclusion that there was no army holier than that of the Jewish people. Its achievements, its strength, and its dedication derived from a sacred decision: Jews would never again go like sheep to the slaughter, never again live on the sufferance of the gentiles. Hence, anyone who dares speak out against Israeli militarism is desecrating something both precious and holy. The army's holy purpose justifies in advance any means it might employ to conquer the land. Eldad finds support for his views in the well-known archaeologist William Foxwell Albright, who, according to Eldad, defended the Torah's commandment of annihilation of the Canaanites.[78] He sees the latter as analogous to the contemporary Palestinians.

In Eldad's view, *teshuva* — meaning either physical return or repentance — is not a condition for redemption but rather follows it. Redemption is not tied to any other ideal. Even the return to the Torah and to faith is not a necessary condition but only something that can hasten redemption.[79] As we have pointed out, Buber was firmly opposed to any distinction between earlier and later stages in the process of redemption, a distinction that could be used to justify invalid interim means in the name of a sacred ultimate goal. Eldad took the opposite position, basing himself on the historical dialectic of which he was so fond and which he claimed was not invented by Marx but found in the Bible and Talmud, exemplified in the story of Jacob's dream.[80] In this dialectic, redemption takes place in a series of stages, each justified as necessary to reach the final objective. This is the meaning of the symbol of the ladder, chosen by Eldad as the name of the journal he published and edited following independence: the first task is to set the ladder firmly on the ground so that we can climb it to heaven. In 1990 Eldad summed up his views as follows: "I want the whole Land of Israel and the whole people of Israel in the Land of Israel. This is my ultimate political ideal, beyond secondary ideas such as problems of government in the State of Israel, democracy, or equal rights for Arabs. . . . In life, one cannot live by all values at once. . . . There is thus a ladder [scale] of values, of importance, and also of times. . . . There are times when heaven takes precedence and times when earth does. . . . The supreme value in my life is the redemption of the Jewish people. . . . When we reach the situation of the United States and France, without enemies and without our very existence being questioned, we can behave like them. . . . But we are still a state in the making."[81]

The distinction between different times is clearly drawn, as is its philosophical justification: "one cannot live by all values at once." There is no room here for balance or compromise between conflicting values, in which there can be at least partial if not full realization of them. Eldad's scale of priorities thus allows us to act without regard to the moral standards accepted among well-established peoples not exposed to the kind of dangers we are. What is more, "we are still a state in the making," so this is clearly not a vision for the near term but for the distant future.

Eldad was undoubtedly influenced by Rav Kook's dialectical thinking about the relation between sacred and profane, but he went further. While Kook accorded a certain legitimacy to secular Zionism as a necessary step on the way to full redemption, he never legitimated a departure from the moral norms of Halakha. What is more, he saw Jewish morality as having universal human significance and therefore stressed the obligation of *ahavat habriot*, loving all our fellow human beings without exception. Not so Eldad. He preached a blatantly nationalistic morality, the only justification for which was that it would ultimately lead to the highest stage of the ladder "set on the ground, with its top in heaven." What is meant by "heaven"? We are left entirely in the dark.

YONATAN RATOSH: THE JEWISH ETHOS AND
THE DESTRUCTION OF THE THIRD TEMPLE

The views of the poet Yonatan Ratosh, too, were espoused a small group of intellectuals, but they expressed the nativist, somewhat "Canaanite" mentality of the preindependence, Palestinian-born generation. (Ratosh himself had been born in Warsaw in 1909 and immigrated to Palestine with his family as a child). As many have stressed, Ratosh's ideology represents the most extreme of the possibilities hinted at in the revolutionary writings of Berdyczewski. It sets up an unbridgeable antithesis between Judaism and the quest for independence and power. Ratosh was deeply influenced by the writings of Uri Tzvi Greenberg and quite close to his view that the Jews would have to undergo a radical psychological change to be able to achieve sovereignty, which could only be done by the sword. Nevertheless, we have here two contrasting readings of Jewish history and especially of the relation of Judaism to power. For Greenberg, only the mythical-historical memory can provide a basis for renewing the Jews' fighting spirit, which Zionism had neglected out of "forgetfulness." For Ratosh, as long as the Jews draw sustenance from their exilic religious tradition, there is no chance of their fighting for their homeland. In other words, for Greenberg the metamorphosis requires a return to the foundational myth of Judaism, whereas for Ratosh it requires a return to an even earlier pagan-Hebrew myth.

The most extreme expression of Ratosh's views is found in his "Opening Address," written in 1943 (namely, when the destruction of the European Jews reached is climax!) as a proposal for discussion by the chapter delegates' committee of the Young Hebrews movement.[82] Ratosh maintains that the Jews have no need for a flag or an independent state. That is for the gentiles. "Hebrew power, in all its purity," is "a power essentially opposed to Judaism" so that "it has no place in the shadow of Judaism."[83] Judaism can undergo martyrdom, but it can never fight wholeheartedly for its homeland. This is proven by "Jeremiah the traitor" and Yohanan ben-Zakkai, the most hallowed and glorious figures in all Jewish history. Ratosh is not enthused over the fighters of Massada or the ghetto uprisings. For him, as for Yudke in Hazaz's story "The Sermon," this is not true heroism because it springs from despair and the lack of any alternative. There is nothing exceptional about the Jewish ability to survive; it is the life force of a spineless worm "that does not feel anything, and is not harmed, [even] when part of its body is cut off." In short, no Jewish liberation movement fighting for statehood and freedom can grow out of "the demanding, alien, treacherous soil of Judaism."[84] Ratosh was convinced that the Zionist ethos if connected umbilically to Jewish tradition would lead eventually to a third destruction of the country. He cast his ideas in poetic form in his great work "Those Who Walk in Darkness," which he began in 1939–40 and completed in 1966. Here he envisions the consolidation of the Hebrew people through a double war, both internal and external, the war of the native-born against the soft, self-abasing, exilic ethos of the immigrants, followed by a war against the foreign conqueror. The war for the conquest of the land in its entirety, from the Nile to the Euphrates, is the principal factor that will draw together the new people to be born on the soil of ancient Canaan.

> I call upon the Hebrews,
> Upon every bold son of the ancients . . .
> Root all that is alien from your heart,
> Until this battered people,
> Pathetic, abased,
> Is of one heart . . .
> Vomit out this poison
> Sucked with mother's milk
> And all old men's foreign wisdom.[85]

The alien poison is an allusion to inherited residues of Jewishness that prevent the "Hebrews" from coming together as one people and must therefore be completely purged. Ratosh was right in foreseeing that war would eventually be a decisive factor in shaping the identity of the "Hebrews" in their homeland but wrong about the nature of that identity: the Jewish residues continue to leave upon it an indelible stamp.

Neither Wolf nor Sheep: The Labor Approach

THE PLURALISTIC CONCEPT OF FORCE

Both Brit Shalom and right-wing Zionist circles had consistent views on the question of sovereignty and the use of force. This was not true of the labor movement. Anita Shapira has dwelt on the affinity of Zionist thinking to political messianism — for example, the belief in an immediate, comprehensive solution to the Jewish problem, a fierce rejection of all alternatives, and a view of the vanguard as having a historic mission.[86] In Shapira's opinion, Labor's eschewing of extreme violence was pragmatic, a result of the need to accommodate reality in a movement whose practical weakness was readily apparent.[87] Yosef Gorny, in contrast, maintains that it was the most fundamental ideas of the movement that from the outset prevented it from developing into a messianic one. I tend to agree with Gorny. Despite messianic tendencies, which were quite pronounced in the early 1920s, the labor movement did not develop in this direction, and its attitude toward the use of force is the clearest evidence of this.

Labor's activism did tap the Jewish messianic impulse, but when it came to practical realization the movement remained within the limits of ordinary history, guided by a strategy of "calculated risk," as Gershom Scholem put it.[88] Gorny rightly stresses the importance of the utopian dimension of Labor thinking. Contrary to the apocalyptic idea of the "last battle" found in the Marxian approach to history, utopianism aims from the very outset at creating a life of wholeness and harmony in the present, not in the dim future; this accounts for its avoidance of extreme revolutionary activity, class warfare, and the unrestrained use of force.[89] The concept of Zionism as a revolution embracing all human spheres, here and now rather than in some unknown, distant future, led to the conclusion that no one value could supersede all others. The freedom of the individual, his creativity, and social solidarity based on relative equality and a lack of rigid hierarchy are the values that must be taken into account in the process of *hagshama* (realization).

In fact, in its social thought, Labor Zionism tried to harmonize individualism and group belonging, personal freedom and concern for the common good. This line of thinking, which represented a kind of continuation of the halakhic tradition, is opposed to the idea, characteristic of political messianism, of sacrificing the individual to the collective. The individual is a value unto himself, not merely a means to achieving collective goals. Consequently, *hagshama* must be seen as a gradual, evolutionary process. What is more, there is objective value in realization here and now, even if it is not subordinated to an external goal. Response to an inner imperative, closely tied to the collective, already has the redemptive meaning of self-improvement. Thus, as Brenner taught his contemporaries, we must make the effort, even if we are not privileged to attain complete redemption; the effort in and of itself entails a kind of individual redemption. This way of thinking is also evident in A. D. Gordon, who was strongly opposed to the idea that the individual coming to the Land of Israel must sacrifice himself for the common good. To be sure, he must make his contribution, but he should view it as a means of self-realization as well. This, according to Gordon (and Katznelson held a similar view), is the difference between Zionism and other social movements: the latter emphasize change in the political or social framework and entirely neglect individual change, whereas Zionism combines the two. This accounts for its integration of the two time frames, present and future, and two values: that of daily action in and of itself and that of work aimed at the improvement of society, the nation, the world. The collective takes on a certain character as it is being created, and Jewish sovereignty is stitched together hour by hour. One should not think that the end result is more important than the intermediate goals: "We, each of us, and each of our lives, are not a means to a distant 'sacred' end, for the achievement of which we and our lives may become 'profane,' according to the principle that the end justifies the means. We are the goal itself, the first link in a string of . . . goals. The goal or string of goals begins with us and our lives . . . and will not end even when our final goal is achieved, for the day this happens life itself will end. . . . There is nothing beyond the path or outside it."[90]

In stressing that "there is nothing outside the path" and that the ideal or norm must be realized here and now and not in some distant future, labor Zionism was following in the footsteps of traditional Judaism. While the vision of the labor movement was total — the creation of a new man and a new society — it was not totalitarian. It did not subordinate the individual entirely to the collective, nor did it sanctify force or maintain that the end automatically justified the means.

The ambivalence of the labor movement toward the Soviet revolution was characteristic. In spite of the enthusiasm and perhaps even adulation the revolution initially aroused in some of the movement's leaders (notably David Ben-Gurion and Yitzhak Tabenkin), the movement had definite reservations about the means the Soviet Union used to achieve its aims. In the early 1930s, Yosef Aharonovitz prophesied, almost in the spirit of Buber, that the Bolsheviks would fail because they employed the methods of their predecessors. The Hebrew pioneer, on the other hand, "does not sanctify the means for the sake of the end but rather uses those means that already incorporate in themselves a large part of the goal."[91]

The relation between means and ends was understood in the labor movement in a flexible manner: what had been defined as an end under certain circumstances could be considered a means under other circumstances, and vice versa. A sense of urgency and distress led, in certain situations, to preferring one goal to the others, but this was not done in the name of an absolute ideological principle. Thus, for example, the movement developed a readiness to fight the Arabs, should it prove necessary, but at the same time made attempts at compromise and dialogue with them. According to Ben Halpern, Zionism was able to avoid many of the pitfalls confronting national movements — especially the danger of fanaticism and extreme violence — because all through the years, at least up to the establishment of the State of Israel, neither sovereignty nor military power was held up as an absolute value but rather, "like any other national aim, either as end or as means, according to circumstances." Halpern notes the unique situation of Zionism that allowed it greater flexibility in realizing its complex goals: "Zionism could afford to be ideologically reasonable, because it was not bound to the nationalist myth of an autochthonous populace aroused to rebellion against foreign rulers."[92]

The labor movement's evolutionary utopianism thus moderated the tendency to use violence as a means of realizing Zionist goals.[93] It distinguished between the distant objective and short-term ones that served as intermediate way stations. As opposed to absolute long-term goals, short-term ones are relative and require ongoing evaluation. Being transitory and relative, they do not sanctify means, and the considerations relevant to them are free of zealotry and dogmatism. They naturally dictate more restrained and morally responsible policies.[94]

Typical in this respect is the contradiction-laden character of Yosef Trumpeldor, who was, along with Jabotinsky, among the founders of the Teamster Brigade and the Hebrew Brigades in the First World War and became a legend within a short time of his demise at Tel-Hai. In his youth he was a pacifist, a Tolstoyan, an anarchist, and a moral vegetarian. In his military service, he emerged as a war hero who scorned fear and death and saw himself first and foremost as a "Jewish soldier," while in his heart he was not a soldier at all. His great dream was to found a commune of workers who would till the soil with their own hands. He rejected the notion of class struggle and the apocalyptic approach to history, adhering to a constructive socialism that avoided violence and bloodshed. On the surface, there was nothing Jewish about his personality; he had grown up in a cantonist soldier's family that, while holding on to its Jewish identity, saw the Jewish way of life as completely foreign. Shulamit Laskov has pointed out the ambiguity in his encounter with Jewishness. Although he based his own Jewish identity on military values, joining the Russian army out of a sense of mission to restore Jewish honor, he consciously despised things military: "In my opinion," he wrote to Ahad Ha'am in 1916, after serving long years in the army and winning recognition as a hero, "I am not a military man, and I am willing to take up weapons only when I cannot see any other alternative."[95] What is more, at a gathering of Jewish soldiers he had recruited to his brigade for defense against the 1917 antisemitic riots in Russia, he felt the need to justify his militarism in these words: "It is a tragic situation that we are compelled to give bone and sinew to an idea that is alien to the spirit of our people and that can be adapted to our life only with difficulty."[96]

These contradictions reflect the duality that accompanied the labor movement from the outset in confronting its Jewishness: on one hand, socialism and faith in man; on the other, Zionism and militarism. The fact that these elements were in conflict did not negate the psychological or moral value of holding onto both: the tension between them restrained the natural tendency to slip into extremism in time of protracted conflict.

The labor movement's belief in democracy, too, served as a brake on uncontrolled outbursts of violence, even though this belief was not free of ambivalence. There is a difference between the military struggle of a whole community that is democratically based and the struggle of a select minority of zealots organized in a military hierarchy. When a democratic community is fighting for a just cause, every tactical step is taken under strict moral scrutiny. Being exposed to criticism, the leadership must restrain itself. This is not the case with an extremist movement; it owes an accounting to no authority outside itself, and it can perpetrate violence without limit, in the belief that it is fighting for a transcendent cause. The fact that Israeli society has remained democratic throughout a period of violent struggle has created the possibility of a moral debate. This debate has naturally restrained the leadership, which has been forced, within certain limits, to consider opposing views. The inclusive outlook of the labor movement, which integrated the needs of the nation with the needs of the individual, stamped Zionism (dominated by Labor) as a movement combining idealistic aspirations with a political realism that was always ready for compromise.

The labor movement shared Jabotinsky's recognition of the need for military preparedness in the struggle for the country. What divided them was their attitude toward the use of force in the realization of Zionist objectives.[97] Jabotinsky saw military power as a precondition for such realization, whereas the labor movement saw it as only one component of the ethos of pioneering *hagshama*. Labor's understanding of power was not limited to the narrow military context but extended to include social and human resources and potential. Jabotinsky's militaristic ideal entailed a readiness for sacrifice at critical moments on the field of battle but not in everyday life. The pioneering ideal of the labor movement, however, entailed a readiness for everyday sacrifice. It did not confine itself to the political or military realm, but expressed itself in all areas of life.

The pluralistic concept of power called for a mutually reinforcing relationship among all the Zionist ideals. The more incentives one had to tie one's fate to Zionism, the stronger it would be. There was a combination of moral and practical considerations, and Zionisms could achieve its objectives only if it could encompass the whole spectrum of human and Jewish concerns.[98] It would not be the Zionist political vision alone that would impel Jews to immigrate to the Land of Israel but also, combined with it, a utopian social message.

The pluralistic doctrine of power went along with strong reservations about both Jabotinsky's militarism and Brit Shalom's near-pacifism. But this doctrine was also sharpened by an internal debate within the labor movement itself when, in 1917–18, the question of recruitment for the Hebrew Brigades—a volunteer effort to help the British conquer Palestine—arose. This was, in effect, the first time in the history of Zionism that the issue of the legitimacy of the use of military force for political ends and not only for self-defense had arisen. The concept of self-defense was accepted by all Zionists without exception, but the idea that the Jews might recover their homeland by force, as other national movements had done, and not just by peaceful construction was alien to some of the leading figures in the labor movement. They feared this step might endanger the very essence of the Jewish rebirth. But could the Jews remain indifferent in the face of a worldwide struggle over their ancient homeland? And is it any wonder that, for more than a few of them, this struggle aroused messianic hopes? The creation of a Hebrew armed force symbolized for them the elimination and negation of exile and the healing, all at once, of the sickly body and soul of the people.[99] Others viewed this enthusiasm as a sign that a "cult of the fist" was taking over the young Yishuv, evidence of a spiritual collapse. It was a betrayal of Zionism's original mission of creating a "humane people" (*am adam*), in Gordon's phrase, a people that would concretize, in its social and political life, the great humanitarian values of mankind and serve as an example to all nations.[100] The difference between Zionism and other liberation movements lay in the fact that it did not postpone the realization of the ideal to the end of days but aspired to achieve it here and now.[101] Nor could good be expected to grow, in dialectical fashion, out of evil.

The position of the writer Joseph Hayim Brenner, who had deserted the Russian army after three years of service, was typically sober. He had profound contempt for everything military but no illusions about the Jews' need to be ready for protracted struggle, and as early as 1913 he reproved his friend Rabbi Binyamin for the pacifist fantasies he had published in the Hebrew press. Brenner maintained that sentimental idealism not only ignored the deepest human instinct; it was also immoral. Jews and Arabs were bitter enemies, so there was no room for talk of love between them. The Arabs were the majority, the lords of the land, and they knew it. The conclusion to be drawn was that the Jews must be ready to use all means at their disposal to defend their lives.[102]

Brenner was among the first of his generation to come intuitively to the conclusion that Zionism could not achieve its aims without the use of military force. In his article "Labor or Militarism" (1919), he argues with those who oppose enlistment in the Hebrew Brigades as a betrayal of the Zionist (pacifist) ideal:

Indeed, those trying to spread the idea of militarism among our young people, to make a cult out of the negative aspects of this phenomenon — the idleness, the poses, the self-glorification, the vapidity, the cruelty for the sake of cruelty, the stupid discipline with its perverse emotions, and the pursuit of imaginary honor for the sake of honor, all these being the result of the professional militarism of every imperial power — . . . [such people] appear to us both ridiculous and accursed. We have no state, we have no work, and [they] preach militarism to us. . . ?! But on the other hand, one who seeks to forbid . . . the taking up of arms, as an absolute prohibition . . . ; one who sees the creation of a small Hebrew army not only as a caricature . . . but as "a human catastrophe and national disaster" . . . ; one who bears coals to Newcastle, preaching to us the ideal of the "lamb" that offers itself for slaughter out of excess piety, the [doctrine embodied in the verse] "not by power but by the spirit" [Zach 4:6] as a supreme virtue — he, too, is painfully mistaken. Such a person fails to comprehend that there is a viewpoint higher than that of militarism [namely, self-defense] as well as lower [namely, passivity]. And our current non-militarism is nothing exalted but the lowest thing possible. It is not that we have transcended militarism; we have not yet attained it. Our nation has not produced its own defenders; we have [as yet] no talented young men [willing] to devote themselves to the service of the people. Should we be proud of the fact that we have no fist?[103]

Negating both the militaristic and the pacifist positions, Brenner's position is most faithful to the Jewish legal tradition, which never entirely ruled out the use of force but rather sought to restrain it. The "viewpoint higher than that of militarism" is that of one who has military power but does not take pride in it or make a cult of it, but rather uses it only when absolutely necessary. The viewpoint lower than the militaristic one is that of one who has no power but who prides himself on the purity of his morals. Only a people that has an army can be "above militarism." Brenner therefore condemns the moral condescension of the Jews toward other peoples, with their claim to be cleaner and purer because they have no "fist." He sees such condescension as ridiculous: one who is in no position to sin cannot pride himself in his innocence.[104] Brenner here exemplifies in its essence the position on the consolidation of a military force taken later, in the 1920s and 1930s, by many in the labor movement. Such consolidation was understood to be a high moral imperative, not unconnected with the other moral and social ideals of the movement.

To be sure, there were in the labor movement figures like Yitzhak Tabenkin who were quite close in their thinking to the militarism of the right.[105] But they were the minority. The struggle between radical militarism and more moderate activism was part of the history of the labor movement from the very beginning. The tension between the two opposed tendencies forced the movement, usually inclined toward moderation rather than extremism, to seek a compromise between them.[106]

The movement's recognition of the importance of military power for realizing its goals went together with a keen awareness of the dangers of using such power. This tension between moral principles and a realistic sense of necessity explains why this movement, more than any other Zionist faction, has been afflicted with misgivings over the use of force. One of the main questions troubling those who shaped the activist ethos of the labor movement was how to educate young people for military struggle while preserving their moral integrity. This dilemma gave rise to the principle of "purity of arms," the meaning of which was primarily moral and educational but which also had a political meaning based on the way military power and moral strength affect one another. The leaders of the movement were afraid that an unrestrained use of force would corrupt those who used it, especially the younger people, and undermine the foundations of Zionism itself. Hence the educational importance of the activities of such figures as Yitzhak Sadeh, the first commander of the Palmah,[107] who stressed the inner connection between moral soundness and military strength.[108] Sadeh opposed the mystification of power by the radical right, for example Uri Tzvi Greenberg and Avraham Stern (known as "Yair"). He warned the younger generation against putting the rifle "in the center of our lives and the place of honor. . . . Whoever takes up such tools should remember that they are meant for emergencies and necessities, that they are tools of last resort, and great is the pain caused when, in spite of us, they rise, under the stress of the times, to a place of honor in our lives."[109] Thus, along with the interest in developing military power, there was a widespread fear in the labor movement that an extreme change might take place in the Jews' character once they acquired the "psychology of shooting" (Jabotinsky), a loss of the moral sensitivity they had developed in exile and a reincarnation of the "lamb" as a "wolf." [110]

OBLIVIOUSNESS TO THE PALESTINIAN ARAB PRESENCE

The political and moral approach of the labor movement was based on the view that the Jews' right to the Land of Israel west of the Jordan was superior to that of the Palestinian Arabs:[111] the latter could satisfy their need for sovereignty in the framework of the larger Arab nation outside the borders of Palestine, represented for them the reclaiming of an obvious right of ownership. The repression was made easier by the fact that when the Jews arrived, Palestinian Arab nationalism was in its infancy, only to crystallize fully under the influence of the conflict with the Jews.

The paternalistic attitude of most Zionist leaders toward the country's

Arabs up until the mid-1930s made it possible for the former to claim that Zionism had benefited all the region's inhabitants, so that the latter had no reason to oppose it. Obviously, the Palestinian Arabs saw Jewish settlement in an entirely different light, as Jabotinsky understood early on.

The political strategy of the labor movement until the establishment of the state thus steered a course between two poles: a refusal to yield what was perceived as a vital national interest — the creation of a Jewish majority in western Palestine — and a willingness to use military force to achieve this, should circumstances require it; and a continuing effort to reach a peaceful agreement with the Arabs, however remote the chances of doing so. This position was articulated with particular clarity by Moshe Beilinson in a 1929 article. He calls upon the Jews to be extremely cautious about "the rights, the feelings, and even the prejudices and preconceptions" of the Arabs. Although he is quite skeptical about the possibility of reaching an agreement with them, he also rules out direct conquest. He knows that the labor movement will have to take the long way around, a way demanding great effort and costing considerable blood and treasure. Nevertheless, he sees this as the "the truest, most humane national course" and "the course of political wisdom," which alone can prevent the poisoning of national sentiment with hatred and contempt for others. Beilinson holds that this course requires combating all actions that could unnecessarily inflame relations with the neighboring people and sincerely seeking ways of living together in peace, "if not for ourselves, at least for our children and grandchildren."[113]

Beilinson highlights the difference between the approaches of the labor movement and the Revisionists: like the Revisionists, the Labor leadership assumed, beginning in the 1930s, that the Palestinian Arabs would accept Jewish sovereignty over the country only when confronted with Jewish power — power in the full sense of the word. But they did not see any point in sharpening the conflict or emphasizing its inevitability; rather, it was of vital importance to begin immediately to educate for future accommodation and peace. The unwillingness to declare violent confrontation inevitable was not just a wise tactic, given the Yishuv's military weakness; it also reflected a moral commitment that force was only to be used as a last resort to settle the conflict. Tactical considerations were mixed inextricably with philosophical ones.[114] Evidence of this can be seen in the fact that the Jewish side showed a certain willingness to compromise when partition of the country was proposed, whereas the Arab side showed no such willingness at any time during the Mandate period. A highly significant educational consideration was at work here: a postponement, wherever possible, of direct confrontation amid a constant search for ways of coming to terms with the Arab opponent that avoided dehumanizing him and narrowing down the options to the use of force.

Many considered this strategy absurd, and at times it was even scored as hypocritical. Yet it did succeed in preventing the dehumanization of the enemy and the entrenchment of hatred for him. It also set up a moral barrier that kept force from being regarded as the only means of settling political problems and an object of cultic adulation.

Examining the principal Zionist positions on the issues of sovereignty and the use of force, we see a clear linkage between attitudes to power and perceptions of Judaism. The religious humanists, of whom Buber was the outstanding representative, emphasized the tension between Jewish identity, on the hand, and the aspiration to power and sovereignty, on the other, and the danger the latter posed for the realization of Zionism's Jewish mission. They therefore advocated treating this aspiration with constant suspicion. Buber's concept of the "line of demarcation," intended to confine political and military power to the necessary minimum, was based on a Jewish religious outlook infused with the spirit of prophecy, as he understood it. Jabotinsky took the very opposite point of view: precisely because he viewed traditional Jewishness as incommensurable with the pursuit of sovereignty, he saw an urgent need to revolutionize the Jewish character by psychological militarization. Uri Tzvi Greenberg and his followers (such as Yisrael Eldad and, later, the spokesmen of Gush Emunim) found a sanction for this revolution in the tradition itself. Power was a precondition for realizing the messianic mission of the Jews, which was, first and foremost, territorial in nature: the achievement of Jewish sovereignty over the whole historic expanse of the Land of Israel. For them, power was not alien to the spirit of Judaism but a basic and authentic component of its worldview.

There was in the Jewish national movement no greater disagreement than that between Buber and Greenberg. Both men sought to revive the ancient Jewish myth while basing themselves on Jewish tradition, yet how great was the distance between them in the way they interpreted these. The two thinkers symbolize two poles in historic Jewish consciousness, two rival powers struggling over Zionism's soul.

The labor movement included figures whose views were close to those of Buber and others who thought like Greenberg. The mainstream saw no contradiction between Jewish identity and the aspiration to sovereignty and power as means of realizing Zionist objectives, but they were keenly aware of the dangers posed by a radical change in the Jewish self-image. Rejecting the image of the "lamb," they nonetheless feared its reincarnation as a "wolf."

10

Reacting to Arab Terror

Jewish Combat Morality

The basic rule of what is called "combat morality," that which serves as the basis of international law, requires that a clear distinction be drawn between combatants and noncombatants. Yet it seems there has never been, in all of history, a war in which this rule was not broken. The harming of civilians in wartime is without doubt one of the most difficult and complicated of moral questions. This is particularly true when the struggle is against an enemy who makes use of terror against one's civilian population while using his own civilian population, sometimes against its will, for cover, support, and protection. In such a situation, it is relatively easy to be drawn into the mind-set of "all is fair in love and war": because the terrorism is an expression of political struggle, the civilian population as a whole can be seen as participating in the battle, and there is no room for the combatant-noncombatant distinction. This view is also based on the claim of "military necessity," i.e., that counter-terror is the only weapon that can be effective in stopping the enemy.

The Palestinian use of terror against Jewish civilians and property has been a constant feature of their struggle against Zionism over the decades. Consequently, the debate over how to respond to such terrorism has been going on all through the history of Zionism, and, in particular, the issue of harm to a civilian, noncombatant population resurfaces again and again in all Israeli debates regarding retaliation.

It was Ahad Ha'am who first raised this issue as a moral problem. In 1921, with bloody Arab riots raging throughout Palestine, a rumor spread that a teenage Arab boy had been murdered in Jaffa in revenge for the murder of Jews. Stunned by the event and close to despair, Ahad Ha'am wrote in an anguished letter to the daily *Ha'aretz:* "Jews and bloodshed? Is there anything more contradictory?" Once again, he expressed his view that the Jewish people had, in its political downfall, rescued the ideals of the Prophets, universal peace and justice, and during its long exile had devoted itself to these ideals for the sake of humanity as a whole. Even when its own blood was flowing like water it did not spill blood, viewing with contempt the bloody hands of its neighbors. Now that we have been privileged to witness the return to Zion and are dreaming of raising the prophetic banner anew, of being "a light unto the nations," he wrote, we encounter this great disappointment. "O God, is this really to be the conclusion? Is this really the goal to which our forefathers aspired and for which they underwent all that suffering? Is this really the dream of 'the return to Zion' that our people has been dreaming for thousands of years, that we should come to Zion and defile its soil by shedding innocent blood?" Without the prophetic ideals for which we suffered, he maintained, all the sacrifices we were making to build up the land would be pointless: "Is it really just to add, in a corner of the Orient, another small Levantine people that will compete in corruption — in the thirst for blood-revenge, . . . etc. — with the Levantines already there? If this is to be the 'messiah,' let him come, but let me not see him!"[1]

Ahad Ha'am was among the writers who had spoken out in the wake of the Kishinev pogrom of 1903, calling upon the Jews to organize in self-defense.[2] He was not a pacifist. In his moral sensitivity he was one of the first in the Zionist camp to pose the dilemma of ends and means in light of the moral aims of the movement. He saw no point to Zionism if its realization could not be based on the moral values of the Jewish tradition and if the Jews simply emulated the behavior of their Arab neighbors in their "thirst for blood-revenge."

Ahad Ha'am's words mark the beginning a polemic about retaliation that continues among Israeli Jews to this day. One of the main aspects of this issue is the question of whether Jews can permit themselves to adopt Palestinian Arab tactics or must confine themselves to methods consistent with Jewish tradition. The Bible warns many times against shedding "innocent blood" (*dam naki*). The halakhic literature deals with the issue of revenge against innocent civilians, particularly in the context of the story of Dinah (Gen 34).

The commentators disagree as to whether the massacre of the Shekhemites by Simeon and Levi, in reaction to their sister Dinah's rape, was legally or morally justified. Given the Halakha's clear condemnation of the shedding of innocent blood and even of execution without due process of law, the question concerning the commentators is whether there are not circumstances, as in war, where it becomes necessary to override these limitations and whether the situation described in Genesis called for such a departure.[3]

Nachmanides in his commentary on Gen 34:13 is unequivocal in his condemnation of the massacre. He explains Jacob's deathbed curse of the two brothers (Gen 49:5–7) as follows: "[It was] because they had committed an act of violence against the people of [Shekhem] . . . and killed those who had done them no harm whatsoever." Maimonides, on the other hand, justifies the massacre on halakhic grounds: the Shekhemites were guilty, not innocent, because they witnessed Shekhem ben Hamor's act of thievery and did not bring him to judgment as they, being children of Noah and obligated to observe the seven Noahide Commandments, one of which is to establish a system of jurisprudence, should have done (Laws of Kings, end of chapter 9). Other commentators, such as the author of *Or Hahayim,* who have difficulty with the slaying of the Shekhemites, try to excuse the act by claiming that it had not been premeditated, but when the Shekhemites ganged up against the brothers, who had come to take vengeance against Shekhem ben Hamor alone, they had to kill all of them. This interpretation, however, runs counter to the actual text: "They came upon the city unmolested" (34:25).

Commentators who justify the act without resorting to Halakha make two types of arguments, the pragmatic and the moral. The pragmatic argument is that revenge against all the inhabitants of the city was necessary as a deterrent. Thus Malbim (1809–1879) puts the following explanation in the mouths of the brothers: "Since we are few in number and strangers in the land, and they have begun to lash out at us, as in this act of treating our sister as a whore, if we keep silent they will do with us as they wish, so we must show them that we are capable of revenge against whoever harms us" (*Hatora Vehamitzva* on Gen 34:31). The moral argument rests on the need to preserve honor by removing the source of shame. This argument is cited by Rabbi Yitzhak Abravanel, who gives great importance to such notions as honor and revenge (see his commentary on Ex 2:12). He justifies the massacre of the Shekhemites in terms of the need for revenge as a way of restoring lost honor: "As a result of this disgrace they had to put themselves in danger, for death for the sake of honor is better than a life of shame and contempt" (Gen 34:31 ad loc.). The Dinah episode often serves as a lynchpin to support one argument or another in the Zionist debate over the morality of vengeance. Later we shall look at some of the opinions of contemporary rabbis regarding this issue.

Before examining the meaning of the term "Jewish ethics," I shall offer some illustrations of its usage. In the following discussion I will focus on two particular debates: that over "self-restraint" (1936–39), in which the principal positions were first staked out, and that over the Kibiyeh incident (1953–54), which was a milestone for the new State of Israel in working out ways of combating terror.

The Debate over Self-Restraint (1936–1939)

In 1936, following a period of accelerated growth in the size and strength of the Yishuv, the country's Arabs launched a series of acts of sabotage and terror against the British Mandatory authorities and against the Yishuv itself. In these actions, which were termed the "Arab Revolt," they sought to force the British to change their allegedly pro-Zionist policy. This objective was eventually realized, when, in 1939, the government published a White Paper restricting Jewish immigration and land purchases. Around the country many Jews were killed in the terrorist actions, and much Jewish property was damaged. The terror stirred up a fierce debate in the Yishuv over how to react.[4] At first the debate was enshrouded in a semantic fog that lumped together two distinct issues. One was whether the Jews should take matters into their own hands and respond directly, that is, act illegally, or whether they should content themselves with passive self-defense and leave the elimination of the terror to the British. This was a political and tactical question. But there was also another, moral one, which will be the subject of this chapter: whether the Jews should resort to the same means as the Arabs, terror against terror, taking vengeance against innocent people.

The leadership of the Yishuv, headed by labor movement leftists, decided in the first stage on a policy of self-restraint (*havlaga*). But the Etzel (National Military Organization) underground (often referred to in English as the Irgun, the first word of its full Hebrew name), under right-wing (Revisionist) influence, rejected this approach in principle and launched a series of retaliatory actions against the Arabs. In fact, such actions were also undertaken by members of the Hagana (the mainstream militia), though they were few in number and against the explicit directives of the leadership. Nevertheless, the policy of self-restraint, as initially defined, was undermined, and the Hagana was eventually forced by pressure from within its own ranks to respond more actively. The line was drawn at actions that harmed women and children, from which the Yishuv as a whole recoiled and which most of the leadership condemned, even as these actions earned praise from certain figures on the right. Instead, modes of response were sought that distinguished between combatants and innocent civilians. The term "self-restraint" thus initially meant not respond-

ing in an active way, but once such passivity was rejected, it referred to refraining from *indiscriminate* acts of retaliation.

The problem was sharply formulated by Robert Weltsch,[5] in whose words
we hear echoes of Ahad Ha'am: "The question before us is terrifyingly serious;
this is a moment of truth, one of those moments that deeply affect the moral
and historical survival of the people and that appear only once in hundreds of
years, on the gravest of occasions. . . . Would we justify the despicable murder
of innocent people, among them women and children, if we were convinced
that by committing it we could win a political victory?"[6]

Those who condemned terrorism tried to draw a clear distinction between
Jewish and Arab codes of battle. Such arguments rested to some extent on
negative stereotypes of the Arabs and the sense of superiority to them that was
widespread in the Yishuv, but they also reflected a strong desire not to dull the
moral aversion to the shedding of blood that had been shaped by Jewish
tradition and historical experience. Thus, for example, an appeal against the
use of terror issued by the Jordan Valley kibbutzim said, "Rivers of Jewish
blood that were shed and are still being shed in exilic communities throughout
the world cry out against the shedding of innocent blood [at our hands]."[7]
David Ben-Gurion, the most pragmatic of the statesmen of the time, like
others in the leadership of the Yishuv, stressed the difference between the ways
Jews and Arabs fought: "We shall not imitate the Arabs or follow in their
footsteps. . . . We must guard our moral purity in all our dealings with our
Arab neighbors, for without a moral basis our power is as nought."[8] Ben-
Gurion points out that "we are judged by a different standard," that people
expect more of us. For him, terrorism is primarily a moral question. But
unfortunately, in a world that does not work according to moral imperatives,
it is impossible to rely entirely on moral considerations and "we must [also]
examine the question from a political point of view, in terms of effect."[9]

The Call for Revenge

By contrast, the rank and file of the Etzel had no qualms about revenge.
In their view, only a violent response, terror against terror, would put an end to
Arab depredations. The policy of self-restraint was attacked as passive, as
turning the entire Yishuv into "an ancient Christian sect." The image of the
lamb extending its neck for slaughter became the stock-in-trade of Revisionist
literature, which dwelt on the themes of Jewish honor and the difference
between the Land of Israel and the Diaspora: the ethic of restraint was a
cowardly exilic one, a return to the humiliation of being "protected Jews"
(*Schutzjuden*).[10] The main psychological problem of the Jews in the Land of

Israel was to liberate themselves from this exilic thinking and develop a readiness for struggle with no holds barred. Hence any restraint should be condemned. This argument was reinforced by the disappointment the restraint of the Yishuv aroused in many Diaspora Jews, who could not understand either the political or the moral motives behind the policy.[11]

The most extreme of all was Uri Tzvi Greenberg. In his well-known poem "One Truth, Not Two," he rejects vigorously the distinction made by the Yishuv leadership between Jewish and Arab codes of conduct on the battlefield. For him, there is one truth, common to Jews and gentiles alike, and that is the truth of conquest by force, symbolized by the figure of Joshua, which during the period of exile was distorted by tradition and in modern times by "traitorous" leaders:

> Your teachers taught: there is one truth for the other nations —
> Blood for blood — but this is not the standard for Jews.
> And I say: there is one truth, not two,
> As there is one sun, and not two Jerusalems.
> Written in the Torah is the conquest of Moses and Joshua
> Unto the last of my wounded kings and lions,
> A truth devoured by the teeth of exiles and traitors.[12]

Hence Greenberg claims to abolish the traditional distinction between the Jewish code of war and that of the other nations. In his poem "When the Time Comes," he cries:

> Blood for blood twice over! . . .
> And manifold indignity for spit!
> For so the culture of the Hebrews teaches us,
> For so the culture of the gentiles teaches us,
> For thus do races repay their enemies,
> In every generation, in every age. . . .

Greenberg here rejects contemptuously the view that there is something unJewish about vengeance, something contrary to Jewish morality. For him, the opposite is the case. Revenge is an imperative going back to Sinai, passed down from generation to generation in the prayers and longings of the Jews until the time came to translate it into reality.

> And each of us, little, knee-high Jews,
> Saw Amalek[13] in his own torturer and abuser:
> Some heathen who accosted him in the street —
> Be it with a punch in the face, making it swell,
> Or spit in the face,
> Whether by snatching a wig

Or threatening to eat him alive —
And each of us, little, knee-high Jews,
Craved vengeance against the enemy ruler,
That [we], too, might have a great king, an army.[14]

Revenge and the cruel deed are for Greenberg necessary if the Jews are to acquire "a lordly character," for they express the race's law of survival. Jewish vengeance is inspired by the example of Simeon's and Levi's attack on the men of Shekhem.

"Purity of Arms"

Berl Katznelson, one of the most eminent leaders of the labor movement, made a signal contribution to defining the difference between retaliation and controlled response. He asks what the political and moral content of the policy of restraint would be: "The idea of self-defense, since the beginning of the Second Aliya, has never been tainted with vengefulness or lust."[15] Katznelson admits that the policy of restraint derived not only "from our deep spiritual attribute, not only from moral considerations, but also from calculation." "Calculation" means political expediency. But he sees no way of separating the two considerations, concluding, like Buber, that morality has great political value.[16] Zionism derives its power from moral norms of combat, different from those common among the Arabs. The enemy does not respect the laws of war, but we are forbidden to emulate him: "We are a people with a great culture; the basis of that culture is a regard for human life, and I doubt that having achieved such respect and appreciation for human life after two thousand years of education, we ought to give them up." Katznelson attributes the vengeful actions of the Jews to cultural assimilation that has weakened their deep resistance to shedding blood. "There is a great distance between our culture and that of our neighbors; a distance of many generations separates us. Deep down, we are afraid of blood." He admits that "this profound trait that has been preserved in us is among the things standing in our way," but "if we want to get rid of [it], we shall not readily be able to do so, and I also believe that if we do, we shall regret it the next day or the day after. . . . If [Zionism] does take up alien weapons, they will do it no good but rather cause its uprooting."[17]

And this is how Katznelson spells out the meaning of "self-restraint": "We stand up to those who attack us, but we do not want our weapons to be stained with innocent blood. . . . Self-restraint is both a political and a moral approach, stemming from our history and our present reality, from our character and the conditions of the war in which we are engaged. If, instead of being true to ourselves, we were to take a different approach, we would long since have lost the battle. And if our actions, instead of being truly heroic, only seemed to be so, we would bring shame upon ourselves and be compelled to pay the highest price."[18]

This terse, instructive summary brings together pragmatic and moral considerations. The argument is that this norm stems from Jewish history and tradition. The main motive is existential: faithfulness to who we are, not betraying our identity. It is no accident that Katznelson distinguishes between imagined and true heroism. He was at work during these years on a Jewish *Book of Heroism,* which would bring together all the instances of Jewish heroism throughout history.

Yitzhak Sadeh, one of the authors of the Palmah code of battlefield conduct, was also concerned during these years with the issue of what constitutes true heroism. Thus, "it is hard for a person blessed with heroism to kill. He comes to this only when there is no way out, when there isn't the shadow of a doubt that killing is justified, the deed necessary for the sake of life."[19] Sadeh makes a forceful case for the close connection between moral and military strength: the rightness of the cause summons up all the powers at a person's disposal, with spiritual power sometimes expressing itself physically.[20] In Sadeh's teaching, a new concept of Jewish heroism emerges, one fusing a resolute defense of life with the conquest of the evil impulse, i.e., restraint that strengthens the defense rather than weakens it.

The polemic over self-restraint gave rise during the forties to a wider discussion of Jewish political tradition. Each camp tried to justify its moral stand on the basis of tradition and claimed to be its legitimate interpreter. The focus of the discussion was the issue of "Jewish morality."[21]

The Religious-Zionist Position

At the time of the debate over self-restraint, Palestine's two chief rabbis and most of the spokesmen of the religious-Zionist camp supported the official leadership of the Yishuv and condemned terrorist attacks against innocent civilians. There was considerable affinity between the arguments used by the rabbis on this question and those of leading nonreligious figures (such as Katznelson).[22] Isaac Halevi Herzog (the Ashkenazi chief rabbi of Palestine) and Moshe Avigdor Amiel (the chief rabbi of Tel Aviv) were in favor of responding actively to terrorism but not if it meant the killing of the innocent. They thus accepted the distinction between vengeance, in the usual sense of the word, and measured response. Rabbi Amiel spelled this out: "We are confusing two separate things; there is self-restraint and there is indifference. We are obliged to show self-restraint, forbidden to be indifferent." He maintained that although the term *havlaga* (self-restraint) was a new one, the idea was quite ancient: "All Jewish morality [entails] self-restraint. . . . Judaism has, throughout its history, taken the path of self-restraint. Always, we were offended but did not offend. . . . 'Thou shalt not kill' is imprinted in the Jewish soul, and thus the slaying of anyone affects the entire Jewish nation."[23] "In its very nature the Jewish soul hates bloodshed, and whenever we see it among the gentiles we are shocked to the depths of our being."[24] A position that subordinates moral values to "the national interest" does not reflect Jewish morality but that of the gentiles, for according to Judaism the individual is an end in himself and not a means to any other end. Jewish morality teaches that "the end does not justify the means, but, rather, immoral means desecrate the holiest of ends" (cf. Buber). The stones of the altar are desecrated if a sword is waved over them;[25] "how much less can we build our national home with a sword that has been waved at innocent people. Such a home is desecrated from the outset."[26]

Rabbi Yehuda Leib Maimon (Fishman) was the only leader of Mizrahi (the religious-Zionist movement) to support the Revisionists' retaliatory actions unreservedly. He based himself on a ruling of Maimonides (Laws of Kings 9:14) justifying the actions of Simeon and Levi against the men of Shekhem, an episode that was, as we have seen, a subject of controversy among halakhic authorities, focused on the question of harm to noncombatants. He held that in wartime, once the killing begins, there is no way of distinguishing between deserving and undeserving victims. "We find this throughout our history."[27]

The rabbis used the term *musar hayahadut* (Jewish ethics) much more than did the nonreligious leadership. It was not understood as a halakhic category but as an imperative derived from scripture, sacred lore, and the historical experience of the Jewish people,[28] or as Amiel put it, "the Jewish way all through history." The term "way" indicates a metahalakhic principle that is both descriptive and normative. Like the nonreligious leaders, the rabbis stressed the prohibition against imitating "those who hate us," seeing retaliation as a violation of the principle that "thou shalt not go according to [gentile] laws" (Lev 18:3) and seeing the restraint of the Yishuv as heroism and a sanctification of God's name.

Some added another reason: acts of vengeance violated the moral norms of the "most civilized" gentiles as well. Rabbi Moshe Ostrovsky, for example, held that we must learn not only from the Torah but also from the non-Jews: "European morality is opposed to vengeance without trial. We should not learn from the example of the wicked gentiles but from that of the most civilized of them."[29] The very use of such a standard indicates the open-mindedness of the era.

Eliezer Don Yihya writes that the openness that religious Zionism had learned from the nonreligious gave rise to a new hermeneutic meant "to give religious, halakhic legitimation to positions that departed from what had been customary."[30] The attitude of the rabbis was a combination of Zionist-style political activism with a universalism anchored in Western culture and socialist ideology. Although the religious Zionists drew upon the religious tradition, they had also been exposed to processes of modernization, which prompted them to take positions that deviated from traditional norms. These positions, however, did not directly contradict any explicit religious law, and they could be reconciled with the Halakha by reinterpretation. As we shall see, this way of open thinking was radically changed in the wake of the Six-Day War.

The debate helped the Yishuv to clarify its basic values and sharpen its self-awareness. The result was the crystallization of positions still current in Israel today. It also gave rise to the doctrine of "purity of arms," which later shaped the Israeli code of combat. "Jewish ethics" was a recurrent motif in most of the opinions voiced, religious and nonreligious alike—the first time there had been a serious public discussion that revolved around this issue. The debate highlighted the difference between the Jewish fighting ethic and that of the Palestinian Arabs, an asymmetry in everything concerning attacks on the other's civilian population. On the Jewish side, an intellectual effort was made to distinguish between combatant and noncombatant Arabs, and terrorist acts committed by Jews were greeted with shock and revulsion. On the Arab side, terrorists were considered national heroes, and the moderates who sought compromise did not speak out against them, whether out of indifference or plain fear.[31]

The Kibiyeh Controversy

As is well known, the 1948–49 war, known in Israel as the War of Independence, gave rise to the problem of the Arab refugees. Those Arab Palestinians who left the country or were expelled in the course of the fighting found their way to camps around Israel's borders, and shortly after the war they began to infiltrate back. Some were trying to return to their homes, but others were bent on sabotage and terror against the Jewish residents of the border areas. The young state had to work out a policy of retaliation.

Compared with the prestate period it was a new moral situation. The moral position of a weak minority living under foreign rule, highly circumscribed in its use of power, is quite different from that of a sovereign state that can wield power in an autonomous fashion. The state must bear all the responsibility for the way its power is used. Its situation differed in another respect from the one that had prevailed during the Mandate period: then, those who engaged in terror could generally be identified, isolated, and punished. This was no longer the case with infiltrators from across the frontiers.

The Israeli government held the neighboring states responsible for the terror, and the Israel Defense Forces (IDF) generally followed a policy of indirect deterrence through collective punishment: counterattacks on the civilian population, intended to arouse fear and thus bring pressure on the rulers to restrain the infiltrators. This was clearly a departure from the tradition of purity of arms espoused by the Hagana and the Palmah during the Mandate period, a departure brought about partly by the pressure of Israeli public opinion, particularly that of the population most directly affected, who demanded revenge.[32]

In October 1953, an elite IDF unit crossed the Jordanian frontier and retaliated against the Arab village of Kibiyeh, from which infiltrators had carried out acts of sabotage within Israel. The order called for a tough response: sufficient destruction of property and life to drive the villagers out of their homes. Several dozen were killed, among them women and children.[33] Moshe Sharett, the foreign minister and a leading Labor politician, called the action a "horror," not only because women and children had been killed but also because of the scale of the operation, which showed that "we can lose control of ourselves" and that "we are a people capable of massive bloodshed."[34]

Public and press opinion abroad expressed abhorrence of the action. Some years later, Moshe Dayan, then chief of the IDF's operations branch, wrote that the Kibiyeh incident had proven for the first time that "what is permitted to the Arabs and other peoples will not be forgiven if committed by Jews or by Israel. The West, world Jewry, and the citizens of Israel expect much more 'purity of arms' from us than is demanded of any other army."[35] And in fact, in response to the criticism, the IDF revised its strategy and began to limit itself to attacks on military targets.

The government, acceding to a demand by David Ben-Gurion, denied that the army had taken part in the action and presented it as a spontaneous outburst by angry, impatient border residents whose persons and property had been harmed by infiltrators from the village. At the same time, within the government many cabinet ministers were sharply critical of various aspects of the action: the way the decision had been taken to carry it out, the fact that so many women and children had been hurt, and the fact that world public opinion had been aroused. Most adamant in his criticism was Moshe Hayim Shapira, of Hapo'el Hamizrahi (a religious-Zionist labor party), who stressed the Jewish aspect of the affair. He rejected Ben-Gurion's attempts to present the action in a positive light, stating: "All through the years we have opposed this. Even when Jews were being murdered in the Land of Israel, we never called for the righteous to perish with the wicked. We were always strict about this." Shapira drew a comparison with the Deir Yassin incident, which had taken place in the heat of the 1948 fighting yet brought an angry response from the Jewish public.[36] "We said this way of doing things was out of bounds from a Jewish point of view. Everyone felt that Jews had committed an unholy act. Jews cannot do such things."[37]

The Kibiyeh incident did not cause the same shock or protest among the Israeli public as Deir Yassin had, probably because of the way the government disguised it. Nor did most Israeli newspapers, including those of the religious parties, dissociate themselves from the action; rather, they sought to justify it in various ways, placing most of the blame on the Arabs or on the European powers, which had not done enough to prevent the terror. Editorials that appeared at the time had a self-righteous tone, preaching to the gentiles that they had no right to criticize the Jews given the way the former had behaved a few years before, when Jews were being slaughtered in Europe. Only the radical left-wing press expressed revulsion at the action.[38]

An exceptionally harsh and probing reaction was voiced in an article by Yeshayahu Leibowitz, "After Kibiyeh," that appeared in the fortnightly *Be-terem*.[39] Leibowitz speaks of the wider significance of the incident. As long we Jews were in exile, living under foreign rule, he writes, we were not responsible for the use of military power. This unnatural situation gave us a spiritual privilege: we could create and develop certain moral values that would never have to stand the test of reality. We saw ourselves, and to some extent were seen by others, as a people that had succeeded in subduing one of the most terrible human impulses, that which leads to intergroup violence. From a moral and even religious point of view, the exilic situation allowed us to evade the true test of morality, which is confronted by "one who is capable of acting and on whom rests the responsibility for acting or refraining from action." Expressing moral reservations about violence without responsibility for the sorts of causes in the name of which violence is committed is "very easy, and therefore hardly worthwhile." For Leibowitz, this incident is "the great test to which we as a nation are put as a result of national liberation," and "this is the true religious and moral significance of regaining . . . the capacity to deploy force. We are now being put to the test. Are we capable not only of suffering for the sake of values we cherish but also of acting in accordance with them?" Recalling the biblical story of Dinah and Shekhem, in which Jacob curses Simeon and Levi for slaughtering the townspeople of Shekhem indiscriminately, Leibowitz appeals to the Jewish public: "Let us not cause our third commonwealth to incur the curse of our father Jacob." In contrast to Buber and his followers, the members of Brit Shalom who were adamantly opposed to the use of force to achieve Zionist ends, Leibowitz recognized the necessity of such use, but he saw the test of the Zionist movement and the Jewish religion in their ability to set moral limits to it. The word *nisayon* (trial) occurs twice in the article, the word *mivhan* (test) three times.

In response to Leibowitz, Pepita Ha'ezrahi calls attention to the "Jewish" side of the episode, the "odd" fact that "on this point our supporters and our opponents, various gentiles and Jews in the Diaspora and in Israel, have made common cause." They are unanimous in claiming, "This deed will not be allowed to the Jews, or justified, or forgiven." She rejects this double standard, maintaining that the Kibiyeh action, while it cannot be justified on moral grounds, should be seen as normal and natural for any people. From this point of departure, she questions the whole idea of the Chosen People, alluded to by Leibowitz, which she regards as a reflection of "our basic arrogance, our primal sin." Kibiyeh put us to the test, and we failed. We turned out to be normal. At last, we have been given the opportunity to see ourselves as we really are. We are no better morally than anyone else. The main lesson to be drawn from this, Ha'ezrahi maintains, is one of humility. We cannot measure up to the double standard, and where we are really at fault is forever pretending that we could.

Ha'ezrahi provoked Leibowitz to clarify his position and take umbrage at the interpretation given to his remarks. In giving the example of Shekhem and Dinah, he had not meant to imply that a special prohibition had been imposed upon the Jewish people by virtue of any moral uniqueness ("Jewish ethics," in Ahad Ha'am's phrase). "I did not say that as Jews we were forbidden to do such a thing, but that it was forbidden [to anyone] to do such a thing. If I chose to illustrate my point by citing the Torah, I did not mean to highlight any specifically Jewish approach. Where else should a Jewish writer draw literary examples from, if not the Torah? The Shekhem incident and the position taken by the Patriarch Jacob illustrate the great moral problematic posed by an action that, however explained, rationalized, and justified, is nonetheless accursed." He blames the Zionist educational ideology for transferring the concept of holiness from the religious to the national realm, thereby bestowing a stamp of approval on actions such as Kibiyeh.[40]

Leibowitz declares "Jewish ethics" to be an extremely dubious idea, and not only because "ethics" does not readily accept a modifier and cannot be "Jewish" or "non-Jewish." The concept itself contradicts the very content and meaning of Judaism. Challenging Shmuel David Luzzato, Ahad Ha'am, and Hermann Cohen, he writes, "Judaism did not produce a specific ethic [*torat middot*] and never presented itself as an ethical system [*musar*] or advocated one. Judaism's only ethic is the strict observance of the Torah and the Commandments, the moral meaning of which is subject to a variety interpretations." The notion of "Jewish ethics" he appears to regard as the invention of secular or assimilated Jews; having rejected the yoke of the Commandments, they have nothing else in which to anchor their Jewish identity.

The Israeli Chief Rabbinate did not react to the Kibiyeh incident. The only immediate halakhic reaction to it (in 1954) was that of Rabbi Shaul Yisraeli, who found a way of "declaring pure something inherently impure," to use a Rabbinic expression for legal gymnastics. For him, there is a "special concept of revenge-war" that applies to the enemies of the Jewish people. In such a war, there is no obligation to take care not to harm women and children, as we see in the case of the biblical war against Midian (Num 25). His conclusion regarding the killing of women and children in Kibiyeh is that the act of revenge committed against this village belongs in the category of "commanded war" (*milhemet mitzva*), and therefore "there is no obligation to refrain from retaliating for fear that the innocent may get hurt, for they will have brought it on themselves, and we are blameless." He hedges this by saying that no *deliberate* harm should be done to children.[41]

Yisrael Eldad, the former Lehi (Stern Gang) ideologue, argues in his own journal *Sulam,* against "alienated" Jews who brandish the slogan of "Jewish morality." Eldad accuses them of a highly selective use of texts. They understand all the psalms and prophecies of revenge as time-bound "literature" that is no longer applicable, and, on the other hand, they have turned the ethical prophecy of the End of Days into an imperative incumbent upon us as Jews today. In fact, Judaism, in his view, cultivates revenge, hatred, and intolerance toward foreigners, especially in the Land of Israel. Jewish ethics, Eldad concludes, is meant to further Jewish survival: "The highest ethical imperative is that of life."[42]

The main question, which is recurrent in most of the reactions to Leibowitz's article, is: Is there to be a specifically Jewish ethical dimension to the way the State of Israel responds to terrorism? I will quote here only the response of the sociologist Amitai Etzioni (living today in the United States), which seems typical in its allusion to an aspect of the affair that Leibowitz ignores or at least avoids, that of self-betrayal:

> Yet, even if the moral imperative "Thou shall not kill" is addressed equally to everyone, it does not follow that there have not been in human history groups of people, and even whole peoples, who related to moral imperatives in a special way. There have been those who said: We shall obey these imperatives

in a world where non-obedience is the norm. And when such a group gets up and does something immoral, it causes disappointment, distress, despair. There is no special, extra immorality here. . . . There was hope that the Jewish people, which, because of special historical circumstances, had imposed upon itself the fulfillment of the moral imperatives, would continue to uphold them even when those historical circumstances changed. . . . The action in Kibiyeh, which did not repel most Israelis, raises the fear that the Jewish people will betray its destiny and turn to the "normalcy" of being "like all the other nations," will adjust to the [prevailing] evil norm at the first opportunity. There is a certain inconsistency in this that evokes despair, even if the inconsistency is not of misleading moral weight. The Kibiyeh action was wrong in and of itself, even without this dimension of self-betrayal.[43]

Unlike Leibowitz, Etzioni distinguishes clearly between the purely moral side of the incident ("there is no special, extra immorality here") and its "Jewish" side, which flows from the special standing of the Jewish people in its own eyes and in the eyes of others. The wrong itself is not made worse for having been perpetrated by Jews, but its psychological and moral effect, the disappointment and the despair it generates, acquire a special dimension "because of special historical circumstances." Thus for Etzioni there is, aside from the moral dimension of the incident, an existential aspect ("self-betrayal') that could be termed a problem of identity or authenticity, not integrally tied to the public moral issue.

The Lebanon War, the Intifada, and the Shift in Israeli Public Opinion

The 1982 Lebanon war and the Palestinian-Arab uprising (in Arabic, "Intifada") of 1987–93 posed severe moral tests for the Jews of Israel, for they necessitated painful confrontations with noncombatant populations on a scale unknown since the War of Independence. Broad sectors of the Jewish population were shocked into a profound moral reckoning. For the first time, the Zionist consensus, whose slogan had always been "There is no alternative," came into question, and society was deeply divided. It was perhaps a sign of the change that later took place in Israeli public opinion over the question of compromise with the Palestinians and recognition of their national rights.

The change of atmosphere was reflected in the report of the Kahan Commission, set up to investigate the cruel Christian Falangist massacres in the Sabra and Shatila refugee camps in 1982. The central question for the commission was whether Israeli authorities were indirectly responsible for the killings. The most revealing part of the report was the reasoning on which it based its conclusions. The commission drew a distinction between legal norms, which it felt did not apply in the situation in which Israel found itself in Lebanon, and "the obligations of every civilized country and the moral principles accepted by all civilized peoples." In terms of the latter, the commission found that the Israeli government bore indirect responsibility for the events in the refugee camps. This finding was substantiated on two grounds. The first was borrowed from Jewish legal tradition, and more specifically the law in Deut 21:1–9 dealing with a situation in which a murder victim is found in an open field and it is not known who committed the crime. According to the Talmudic interpretation, this law regards the "elders" (judges) of the city as indirectly responsible for bloodshed occurring within their jurisdiction. The second ground is found in exilic Jewish history: as a persecuted minority, Jews always held their host governments responsible for attacks against them, and not just the attackers themselves.[44] Here we have a good example of the kind of moral discussion being carried on in Israel, where widely accepted norms governing relations among "civilized peoples" are combined with norms drawn from the Jewish tradition.[45]

The Intifada provides other examples of how Israeli public opinion was challenged by events. Shortly after its outbreak (December 1987), Yossi Sarid, a left-wing politician, declared from the Knesset podium that the brutal suppression of the uprising would also put an end to Israeli democracy and that the means the IDF was using to suppress it were "not justified, not effective, and not Jewish."[46] Likewise, in reaction to an incident in which Israeli soldiers buried a Palestinian alive, the journalist Yoel Marcus wrote: "Even those willing to give up the territories [occupied since 1967] in exchange for peace accept the necessity of holding on to them so that we have something to give in exchange for peace. But there are things we cannot and need not do, because all through history we ourselves have been victims of the selfsame tactics. Because we as a people have experienced in our own flesh how ordinary people [we knew] from the neighborhood, from the workplace, from social contexts, turned into animals — as individuals and, when it became government policy, as a society. As rulers, let us always be handicapped. Let us never be perfect in imposing order. It is better that way. What happened last week will leave a stain on the life of a people meant to be a light from Zion unto the nations."[47]

Diaspora Jewry, which also took part in the debate over "Jewish morality," was as divided in its views as Israelis were. Liberal Jews voiced shame and profound revulsion at actions they saw as contrary to "Jewish morality." On the other hand, American Jews, who identified more with Orthodoxy or the Republican Party, supported the forceful suppression of the Intifada unreservedly.[48]

It is apparent from the ongoing debates amongst Jews, both in Israel and in the Diaspora, that for many the connection between morality and power is not an abstract question but one that must be viewed in light of Jewish tradition and history. Nor do they rest content with condemning certain kinds of behavior as immoral; they add that the latter are "un-Jewish," an epithet that seems to lend greater weight to the condemnation. Thus, for example, a group of prominent American and British Jews sent a letter to the *New York Times* in early February 1988, condemning the Israel Defense Forces' mode of response during the Intifada and calling for negotiation with the Palestinians. They concluded their letter by declaring, "We believe this is the democratic, the humane, and the truly Jewish way."[49] Although arguments based upon history and self-image are often found among other peoples (in the United States, for example, the Supreme Court uses the term "American ethos" as an argument for its decisions), the Jews seem to attribute particular importance to such considerations. Clearly, then, Jewish ethics has come to play a significant role in Israeli public discourse, especially over the reactions to the Palestinian terror.

The term "Jewish morality" or "Judaic ethics" (*musar yehudi* or *musar hayahadut*), which does not appear in medieval Jewish philosophical literature, became popular among the newly emancipated Jews in the nineteenth century, for whom it served mainly apologetic purposes. Seeking to integrate into the surrounding society while preserving their uniqueness, they tried to dispel prejudices against Jews by presenting their unique contribution to European culture: Judaism embodied the purest of moral ideals and was *the* universal humanitarian religion. With the appearance of the Zionist movement, a new dimension was added to the use of the term, particularly as a result of the debate over Ahad Ha'am ideas, in which the term "national morality" played a central role in defining national identity.[50] Thenceforth the term "Jewish morality" was used mainly in an internal context, whether it was the debates between the Zionists and their liberal opponents or those that divided the various factions within the Zionist movement itself. What meanings does the term have in this context?

Jewish Ethics and the Consciousness of Being Chosen

Orthodox thinkers, such as Leibowitz, tend to claim that the term "Jewish ethics" has no normative meaning but only a descriptive or historical one, encompassing the totality of laws and imperatives to be found in the Judaic tradition (Halakha). In my opinion this definition is incomplete, for the term, as it is used by both religious and nonreligious Jews, has a normative as well as a descriptive meaning.

There is no doubt that for many Jews the term "Jewish ethics" is predicated on the age-old Jewish sense of chosenness. This notion does not imply that the Jews are morally superior to others. Rather, it points to a certain moral self-claim, anchored in a particular identity, memory, and moral sensitivity acquired during a long history as an oppressed minority. Chosenness in this context is understood by Jews as a reminder of their obligation of loyalty to themselves, to the destiny they took upon themselves.

As Levinas claims, every truly moral action is bound up with an awareness of "being chosen" because I demand of myself more than I demand of the other. My basic intuition is that I am different from him, not like him, and therefore I have more responsibility. "Where there are no men, strive to be a man."[51] I believe it was the intuition of the Zionist pioneers who came to settle the Land of Israel in the first half of the twentieth century. This intuition applies to both the interpersonal and the international realm. If chosenness takes on national garb, it is because that is the only way to establish a civilization, to keep it alive and pass it on.[52] Perfecting the world requires being aware of an inequality of obligation. Every nation worthy of the name is chosen in the sense that it has a consciousness of having a unique destiny. It belongs to a supranational order and has an ineluctable responsibility: it must conduct itself as if it alone would be held accountable for all the others.[53]

According to Levinas, the sense of being responsible for the fate of humanity is the origin and root of the Jewish sense of chosenness. Chosenness means accepting this responsibility, which transcends any formal duty because it is not based on mutuality and expects no reward. The Jewish people's relation to the rest of humankind is one of obligation without mutual expectation. Thus, Jewish particularism is essentially universal, as Levinas states: "There is no moral awareness that is not an awareness of this exceptional position, an awareness of being chosen. Reciprocity is a structure founded on an original inequality. For equality to make its entry into the world, beings must be able to demand more of themselves than of the Other, feel responsibilities on which the fate of humanity hangs, and in this sense pose themselves problems outside humanity. This 'position outside nations,' of which the Pentateuch speaks, is realized in the concept of Israel and its particularism. It is a particularism that conditions universality, and it is a moral category rather than a historical fact to do with Israel, even if the historical Israel has in fact been faithful to the concept of Israel and, on the subject of morality, felt responsibilities and obligations which it demands from no one, but which sustain the world."[54]

This view is also implied in Maimonides' halakhic code. When referring to supererogation, actions "beyond the call of duty," he uses the phrase "the way of Israel" as against "the pagan way." In four different places he describes cruelty as a pagan, not a Jewish attribute.[55] In two of these instances he goes so far as to claim that a person who behaves cruelly and without mercy is to be suspected of being of non-Jewish ancestry. In one such passage he writes:

> It is permitted to work a heathen slave with rigor. Though such is the rule, it is the quality of piety and the way of wisdom that a man be merciful and pursue justice and not make his yoke heavy upon the slave or distress him, but give him to eat and to drink of all foods and drinks. The sages of old were wont to let the slave partake of every dish that they themselves ate of. . . . Nor should [the master] heap upon the slave oral abuse and anger but should rather speak to him softly and listen to his claims. So it is also [illustrated] in the righteous ways of Job, on which he prided himself: "Did I despise the cause of my manservant or of my maidservant when they contended with me? . . . Did not He that made me in the womb make him? And did not One fashion us in the womb?" (Job 31:13, 15). Cruelty and effrontery are not frequent except with heathens who worship idols. The children of our father Abraham, however, i.e., the Israelites, upon whom the Holy One, blessed be He, bestowed the favor of the Law and laid . . . statutes and judgments, are merciful people who have mercy upon all. Thus also is it [evident in] the attributes of the Holy One, blessed be He, which we are enjoined to imitate: "And His mercies are over all His works" (Ps 145:9). Furthermore, whoever has compassion will receive compassion, as it is said: "And He will show you mercy and have compassion upon you and multiply you" (Deut 13:18).[56]

I believe we see here the deepest roots of the notion of "Jewish ethics." First, there is no distinction made here between the descriptive and normative; the two are combined in what is called behavior "beyond the call of duty" (*lifnim mishurat hadin*). "It is permitted to work a heathen slave with rigor" because he is not a Jew, but this would not be "the quality of piety and the way of wisdom." Maimonides bases this normative statement on two different arguments. The first argument concerns the historical identity of the people of Israel: citing scriptural examples of the conduct of the early sages, he concludes that "cruelty and effrontery are not frequent except with heathens who worship idols," whereas the people Israel, who were privileged to receive a Torah enjoining upon them [just] statutes and judgments, are merciful people who have mercy upon all." On the face of it, this is a descriptive statement, but it is not merely descriptive. Maimonides certainly does not believe all Jews are compassionate and all pagans cruel, for he recognizes the existence of righteous gentiles (Laws of Kings 8:11). "Israel" is thus not something empirical. Compassion is not a racial or congenital trait of the Jews. Rather, one who behaves compassionately demonstrates that he is part of the *ideal* Israel, which is said to be ever mindful of the importance of showing mercy. Maimonides is thus positing compassion as a necessary, if not sufficient condition for membership in the Jewish collective. Whoever does not behave mercifully, whoever is cruel, effectively excludes himself, for this is not "the way of the seed of Israel" (Laws of Repentance 2:10). The statement has a distinctly exhortatory quality. What we have here is thus both a descriptive and a normative statement.

Maimonides' second argument is a theological one, relying on citations from Job and the Psalms. Unlike the pagans, Israel are "merciful to all" because they have "[just] statutes and judgments" enjoining them to imitate the attributes of the Holy One Himself, whose "mercies are upon all His works." Shalom Rosenberg has shown that the idea of *imitatio dei* is, for Maimonides, a metaethical one that bursts the bounds of expediency of group ethics (or transcends the sociologists' distinction between "internal" and "external" morality). Its meaning is that "there are moral criteria by which the laws of the Torah and the conduct of the people of Israel can be judged, and these criteria are in accord with the attributes of the Holy One, blessed be He."[57] Maimonides' theological argument sheds light on the process by which a particular historical tradition develops a mechanism of moral self-criticism. The bounds of particularistic morality, often tantamount to group self-interest, are broken in favor of universal human solidarity. Or, to put it more precisely, universal morality itself now becomes a hallmark of the particular group. Maimonides draws his ethical principles from Greek philosophy, but as a leader he bases his moral critique not on a certain norm considered valid halakhically, but on a metahalakhic principle implicit in the tradition itself, that of solidarity ("His mercies are over all His works"). This is the same principle we have found in Levinas's thought. This principle is to be found at the root of all historical traditions and is created by them, as Hans Gadamer has shown.[58] It is thus neither merely descriptive nor merely normative but combines the two.

Maimonides identifies "Israel's way" with "mercy," that is, with a set of norms Jewish tradition calls "beyond the call of duty." He thus presents mercy as a normative demand addressed not only to individuals or an elite but to all of Israel.[59] Actions "beyond the call of duty" have to do with moral character, the virtuous personality.[60] Being a function of character, which is shaped by cultural and historical tradition, they lie beyond the scope of our routine moral obligations. They reflect sensitivity, intuition, and imagination learned not from abstract law, but through imitating lofty historical models.[61] Members of historical communities also learn the meaning of moral life through narratives, institutions, and symbolic actions.

The Jews have excelled in cultivating their collective memory. This phenomenon is almost certainly based on the tradition, beginning in the Torah, of using the history of the Jewish people as a basis of exhortation: "You shall not oppress the stranger, . . . for you were strangers in the land of Egypt" (Ex 22:20). Over and over, the Torah commands the people to rehearse their past, for knowledge of the past is the key to moral renewal in the present. To remember is to feel moral claims and responsibilities. It is as a people with a historical identity that the Jews are responsible for observing the moral commandments. Moral action is in itself a confirmation of this identity, rooted in the ancient Covenant.

As we have noted, the preservation of identity depends on what the philosopher Bernard Williams calls "integrity," meaning a set of principles according to which men strive to mould their character.[62] A person feels loyal to the self-image he has created and to the principles on which it is based, for, in a sense, it is the preservation of that image that gives meaning to his life. This loyalty thus becomes a guiding principle in all that he does, and when forced to act contrary to it he is beset by deep misgivings. Furthermore, the integrity of the self, or what is called personal identity, presumes the integrity and continuity of the narrative in the framework of which his moral acts gain meaning. To speak of our identity means to speak both of who we are and who we want to be; the descriptive aspect cannot be separated from the normative one.[63] The question of what kind of Jews we strive to be is answered through the hermeneutics of the tradition. It is precisely for this reason that the term is so controversial, for tradition lends itself to a variety of interpretations.

The secular Zionists' attitude toward the idea of chosenness was ambivalent from the outset, ranging from utter rejection to indifference to enthusiastic espousal.[64] Zionism strove for "normalization." Relinquishing the idea of chosenness is one of the hallmarks of secularism. A people's existence needs no metaphysical justification, nor does a people need a destiny. All attempts to impose a mission upon the Jews reflect the "pathology of exile."[65] Such Zionist thinkers as Berdyczewski and Brenner maintain that adhering to the idea of chosenness under the humiliating objective conditions of Jewish life in exile is contemptible and ridiculous, a rationalization on the part of the weak (here we see the influence of Nietzsche); for there can be no true morality when there is no freedom of choice, no possibility to do wrong. We cannot claim that we are a chosen people as long as we are not a people, as long as we cannot demonstrate this in the way we live.[66]

Alongside this vigorous rejection of chosenness, there were some schools of Zionist thought that held on to traditional notions of Jewish destiny, in which the redemption of Israel is bound up with the universal redemption of mankind. There was an expectation that the Jewish people demands much of itself, the expectation that whatever the Jews do in their homeland serve in the future as a guidepost for mankind as a whole. But those who nurtured such expectations, like Ahad Ha'am and Buber, did not base them upon belief in any wider mission but only upon demands Jews should make of themselves out of existential loyalty to their heritage, and Gordon, considered the foremost advocate in secular Zionist circles of the idea of chosenness, maintained that there was no need for the Jewish people to justify its existence in the eyes of the world on the basis of its contribution to humanity; nor did he regard the idea of chosenness as a tool for educating others. Moral chosenness was an end in itself, the result of the people's faithfulness to its heritage.

The call for moral excellence was an inseparable part of the national consciousness of many Zionist thinkers and statesmen, religious and nonreligious alike, from Moses Hess to Rav Kook, Hayim Weizmann, and David Ben-Gurion. This is why social utopia played such a significant role in both the ideology and the practice of Zionism. The Zionist vision was not limited to politics; it included the building of a new society in the spirit of the Prophets. Since morality is a dominant component of Jewish identity, Zionist thinkers attributed great importance to the question of whether their moral views on current Jewish issues were compatible with the age-old teachings of the Torah. This explains why secular-minded Jews have turned to religious sources for a stamp of approval, as it were, for their moral views.[67] We may well ask whether anchorage in tradition lends special validity to a moral norm. From the point of view of universal morality (Hegel's *Moralität),* the answer is no; but from the point of view of "national morality" (Hegel's *Sittlichkeit*), this was quite a natural desire to preserve identity and to find historical continuity within the development of the tradition. "In the nation-state," Ruth Gavison writes, "it is only fitting that there be an attempt to emphasize and develop particularistic elements — in style, emphasis, and traditions — that give the system of social norms and the legal system derived from it their special vitality."[68]

Thus far we have presented "Jewish morality" as a concrete rather than abstract term in which Jews express what they see their historical identity as requiring of them. It is precisely for this reason that the term is so controversial, for tradition lends itself to a variety of interpretations. In any event, the interpretation Israeli Jews give to "Jewish morality" is derived from a sense of Jewish chosenness. The latter idea thus continues to serve as a point of controversy in Israeli political and moral discourse. This controversy reflects Israel's struggle over its Jewish and humane character. Advocates and opponents of this idea are to be found on the right and the left alike, each having his own arguments, depending on how he understands the meaning of the idea. Evidently, the sense of uniqueness arising from Jewish history continues to operate not only among religious Zionists, but also among secular-minded people, to the extent that they have a strong historical awareness.[69] Gershom Scholem may have been right when he said that deep faith in the moral uniqueness of the Jewish people, a uniqueness which makes its history important to the world as a whole, "transcends the sphere of pure secularization."[70]

I I

Halakha and Morality in Religious Zionism after the Six-Day War

From Universalism to Particularism

During the century of its existence, religious Zionism has undergone a profound change in its attitude to politics and power. It has gone from advocating strong restraints against the use of power for political ends to sanctioning warfare as a means of redeeming humankind, from open-minded universalism to a narrow parochialism that sees Jewish morality as being utterly different from that of the gentiles and the championing of Jewish sovereignty over the whole Land of Israel as the test of Zionist, and even Jewish loyalty. For the movement's first thinkers, national redemption was linked to universal redemption. It was not military power but the spiritual and moral power of the Torah, with its vision of world peace that was necessary for realizing Zionism's religious purpose.[1] The founding fathers of religious Zionism, such as Reines, Kook, and Amiel, had reservations as to whether Zionism, in its struggle for redemption, should make use of force.[2] To some extent, this was simply a continuation of the traditional view, which had for centuries served to restrain, if not suppress, any tendencies Jews might have had toward military activism. Although these thinkers were not true pacifists, they made much of the contrast in principle between the ways of Jacob and those of Esau, between the Jews' "culture of the book" and the gentiles' "culture of the sword." They believed it was the destiny of the former to supplant the latter. They rejected the possibility that the Jewish people's return to its homeland would necessitate bloodshed or the use of force against the country's Arab inhabitants. In fact, the redemption of the Jews and of humanity as a whole would come only when the rule of Amalek, meaning the culture of the sword, was abolished.[3]

These thinkers were aware of the dangers of nationalism, and they sought ways to avert them. In fact, they understood modern nationalism as an idolatry to be rooted out. Thus, while critical of the exilic life, they also called attention to the positive values that it had given rise to, especially the abhorrence for violence and bloodshed. Judaism, as they understood it, was the only thing that would prevent Zionism from becoming aggressively chauvinistic. If Zionism were nourished by the spirit of the Torah, they thought, it was certain to be different from other nationalist ideologies.

The problem is that one looks in vain in the writings of these figures for any serious grappling with political realities, such as Arab opposition to Jewish aspirations. Indeed, they do not even begin to engage in political thinking. (Of all the religious-Zionist leaders, only Rabbi Hayim Hirschensohn provides an exception in this regard.) It did not occur to them that one day it would be the religious Jews who would be the standard-bearers of an aggressive policy that did not recognize the rights of the country's other inhabitants. In this sense, they were naïve even more than many of the secular-Zionist leaders.

Anyway, the universalistic sentiment characteristic of the first religious-Zionist thinkers was shared by influential figures in Hehalutz Hamizrahi (the Oriental Pioneer), the settler-worker wing of the movement, and its most active faction during the prestate period. This faction claimed ideological affinity with the secular pioneer movement, identifying in large measure with its universalistic values.[4] This is evident from its educational program, its efforts to establish collective settlements, and its moderation concerning the Arab question, as demonstrated, for example, during the debate over self-restraint.

Until the Six-Day War (1967), religious Zionism did not take a distinct stand in any of the great political or moral controversies that wracked the Yishuv and the newborn state. Although the movement's views about Jewish entitlement to the Land of Israel were always closer to those of the right than the left, on a pragmatic level it took a moderate line, and once the state was established (1948), it narrowed its efforts to strictly religious matters, such as education and public violation of the Sabbath and the dietary laws. It said almost nothing about the struggle with Israel's Arab enemies, the question of how Israel was to treat its Arab minority, or major social issues. It did not speak out after the Israeli massacres at Deir Yassin (1948), Kibiya (1953), or Kafr Kassem (1956).[5] "It must be admitted sorrowfully," Tzvi Yaron, himself a religious intellectual, wrote in the early seventies, "that the purely religious contribution to [public] thinking about the new moral issues [facing] Israel has been quite meager."[6]

The messianic atmosphere that pervaded the country after the Six-Day War and the conquest of Judea, Samaria, and the Gaza Strip led the religious leadership to break its traditional silence and moved the religious-Zionist public as a whole from the fringes to the center of political activity. The messianically oriented faction within that public now became dominant. It was the time of the birth of political messianism in Israel in the form of Gush Emunim (the Bloc of the Faithful). From that point on, there were more and more public statements by religious leaders on the Israel-Arab conflict. What they said reveals a full-scale retreat from the universalistic tendencies of pre-state religious Zionism and an entrenchment in particularistic positions.[7]

Rabbi Tzvi Yehuda Kook, the spiritual leader of Gush Emunim and son of Avraham Kook, ruled that the Commandment to settle the Land of Israel was "essential and fundamental and encompass[ed] the entire Torah."[8] Consequently, it was an even more important Commandment than the three cardinal prohibitions (murder, idolatry, and fornication) which, in Jewish law, may not be violated even on pain of death. Unlike most other Commandments, it took precedence over the saving of human life, so that we might well have to go to war and sacrifice our lives for its sake.[9] True redemption would depend on extending Jewish sovereignty to all parts of the biblical Land of Israel. This is the younger Kook's essential theological innovation and one that is unprecedented in the Jewish tradition, legal or extralegal. Unlike Maimonides, Kook claims that the redemption of the people and the land are not dependent on a return (*teshuva*) of the Jews to God or religion. Such a return need not precede the messianic age but will, in fact, follow upon it once the political redemption now underway is complete.[10] Kook's new departure, influenced by the thinking of his father, lies in seeing the present, this-worldly redemption as actually being the messianic one. Redemption is taking place before our very eyes, not in supernatural occurrences but in processes that seem quite mundane.[11] The State of Israel is the state envisioned by the Prophets, and it serves as proof that we are in the midst of the process of redemption.[12] This process is being effected primarily by the military power of the state, and it is the army's successes more than anything else that reveal the workings of the Lord.[13]

Historically speaking, political messianism is the most radical expression of a major motif of Zionism: the need for activism, for taking Jewish fate into our own hands. Thus, for Kook, the fact that the present reality is a messianic one obligates the Jewish people to a prodigious effort to "force the End." Since the main aspect of the redemption is political and military, the state and its army are, for Kook, "holy," and all the wars waged by Israel are to be considered divinely ordained.[14]

The only war that was considered to be holy in the Jewish tradition was the Joshua's war of occupation of the Land of Israel. Recently, however, it has been changed by Zionist rabbis: following Kook, several Zionist rabbis have maintained that the wars of Israel all have a theological meaning: Gentile attacks on Israel are attacks on God, but because they are not capable of fighting Him they fight Israel instead: "There is a constant struggle being waged in the world between the Lord's people, who seek to make [His] kingdom evident in the world, and 'all the nations oblivious to God,' who wish to make the world forget the Lord's name. . . . The enemies of the Lord want to fight Him, as it were, and they do it by making war on His people, the people of Israel; they therefore attack the Holy Land, the Land of Israel, by polluting its soil with all sorts of idolatry and the like. . . . This final struggle against holiness in the world is a lost cause, a last spasm before holiness appears in all its glory. These are desperate attempts to hinder the redemptive process, which is becoming more and more evident."[15] The struggle between Israel and the other nations thus takes on a cosmic, demonic character. As in other contemporary fundamentalist movements, this is a struggle for the victory of the divine idea over secular Western culture, which symbolizes all the impurity in the world.[16]

Peace in and of itself is not an ideal in Judaism, or at least not a short-term goal, as long as the entire Land of Israel is not in Jewish hands and the entire people of Israel is not living in the Land. Hence, "even if there is peace, we must initiate a war of liberation to conquer [the Land]."[17] True peace will not come without an educational and moral revolution on the part of the Arabs, that is, until they recognize the uniqueness of the Jewish people and accept the seven Noahide Commandments (those which, according to Jewish teaching, apply to all human beings).[18] Thus peace represents the end of history, the utter perfection that will only appear in the time of the Messiah.[19]

The Sense of Moral Superiority

For some spokesmen of this new messianic Zionism, the election of Israel now takes on not only an ontological, metaphysical meaning (which it already had for the medieval thinkers Yehuda Halevi and Yehuda Loew of Prague) but also a political and moral one. As the Chosen People, Israel is morally superior to the other nations and is thus entitled to use its military power to fulfill its political and moral mission in the world. The Jewish people is the only people that is prepared to institute a new political order and is unwilling to give in to wickedness and blackmail. It bears responsibility not only for itself but for all humanity and, of course, also for the neighboring people (the Arabs), which needs to be taught to recognize its own best interests. An outstanding example of this approach is provided by Rabbi Eliezer Waldman, head of a yeshiva in the newly captured city of Hebron. In his view, acquiring power and honor is a condition for fulfilling the Jewish people's moral mission. "The people of Israel must first gain respect in the world; otherwise, it will not be able to teach the ways of truth, the ways of righteousness and justice. And because it was for so long a despised people, vilified and abused, our people, even more than others, must, for its very survival and then for the content of that survival, attain a position of strength. [It must become] a people that cannot be scorned, despised, or attacked because it can defend its existence and its honor. . . . The nations of the world know in their hearts that we have a moral sensitivity, a sense of justice and righteousness, a compassion. They are aware of our sensitivity about human life (which they do not share). . . . The knowledge that we are different from them gives them feelings of inferiority, expressed in their blaming us for a lack of morality."[20]

Playing the educational role of "light unto the nations" requires, first of all, being strong, for "a wretch's wisdom is disdained," and only one who is forceful gains a hearing. Under the conditions of exile it was not possible to exert any influence, to radiate light. Only now that we have become heroes who know how to stand up for ourselves do we have a chance to affect the world. This is what gives a positive dimension to Israel's wars. Israel's wars are part of the struggle for world peace and the redemption of humanity. There will be peace in the world only when all nations acknowledge the Jewish people's exclusive title to the Land of Israel and this land's centrality in the world. "All humankind will be blessed by the people of Israel living a full life in [the whole of] its land."[21]

Waldman contends that the Arab masses have been incited against Israel by their leaders and thus prevented from recognizing their real interests. Our task as Jews is to help them and teach them about the motives of their leaders.[22] That is, through appropriate propaganda the Arabs' approach to Zionism can be changed: they will recognize that what is taking place here is a redemptive process of global import. When they do, they will cooperate of their own accord in furthering the Zionist undertaking.[23] Thus, the theological argument that stresses the election of the Jewish people justifies moral paternalism. According to this approach, Jewish domination of the Arabs will not, in the end, cause them suffering but bring them benefit. Although they do not recognize this as yet, they will in the future acknowledge the justice of the Zionist cause. Such paternalism, familiar to us from the history of colonialism, provides ideological legitimation for denying the Palestinian-Arab people's right of self-determination. The brute assertion of power receives religious sanction as a tool for propagating elevated moral values among the morally and culturally inferior "natives."[24]

Moral condescension precludes any possibility of self-criticism. The sense of chosenness and the belief in the Jews' absolute, exclusive entitlement to the Land of Israel provide a comfortable platform for the development of a simplistic approach to the Arabs. Because, morally speaking, we are superior to all the other nations, our treatment of them is above criticism. This tendency is reflected in the mentality of today's religious-Zionist young people who are loyal to the Land (and not only the State) of Israel and who, unlike their nonreligious counterparts, have no misgivings about the Jews' right to the land or the justice of their stand in the conflict with Arab nationalism because they see themselves as exempt, a priori, from such reservations.[25]

The Jewish ethic is infinitely superior to those of the other nations. "Our morality is no human creation; it is not autonomous but heteronomous, or, more precisely, theonomous." It is because of this moral superiority that "the Jewish people . . . cannot abide immoral behavior in the Land of Israel, the cradle of prophecy . . . and morality for the entire world." The Jews thus call upon all their neighbors to observe the seven basic moral principles (the Noahide Commandments).[26] The Jewish people's subjection to the "higher morality" implies that the Commandment that it conquer the Land "transcends any human moral qualms about the national rights of gentiles in our land," for the happiness of the whole world depends on "the Jewish people being restored to health and to normal residence in the whole length and breadth of its country."[27]

In short, the sense of chosenness is translated into a moral outlook that does not recognize Jews and gentiles as equals, indeed, opens an unbridgeable gap between them. Underlying this position is the view that human rights are a purely European idea, alien to Judaism. The extreme view of the disparity between Jews and non-Jews leads to the conclusion that the latter not only have no national rights in the Land of Israel but have no human or civil rights, in the usual sense, either. This does not necessitate actually expelling them — as the extremist Meir Cahane, for example, thought — but as long as the Arabs do not recognize the mission of the Jewish people, they cannot partake equally of Israeli democracy.[28] The halakhic category best suited to defining the status of minorities in the Land of Israel is that of the *ger toshav* (resident alien), who does not have equal rights with the country's legitimate proprietors but is permitted to dwell there as long as he accepts the seven Noahide Commandments.[29]

The position of the Ashkenazic Orthodox leadership in Israel regarding relations with non-Jews does not appear essentially different from the position it took in Eastern Europe in the nineteenth and twentieth centuries: moral superiority mixed with fear and suspicion of the *goi*. But these leaders have overlooked the historical change that has taken place: Jews now have power and are not dependent on the gentiles. The rabbis are speaking out on crucial public issues involving war and morality, basing themselves not on a thorough understanding of these issues or the changes wrought by the Zionist revolution, but on a superficial application of past experience.[30]

The messianic interpretation of events, along with the dichotomy between Jewish and human morality, makes for a tendency to shrug off responsibility for the consequences of one's actions. Because the process is historically necessary and redemption a present reality, we need not be concerned with the moral and political effects of what we do. A way of thinking that sanctifies the political status quo and gives a religious stamp of approval in advance to everything done in its name leads inevitably to the swallowing up of politics by religion, or of religion by politics. It is an approach that refuses to recognize the limits imposed by either reality or conventional morality. The great historic "right" of redemption provides a cover for the little (and not so little) wrongs committed in everyday life. The main danger recognized by this approach is not that of the moral corruption that can result from an unrestrained use of force but the weakness of faith implicit in concessions and compromises with our enemies under pressure from outside powers. Our relations with other nations should be based on a belief that "if we are firm we shall succeed." That is, these relations depend on us alone, and "if we believe in ourselves and the rightness of our course, we shall convince them as well."[31]

These ideas betoken a return to a fundamentalistic understanding of scripture. Such power-related terms as "vengeance," "expulsion," and even "annihilation," which had been softened somewhat by the Jewish exegetical tradition, have become once again a legitimate part of religious discourse.

The Issue of Harming Civilians

The most conspicuous change in the moral outlook of religious Zionism after the Six-Day War was on the question of causing harm to the civilian population of the enemy. In contrast to the unequivocal condemnation of this practice expressed by the religious leadership in the 1930s, more and more rabbis in this camp ruled such harm permissible after the fact or even saw it a positive religious duty as part of the struggle against Arab terror. Such views became particularly widespread during the Lebanon war (1982) and the Intifada (1987–93). A concept of vengeance that did not distinguish between the

innocent and the guilty gained ground among religious Zionists. "Jewish ethics has no room for excessive righteousness." Such pangs of conscience are not
rooted in the Jewish religion.[32] The struggle is with "Ishmael" in general, i.e.,
all the Arab peoples bent on our destruction, and not only with the actual
perpetrators of terror. The view that we should not imitate our enemies, which
dominated the earlier debate over self-restraint (1936–39), was now explicitly
rejected in favor of a "biblical" view that insisted on "speaking the enemy's
language and using his own weapons against him." Relations with neighbors
should be based on reciprocity, which justified collective punishment,[33] and
there can be no doubt that the Israel Defense Forces' actions in the occupied
territories are "compatible with Jewish ethics."[34]

The operative conclusion of this ideology is a rejection of the army's traditional concept of "purity of arms." The Jewish people was commanded to be
"holy," not "moral" according to gentile standards. There is a tendency among
the religious-Zionist leaders to distinguish between the Torah's code of conduct in war and the "gentile" code, which they condemn as hypocritical and
false. Rabbi Yehuda Gershuni writes that, according to the laws of the Torah,
prisoners captured during the Lebanon war should be executed since most of
them are members of the Palestine Liberation Organization and, as such, can
be assumed to be bent on spilling Jewish blood. But in our present situation,
"as a small, poor people, dependent on others, we are not free in our political
decisions and cannot carry out the dictates of Jewish law to the letter."[35] Rabbi
Shimon Weiser states that the Geneva Convention is to be considered "gentile
law" and thus not binding on Israel's army. In time of war it is permissible to
shed a gentile's blood, "unless it is clear that he has no evil intent. It is this
principle that, from the point of view of Halakha, defines 'purity of arms.' "[36]

Rabbi Dov Lior, of Hebron Yeshiva, too, holds that "we should not go
overboard in adopting the standards of foreigners." Not everything said by the
gentiles about Israel is said from a moral point of view; much is said out of
hatred for Jews. "So let us not adopt their morality, [but rather] rely on the
Halakhic sources." He is confident that "whoever goes to war out of a conviction that he is saving Israel from a holocaust shall not be morally compromised
in the least."[37] The underlying assumption is that for a religious Jew faithful to
the Halakha there can never be a contradiction between it and morality because it is the Halakha that determines what is and is not moral. "For a
believing Jew there can never be a moral problem in wartime, because [for
him] going to war is always the expression of a divine will to protect the
community, and whatever is required and needed for such protection automatically becomes moral, even if it be the cruelest of acts, such as murder
itself."[38]

All in all, one conclusion is clearly to be drawn from the sacred texts: "Israel's Torah and modern atheistic humanism have nothing in common. . . . A Torah that calls for vengeance in such terms as 'A blessing on him who seizes your babies and dashes them against the rocks!' (Ps 137:9) — such a Torah is not humane. It is based on moral principles utterly different from those accepted today in the Western world, and it makes no difference whether these laws are applicable today or not; the eternal [underlying] principles do not change."[39]

This sharp distinction between atheistic, humanistic morality and that of the Torah raises afresh the question of whether there is any moral difference between the murder of a gentile and a Jew. The issue came to the fore with the exposure of an anti-Arab Jewish underground in Judea and Samaria in 1983, when there were those who distinguished between the shedding of Jewish and gentile blood. They cited the great late-medieval halakhist Rabbi Yosef Karo, who, commenting in his *Kesef Mishna* on Maimonides' code (Laws of the Murderer and the Saving of Life 2:11), rules that the punishment of one who murders a gentile is in the hands of God, not a human court. For Rabbi Sha'ul Yisraeli, considered one of the most important authorities of the religious-Zionist movement, there is an ontological difference between Jewish and gentile blood, and this view is accepted by other rabbis.[40] Rabbi Yisrael Ariel examines this issue halakhically and concludes that the prohibition "Thou shalt not kill" does not apply to a Jew killing a gentile but is limited to the killing of one who shares one's commitment to the Torah and the Commandments, i.e., a fellow Jew.[41]

The most vigorous opponent of harming noncombatants was the late Rabbi Shlomo Goren. For many years the chief chaplain of the Israel Defense Forces, Goren drew a halakhic lesson from the story of Dinah (Gen 34) for the behavior of present-day Israeli soldiers in wartime. He pointed out that, on the question of harming noncombatant populations, the "two lights of the world," Maimonides and Nahmanides, disagree as to whether Simeon and Levi, in that episode, acted according to Halakha. He tries to reconcile the two: Maimonides' ruling is that "Simeon and Levi's act was halakhically correct, but only according to a strict construction of the law, and it was not morally correct" because "wherever laws concerning capital punishment are concerned, there is a pious way of ruling that sometimes runs counter to Halakha, . . . and in this case the pious way of ruling should be followed." In Jewish capital law regarding gentiles, too, "there is a pious way of ruling, based on compassion, that is to be followed even in wartime and that we should study as being derived from an attribute of the Holy One, blessed be He." That is, for Goren "beyond the call of duty" displaces "duty," and "moral" rectitude displaces "halakhic" rectitude because the pious way of ruling "is also Torah," and in capital matters it transcends Halakha. This leads Goren to the far-reaching conclusion that it is forbidden to harm a noncombatant population "and certainly forbidden to harm women and children who are not participants in the fighting." The only exceptions are the wars the ancient Jews were commanded by the Torah to wage because in those cases the enemy had treated them cruelly. But no lesson should be drawn from those wars regarding others taking place in our own time.[42] Goren called upon other rabbis to warn against harming noncombatants, "particularly since the Halakha is clear and definitive on the subject, lest, heaven forbid, God's name be profaned by it being said that the Torah permits the indiscriminate killing of the innocent together with murderers."[43]

Halakha and Morality

It is thus rare for the fathers of religious Zionism to voice moral misgivings about the use of force against Arabs. There have been those among them who criticized fundamentalism, intolerance, and narrow-mindedness, both in regard to other Jews who held different opinions and toward Arabs. But such voices are a minority within a minority, and they have had little public influence. Yeshaya Leibowitz pointed out the "glibness and simple-mindedness," the "shallow dogmatism" displayed by the religious authorities in their discussions of how to react to violence, which he saw as "a matter that goes to the root of human consciousness and conscience" and has been debated inconclusively since time immemorial.[44]

What is the source of this lack of sensitivity to the suffering we cause others, and how is it that there is so little moral concern about violence on the part of a public educated in the Torah, which stresses time and again the importance of justice and mercy? This would seem to be a sign of a broader phenomenon: in Orthodox Judaism, especially its Ashkenazic variety, recent generations have seen a progressive detachment of religion from morality in all spheres.[45] This process can be explained as a defensive reaction to modernity and to the secularization of societal norms.[46] The unraveling of the connection between religion and universal norms—a connection that was self-evident to earlier generations—indicates a crisis in religion in our time, in which religion no longer encompasses the totality of life. The same phenomenon is to be found in Protestant Christianity, from Kierkegaard to Barthian "dialectical theology," which stress faith's revelatory, transcendent character, so alien to accepted human values.[47] The rejection of religion's moral dimension was meant to shore up its autonomy and highlight its uniqueness at a time when the boundaries between religion and culture had become blurred.

As we have seen, contemporary Orthodoxy tends to identify morality with Halakha. In this approach, all decisions, including those on public matters, must be made on a purely halakhic basis. At present, this is also the approach of a large part of the religious-Zionist camp, which has, in effect, followed the ultra-Orthodox. This is an ironical development, for it represents a marked departure from the original teachings of Rav Kook and the universal values of early religious Zionism in favor of a narrow particularism. Kook, after all, incorporated universal human morality into his thought in a profound way, maintaining that the Torah was based upon natural morality, which the God-fearing were forbidden to disregard.[48]

This retreat is a dialectical expression of processes underway in Israeli society since the establishment of the state and of the problematical position of religious Zionism, caught between two camps — the anti-Zionist ultra-Orthodox and the nonreligious Zionists — toward both of which it has always been ambivalent. As I have written elsewhere, religious Zionism always had trouble achieving "a comprehensive synthesis of Zionism and religion. . . . In relation to ultra-Orthodoxy it saw itself as religiously inferior, while to secular Zionism it saw itself as inferior from a Zionist point of view."[49] The way out of this bind, which first became evident after the Six-Day War and the wave of messianic sentiment it stirred up, is a mixture of nationalistic, messianic ideology and a personal way of life that tends toward halakhic stringency. This mixture is intended to draw the two poles together and to give religious Zionism a central role in the society as a whole. As secularization proceeded apace in Israel, accompanied by the growing alienation of the nonreligious public from both the Jewish religious heritage and the labor ethos, the time for such a melding seemed ripe. These processes had produced a polarization of the two moral worldviews: precisely because so many people in the nonreligious camp stressed social and political — or, if you will, universal — morality, many religiously observant Jews did not regard such morality as "Jewish." A significant part of the religious-Zionist public saw its Jewishness expressed in purely particularistic terms: the world of Halakha, on one hand, and faithfulness to the land and people of Israel on the other. Gravitation toward the ultra-Orthodox pole, with its stress on the ritual side of religion, and extreme nationalism, with a concomitant stress on Judaism's ethnic elements, are two sides of the same coin: the suppression of the dimension of universal morality in Jewish religion. We have seen various aspects of this phenomenon in the ideology of Gush Emunim.

Detaching the Halakha from universal human morality means regarding it as independent of any other worldview or moral philosophy. Faithfulness to the Halakha in the narrow sense frees one of the need to think and weigh independently, indeed, to consider moral questions altogether, for it is the

Halakha that determines what is moral and provides the only guarantee, as it were, of appropriate moral behavior. Universal morality is seen as a secular, Western concept, alien to the Torah. This leads to a demonstrative rejection of all moral norms originating in the non-Jewish world, which is only ostensibly humane. It can also lead to discrimination between Jewish and gentile blood. Extreme particularism, wrapped in universal garb, and unquestioning faith that whatever serves the interests of the state and people of Israel is inherently good for humanity at large account for the defense by certain Zionist rabbis of such Israeli behavior as that in the 1982 Sabra-Shatila massacre, the actions of the Jewish underground in 1983, and the Hebron massacre of 1994.

What is more, as a corollary of the absolute authority given to Halakha vis-à-vis individual moral conscience, there is increased reliance in the religious-Zionist community on *da'at Torah* ("the opinion of the Torah"), the views of halakhic authorities on extra-halakhic issues, which are seen as superior to ordinary human considerations. This is not the place to discuss the reason for this phenomenon.[50] When it spreads to the political realm, however, the result is a swallowing up of politics by established religion. *Da'at Torah,* which was unknown in Jewish tradition until the last few generations, is now even more authoritative than a halakhic ruling, for it need not be based on earlier sources, which are open to argument. It falls under the heading of a *gezera* (decree), based on what is called "trust in the sages" (*emunat hakhamim*), and is not subject to questioning as to how it was derived. This means blind obedience and a suspension of independent, spontaneous thinking and conscience.[51]

Ideology and the Problem of Halakhic Interpretation

Criticism by religious Zionists themselves of the view that sees the Halakha as completely independent of universal human morality comes from two directions. One, theological or philosophical, holds that regarding Halakha as totally distinct from human morality contradicts our concept of God and His relationship to man. The other, empirical, examines the methodology and technique of the Halakha itself, as it has crystallized down through the ages, and shows that its arbiters, in their rulings, employed moral considerations and norms drawn from outside the Halakha in the narrow sense, i.e., they recognized general human morality as a factor in the halakhic system.

The point of departure of the theological critique is that the concept of the commanding God in Jewish tradition assumes both His goodness and man's ability to recognize the good independently of Him. Hence, despite the Halakha's divine origin in the Torah, man is not expected to suppress his moral or intellectual awareness in deference to its authority. The Covenant between man and God presumes mutuality and does not demand that man give up his spiritual independence but rather that he take responsibility for his actions. The halakhic system is not immune to the weaknesses and limitations of all human knowledge, and thus it must be sensitive, like all human knowledge, to the judgment and criticism of others, especially in the case of commandments that have a moral import.[52] From a philosophical analysis of the necessary consequences of God's goodness, Daniel Statman and Avraham Sagi conclude that Jewish tradition does not admit the possibility of a contradiction between human morality and the word of God. Morality does not depend on religion, but it is not opposed to it either. The two are congruent with one another. The commanding God is a good God. The believer's world is not shaped exclusively by the divine imperative. "There are values which are valid independently of the divine command, [values] which man is capable of knowing independently of God and to which he is deeply committed." They see this conclusion as flowing from the Jewish hermeneutical tradition, which seeks in various ways to overcome conflicts between religion and human morality, believing in the righteousness and benevolence of God, whose Torah is one of life and loving-kindness ("Its ways are ways of pleasantness." Prov 3:17). This accounts for the willingness of certain commentators to detach the sacred text from its plain meaning in order to avoid offending our moral sensibilities. They approach the text with the conviction that the word of God cannot contradict our basic moral intuitions. Furthermore, since man is commanded to imitate God, his obligation goes *beyond* the law (*lifnim mishurat hadin*); the idea of *imitatio dei* gives the commentators a metahalakhic basis for speaking about moral obligation.[53]

The view that regards the morality of the Torah as entirely different from accepted human morality thus flies in the face of what we find in the sacred texts themselves. The views of the sages down through the centuries until modern times were anchored not only in these texts but also in what was accepted by the nations among whom they lived. There were two justifications for this. One was a concern about "sanctification of the divine name" (*kiddush hashem*) and "desecration of the divine name" (*hillul hashem*), i.e., the assumption that Jews' moral behavior determined the standing of the Jewish religion, and thus of God Himself, in gentile eyes. The other grew out of the halakhic principle that the social setting in which Jews live must be taken into account in deciding the law. In fact, most of the leading Jewish thinkers assumed that it was upon human morality that the laws of the Torah were built. Avraham Sagi cites Rabbi Hayim Hirschensohn: "There is no rule or law in the Torah that is contrary to the ways of true civilization" (*Malki bakodesh* 1:21). Hirschensohn goes even farther, holding that it is forbidden to violate international law. Jacob cursed his sons Simeon and Levi for doing so by killing innocent people (*Ele divrei habrit* 1:70). Thus, while human morality and Halakha are not identical, there is no contradiction between them. Furthermore, moral considerations should be an integral part of halakhic reasoning.

In a wide-ranging article on halakhic methodology, Eliezer Goldman shows that "[Present-day] Orthodox ideology concerning halakhic decision-making does not reflect what authorities did [in times past]. . . . This is a [new] construction, shaped by the battle against reformist tendencies. In addition, it reflects a sociological situation in which the Torah has become the property of those who frequent the study-halls but has ceased to shape public life."[54]

Goldman thus rejects the Orthodox ideology according to which Halakha is something completely autonomous and unrelated to other sets of norms, and he shows that this approach does not jibe with the way the Halakha has always operated. Traditionally, value judgments made by the teacher and judge play a not insignificant role in halakhic decision making. Therefore, metalegal (or metahalakhic) norms mediate between these value judgments and the Halakha proper, guiding us in the interpretation and application of the latter. The Rabbinic authority's readiness to widen or restrict a halakhic norm, or his readiness to interpret the Halakha according to a given extra-halakhic principle, depends on value judgments concerning the situation under discussion, which naturally gives added importance to the ideological dimension of halakhic decision making.[55] The worldview of the rabbi, his sensitivity, and his familiarity with the human problems of the day are thus crucial. He cannot be oblivious to historical developments, imposing old standards simplistically upon the new reality, or he will fail to bring that reality under the aegis of the halakhic way of life. The multiplicity of halakhic sources and the existence of extra-halakhic norms both help him grapple with unexpected cases and situations. While in making use of an extra-halakhic norm the authority does not introduce new law or set up his autonomous value judgments as opposed to the Halakha, such judgments do, nevertheless, guide him in the rulings he makes based on legal texts.[56]

The Halakha itself recognizes the legitimacy of using various human values in legal decision making, so that it would be incorrect to view it as a monolithic system. A difference of extra-halakhic views, which may be ideological in nature, can lead to a difference in halakhic rulings. Nor does the Halakha supply an unambiguous answer to every human problem, something which only a lack of faith or embarrassment prevents us from recognizing. "The Halakha" Goldman says, "was attended by uncertainty from the moment the Torah was given to us." The textual sources are not unambiguous, there is no uniformity of thinking, and we can never be absolutely sure what the Torah's intention is.[57]

The Crisis of Religious Zionism

Religious thinkers like Julius Guttmann and Ernst Simon, who had been educated in the tradition of European humanism, believed that the return of the Jewish people to its homeland and the establishment of an independent Jewish society opened up new opportunities for Jewish religious expression, especially in terms of Judaism's relationship to the world at large. Living in exile as a minority struggling to preserve its distinctiveness had imposed a certain narrowness on the Jewish religion, in terms of both intellectual receptivity and political activity. Assimilative pressures had compelled Judaism to play the sociological role of a protective shell for Jewish life, while prolonged inequality and persecution had fostered in it a certain intolerance and parochialism. An example is the distinction in Halakha between the moral standards to be applied in relations with Jews and non-Jews, which Jacob Katz has referred to as the distinction between "internal" and "external" morality. These thinkers hoped that the return to the homeland would liberate religion from its traditional sociological function; once Jews were reunited on their native soil, concern about Jewish survival would cease to be central to them and, as a result, Jewish religiosity would be capable of a freer, more natural attitude toward Western culture.[58] Simon thought Zionism was creating the basis for more civilized relations between the Jewish people and the rest of the world, grounded in equality and shared values, thus enabling Judaism to express fully and freely its inherent humanism and universalism.[59] Such expectations were not very far from those of the founders of religious Zionism.

And, indeed, it seemed at first as though these expectations would be fulfilled. But gradually, as we have shown, a profound change took place which has had the opposite result: it is precisely in the State of Israel, where the Jews are a politically enfranchised, empowered majority, that their religious conviction has taken an extremely particularistic turn. And religious Zionism has not yet come to terms with the two demons it confronts within Jewish tradition: explosive apocalypticism and the negative image of the gentile; nor has it defined its position regarding the concept of democracy.

The expected positive turn may well have been prevented by two interrelated existential problems: the place of religion in Zionist identity and the confrontation with Palestinian nationalism.[60] Both have had the effect of strengthening the particularistic element in Israeli Judaism.[61] Religion thus continues to play a significant psychological and sociological role, though different from the one it played in the Diaspora. It is no longer a protective shell but the indispensable ideological foundation of a people's struggle for its historic homeland. As long as the Arab-Jewish conflict continues, religion will not be able to extricate itself from this bind or develop an open, critical approach toward the sacred texts that will allow for a reinterpretation of them in light of the new relationship between the Jewish people and the family of nations.

So it happened that, as Hayim Be'er has said, "Judaism has failed miserably in its contact with the state, with power, and with modernity."[62] Its greatest failure has been in its mystification of power. This is perhaps the central paradox of Zionism, testifying simultaneously to the success of its moral revolution and to the dangers that revolution carries. As we have seen, religious esteem for power derives from a fundamentalist reading of scripture and also from halakhic sources. The religious-Zionist messianic zealots see themselves as being in the forefront of the camp, and they do not shy away from the use of force. "Paradoxically enough," Menahem Friedman writes, "this zeal is an [integral] part of the Zionist revolution, which demands sovereignty and is prepared to take up arms without hesitation in pursuit of its aims."[63] The coupling of halakhic sources in which a justification can be found for murder, pure and simple, with the modern ethos of power politics enormously increases the potential for violence. This danger looms especially great when we consider the widespread demand by religious leaders to give the Halakha precedence over democratic law, a demand meant to silence all moral criticism.

Many of religious Zionism's spokesmen regard any willingness to compromise for the sake of peace as, prima facie, a sign of the weakening of Jewish identity. Such an approach is not unique to them, however; it now characterizes large parts of the non-Zionist religious public as well. Ultra-Orthodox Jewry has been deeply influenced by the idolization of power. It is proud of the fact that Jews have power, although this pride is unconnected to Zionism's ideological underpinnings. First and foremost in the latter category is the Habad movement, which draws a simple comparison between faithfulness to the Torah and faithfulness to the Land of Israel. The greater a Jew's faithfulness to the Torah and the deeper his connection to it, the greater will be his opposition to territorial concessions. For Habad, devotion to the Torah and the Commandments implies an uncompromising assertion of power, which alone can guarantee the survival of the state and the health of the Jewish people in their homeland, while preventing a renewal of soft, exilic thinking. Even conceding that the assertiveness of the Orthodox Jews in Israel is, to some extent, a reaction to the "defeatism" of the left, which is largely estranged from Judaism, the simplistic identification of Judaism with power, in the sense of violent domination, is still astonishing.

The crisis of religious Zionism would appear to have arisen in the same area as the crisis of secular Zionism, though with opposite results. In both camps, there has been a failure of reinterpretation: the founding generation failed to transmit its spiritual legacy to the generation that followed. But whereas the founders of secular Zionism did not pass on their *Jewish* experience to their children, the founders of religious Zionism failed to translate their *humanitarian* values into normative, halakhic terms, so that, in the next generation, a gulf opened between Halakha and morality. The religious Zionists, who had made their accommodations to modernity, refrained from taking the decisive step that their model called for: "legitimating religious change by getting the religious public to adopt it, even without the approval of the rabbinic authorities."[64] As long as the Halakha is conceded to be completely autonomous, based only on internal Jewish sources, the fundamentalists will have the upper hand. They can claim, quite rightly from their point of view, that the humane ethos espoused by the devotees of modernity is a compromise and accommodation stemming from a desire to imitate Western culture or assimilate to it, not something inherently Jewish. Thus Ya'ir Sheleg was right to maintain that modernist Orthodox society could not resist fundamentalism because it had painted itself into a corner: "This society lives a two-faced ideological life: on the one hand, it conducts its daily affairs in a such a way that the traditional norms of thought are important but not exclusively so. This is a way of life no longer based entirely on authentic midrash but [also] on [contemporary] values and viewpoints, and in the practical realm it is full of foreign influences. On the other hand, since faithfulness to the sacred texts is still of the highest importance to all sectors of Orthodox society, it continues to pay lip service to these texts, as if its whole way of life flowed from them and from their interpretation alone.[65] To get out of the endless wrangling with the ultra-Orthodox over the interpretation of the sacred texts, modernist Orthodoxy must admit openly that it too, and not only secularism, "fixes the bounds of its world according to the Bible and [other] traditional sources, but not only according to them." The question is to what extent the authorities will have the courage to innovate in these ways.[66]

Persecuted or Persecutor?

The protracted conflict with the Palestinians forces the Jews of Israel to come to terms with their past. In an almost paradoxical way, they draw contradictory conclusions from it. Long-term exposure to degradation, violence, and the danger of annihilation in the Diaspora, and the ongoing existential threat to the state from the Muslim world have tended to foster the view that military power is the only way to ensure survival. Over time, Israelis have developed an image of themselves as victims and targets of aggression, an image that has deep roots in Jewish history. But the long history of Jewish agony also serves as a permanent reminder of the importance of universal human solidarity. A people that suffered so long as an oppressed minority cannot remain indifferent to the sufferings of other peoples, particularly when it is responsible for these sufferings. Consequently, it feels uneasy at the use of force and at the possibility that the "lamb," the eternal victim, might turn into a "wolf," that the persecuted might become the persecutor.

Tension between these contradictory lessons of the past characterizes public rhetoric in Israel and the imagery by which Jewish society understands itself in relation to the outside world. The positions of the various political camps in Israel in regard to the Palestinians range from extreme self-justification on the right, which places all the blame on the Palestinians and refuses to recognize them as having any rights, to extreme self-accusation on the left, which ignores the actual contribution the Palestinians have made to the conflict. On the right, there is a stronger existential fear of the possibility of future annihilations and greater suspicion of non-Jews. In rightists' view, there is no chance that the latter will ever change their attitude toward the Jews, and thus Jews must be assertive toward them, never betraying any sign of doubt, concession, or weakness. On the left, on the other hand, feelings of guilt at the need to use force predominate. The left tends to downplay the severity of this protracted conflict, seeing it as an ordinary dispute between nations that happens to stretch back one hundred years and ignoring its Muslim religious dimension. Thus, in the leftist view, normalizing relations with the Palestinians seems a relatively straightforward matter, dependent mainly on our will and conduct and not on the events of the past.

The Image of Victim

In the first years after the establishment of the state, the prevalent ethos in Israel was that of *mamlakhtiut* — conduct appropriate for a sovereign people — associated with the name of David Ben-Gurion. Having striven his whole life for the normalization of Jewish existence, Ben-Gurion sought to ground Israel's foreign relations on equality, mutual aid, and shared interests and to disentangle them from all feelings of shame, sympathy, and appeals to morality or conscience. He saw the conflict with the Arabs, too, as one of interests, not unlike disputes between other sovereign states, rather than as just another front in the historic struggle between Jews and gentiles. "From the point of view of *mamlakhtiut*, the creation of the state represented a break with the Diaspora Jewish fate of suffering and persecution, and thus this approach steered clear of anything that might be interpreted as assuming the role of 'victim' in relations between the state and the Jewish people [, on the one hand,] and the rest of the world, [on the other]. . . . The notion of *mamlakhtiut* fosters the image of the State of Israel as strong, confident, and self-reliant and at the same time deserving of the support and confidence of other states. This image was not compatible with the traditional one of 'a lamb among wolves' or of 'a people that dwells alone.' "[1]

Ben-Gurion believed that if the Jewish people could acquire political and military power, it could free itself of its "exile complex" in its relations with other nations. There were two developments, however, that led to a gradual return to the image of Israel as victim: the protracted, violent struggle between Israel and the Arab states, accompanied by repeated threats of annihilation from the Arab side; and the growing power within Israel of the memory of the Holocaust. Both these developments deepened Israel's feeling of isolation and vulnerability and prepared the ground for a suppression of the idea of normalization in the late 1960s in favor of more traditional images like "a people that dwells alone," which many Israelis had wanted to shed.[2]

In the minds of Israeli Jews, the memory of the Holocaust becomes emblematic of their present existential situation and strengthens their sense of solidarity with each other. At the same time, it makes them more suspicious of non-Jews and more inclined to rely on themselves alone. There thus develops a psychological and political climate favorable to the recrudescence of traditional Jewish-gentile imagery among wide circles of the public that have generally distanced themselves from it. This imagery has, as Charles Liebman points out, given expression to an ideology with an authentically Jewish cast that also fits reality as secularist Jews experience it.[3]

The transformation of the victim into a mythic symbol reduces the fear of death in a way that is vital for a society fighting desperately for its life. The victim becomes the focus of a sacred cult, and the story of his sacrifice becomes a paradigm that gives the community confidence in its final victory. It is thus no accident that most of the symbols that have sustained the Zionist cause in the past have been taken from narratives of defeat: Massada, Beitar, Tel Hai, the Warsaw ghetto, and the Holocaust itself, the greatest of all Jewish reverses. They all express defiance of fate, weakness turned to strength. Thus, according to Yisrael Eldad, Israel may be the only country in the world where the three most important national monuments — Massada, the Western Wall, and Yad Vashem (the national Holocaust memorial) — all recall destruction and defeat rather than victory.[4]

But there is a decisive difference between the way the victim image functions for a powerless minority struggling against an oppressive majority — like the Jewish people in exile — and the way it functions in a sovereign polity possessed of military power. In the former case, the narrative of victimization serves as an ideological weapon, a source of comfort and solace to a defenseless group. But in the latter case it can serve to legitimate and encourage indiscriminate violence. The victimized community can gradually be transformed from the persecuted party to the persecuting one. Having assumed for itself a monopoly on suffering, the victim-community becomes indifferent to the suffering of the other. Furthermore, it expects the world to sympathize entirely with its position, as a way of repaying a moral debt and atoning for wrongs done it in the past. It refuses to consider at face value any accusation made by others, seeing in such accusations merely another link in the chain of hatred, suffering, and degradation that is its exclusive inheritance. Being in constant danger, it also rejects all demands from inside for self-criticism and moral accounting with the claim that they are likely to weaken its resolve to stand fast. Moral criticism is taken as a sign of weakness or lack of faith in the rightness of the struggle, and it is thus branded as hypocrisy or falsification. In this way, the community may gradually lose not only its moral sensitivity but also its awareness of the limits of its power.[5]

Guilt in Post-Independence Hebrew Literature

Let us turn now to the other end of the spectrum: the left and its guilt feelings. Moral misgivings about the Arab question accompanied the Zionist movement right from the outset of its settlement activities in Palestine. But until the War of Independence (1948–49) there was no feeling of guilt toward the Palestinian Arabs because Zionism understood itself as the struggle of a small, relatively weak society for the right to a foothold in its own homeland. The feeling of "living on the edge" that Alterman expressed in his poetry, the feeling that the Zionist struggle was a matter of life and death, gave the Zionist vision a powerful moral pathos. In such a struggle there could be no room for guilt toward the enemy. The Zionist mind may well have had an "internal defense mechanism," as Shlomo Avineri termed it: since most of the Zionist leaders were idealists (and perhaps even optimists), repression of feelings of guilt was, in their case, an unavoidable necessity. Failing such repression, it is doubtful that they could have adhered to the goals of Zionism as unwaveringly as they did.[6] It was only when the Jews, with their growing military power, began to defeat the Arabs and it became obvious what the bitter upshot of the conflict would be for the latter, that there began to be room for guilt feelings. The saying "Sorry we won," commonly voiced in a sarcastic tone after Israel's victory in the Six-Day War (1967), was at the same time an authentic expression of the change that had taken place in the national consciousness: the acquisition of power and the victory that it made possible were connected with the emergence of a new feeling, that of responsibility toward the vanquished, the weak.[7] The feeling of guilt was a sign of this sense of responsibility, which found its clearest expression in the volume *The Seventh Day*.[8] In a series of essays published in the late sixties and early seventies, the writer Ehud Ben Ezer reveals the increasing expression in modern Hebrew literature of guilt vis-à-vis the Arabs. S. Yizhar's war stories "Hirbet Hiz'a" and "The Prisoner" are the most important but not the only instances. Ben Ezer marshals a long series of examples to prove his thesis that beginning with the War of Independence, the Arab had become a moral problem in Israeli writing.[9]

Similarly, the writer Binyamin Tammuz, who deals with the problem of guilt in a number of his books, maintains that the drama of modern Hebrew literature is characterized by a penetrating sense of guilt. The more we strike the Arabs, he writes, the deeper our sense of guilt over their humiliation and expulsion. Tammuz gives many reasons for this feeling, but the main one, in his view, is the confusion the Arab problem caused Israelis who had lost the spiritual legacy of their forefathers.[10]

The critic Yosef Oren points out that the fighter as portrayed in the literature of the War of Independence, the soldier of "the 1948 generation," is a singularly soft-hearted figure, full of qualms and deep misgivings. "In his ruminations, military victory brings [a sense of] moral defeat and pangs of remorse." This literature is devoid of expressions of pride or joy at the defeat of an enemy who has just threatened Israel with destruction and who, if he had been victorious, would almost certainly have carried out this threat. Instead, the Jewish fighter feels compassion for the defeated.[11]

Oren, Ben Ezer, and Tammuz agree that the literature of the 1948 generation is characterized by a deep sense of guilt toward the vanquished Arabs and that the resulting confusion presents a serious problem for the emerging Israeli identity. Where they disagree is over the causes of these feelings. Ben Ezer sees the guilt as the result of a contradiction between the Zionist ideology on which the native-born Israelis had been raised, according to which the return to the homeland was to be accomplished by peaceful means, and the necessity of waging war that had been imposed upon them. He sees the root of the trauma in their spiritual unpreparedness for the cruelty of warfare, owing to an idealistic (and perhaps naïve) education that had ignored the bitter reality. Oren concurs but goes further: for him, the ideology was weakened not only by its innocence but also by being detached from its Jewish roots and Jewish historical purposes. The war was not seen as one of national liberation but as one meant primarily "to expel and despoil the Arab population."[12] In contrast, Tammuz sees the guilt feelings as the expression of an exilic Jewish complex from which the native-born Israelis, however secularized and cut off from the faith of their fathers, have not succeeded in freeing themselves. It is atavistic psychological residues, instilled by an inconsistent Zionism, that prevent the Israelis from taking possession of their homeland in a simple, natural way and may yet cause them to lose it. This is the message of many of Tammuz's works and especially of the story "The Grove." Oren believes it is because they are not Jewish enough in their thinking that the members of the 1948 generation feel guilty, whereas for Tammuz it is because they are too Jewish, too "exilic."

The historian Barbara Tuchman describes well the contradictory sentiments of many Israelis after the great victory of the Six-Day War: "[Israel's] people, so long and so often the victims of violence, have had to become, against their ethic, against the hope that brought them back to Zion, users of violence. . . .

Notwithstanding the pride . . . in a job well done, many people in Israel are profoundly troubled by their new role and their own success in it."[13]

In fact, just after the Six-Day War Aharon Megged wrote that the new image that had taken us by surprise, the image of the mythological hero who crushes his foes, would never prevail among us. It would not have the strength to overpower images that had proven themselves over thousands of years of history. These humane images, so different from those found in the stories of valor and lust, cruelty and mystery so common in the myths of other peoples, are not exilic but rather "ancient, archaic, leaving their impress like the great archetypes in the history of human culture." Megged maintains that any attempt to change these historic images would be doomed to failure, as the literature of the 1948 generation demonstrates. "The generation that has grown up in this country and never known exile, even this generation, contrary to the accepted view, lives by the selfsame image. If to judge by the literature, it would appear that from 1948 right up to today there have been few stories written by the members of this generation that do not identify emotionally, not only with ourselves, but also with the fate of the vanquished, the refugee, the prisoner, the uprooted. Jewish 'perversity'? Jewish 'morbidity'? Perhaps. But to me it seems that we can take pride in such sicknesses."[14]

While Megged takes pride in the sense of identification with "the fate of the vanquished," the writer Yehoshua Bar-Yosef sees it as a cause for concern. He, too, takes note of the psychological difficulty Israelis have breaking with the traditional image of the Jew, but he draws completely different conclusions: "Practically every Jew, insofar as he is a Jew, is shocked at the sight of blood. Until now, it was mainly shock at the sight of his own blood. Now that we have begun to defend ourselves by force, we are shocked in a new way: by the blood of the one who sought to kill us. And I do not know which shock is greater. When it is our own blood, we can take comfort, somehow, in self-pity, but when it is the blood of our would-be killers, we feel guilty as well. We suddenly see ourselves as a kind of people that we hate and despise, as murderers . . . , like all those contemptible, despicable gentiles."[15]

Bar-Yosef recommends, however, that Israelis swallow this bitter pill in spite of themselves, that they make their peace with the horror and try to live with it in their own way. For him, this exaggerated sensitivity, a product of the heritage of exile, should not be allowed to influence the course of our struggle in any way. He is not alone in thinking that the Jews of Israel need to free themselves completely from guilt feelings, because they sap their fortitude and their faith in the justice of the Zionist enterprise.

In the works of young native-born Israeli writers there is a growing concern that the image of the persecutor will replace that of the persecuted. At its most extreme, this literature tends to present the Arab as victim and the Israeli as aggressor. (Interestingly, this phenomenon has its counterpart in the adoption by the Palestinian Arabs of Zionism's victim image.)[16] There are those who would interpret such harsh self-criticism as a pathological expression of self-hatred or even of self-destructiveness.[17] But extreme expressions in literature and art do not come out of nowhere; they reflect the hidden or unconscious sentiments of many. As long as Israel was a weak country, standing alone against a hostile Muslim world, there was great resistance to discussing Israel's responsibility for the problem of the refugees, not only because of the usual psychological difficulty of admitting guilt, but also because of the fear that such an admission would cause serious political damage to Israel's image in the eyes of its friends, be they Diaspora Jews or other states, and give aid and comfort to its enemies. Only after it had attained military power and a strong international standing could Israel allow itself to discuss this issue openly and critically. Thus, the imaginative literature anticipated historical research by decades, preparing the ground for a critical examination of the question of Israel's responsibility in the creation of the Arab refugee problem.[18] Such an examination can bring about a more balanced view of the conflict, and it thus has great political and moral value: on the one hand, it can promote peace and reconciliation with the Palestinians when they, for their part, are prepared to acknowledge their own responsibility for their disaster; on the other hand, this examination is a necessary condition for maintenance of our moral integrity.[19]

Although exaggerated guilt feelings, especially those of a neurotic nature, can inhibit a person from taking any action at all, a certain capacity for feelings of guilt is vital to the moral stability of both the individual and the collective. As with all emotions, the power of the feeling and the nature of the deed must be in proportion.[20] Guilt feelings serve as a warning against turning necessity into a norm or habit.[21] They are an important component of our moral character. An action contrary to the values on which our world is predicated and from which it derives meaning can undermine our human identity.

Every nation that wishes to survive must, on occasion, breach the rules of absolute morality. But, as Buber rightly stresses, the fate of a nation depends on whether, from time to time, its leaders are willing to make a thoroughgoing moral reckoning. It is this that determines whether the nation will grow stronger or decline. On the other hand, "because of their excessive guilt, both men and nations are wiped off the face of the earth. Great statesmanship, which is directed by the true interest of coming generations, is a policy that ensures that the nation does not heap upon itself too great a degree of guilt."[22]

Collective guilt is a rare phenomenon. What is more common in relations among peoples is the placing of mutual blame rather than recognition of one's own failings. One of the things that distinguishes one culture from another is the degree of willingness to commit far-reaching violations of the moral law and, concurrently, the degree of guilt that is felt when doing so.[23] After the Second World War, Germany, with its pietistic Christian heritage, was able to acknowledge its guilt and even demonstrate, in various ways, a willingness to atone (the reparation payments to Israel are an example). But Japan, in whose culture shame plays a central role, refused for many years to apologize for Pearl Harbor or the cruelties perpetrated by its soldiers during the war.[24] Only lately has it taken some steps in this direction.

The Jews have always cultivated a sense of guilt toward their God, which completely displaced any sense of shame vis-à-vis other peoples. Zionism rebelled against this Jewish self-criticism, reviving among Jews the sense of shame, and this, in turn, served as a catalyst for the restoration of their feeling of national dignity. Undoubtedly, this goal could not have been attained without regaining military power. The Jewish psychologist Erik Erikson was right in seeing the charge that Jews did not fight because they could not do so as an important source of popular antisemitism.[25] Not having the opportunity to use violence for so many generations, the Jews had become vulnerable, not only because they could not defend themselves but also because their weakness provoked the aggressiveness of their neighbors. One of Zionism's most impressive achievements has been its success in changing the popular image of the Jew to one that inspires respect and admiration among non-Jews. Thanks to the State of Israel, Jews all over the world, whether or not they admit it, enjoy greater self-respect, pride, and security. They feel themselves to be equals and need no longer be ashamed of being Jewish or try to hide it, as they did until quite recently. Shame has thus been a significant factor in strengthening Jewish identity in the modern world.

Because of the new Zionist stress, shame displaced guilt as the primary factor in Jewish consciousness, but it did not eliminate the special Jewish sensitivity to the question of guilt entirely. Rather, this sensitivity was now transferred from the realm of relations to the divine to that of relations between Jews and their neighbors.[26] Unexpectedly, it was only at the expense of the suffering of another nation that the Jews were able to win their sovereignty as a nation. Consequently, the guilt feelings that had, understandably, been repressed by the founding generation returned to haunt their children. Though war had been a historical necessity, this fact by itself did not relieve the anguish, which has continued to weigh heavily on all those contemptuously referred to in Israel as *yefei nefesh* (bleeding hearts).[27]

Every civilized nation needs a certain amount of guilt feelings. How much more so we Jews, for without recognizing our guilt not only will we not succeed in building a well-run state, but it doubtful that we shall remain Jews. The assumption that we are always in the right and that all blame is to be placed on the enemy rules out any possibility of dialogue with him. "He who sees himself as entirely innocent," wrote Ben Halpern, "will never reach agreement with his fellow-man. . . . There can be no real accord or lasting arrangement between two parties unless they realize that they are obligated to each other; and before there can be a sense of obligation there must be a sense of guilt."[28] But the sense of guilt cannot be one sided. The moral questioning that characterized Zionism at every step of the way, be it over the right to the land or the limits of the use of force, has not been paralleled yet on the Palestinians' side. So long there is no mutual sense of guilt, it is hard to believe in the possibility of establishing a solid neighborly relationship with them.[29]

13

Challenging the Zionist Ethos

"Why Did the Dreams Fade?"

HAGSHAMA: THE DIALECTICS OF
"WORLDLINESS" AND "SPIRITUALITY"

Hagshama, practical realization, is one of the key terms in modern Hebrew literature and Zionist thought beginning with the period of the Second Aliya (1904–18), particularly in the writings of the labor movement. In the years following the Balfour Declaration (1917), hagshama became a watchword for both the religious and the nonreligious pioneering youth movements. It was a term that conveyed the essence of Zionist resolve and activism, the effort to give life to the spirit and concrete expression to an age-old dream.

Philosophically speaking, hagshama signifies the desire to meld opposites, the *vita contemplativa* and the *vita activa*. In this sense, there is a similarity between the Zionist concept of hagshama and the Marxist notion of praxis. For Marx, revolutionary activity should combine the analytical and critical with the practical, the assessment of reality in light of the ideal with the realization of the ideal that creates a new reality. Zionism, too, looked at the Jewish condition in relation to a dream and found that the realization of that dream would require a revolutionary change in the condition. But it also recognized that without the dream there could be no realization, that the effort would have no meaning. Hagshama thus connoted a constant tension between absolute devotion to the ideal and a pragmatic consideration of the contradictions and difficulties imposed by reality. Immersion in the ideal could lead one to ignore reality and could detract from the enormous energy required to take the first step, to lay the cornerstone of the new edifice. But excessive immersion in the work of construction could also lead one to forget the purpose of the edifice.

The dialectic between "spirit" and "life," between "spirituality" and "worldliness," preoccupies Zionism and is reflected in the thought, fiction, poetry, and drama that have accompanied the movement of Jewish rebirth from the outset. Modern Hebrew literature, especially that which appeared in Eastern Europe and was one of the main factors giving rise to the Zionist movement, aspired to reclaim the worldly realm for the Jewish people and, in the process, questioned the thoroughly spiritual mantle which Jewish existence in exile had assumed.

It was this worldly frame of mind that gave rise to Zionism's new social ideal, that of the *halutz* (pioneer). Unlike the contemplative, spiritual ideal of the traditional scholar, who sees as his life's purpose the preservation, development, and transmission of religious tradition, the halutz was an activist and a doer in those spheres that Jews in exile were thought to have neglected. The halutz was an ideal type (in the Weberian sense) that embodied the ethos of Zionist hagshama. This ethos was made up of norms of behavior, speech, and action, all directed toward one central goal: the settlement of the Land of Israel and the building of a new society there. It was an ethos based on the optimistic faith that energetic, persistent devotion to the establishment of a worldly foundation would eventually bring about a rebirth of the Jewish people and the Jewish personality, and perhaps humanity as a whole.

Yet alongside this optimistic outlook, in Hebrew literature there is also "a fear of realization," a constant concern that once the Jews re-establish their life on a worldly, secular basis, they will lose their distinctive spiritual identity and their ancient dream of redemption. Is this revolution doomed to failure if it tampers with the source of its visionary inspiration?

The depth of these fears can be seen, not only in the Orthodox leadership's stubborn opposition to Zionism (as well as to messianic movements in the past), but also in the opposition of many of the best writers during the period of the Hebrew Revival, which paralleled the early period of Zionist history. According to Stanley Nash, "what characterized Ahad Ha-am, Berditchevski, [Shmuel-Yosef Ish] Horowitz and others like them was a longing that was afraid to be satisfied. . . . This is a viewpoint that prefers eternal tension, which fructifies and sustains, to grey realization."[1] Nash quotes the view of Horowitz, one of the first Hebrew writers of the Lovers of Zion period: "The return to Zion is a beautiful and charming thing so long as it remains an aspiration. It fortifies, encourages, shores up the faith of the faltering and the hope of the impotent. . . . But as soon as it comes close to becoming a reality, all the obstacles in its path and the lack of strength to realize it become apparent."[2] Some dozen years later Horowitz wrote: "When the candle is extinguished, its life-forces, the forces of illumination within it, are hidden in its depths. . . . And such a situation can go on indefinitely. Once you kindle it, of necessity the life forces within are revealed, but also, of necessity, they burn and are used up. . . . Therefore, I say: be careful not to waste the last penny in your pockets! *The Zionist idea need not be realized*. It must serve as a guiding star for all the aspirations, activities, and deeds of the people of Israel in the lands of its dispersion. This is the messianic idea, the greater idea, which created the spirit of Israel, and this is the secret of [Israel's] survival (emphasis added)."[3]

A similar idea was expressed by David Frischman (1859–1922). For him, Judaism is an eternal ideal to which we must continually aspire. The main thing is not the realization but the aspiration. Realization negates the ideal and corrupts it. Zionism has taken an ideal and made it something to be realized. In doing so, it threatens to eliminate that ideal from the world.[4] It is the great fear that the ancient dream may be dashed by distorted realization that brings a thinker like Hillel Zeitlin (1871–1942) to renounce Zionism as a way of rescuing the Jewish people and to embrace territorialism instead. (Cf. chapter 7, above.)

No Hebrew writer expressed this problem as deeply — or as tragically — as Micha Yosef Berdyczewski (1865–1921). In his writing we find most sharply delineated the clash between the "earthly" and the "spiritual" (or the "heavenly"), a clash that is not only inevitable but leaves no room for compromise: traditional Judaism (the "spiritual") is beyond repair or change; it is an obstacle to be overcome and rooted out. "For we have built for ourselves too many pathways to heaven; for we are overly spiritual people. . . . And I call for the defeat of the regime of the spirit and the enthronement of matter, so as to restore our strength and daring and make us people who know life and are not mere clerics."[5]

This rebelliousness was imbued with a revolutionary view of the Jewish past and Jewish culture. For Berdyczewski, exile is not a punishment from heaven or a political catastrophe imposed on the Jewish people from without; rather, it is the result of a sin inherent in Judaism itself, the result of the traditional Jewish worldview.[6] The rabbis managed, through their spurious spirituality, to impose upon the Jewish people "the culture of the book," so foreign to its spirit.[7] They preferred "Yavne" to "Jerusalem," assuming it would be easier for Judaism to prosper in exile than in the homeland.[8] Consequently, for Berdyczewski there can be no redemption from exile without redemption from Judaism itself. Zionism will never succeed if it does not turn its back altogether on exile and reconnect with the ancient era when Israel still held aloft the flag of this-worldly redemption.[9]

The "negation of exile" here receives its most radical interpretation. In it, Berdyczewski, more than any other Hebrew writer, lays the foundation for the powerful Zionist myth of the "new Hebrew." Although the myth is not as yet fully delineated, it is clearly opposed to historical Judaism and close to the thinking of Nietzsche. All of Berdyczewski's scholarly, literary, and philosophical work was devoted to providing an undergirding for this myth in the remote past and in Diaspora life. Berdyczewski never immigrated to Palestine, but he was well aware that the practical realization of this myth could come only at the price of a break with Judaism, which, in turn, could mean a loss of identity. He was fearful that the result would be destruction rather than rebirth. But his disciples were much less ambivalent, and his great negation inspired them to creativity and hagshama.

THE LONGING TO UNITE "HEAVEN" AND "EARTH"

Berdyczewski stresses the importance of irrational forces for the renewal of Jewish life. This becomes the approach of a broad, perhaps dominant body of Zionist thought and Hebrew literature in the early twentieth century. The desire for this-worldly life in the here and now, as opposed to the otherworldliness of traditional Judaism, which is seen as the cause of the Jews' loss of spontaneity and personal freedom, is common among many Hebrew writers.[10] As Eliezer Schweid has written, the Jew longs for full, natural life, life in the wider world. This goal, generally sought in the religious experience that lifts man from the earthly to the heavenly plane, is here reversed: we seek to be lowered from heaven to earth.[11] This is the meaning of the turn from the old to the new: holiness is now to dwell not in heaven but on earth.

But alongside these sentiments, we also find among such writers as Buber, Gordon, and Kook a desire to bridge the gap that has opened between heaven and earth in exile and create a new unity. Significantly, Berdyczewski himself was one of the firsts to express this aspiration. We thus find in the undergirding of the Zionist utopia some of the old religious longing for unity, for the perfecting of man and of life. We see here the deep connection between the ideas of Zionist realization and utopia. The stress on concreteness is not merely a matter of reconciling oneself to this world but of reshaping it in the spirit of the dream. It was this drive that made Zionism, even at its most antitraditional, a redemptive movement in the original religious sense.

Here lies, in all likelihood, the source of Kook's optimism about the Zionist revolution. He accepts the main thesis of secular Zionism, that exile has caused the Jewish people to neglect the physical side of its existence and become overly spiritual.[12] But for Kook, in contradistinction to the secular Zionists, the long exile was a necessary stage in the education of the people to fulfill its destiny in its own land. In our own time, however, exile is dangerous for Jewish survival. With the balance upset, not only has the "natural" strength of the nation been sapped, but the people's spirit, too, has begun to flag. We are therefore seeking a way to recover our lost unity.[13] Our unnatural situation requires, as a remedy, a temporary stress on the physical. But just as the Jewish people can no longer tolerate exaggerated spirituality, it cannot bear empty physicality either. As soon as the pioneers finish their work of throwing off the former, they will proceed to eradicate the latter, the false god of materialism, as well. The national movement can thus bring about a healthy new equilibrium and abolish the opposition between sacred and profane.[14]

Most of the pioneers of the Second and Third Aliyot (1904–24) undoubtedly saw the Zionist vision as an exalted, authentic expression of ancient Jewish eschatological longings translated into worldly terms. This view receives rich expression in the Hebrew poetry and prose of the period. Yet there remained a gap between old and new symbols and ideas. In retrospect, the secular rebellion against tradition seems to have brought about a suppression of the very Jewish sources upon which that rebellion had been nourished.

Almost all revolutionary movements take a one-sided, simplistic view of reality. This is a source of strength but also of weakness. In the case of Zionism, it was only the fiction of the time, beginning with the Second Aliya, that noticed the ambiguities in the fateful decisions that had to be taken and the price that might have to be paid for them. Bialik, for example, seeing the spiritual poverty that threatened people who were investing most of their energies in the physical settlement of the land and very little in the deeper meaning of that activity, warned against a narrowing of the idea of redemption.[15]

Even more skeptical was the novelist Hayim Hazaz. The dialectical character of his work has been pointed out by most of the critics.[16] Gershon Shaked has shown that Hazaz, more than any other writer, exposes Zionism's inner contradictions.[17] Although Hazaz the orator and pamphleteer was a fervent Zionist—he would eventually even become an advocate of retaining "the whole Land of Israel"—Hazaz the writer knew no certainties or clear-cut solutions, and he was haunted by doubts concerning the Zionist enterprise. A recurrent theme in his work is that of the tension between heaven and earth, seen most often in his descriptions of landscape. The Land of Israel, unlike the

Diaspora Jewish villages, is described as a place where this tension breaks down. Heaven and earth (i.e., spirit and land) commingle and kiss, a mixing which is, of course, essential to messianic fulfillment. But this erotic mingling causes Hazaz the gravest doubts and fears. According to the critic Dan Miron, the land has an abysslike quality, and the erotic penetration of it leads to a casting off of the burden of Jewish tradition and entry into a new realm of instinctive life completely divorced from Judaism.[18]

In one of his stories Hazaz writes: "Time — that is the locus of our vitality, just as space is the locus of the gentiles' vitality. . . . And this is the very essence of Judaism and what sets Jews apart from gentiles. . . . Now we have traded time for space, . . . the spiritual realm for [that of] grim physicality, ordinariness, and this-worldliness, with all its base lusts and desires. . . . Here lies the danger to the Jewish people, a danger of decline [and] decadence."[19] The great change taking place in the life of the people, Hazaz warns, could not only damage its spiritual identity and obliterate its uniqueness; it could bring about its decline. This is the dialectic inherent in Zionism. The very effort to realize the dream can lead to its demise. An exclusive intoxication with the physical work of construction can lead us to forget the purpose for which we are building — the revival of Judaism — and worldly achievement can become a value in itself.

Exile entails a longing for redemption, but redemption entails a new exile.[20] The elimination of exile requires the elimination of its spiritual underpinnings, and since the Torah is the basis of the Jewish people's existence in exile, redemption entails the negation of the Torah.[21] This is the Zionist paradox: construction entails destruction and could lead to collapse. The Land of Israel in its concreteness is the opposite of the Land of Israel of the dream. Hence the preferability of the dream over its realization; hence the dread of the very possibility of realization, for the idea realized is the idea contradicted.

In some of his works, Hazaz puts into his characters' mouths opinions astonishingly similar to those of the most vocal opponents of Zionism, such as Hermann Cohen and Franz Rosenzweig.[22] For Moroshka, the hero of the story "A Muddy Barrel," exile is a historical phenomenon that has set the Jews apart, "third [in importance] after the revelation at Sinai and the settlement of the Land of Israel." "It is slavery but also freedom, lowliness but also heroism, the highest heroism of completely free people, the heroes of a worldwide war — who among the nations can match our heroic deeds?" The gentiles are "provincial": "their horizon is narrow, and their world is like an egg." Their life and culture turn mostly on "the fist," in which they take pride. What the gentiles lack to be truly free, free of the dictates of their instincts, is the experience of exile. "Exile that will chasten them and teach them to see and grasp what the world is, what man is, what human life is, what truth and justice are."[23] Once the other nations undergo this educational experience, "there will be no more war in the world, no competition or hatred or jealousy between nations, no enslavement of one man by another."[24]

As a storyteller, Hazaz is unsparing in his criticism of the Zionist movement for making the establishment of a state its ultimate objective. "Is it over this that we anguished these two thousand years, for this that we suffered exile, persecution, harsh decrees, tribulation, and martyrdom, so that we could, in the end, make for ourselves some sort of state? . . . A state! All this — and then a state. . . . Ach, it's a gentile's perception."[25] "Every people has its state, but we, only we, had exile."[26] In light of this, the Land of Israel represents not ascent (*aliya*) but descent, "failure and despair," for it is in this land that the Jews have become like all the other nations. Even in the early 1930s, he foresees the possibility that in the Land of Israel of all places, the Jews will undergo complete cultural assimilation.[27]

No wonder such sentiments provoked the critic Yeshurun Keshet to ponder "which is greater here, the skepticism about the fate of our attempt to redeem ourselves or the love of that anarchic extra Jewish soul [such as the one a Jew is said to acquire on the Sabbath], which prevented us from ever finding a resting place in this world?"[28] The dialectic Hazaz referred to in his fiction placed a question mark on where hagshama would lead, and, in a sense, he prophesied cultural changes that did take place in the generation following the establishment of the state.

THE TRIUMPH OF WORLDLINESS AND ITS PRICE

It is probably beyond dispute that in the struggle in the Zionist movement between worldliness and spirituality, the former has won out. Worldliness, which required a break with the Diaspora and the Jewish heritage, was evidently more in tune with the concrete needs of the time. In the years before the establishment of the State of Israel, the wide influence among Palestinian Jews of the "Canaanite" ideology, which advocated such a split in an extreme way, was one of the signs of the triumph of the new Hebrew.[29]

The literature of the 1948 generation is rife with the stereotype of the *Sabra,* or native-born Israeli, which resembles in many ways the image Eastern European Jews had of the gentile. Although the reality was much more complex, the stereotype served, in Gershon Shaked's words, as "a response to the expectations of the parents' generation, which wanted its children to be as different as possible from the image of the old, exilic Jews." All qualities that did not fit the ideal image of the young fighter and pioneer were scorned.[30] The reading public cultivated in real life the personality of the new Hebrew — anti-intellectual, down-to-earth, and energetic — that corresponded to the literary image. His life was devoted to physical activity, heroism, and adventurism that reflected a spontaneous affinity for the landscape, and his mental world did not extend beyond the country's boundaries. The native-born Israeli was to excel in all the qualities the exilic Jew did not have: robustness, simplicity, rooted-ness in the soil, and purposiveness. He would thus do well in the military or quasi-military setting, which called for precisely such qualities. Lacking spirituality and intellectual sophistication, he would be largely indifferent to the fate and cultural heritage of the Jewish people. Indeed, he would feel no connection to the chain of the generations, with its age-old longings and hopes.[31]

This image as it emerged in literature was delineated by a contemporary writer, Matti Megged, as early as 1950. "At bottom, the worldview of the Israeli of this generation contains him alone: his memories, childhood experiences, vocabulary, and the like — all characteristic products of the country and its rebuilding, but lacking a sense of continuity with the past. The problems with which he struggles are not laden with the wearying burden of previous generations, and even the generation immediately preceding him, which has certainly played a major role in laying the groundwork for new activity, hardly shares these problems." For Megged, the literary figures are ultimately shallow, "lacking any significant spiritual life, any great love, any ideas or vision." They excel in acts of daring but cannot "build anything grand in the way of a humane vision." They are products of a situation, not necessarily masters of it. Faced with critical problems beyond the narrow realm of practical activity, they stand "empty-handed, without human or Hebrew culture and without vision." In this way, their break with "historical continuity" takes its vengeance.[32] A similar picture of the disconnectedness from history is revealed in the fiction of S. Yizhar, the greatest writer of the 1948 generation, as Dan Miron pointed out.[33]

Anita Shapira has characterized the young people who established the state as having a combative activism lacking in their forebears. The native-born generation's national loyalties were based upon a concrete attachment to the land, not on any romantic or messianic mysticism. "In the last analysis, their world was a narrow one, limited to the confines of the Land of Israel. They were doers, without intellectual pretensions."[34] It is not difficult to see in this characterization the achievement of the "normalization" aspired to by this-worldly Zionism. But, as Shapira points out, it is doubtful "that this was the kind of new generation the Zionist thinkers had prayed for." In all of Jewish history there had probably been no generation upon which so many hopes had rested as the first and second native-born generations here. But was this load not so heavy as to overwhelm them? Could the parents' messianic dream, complex and fraught with contradictions as it was, ever be realized by their children?

A typical example of this ambivalence is to be found in the poet David Shimoni, of the Second Aliya. In his idyll "The Damp of Night" (1936–39), in the chapter "Unformed Children," he expresses the misgivings of the pioneer Yehuda about his son Gideon. The former is enthusiastic about the "blessed freshness" of this generation, which "draws the vitality of its existence straight from the roots"; about the Hebrew it speaks, its practicality, its unmediated love of nature and the homeland, which makes it ready to come to its defense "out of the simple feeling [for their country] that ignorant people have." But when Yehuda gets used to this freshness, "something like disappointment" begins to trouble him, and "a piercing doubt secretly weighs on his heart."

> Might . . . the free children of rebirth
> Be more downtrodden and impoverished of spirit than the wrung-out
>   children of exile?
> They lack the depth that only the tormented can attain,
> The splendid longings, that only those who dwell in darkness know,
> The yearning for redemption, with its uniquely sweet anguish,
> That sustained generation after generation with heroic devotion,
> With a craving for holiness and purity and something more exalted than life.
>   . . .
> They lack the gravity and passionate intellect
> That always marked Israel's children in exile.
> They are too shallow and frivolous, and their mental horizon is too narrow.

The younger generation does not "bend over books," but, Yehuda consoles himself, "is that not what we prayed for?" In fact, his son Gideon is the paragon of the Diaspora Jews' dream, and the "depth" he lacks now will undoubtedly come with time, unexpectedly, from his unmediated connectedness to the homeland. He will then take upon himself the exalted destiny of reopening the "eternal bridge that had been cut."[35]

With the establishment of the state, the ethos of hagshama gradually ran out of steam. Beginning in the 1960s, there were signs in Hebrew literature of a cooling to the worldly ideal and to the cult of the state that, under Ben-Gurion's influence, had been dominant in Israel in the fifties. The escalation of the conflict with the Arabs, together with the growth of materialism in the society, led quite a few native-born authors to question the very validity of the Zionist ideal, or at least the way it had been realized, and to wonder about the spiritual price the Jewish people would have to pay for statehood.[36]

Such concerns grew in the seventies and eighties, leading to what is now called "Post-Zionism." The figure of the alienated individual resumed its central role in Hebrew literature, and the new Hebrew was relegated to the sidelines. Here is how the critic Yosef Oren summarizes the "Israeli situation" as reflected in the literature of the seventies, particularly after the shock of the

Yom Kippur War: "The state is hastening the decline of distinctively Jewish traits, especially in the spiritual realm. In their place, it fosters practical traits that are needed to defend the country's borders and to meet the other needs of physical survival in a hostile environment. We are declining as the originators of culture, as a people that has always excelled in its intellectual gifts. Under the influence of the state, the Jewish people is losing [the] genius that gave it a special place among the nations. This aspect of the 'Israeli situation' is presented [in the literature], in the theme of decadence, as a threat to Jewish survival, not from enemies without but as a process of decline and loss within."[37]

Oren bases himself on the works of two prominent authors, Binyamin Tammuz and Amos Oz. The writings of Tammuz, who was once considered one of the "Young Hebrews," may be the most glaring example of disappointment at the realization of the Zionist dream. In his article "The Silence of the Violin Comes to an End," he maintains that the state has hastened the "process of breaking away from the Jewish people by focusing solely on hagshama." "The patent worldliness of the actions required to secure physical survival in the Land of Israel has left no mental room for the development of a tie to the people that gave birth to Zionism, financed it, and nourished it in the most recent past, in literature, . . . religion and philosophy."[38]

In his novel *Jacob,* Tammuz declares that "Judaism is Diaspora." Earthly sovereignty takes Jews far from Judaism, diluting the spiritual and cultural power that enabled them, in the Diaspora, to cope with the gentile world. The Jew's true province is that of the spirit, which is not limited to earthly boundaries. The use of physical force is against his nature, for the hallmark of Judaism is the ethereal dream, and any attempt to realize the latter destroys both the dream itself and the people to whom it was entrusted.[39]

Tammuz is at his most pessimistic about worldly political existence in his novel *Requiem for Na'aman.* The moral of the story is the bankruptcy of the idea of normalization. Not only is worldly existence unworkable; it brings spiritual and cultural disaster down upon the Jews, who were never meant to be like other nations. One of the main characters says, "I only came to remind you . . . of something that should never be forgotten. . . . Our strength is not in strength but in the spirit. . . . The Jewish people has but one face . . . [and it is] toward Sinai."[40]

NORMALIZATION VERSUS MESSIANISM IN THE WRITINGS OF AMOS OZ

While Tammuz's judgment about the future awaiting the Jewish state is unequivocal, in the work of Amos Oz there are merely misgivings about the psychological and spiritual price to be paid for the success of Zionism. Oz is the analyst par excellence of the Zionist dream of redemption, and he often questions whether that dream had negative elements that came to light only when it was realized. The picture he draws is both of the reality of Israel as it is and also of the inner processes that have shaped Israeli society all along, since the beginning of the twentieth century.

As Tzefira Porat has pointed out, Oz's native-born-Israeli characters are strangers in their own country, unable to reconcile themselves to the reality around them that is so different from the utopian dream on which they were raised. They are restless, bedeviled, and unable to live simple, normal lives. They no longer believe in the Messiah, but a world devoid of redemption is repugnant to them. Their yearning for redemption makes it difficult for them to come to terms with their homeland as it is or to develop a sense of belonging to it. Wanderlust is the only "Jewish" trait Zionism has left them. What is more, they are ignoramuses when it comes to Judaism and its texts, though amazingly conversant with the books and symbols of other religions.[41]

A principal theme of three of Oz's novels, *Perfect Peace, Black Box,* and *Fima,* is the unwillingness or inability of the second generation to embrace its parents' legacy. The young cannot fulfill the older generation's expectations; they refuse to grow up and become parents themselves. And no wonder, for one who cannot inherit will not be able to bequeath; one who has never learned to be a son can never be a father. But ironically, the children do fulfill a certain aspiration, albeit an unconscious one, of their parents: they are a new, different kind of Jew, unconnected to the life of exile and all it entailed. They were not meant to be a link in the endless chain of history but its end product, the first redeemed generation.

In an early story, "The Way of the Wind" (or "The Way of the Spirit" — the Hebrew carries both meanings), which Oz wrote in the sixties, the dream is presented as a tragicomedy. The father hopes to found a new line "free of deformities." He aims for a "wonderful synthesis" of spirit and flesh, heaven and earth. His son Gideon (the name of a biblical hero) is chosen to be the founder of the new dynasty. Although he has the gentle soul of a poet, he tries to live up to the expectations his name implies. He enlists in the paratroops in order to become a "proper he-man." The symbolic conclusion of the story brings the dream to a tragic end: in a demonstration jump by his company on Independence Day above the fields of his kibbutz, the son's parachute gets caught on a high-tension wire. He is electrocuted — intentionally? — and remains dangling from the wire upside down, "like a slaughtered goat on a hook." The figure of a man hanging head-down between heaven and earth is, in Yigal Schwartz's words, "a grotesque realization of the 'wonderful synthesis' between the worldly and spiritual."[42]

At the center of the novel *A Perfect Peace* is the author's perplexity at the contradiction between the dream and its fulfillment: "In times gone by, everything was done here with enormous devotion and sense of purpose, sometimes even self-sacrifice. Audacious dreams were brought to fruition. The free Hebrew state came into being. A second and third generation grew up, tanned and striking, to take over the machinery and the weapons. How is it that the world has paled and the dreams faded?"[43]

The answer would seem to lie in the character of the second generation, which, while successful in a practical, material sense, is absolutely lacking in the vision the first generation had, and the reason for this is that it denies any connection with the past.

> Just who are these youngsters anyway? What is going on in their heads? They're first-rate farmers, no doubt about it. What we ourselves did with enormous effort, they toss off without any sweat. Presumably they're brave and proficient soldiers. Yet always with an air of melancholy about them. As if they stemmed from another race, an entirely different tribe. Neither Asiatics nor Europeans. Neither gentiles nor Jews. Neither idealists nor on the make. What can their lives mean to them, raised in this whirlwind of history, this place-in-progress, this experiment-under-construction, this merest blueprint of a country, with no grandparents, no ancestral homes, no religion, no rebellion, no *Wanderjahre* of their own? With not a single heirloom — not a chest of drawers, not a gold watch, not even a single old book. Growing in a place that was hardly a hamlet, in tents and shacks, amid pale young saplings. Just a fence and searchlights, howling jackals and distant shots.[44]

In short, the next generation had no spiritual identity. But had these young people not fulfilled their parents' dream? Had it not been that, in the words of one of the characters, "all the foundations [were] rotten to begin with"?[45] Was the spiritual sterility of the younger generation, symbolized by biological sterility, not a fulfillment of the older generation's aspirations? It was "a new generation of biblical Gideons and Nimrods, . . . a pack of wild prairie wolves instead of little rabbis. No more Marxes, Freuds, [or] Einsteins; no more Menuhins [or] Jascha Heifetzes; not even any more Gordons, Borochovs, [or] Berls — no, from now on nothing but sunburned, ignorant, illiterate warriors."[46]

Oz puts these words into the mouth of a father who, deeply disappointed with the fruit of the pioneering ideal in his own family, blames only himself. The image of the Sabras — "bronzed, ignorant, stupid warriors" — is far removed from the spiritually rich personalities produced by the Diaspora. Here, then, is the key difference between the first and the second generation: although the former detached itself from the Jewish religious tradition, it remained experientially linked with it; as a result, it could see itself as both revolutionary and conservative. Its Zionism comprised universal human values that were seen as being, in some sense, the essence of the utopian values of the Jewish tradition itself. With the younger generation it was different. It had grown up without any sense of connection to the past that could serve as the basis for a distinct cultural identity. Oz's book suggests that because the Sabra is devoid of the least spark of Jewish spirituality, he has no dreams or ideals, and there is no hope of historical continuity through him. The only chance of carrying on the Zionist enterprise lies in the Diaspora Jewish genius, which alone can produce dreamers and achievers like the pioneers of the Second and Third Aliyot. There must therefore be a recurring revolution, which will revive those exilic spiritual qualities that both parents and children had rejected, at the beginning of Zionism, out of a sense of superiority to the Diaspora Jews.[47]

Thus the circle is closed: the decline of the Sabra makes way for the rehabilitation of the Diaspora Jew. But now the latter is nothing like the negative stereotype so common at the beginning of the century. He is not inferior, weak, or passive but more "rooted" than the unconnected Israeli, and he is willing to shoulder the responsibility for Jewish survival.

The fading of the dream means the death of the utopian element in Zionism, which drew its passion from messianism. Consequently, Oz's analysis of the process of Zionist realization leads him to wonder about the fate of the messianic idea in Israeli society. His ambivalence toward messianism stems from the polar alternatives it seems to him to present: on one hand, a megalomanic fantasy of greatness that can bring total catastrophe; on the other, renunciation of the vision, which leads to a decline into petty ordinariness. Avner Holtzman notes the conflict in Oz's thinking between his attraction to messianic mysticism, leading to a zealous activism, and his attraction to rational level-headedness. At the same time, he sees in Oz a religious yearning for the synthesis or harmonization of opposites.[48]

In his volume of essays *In the Land of Israel* (1983), Oz portrays a society riven by polarities: "It may be necessary [for us] to pull in now and forego all our messianic dreams," to proceed more modestly. In contrast to the grand ambitions of Gush Emunim (the Bloc of the Faithful, a movement devoted to Jewish settlement in the areas occupied in 1967), he points to the new Mediterranean port city of Ashdod, "a city on a human scale" well within the bounds of pre-1967 Israel, as symbolizing not "the grandiose fulfillment of the vision of the Prophets and dream of generations," but the acceptance of reality that he advocates.[49] Elsewhere he says, "I would like to make my peace with the Land of Israel. I would like it to be calmer, a little less Jewish." Oz knows it is "a terrible thing to say," but he feels we "must change something deep in our soul." Yet he has no formula for doing this.[50]

The novel *Black Box* (1987), too, is an effort to diagnose the Israeli situation. It describes the decline of a family over three generations, symbolizing, in effect, the spiritual decay of Zionism. Three of the characters represent three options facing the society, none of which is entirely appealing. One option is that of Alexander Gideon, whose father Volodya immigrated to Israel after experiencing real antisemitism. Alexander was supposed to have grown up to be a proud Sabra, rooted in the soil of the homeland, but instead he becomes "detached." Unable to embrace his father's legacy, he goes abroad, where he settles down to study the phenomenon of messianic fanaticism. He writes a book that is described by one critic as "an ice-cold analysis of messianic passion in both its religious and its secular garb." Faith is presented as a pathological and even immoral phenomenon. "All world-reformers since the dawn of history have actually sold their souls to the Devil of fanaticism."[51]

The second option, an outgrowth of the first, is embodied by Boaz, Alexander's and Ilana's son. He is a contemptible, spiritually impotent hippie type, interested only in having a good time, keeping a low profile, and staying out of the fray.[52] Whereas the son, Alexander, had some spirituality in him, however distorted, there is none left in the grandson; he is the personification of decadent worldliness. The antithesis of fanaticism is not sanity but bestiality: "Eating, working a little, fucking." This is worldliness at its most grotesque and repulsive. Complete abandonment of the vision, living only in the present, thus leads to a disaster no less terrible, and perhaps more so, than the messianic option symbolized by the third character in the novel, Michel Somo, Ilana's second husband, who is close to Gush Emunim.[53] Oz hints at a future fight between Boaz and Somo.[54] It will be the great battle over the fate of Zionism: can it live without an animating vision, or with a messianic one, with all that this entails?

Oz has gradually come to the conclusion that we cannot do without either of the two opposing sources of energy. In a 1990 interview, he calls for reconciliation between them, with an eye toward a "mystical union" of the two, though without spelling out what that might be like. "We are dependent on dangerous forces, without which there would be nothing at all. Therefore, [the beasts] should not be slaughtered but domesticated. . . . There is no source of strength in Judaism that I would not like to domesticate, including the messianic idea."[55]

It is this domestication that Fima, hero of the novel of that name, called in the original Hebrew *The Third Condition*, aspires to. The "third condition" is an intermediate one between two extremes on the political scene: "One group pisses on the state and says it's illegitimate because the Messiah hasn't come yet; the other group pisses on the state and says it's just a temporary scaffolding that we can dismantle now that the Messiah's standing at the gate."[56] For Fima, "the Messiah is our angel of death";[57] because of the madness he brings with him, the state is crumbling.[58] Our greatest problem, Fima believes, is "how to exist and operate in interim circumstances that can drag on for years, instead of reacting to reality by [just] sulking."[59] So Fima awaits some sort of miracle, some kind of illumination that will restore our lost wholeness.[60] The "third condition" he hopes for is one in which messianic intoxication and ecstasy are joined to rationality and sobriety.

A FLEETING PASSION

The question of why the utopian element in Zioniam and in its ethos of hagshama have died has been taken up by historians, sociologists, and literary critics, so I will merely try to round out the picture with a few personal reflections. The establishment of the state brought with it rapid bureaucratization and socioeconomic differentiation, a development that ran counter to the pioneering, volunteer ethos. The passion for Zionist realization, which for an earlier generation had been full of spiritual meaning, lost much of its validity in the eyes of the new generation as the task of pursuing many of the national objectives passed from voluntary bodies to the organs of the state. This was the background for the emergence of careerism and the insistence on quick rewards, seen as compensating, in some sense, for the heavy sacrifices made earlier. A great gap opened between the official ideology and the actual behavior of a great part of the Israeli elite. The absorption of the new, mass immigration was marked by harsh social deprivation. The quasi-messianic expectations that had, with Ben-Gurion's encouragement, been attached to the establishment of the state were not fulfilled, and many young people began to feel a sense of profound disappointment. Zionism's pretenses of being the purveyor of speedy redemption proved false.[61]

A decisive change was brought about in Israeli society by the increased social and political weight of the immigrants from the Arab world. Their acculturation was different from that of the earlier European immigrants, for the Arab immigrants had none of the negative feelings about Diaspora life or tradition that the European pioneers had brought with them. On the contrary, this population retained a strong attachment to Jewish tradition and was indifferent to the ideas of the socialists. The ideological issues of the society's formative period were alien to it. It understood its Jewishness primarily in terms of religious and folk tradition, not in terms of nationality. The gap between it and the largely secular "host" society was widened further by the differences of economic status and class between the new immigrants and the veteran population.

More than fifty years ago, Martin Buber made the observation that a utopian program not anchored in tradition is bound to run out of steam. He claimed that the pioneer's devotion to hagshama did not come from within himself, from the times in which he lived, or from his socialist convictions. What really motivated him, wittingly or unwittingly, was the ancient Jewish longing for community. But because of the decline of Judaism in the preceding generations, the pioneer acquired his enthusiasm for hagshama in an antireligious spirit, and he was cut off from Jewish tradition. This led, in Buber's view, to a contradiction between being and consciousness: in the pioneer's being, this tradition was at work unconsciously; in his consciousness he had severed his connection with it and even opposed it. The world of the pioneer became "painfully down-to-earth and present-oriented," i.e., devoid of history. He sought legitimacy from the imperatives of the moment alone, rather than from any connection with the past. The pioneer's passion for hagshama would thus be fleeting; he would not be able to pass it on to the next generation.[62]

Buber's prophecy came true: the social and intellectual elite that established the state was unable to transmit its ethos to its heirs because that ethos had been detached from its historical and religious roots. We have already pointed out that although the pioneers understood the Zionist vision as an authentic expression of age-old yearnings, no educational effort was made to relate the new (Zionist) values to their sources in the old (Jewish) ones. The secular national ideology, with its values and symbols, remained alien to the mythic experience on which it was based. Hence the power of that experience petered out after one or two generations, and there was a demythologization of Zionism, a process that began with the founding of the state.

The sociologist Yonatan Shapira has also pointed out that extreme negativity toward Diaspora life had prevented the older generation from transmitting to its heirs the Jewish and wider, non-Jewish dimensions of that life. Education had been completely subordinated to national goals and thus suffered from dogmatism, a tendency to rigid indoctrination, and a simplistic view of reality.[63] The anti-intellectualism of the pioneers found expression in the values they chose to pass on: obliviousness to the sources of Jewish culture, emphasis on the physical and simple over the metaphysical and complex, encouragement of pragmatic values, and a preference for blunt behavior and speech.[64] The Zionist ethos was shaped by cosmopolitan people who stood at a crossroads between Jewish and European culture and had to make difficult, fateful choices between them. This meant that their devotion to this ethos, once they worked it out, was a product of deep conviction and historical awareness. The next generation, however, had a narrower perspective and no misgivings. A gap thus developed between the older generation, that had applied its cultural riches to hagshama, and the younger, that took hagshama for granted without having internalized the cultural matrix out of which it had grown.[65]

Although in the view of Herzl and most of the Zionist leadership Zionism was an "open-ended ideal," nourished from the depths of Jewish messianic longing, for many Israelis it became something finished, a goal already realized. It is thus no accident that the question of whether or not Zionism has completed its task occupies a central position in the current ideological debate between Zionists and Post-Zionists. This debate also casts its shadow over much deeper cultural questions, among them the sense in which Israeli society is to be Jewish and how it is to relate to the Judaic as opposed to the larger Western tradition. The proponents of messianic activism are today concentrated in the religious camp. For them, Zionism must carry on with the great endeavor it began in the prestate era. But because of their adherence to the vision of what is called "the whole Land of Israel" at the expense of other aspects of Zionist utopianism, they tend to avoid grappling with practical realities. On the other hand, many of the "realists" of the secular left, put off by mystical, messianic attitudes to the territorial question, tend to jettison the utopianism that characterized the mainstream of secular Zionism in the past. The result is a deep polarization of Israeli society, between visionaries who cannot face reality and realists who have no vision.[66]

In a sense, then, the very element that served as one of the main sources of Zionist strength has become a source of its weakness. As in other utopian movements, this element was very effective during the revolutionary phase and even for a generation beyond it, but it lost its power once it presumed to take the place of the previous tradition. The struggle between the conflicting tendencies within Zionism is still unresolved. Early on, Gershom Scholem raised the key question: can there be a fruitful synthesis between these tendencies without their canceling each other out? Like Kook but with a different point of departure, Scholem saw as positive the tension in Zionism between the desire to make a radical break and the desire to perpetuate. For him, any one-sided choice would be fatal for the Jewish people.[67] Secularization was necessary and unavoidable, but it carried many dangers with it. Hagshama meant primarily solving practical problems and meeting current needs, and as a result it unintentionally stripped the concept of exile of its redemptive potential.[68] In any event, Scholem believed that Judaism would have to pass through a crisis in which it would shed old forms and take on new ones. Secularism should not be seen as the last word but as a transitional phase. This is an era in which God's face is hidden, but out of the crisis in which Zionism finds itself, God will reveal Himself all the more strongly.[69] The Jewish people cannot content itself with mere worldly, political existence but is always driven toward the pursuit of some transcendent ideal. Thus the quest for normalization, being "a people like all peoples," will not succeed.[70]

Of course, there are many who doubt the possibility of the kind of synthesis Scholem proposed and who demand a decision one way or the other, but most Israeli Jews reject this demand. The fate of Zionism will therefore probably be decided by the degree to which this synthesis — between heaven and earth, between rebellion and renewal of tradition — can be achieved. The chances of the revolution succeeding may hinge ultimately on its ability to maintain a vital connection with the dream out of which it was born.

"Zion's Guilt": The Post-Zionist Critique

In recent years there has been a tendency among a group of Israeli historians and sociologists referred to as "Post-Zionists" to subject Israel's myths to historical and moral criticism. This group, identified with the political left, is calling for revision of our understanding of the Zionist past and consequently of Zionist identity. One of the principal concerns of these scholars is to reassess the degree of Zionist guilt in the ongoing conflict between Israel and the Palestinian Arabs. In their view, the Zionist narrative gives a distorted account. There is a profound discrepancy between the rhetoric and self-image of a peace-loving people that is in the right and has been subject to repeated attack and its own purportedly brutal use of force. The critics are trying to demolish the myths underlying this image and prove that Zionism intended from the outset to take over the country and systematically evict its Arab inhabitants. What is more, they say, Israel's territorial ambitions have caused it to pass up chances for peace and given rise to a nationalistic, militaristic society indifferent to humane, liberal values.

The Post-Zionist critics make two principal claims regarding earlier accounts of Zionist history. First, they were ideological constructions, intended to support Zionism and the Zionist establishment by legitimating the Zionist myth. The actions taken by the Jews in Palestine were presented in too favorable a light and the wrongs done to the Arabs ignored. Second, when the Zionist movement is examined according to sociological categories, it turns out that it is not a unique phenomenon but a colonialist movement, marked from the outset by a proclivity for the use of force. It is not essentially different from other migrations to undeveloped countries aimed at exploiting their resources and indigenous inhabitants. Although the Zionists have continually insisted that they did not come to impose their rule over the Arabs by force or to exploit them, this is only a tactic meant to conceal their true aspirations from themselves and from others, so as to win the support of the Jewish people and world public opinion.[71]

There are, no doubt, political motives underlying the Post-Zionist claims, notably a desire for reconciliation with the Palestinian Arabs, for which doing away with the Jewish, Zionist character of the state is often thought to be a necessary condition. Some regard this criticism of Zionist myths as a sign of maturity, of the liberation of Israeli society from the ideological shackles of the founding generations. But others see Post-Zionism as self-destructive, or at least as aimed at delegitimating Zionism itself, out of a sense of alienation and self-hatred. There is some truth to each opinion. Certainly Zionism, like all social movements, needs to be self-critical; accurate self-understanding is always essential to further progress. But has this particular critique been a fair one, done with sympathy and intellectual integrity? Let us examine some specific Post-Zionist claims with this question in mind.

ZIONISM AS A COERCIVE MOVEMENT

There is a strong tendency in Post-Zionism to assess the true intentions of the Zionist ideologues according to the practical outcome. Their *declared* intentions are unimportant, and the terms they employ are mere euphemisms. Euphemism can, of course, serve legitimate purposes, for example, as a mode of polite discourse, but when employed as an ideological tool it represents a kind of ruse or hypocrisy. Thus, "redeeming the land" referred, in fact, to expelling the Arabs from it, and "settlement" meant colonization pure and simple, it is claimed. To be sure, the Zionists did not invent these terms — they inherited them from Jewish tradition, of which they saw themselves as heirs and which they believed legitimated their return to the Land of Israel — but this matters little to the Post-Zionists, for whom all these terms are mere rationalizations of self-interest, meant to serve the sole purpose of oppression and displacement. The proof is in the practical results.

The Post-Zionists ignore that these results depended on the intentions of both parties to the conflict, which must be juxtaposed to each other and not only to the outcome. Their reasoning is ex post facto: if Zionism began to use force at a certain stage in its career, this means not that circumstances had compelled it at that point to do so, but that it had intended to do so from the outset. If, as a result of the 1948 war, Arabs were driven out of the country, it means the Zionists had always wanted to do this and were only awaiting an opportunity, no matter what they thought or said. Whereas the Zionist slogan "There is no alternative" had shifted all the blame onto the enemy, the Post-Zionists lean toward the opposite extreme, hunting feverishly for any evidence that will incriminate the Zionist leadership. There is no room for innocence or tragic necessity; the leaders were never torn by insoluble dilemmas; there is nothing but villainy and plotting.

This simplistic view of history is vastly different from that of Jacob Talmon, the astute analyst of modern nationalistic violence. For him, "the Jews were completely sincere when they claimed that they had no intention of [displacing] a single Arab. They had not come to take the place of the Arabs but to create new opportunities, reclaim the desert and the marshes, and settle alongside [them]."[72] "A minority aside, all adherents of Zionism did their utmost to achieve their aspirations without using force. . . . But it was the fate of our liberation movement — the most humane national movement in history — to be drawn into a tragic clash with a neighbor, to be embroiled in a bitter struggle with the powerful forces and fanatical aspirations of a violent age."[73]

Talmon does not entirely exculpate Zionism, but he regards its "sins" as calling "not for censure alone but for compassion, as unavoidable tragedies."[74] Most Zionists undoubtedly failed to gauge correctly the depth of the Palestinian Arabs' opposition, the power of the nationalistic forces at work among them (which Zionism itself had helped to arouse). Gershom Scholem, a member of Brit Shalom, saw in this a dialectical process that only became evident after the fact. "A reality emerged which had developed in the course of our activity." Consequently, Scholem opined in 1970, there was no point in blaming Zionism for what it had failed to do sixty years earlier. "Did the Zionist movement miss opportunities? . . . It is not for me to cleanse the Zionist leadership of its iniquities. But retrospectively, as a member of Brit Shalom, I doubt today whether it would have made much difference if we had done one thing rather than another."[75]

Because the protagonists in historical processes are human beings, the historian cannot refrain entirely from moral judgments; he cannot avoid the question of who is *responsible* for what happens. If his judgment is to be credible, however, he must try to understand the situation and motives of each party to it. The writing of history cannot be detached from the experience and awareness of those who made it, interpreting it as they went along. The deeds and interpretations of the protagonists can, of course, be viewed in a critical light, but the criticism must try, first and foremost, to understand them with empathy, without moral condescension, in the context of their times and not the critic's own.

A historian who judges from results and dismisses declared intentions is exhibiting the wisdom of hindsight. For example, he "knows" for certain that there were ways to avoid war but that Israel preferred to ignore them because of a penchant for the use of force. He even "knows" that in 1948 the State of Israel was not in serious danger, for the Arab forces were small and poorly equipped in relation to those of the Jews — albeit six hundred thousand against forty million! — and therefore there was no reason for the Yishuv to be afraid despite the declared intention of the Arabs to "throw the Jews into the sea." Thus, using supposedly objective, quantitative methods, it becomes possible not only to demolish the myth of "the few against the many" and explain this myth as a tool of manipulation used by the Yishuv leadership, but also to prove Israel's coercive intentions and its refusal to compromise with the Arabs after defeating them.

ZIONISM AND COLONIALISM

Colonialism is the use of the wealth and power of a mother country to dominate and economically exploit territories that never belonged to it. But the Land of Israel, unlike other countries of immigration, held no economic attraction at the time when modern Jewish settlement began there. The Zionists' purpose, rather, was to create there a new basis for Jewish identity, which had been cast in doubt by the process of modernization. It was the utopian element in Zionism that drew them to this particular land. The Post-Zionists detach Zionism from its specific historical roots. This makes it possible for them to see Zionism as just another colonialist movement or wave of migration.

The term "colonialism" is also misleading in that it ignores the idea of historic right, a part of the right of self-determination, which is based on the group's past. To be deprived of historic right is to be deprived of the right of self-definition, which is certainly an injustice.[76] Thus, such commonly used Zionist terms as *aliya* ("ascent," i.e., immigration by Jews to the Land of Israel), *hitnahalut* ("recovering one's patrimony," i.e., settlement of the Land of Israel) and *ge'ula* (redemption) cannot be separated from our understanding of Zionism. These are not rationalizations or euphemisms meant to conceal the Zionists' true aims from others or from themselves; rather, they are an exact expression of the historical outlook upon which the Zionist claim to national self-definition rests.

The choice of a particular terminology is not a neutral matter; often it implies value judgments. For example, such statements as "Zionism is a coercive movement" and "Israeli society is militaristic" are not merely empirical but imply a condemnation of the phenomena in question. There is no doubt that in common parlance today, at least in certain academic circles, these expressions have negative connotations. "Coercive" is not a merely empirical term, referring in neutral fashion to the struggle for power, but implies a certain moral stance that allows me to seize by force something that is essentially not mine and to which I am not entitled, or that regards as illegitimate the means I use to seize it. It is only fair to ask whether Zionism was power-oriented or militaristic in the same sense as fascism, for example, was, or whether finer distinctions must not be drawn.

The Post-Zionist critics see the essential evil of Zionism in its ethnocentricity. Herein, they say, lies the source of its tendency to coercion. In my Introduction, I have shown how such views are based on the faulty assumption that liberalism and nationalism are contradictory and that the latter must be abandoned if the former is to be upheld. What we have here is a narrow, simplistic view of both nationalism and liberalism and hence also of justice and the legitimate exercise of power. Being under the spell of Foucault's negative concept of power — any kind of power, no matter to what end — the Post-Zionists tend to see any use of force by the state as oppressive and unjust. The belief that the Jewish people in Israel can sustain its national identity among hundreds of millions hostile Muslims without power seems to me a dangerous illusion. Also, the Post-Zionists disregard the vital symbolic meaning that the Jewish state as such has for the Jews in the Diaspora and the need for a shelter for persecuted Jews so long as there is antisemitism in the world.

SPARTA OR ATHENS? MILITARISM IN ISRAELI SOCIETY

After the Second World War, Jewish intellectuals like Judah Magnes, Ernst Simon, and Hannah Arendt warned against establishing a Jewish state against the will of the Arabs. They feared that such a step would lead to a protracted conflict and that the new state would become a kind of modern Sparta, losing the humane values that had been an inseparable part of the Zionist message. In the history of the West, Sparta represents a society that educates its sons to a way of life completely based on military values. The Spartan citizen was a soldier on leave, liable to be called up at any time, and his personal life was not his own but belonged to the totalitarian state.

Arendt, who foresaw the worst for the Jewish state, observed with trepidation the militant activism of the Palestinian Jews in the wake of the war. She saw their armed opposition to the British and the violent struggle they were expected to have to wage against the Arabs as suicidal, the end of the Zionist dream. She predicted that the new state that would arise as a result of the war with the Arabs would be attacked by a hostile world and turn into a fortress, isolated and hysterically afraid within vulnerable borders. It would be completely preoccupied with defending itself in a way that would, of necessity, suppress all other kinds of activity and interest. The flourishing of Jewish culture would cease, and all the Zionist social experiments would collapse. Political thought would focus entirely on military strategy, and economic development would be determined by military needs. The Palestinian Jews would be cut off from the Diaspora, emerging as a new and distinct nation. A

Balkan chauvinism would make vulgar use of the religious idea of the Chosen People, and the Jewish people as a whole would decline into being just another small, warlike tribe like the Spartans.[77]

Arendt's bleak vision can serve us as a point of departure for considering whether Israeli society, despite having to divert much of its economic, social, and cultural resources to the protracted struggle with the Arabs, has managed to cultivate humane, democratic values or whether it has failed to do this and become a militaristic society, a modern Sparta. Israeli sociologists are divided on this question. One school, that of Moshe Lissak and Dan Horowitz, holds that militaristic values do *not* occupy a prominent place in Israeli society; rather, Israel offers living proof that "it is possible for a society to maintain a high level of allocation of resources for national security and a value system which perceives collective security as central without this having adverse effects on political pluralism or on the perception of social conflict and political controversy in other spheres as legitimate."[78] The reason for this lies not only in the near-pacifism of the society's founders but also in the fact that the near-universal participation of civilians in the army gives civilian norms an entree into the military sphere.[79] These observers point to features of the Israeli army — the stress on solidarity, the comradeship between soldiers and officers, the preservation of such values as equality and pioneering, and others — that are opposed to the rigid formality, hierarchicalism, and authoritarianism usually associated with militarism. There is reciprocal influence between the civilian and military spheres, but, according to this school, the influence of the civilian sphere on the military is greater. "Paradoxically, we may say that the involvement of the military in civilian life, in areas related to national security, is what has made possible the survival of democratic procedures and a civilian routine."[80] The army is not an exclusive coterie, and it does not set public policy. Although Israel is embroiled in a protracted, violent conflict, and most of its civilians are soldiers on leave, no militaristic ethos or cult of war has arisen here. Israeli society remains a relatively open, democratic, pluralistic one and does not behave as though it were under siege. In short: "[Israel's] democratic form of government and the pattern of life of its citizens are not suited to recurrent emergencies and 'living on the verge of extinction.' Israel has not become a Spartan garrison state ruled by 'experts in violence,' where all aspects of life are subservient to the need to respond to the challenges posed by the external threat. It is closer to the model of Athens, which, though it was involved in wars, perhaps no less than Sparta, maintained a democratic regime and cultivated 'civilian' ways of life during periods of quiet."[81]

Opposed to the school of Horowitz and Lissak is one that sees Israeli society as fundamentally militaristic. The leading spokesmen of this point of view are

Barukh Kimmerling and Uri Ben-Eliezer. Kimmerling believes Zionism is a colonialist movement in the full sense of the word, and this is the source of Israel's militarism. To be sure, the latter differs from the militarism of fascist and totalitarian regimes in being civil, cultured, sophisticated, and prevalent throughout the society rather than restricted to a ruling elite. Israeli militarism, in this view, is largely a mental phenomenon: seeing all reality from a military point of view. According to Kimmerling, the militarization of Israeli society has had three distinguishing features:

1. *The army is central to collective experience and identity.* The unifying factor in Israeli society is war and military service.[82] The army is one of the collectivity's central symbols, an embodiment of pure patriotism. Its stature is hallowed, as we see in the rituals and terminology with which it has been surrounded, and it is regarded as the sole safeguard of Jewish existence.

2. *The blurring of the boundaries between society and army is not a positive factor,* promoting the favorable influence of society on the army, but a negative one, promoting, mainly, the militarization of the civilian population. The politicians, all of whom have served for greater or lesser periods of time in the army, espouse military ways of doing things, which, in effect, dictate state policy. This is the translation into practice of the slogan "There is no alternative." The military approach is internalized, not only by most politicians but also by the public, consciously or unconsciously shaping its thinking.[83] Military considerations take precedence over all others, and security is the highest social priority. In other words, the doctrine of national security dictates all social decisions and encompasses all spheres of national life.

3. *Israeli culture bears a militaristic stamp.* Common speech, laden as it is with military terms and simple slogans, as well as the country's general ambience, are reflections of army life. Symbols and images connected with the conflict with the Arabs permeate the cultural codes themselves, as seen in the commemoration of the Holocaust and in the Israeli self-image, a mixture of strength and weakness. Unconsciously, the military way of doing things becomes part of the political culture and collective moral code.[84] By seeing itself as a society under siege, living in a perpetual state of emergency, Israel fosters an exaggerated sensitivity to both internal and external criticism and a chauvinistic atmosphere accompanied by xenophobia and ideological intolerance.

Ben-Eliezer has done a historical analysis of the roots of Israeli militarism. Unlike other scholars, he does not claim that a penchant for the use of force characterized Zionism from the outset. Its militarism derives, rather, from the social and ideological revolution wrought by the native-born Palestinian Jews in the 1930s, against the background of the worsening conflict with the Arabs. These young people, who saw themselves as a superior breed for having freed themselves of the exilic complexes of the preceding generation, found their path to power blocked by their parents. They therefore used the military as a springboard to positions of leadership in the society. Gradually, they were able to impose their pragmatic, Sabra (native) worldview and their coercive ethos on the society as a whole. In this, they were assisted by the dominant group, headed by Ben-Gurion, which supported them in order to hold on to its own hegemony in the Yishuv. This ethos, based on a view of reality "through the gunsights," still predominates in the society, shaping foreign and domestic policy alike.[85] Israel is, in Ben-Eliezer's phrase, "a nation in uniform," and militarism is one of the central organizing principles of Israeli society.[86]

Ben-Eliezer's thesis is thus the antithesis of "no alternative"; the military approach, rather than being the result of political circumstances in the late 1930s, was, he says, the result of a new ideology devised to serve the adventurism and penchant for the use of force of young people aspiring to dominance and heroic greatness. These tendencies were given full expression later on, in Israel's wars.

Kimmerling and Ben-Eliezer never draw a comparison with Sparta, but their analysis points in the direction of this model. Has Israel, in fact, become another Sparta? Zionism's main ideal type, in its formative years, has not been the soldier but the pioneer, he who worked a revolution in the moral and personal spheres by uprooting himself from the life of exile, forging a new culture and way of life, and creating new social frameworks. It is true that the image of the laboring pioneer was shunted aside during the years just before the establishment of the state, when that of the fighter became the educational model for all sectors of the society. The question of security became the focus of national concern, and those who served it gained great prestige. War and military service took on a central role in the national consciousness, and the army became the crucible of the emerging society.[87] But these phenomena are insufficient in themselves to justify describing Israeli society as militaristic. Rather, they appear at a certain stage in the history of every people, that of its struggle for independence. Attributing Israeli policies during the period of the establishment of the state to a single motive, as Ben-Eliezer does, is simplistic and unconvincing. The same is true of his portrait of Israeli youth. His style is marked by a tendentiousness and condescension that ignore the moral dilemmas faced by that generation, such as we see in their fiction, poetry, and diaries. Contrary to the prevailing notion that the Sabra character type is nationalistic and prone to the use of force, the sociologist Oz Almog maintains that in the literature of the Sabras themselves the picture is altogether different: "On the whole, the mythic profile of the fighting Sabra is made up of anti-chauvinistic and anti-militaristic elements." There is no power madness or triumphalism. Death on the field of battle is not held up as an ideal, even when it takes on a metaphysical, moral meaning.[88]

In my opinion, the crucial question is whether army and war are the basic unifying factors in Israeli society, as Ben-Eliezer and Kimmerling claim. It seems to me the answer is in the negative. The army could play a unifying role (that of melting pot) only because it was based on humane values instilled by the prestate leadership, values which may be seen as a legacy of Diaspora Jewry: equality, solidarity, mutual responsibility, and a readiness to volunteer for the common good. The Lebanon war (1982) demonstrated that war can only serve as a unifying force if there is an existing basis for solidarity. It is not a spirit of discipline and blind obedience that animates the army but one of voluntarism and responsibility. Civic virtues may take on military garb but are not, in their origin, military.[89]

It is thus no accident that the Israeli military ethos emphasizes such values as camaraderie between soldiers and officers. The army itself teaches citizenship, and the commanding echelon is committed to democratic values. The claim that the military approach has dictated state policy can be proved or disproved only after we have a clearer picture of the motivations of the other party to the conflict, i.e., after its archives, too, are opened. Nor is the claim that security considerations dominate all aspects of Israeli life correct in view of the great variety of economic, social, and cultural activities in Israel that have nothing to do with military objectives.[90]

We can state with a fair degree of certainty that, despite the prolongation of the Arab-Israeli conflict and the fact that most of the citizens of the young state came from countries that had no democratic tradition, democracy in Israel is developing rapidly, and the country is much more democratic today than it was thirty years ago. The army is gradually losing its value as a melting pot and as an obligatory rite of passage for Israeli youth coming of age.[91] Civilian oversight of the security services has also improved greatly since then. It is a clear indication that Israeli society is freeing itself from whatever militaristic patterns it might have picked up along the way.

A sober assessment of the moral character of the army itself also leads us to the conclusion that militarism is not deeply rooted in Israel. The army in a militaristic society is certainly not distinguished for its moral virtues. It is largely devoid of any sense of the moral limits of the use of force, and it is not selective in its choice of means. It tends to view the enemy as an object to be destroyed without mercy. The Israeli army, on the other hand, has generally felt a moral obligation to limit its use of force. For most of its history its moral code has been based on the principle of "purity of arms," in which war is seen as an unavoidable necessity, a last resort. As Rotenstreich puts it, "an attempt has been made here to foster loyalty and dedication [to military objectives] despite a negation of war in principle."[92]

Most Zionists undoubtedly failed to gauge correctly the depth of the Palestinian Arabs' opposition, the power of the nationalistic forces at work among them. There can be little doubt that Israel's erstwhile obliviousness to the existence of a Palestinian-Arab people took a heavy toll in wrongdoing and bloodshed that might have been prevented had an awakening come sooner. But the question remains — and on this scholars differ — whether such an awakening would have contributed much to achieving an agreement between the parties to the dispute in view of the fact that, until recently, the *Palestinians* showed no sign of willingness to compromise.

For a long time the Arab enemy was seen in stereotypic terms, often along the lines of the traditional exilic Jewish picture of the gentile foe. Similarly, the "white man's" view of the Orient — at least among Israelis of European extraction — and the heritage of Jewish "chosenness" made for a patronizing attitude toward the Arabs and their culture. But to judge from the literary testimony of the period, there was no blind hatred of the enemy, nor was the desire for revenge that wells up in wartime given vent. This does not mean there was no brutalization or demonization of the enemy in Israel's wars; there was, in all of them. But the fact is that the army did not usually endorse them, and they never assumed the massive proportions we see in other modern national struggles. Generally speaking, the army has never been morally corrupt, nor has military power corrupted Israeli society, although this power has sometimes been misused in a way that aroused fierce moral debate. It is thus not surprising that the deep moral shock experienced by Israelis during the Lebanon war and the Intifada (1987–93), as a result of the need to confront the Palestinian civilian population at close quarters, opened the eyes of the country's political leaders to a truth that could no longer be ignored, the truth of this people's existence and the necessary need for compromise. Whether such a change has also occurred on the other side is still a question.

The story of Israel is therefore, above all, the story of a dramatic struggle over the limits of the legitimate use of force. Militaristic and antimilitaristic tendencies have been at loggerheads all through the history of Zionism, but militarism has never gained the upper hand. Israel has belied most of the gloomy prophecies of the Diaspora Jewish critics. It has not become another Sparta, though it is still a long way from being an Athens.[93]

Conclusion
Politics in Israel as a Test of Judaism

We have seen that the reference to "Jewish ethics," which alludes to the sense of chosenness, has been very common in the Zionist political discourse. In the controversies over how to carry on the struggle with the Palestinian Arabs, beginning with the debate over "self-restraint" in the late 1930s, the question has arisen again and again of whether to adopt the enemy's norms of combat or conduct ourselves according to the more restrictive, traditional Jewish morality. Clearly, it is a certain sense of Jewish identity that gives rise to these moral concerns.

But since the Yom Kippur War of 1973, and especially since the Oslo Agreement (1993), the internal debate over public policy in Israel has been sharply polarized in a way that endangers the consensus on which the state itself was founded. The right wing, which includes the majority of Orthodox Jews and neotraditionalists, tends to base its claims on traditional Jewish archetypes and collective memory, while minimizing the value of universal concepts and even going so far as to ignore those elements within the Jewish tradition that call for solidarity with mankind as a whole. The left wing, which is made up mostly of secular Jews, favors such universal values as "human rights" and "democracy," which still have an alien ring for the traditional Jewish ear, while minimizing the use of figures of speech, images, and myths drawn from the Jewish tradition, which it considers chauvinistic. In this, today's left differs from the earlier Zionist Labor, which, in its thinking and rhetoric, always combined a grounding in the Jewish heritage with universal, humanistic values.

Although it would be a mistake to present the internal debate between particularism and universalism as a struggle between religion and secularism — there is a tension between the particular and the universal in the hearts and minds of the majority of Israeli Jews, be they religious or not — it is a fact that, in contrast to the past, current leftist moral criticism of the state's policies totally disregards the argument from Jewish ethics. In doing so, it knowingly cuts itself off from the context of Jewish history and weakens its own case. On the other hand, the religious right interprets Jewish ethics as completely opposed to universal norms. As long as the argument is between Jewish culture and an abstract, universal culture, there will be no common basis for political or moral discourse between left and right, and the ideological groupings in Jewish society will remain painfully polarized.

Questions of right and wrong over which society is deeply divided must be decided on the basis of the broadest possible cultural common denominator. This common denominator cannot be fixed in advance but must result from a give and take, based on mutual respect, among all the groups that make up the social fabric, Jews and non-Jews alike. And because the State of Israel defines itself as both a democratic and a Jewish state, it is only fitting that the political discourse and decisions of the majority be based on both the democratic and the Jewish traditions.

The question of how the State of Israel can be both Jewish and liberal, or how Western and Jewish legal norms can be combined, will no doubt be decisive for the future of the country and of Jewish culture both here and in the Diaspora. In the past, Jews found ways of integrating values from the surrounding culture into their own. Israel's political culture must be based on the assumption that such an integration is still possible, for without this assumption, the ideological groupings in Jewish society will continue to be painfully polarized and lack any foundation for shared discourse.

Zionism has given the Jewish people a framework for dealing with the full range of political and social problems. In doing so, it has made it possible for the Jew to meet "the other" on an entirely new footing of equality and human solidarity. By regaining for the Jewish people the capacity to deploy force, Zionism put the Jews and Judaism to the supreme test. It is no accident that some prominent Zionist thinkers have seen the movement's attitude toward the Palestinian Arabs as the highest test it has had to face in the present generation.

Indeed, with the passage of time, this test has become more difficult rather than less so. Many Jews in Israel believed that the Oslo Accords would open a new page in the history of the relations between Israel and the Palestinians, one based on mutual recognition and trust. But they were disappointed: not only has terror against Israeli civilians remained the main weapon of the Palestinians in their struggle, but its use has become even more ruthless. And as in the past, there are still very few among them who are prepared to condemn this tactic. Unlike the Israeli society, Palestinian society still does not show much readiness for self-criticism.

The establishment of the Jewish state and the use of force by Jews have provoked considerable moral consternation in the world. For many non-Jews, Israel symbolizes the hope for universal peace and justice. They expect it to behave in accordance with this ideal and judge it more harshly than other nations The disproportionate amount of attention given to Israel in the world media reflects a deep concern with the behavior of Jews, as if they were permanently on trial. Jews as Jews are held to a higher moral standard, and as a result Israel has always been accused of the excessive use of power.

Many Israelis reject this double standard, seeing it as a form of hypocrisy and veiled antisemitism. It is hard to deny that accusations are often leveled at Israel out of antisemitic motives. For Christians, Israel embodies a constant reminder of their own wrongdoing, and their conscience can be quieted by finding fault with it. Nevertheless, it must be recalled that Zionism itself presented the uniqueness of Jewish morality as supporting the Jews' claim to self-determination in their historical homeland. And it is difficult to see how Israel can retain its Jewish character if it does not remain faithful to the inner demands of the Jewish heritage out of which it was born. In this sense, the expectations the gentiles have of the Jews are important primarily as a reminder rather than a motivation; they help Israel to recall its obligation, not to them, but to itself.

Ernst Simon wrote that during the period of exile, the Jews assumed for themselves the role of God's witness under conditions of subjugation, but this unusual condition was, to some extent, forced upon them: living as they did under abnormal political circumstances, it was easy for them to present themselves as exceptional. For this reason, some Jewish thinkers believe it is easier to fulfill the Covenant in exile than in an independent homeland; it seems to them that in the Diaspora there is less of a threat to the essence of Judaism. Particularly in the modern period, it was relatively easy for Diaspora Jews to swim with the prophetic current in Judaism and present its universalistic demands to the world, for they were not responsible for the fulfillment of those demands. The question for Simon is whether we can remain God's witnesses under the conditions of a normal, modern state of our own.[1] When the Jewish sage in the *Kuzari* (1:114) takes pride in the moral virtue of the Diaspora Jews, his interlocutor, the king of the Khazars, gives him the ironical reply that the Jews can take pride in being meeker than the other nations only because they do not have the opportunity to kill. But when they do have that opportunity, they too will do so. Only by having their own state do the Jews have a chance to disprove the Khazar king's incisive pronouncement about them, on condition that they retain the moral sensitivity acquired during their history as an oppressed minority.

It is in this context that we may evaluate afresh the views of Jewish thinkers who, in the prestate period, opposed the Zionist enterprise, rejecting the goal of sovereignty and viewing exile as the ideal setting for the Jewish people to fulfill its destiny. One finds in their writings a great deal of romanticization and idealization of exilic life, a disproportionate stress on its positive aspects and an almost total disregard for its drawbacks and dangers. Most of these writers formed their views before the rise of Nazism and the Holocaust. They did not see antisemitism as endangering Jewish existence, and they believed that the chance for a spiritual renaissance was greater in the Diaspora than in Israel. Certainly, Zionism was more realistic about these things. Yet, these writers may yet have something to teach us.

Whereas the non-Zionist writers show a deep understanding for the positive role of exile in the shaping of Jewish identity, the Israeli ethos grew out of a negation not only of exile itself, but of the Jewish culture that developed there. Even if we admit that such a negation was necessary at a time when a whole generation was trying to extricate itself from exile and needed a powerful ideological rationale for doing so, we must still ask ourselves whether such a view is still justified, whether exile should still be seen as an unmitigated disaster, or whether it should also be recognized as a source of some positive values. It seems to me that one of the key questions facing Jewish culture in Israel today is how to translate the historical experience of exile, in a positive way, into the context of an independent state. We are in need of a fresh self-appraisal, a revision of the Zionist outlook that was so bound up with the negation of the exilic cultural heritage or with indifference to it. Given the destructive potential of modern nationalism, this heritage looms ever more important as a counterweight to the temptations of military and political power and as a much-needed foundation for shaping our self-image as a sovereign people.

An impressive attempt to integrate the Zionist ethos with the ethos of exile was made by Nathan Alterman, the poet of the rise of Israel. In several of the poems in his *City of the Dove,* and particularly in the cycle "Physiognomies," he gives an accounting of the exilic ethos.[2] He announces that it is not his intention to glorify exile or its "supposed splendor," but, in fact, he showers praise upon it for the tremendous power with which it shaped a unique culture and ethos. Like Hazaz, he stresses the ironical attitude of the exilic Jew to worldly politics. This Jew is like a wayfarer who "makes light of scorn [and of] distance / From states and their affairs . . . , from royal quarrels, from the whole exhausting tumult."[3] Diaspora Jewry "wrapped itself in powerlessness," so as not to give other nations' power a handhold. It knew that if it were to "make itself iron [weapons]" it would be obliterated. The history of the Jews was made not, as with other peoples, by those who ruled over them, but by the unbroken chain of generations of the Jews themselves, for the strength of this people was not in its rulers but in the masses of individuals who cleaved willingly to it. The collective ethic lay in the ethic of the individual. Therefore, in the case of this people, "wiped clean of the image of the machine and the idol," "the concept of nationhood, so distorted in the annals of humankind," was redeemed.[4] It kept this concept "alive and full of fundamental power" by virtue of its having been "stripped of all the glory of a nation's life." The greatness of the Jewish people in exile lay in its success at creating a model of pure nationhood, without "the trappings of sovereignty" that make the concept of nationhood "dreadful in its instruments of destruction." In its history it represented a "wonder-nation," in which "nationhood, so distorted in the annals of world history, was redeemed."

Alterman expresses foreboding that in its very return to its homeland and recovery of self-government there, the Jewish people will lose the distinctive identity it acquired in exile. The penetrating question posed in this poem cycle is whether the people will betray its essence, "the powerful distinctiveness which has known no like / Till now in the whole history of the nations"; whether, in the course of acquiring the "instruments" and symbols of "dominion," it will lose its character and come to resemble its persecutors and enemies: "A people risen from among foes / Shall perceive its own face to be the face of strangers."[5]

The return of the Jews to power and the use of weaponry could distort their distinctiveness as a people: "The faces of its persecutors, who shed its blood, / Now emerge from its own image." To adopt the sword means to build a bridge "over the chasm between the blood of the persecuted and the blood of the persecutor." War creates a covenant between the people and its attackers; the people grasps at what is given, at physical survival, at the price of "sin in return for sin."[6] Is it any wonder, then, that this poet of Israeli resurgence and celebrator of its armed might, like Bialik earlier (in his poem "It Is Not That You Have Hemmed Us Tightly In"), feels he must apologize for the fact that the Jews are compelled to take up the sword, rather than the ploughshare, in order to establish their state?

You alone — those who fall in your name attest —
Sought to the end to arise by the ploughshare
And not by the sword. But from you arose as one
Redemption and destruction.[7]

But if such is the nature of exile, what justification can the poet find for the Jews taking up "the trappings of sovereignty," such as will establish a covenant between them and their persecutors? The answer is: only political sovereignty offers any guarantee of justice for the Jewish people in our time. Without a state, "there is no judgment or punishment for sin," for it is the state that holds "the sword and scales of justice" that assure that the principle of retribution, the accepted principle of international relations, will be upheld.[8]

In this light, Alterman saw the Eichmann trial as a great event in that it "incorporate[d] for the first time into the life-story of the Jewish people the express judicial legality of justice and retribution." It is germane to point out that Alterman also saw the trial as a chance to settle accounts with those who pined for the times when Jewish existence lacked the trappings of sovereignty and was therefore more "spiritual," free of the limitations of politics. For him, there is a place for such thinking in the abstract, when it is just "a longing for a distant global future, a future in which humanity is whole and united," in which it is not the trappings of sovereignty that divide nations from one another. But such thinking is not valid if it implies disrespect for the trappings of sovereignty today, presenting past exile as preferable. Alterman points to "an inhuman, chaotic emptiness" hidden within the history of the Jewish people in exile. "[The right to conduct] a criminal trial is not only needed for the self-preservation of human society. It is also needed for the preservation and moderation of the laws of God, nature, and man, without which a life-history is deprived of logic." By the capture and trial of one who shed the blood of the nation, the State of Israel presents itself to the Jewish people as a whole as asserting the validity of those laws for the first time. Here we see a new dimension that the establishment of the state gave to Jewish life, in place of the inner chaos thitherto evident there.[9]

Alterman is well aware of the dialectics of power, in which there is a guarantee of retribution and justice but also the potential of corruption, so that spiritual brakes must be developed to control its use. Thus, unlike many in his generation, Alterman could call for shedding the morbidity of exile but at the same time wonder

whether in this sickness there is not evident
A spark worth keeping unhealed . . . ,
Lest it be expunged from our blood,
A spark of resistance and rebellion
Against the ways of the nations' history and the lusts of their regimes.[10]

Alterman thus hopes that the people will continue to bear the stamp of exile, even when they take on the character of their enemies. He wants their exilic past to give them an added sensitivity, a capacity for self-criticism that will allow them to assess "the value of deeds and names," for *raisons d'état* will never prevail over "the justice of God and man."[11] His vision is a synthesis of the old and new images of the Jew, in which a sense of belonging and patriotism are combined with the critical attitude toward the claims of politics which the Jews developed in exile.

> Though they who dwell in you shall quarrel,
> You will always be their haven,
> And they will never leave you, for they desire life.[12]

Alterman hopes that the new self-image the Jewish people is assuming will not completely efface the old one but continue to be recognizable to the other nations as it makes its way among them "as a wayfarer and a stranger," bearing "the seed of another world," "the end-time nation, unmarked by domination or brutality."[13] That which thinkers like Dubnow, Frishman, Hermann Cohen, and even George Steiner advocated in the Diaspora was also advocated in the Land of Israel by Alterman: a people that, in its very existence, would symbolize pure nationhood and eschatological fulfillment.

Herein lies the relevance of those thinkers to the question of Israeli Jewish identity: in the alternate interpretation they suggest to Jewish history they help us to free ourselves from the narrow, perhaps even dogmatic Zionist reading of it. They remind us that sovereignty in and of itself is not Judaism's vision, and the attainment of it carries a heavy moral price. But the lack of sovereignty also carries a moral price. The question of which price is greater has been, and remains, at the center of the debate between Zionism and its radical critics, like Steiner.

At the beginning of this book I suggested that the image of Jacob, whose character is so profoundly different from that of Esau, had an archetypal significance for the Diaspora Jewish consciousness and self-image. As we see in Isaac's blessing, Esau's characteristic skill is that of war: "You shall live by your sword" (Gen 27:40). Jacob, who steals away from Laban and dreads meeting up with his brother Esau because he has defrauded him of his birthright/election, is the archetype of the Diaspora Jew. He is to exchange his identity as Jacob for that of Israel after wrestling with an angel at the Jabbok River, his last stop in exile before entering the Promised Land. According to the commentary of Rashi, based on the Midrash, this is *Esau's* guardian angel. Though Jacob, mustering all his physical and spiritual strength, is able to overcome the angel, the price of his victory is a permanent injury, the disloca-tion of his thigh, which will thenceforth prevent him from devoting himself completely to war or seeing it as his raison d'être. It is not merely a physical defect but the symbol of a new spiritual and moral identity. The dialectic inherent in this identity will henceforth characterize Israel, as the ancient midrash grasped so well in its reading of the verse referring to Jacob's mood before meeting his brother: " 'Jacob was greatly frightened and anxious' (Gen 32:8): 'Frightened' lest he be killed, 'anxious' lest he kill. He said: If [Esau] overcomes me he will kill me, and if I overcome him, I will kill him" (Genesis Rabba 76:1). In other words, even when fighting for his life, the possibility that he will have to shed the blood of his brother/foe causes him great distress.

This dialectic reappears at the threshold of the modern era in Heine's poem "To Edom" (1824):

> For millennia now, as brothers,
> We've borne with each other an age;
> You bear the fact I'm still breathing,
> And I — I bear your rage.
> But often you got in strange tempers
> In dark times since the Flood,
> And your meekly loving talons
> You dyed in my red blood.
>
> And now our friendship grows firmer
> And daily increases anew,
> For I too have started raging —
> I'm becoming much like you![14]

Heine is describing the complex interrelations between the Jewish people and the Christian peoples of Europe, the midrashic metaphor for which is Edom (another name for Esau and a Rabbinic code name for Rome). They are relations of dependency combined with mutual tolerance and a certain amount of brotherliness. Esau "bears" Jacob's existence but sometimes is seized by an ostensibly religious zeal that drives him to shed his brother's blood. Jacob, for his part, "bears" the wild Esau, but of late — Heine is alluding to the period of the Emancipation — the friendship between the two brothers has grown so much stronger that Jacob has himself begun to behave wildly and almost resembles his brother. Heine fears that the convergence of the brothers in the modern era means, among other things, that Jacob is assuming Esau's violent character.

A century ago, when the Jews began to return to their homeland, they were gradually forced to learn Esau's martial skills. But remaining true to the ancient command "You shall not follow their laws" (Lev 18:3), many of them tried to steer clear of the danger to which Heine is alluding: "Comradely love and a single law for all—we shall hold fast to these commandments which the Torah of Moses and the Torah of the heart enjoin upon us, as we undertake to establish our country. . . . Let us keep away from the worship of alien gods and from bowing down to the Golden Calf, lest we be afflicted with the Lord's curse of being left to wander in the wilderness forever. The Roman principle granting sovereignty [on the basis of conquest] was invented by a warlike people. It was Roman spears that drove us from our land. In returning to it, let us not follow their laws."

These words, written at the turn of the twentieth century in German by the Zionist sociologist and economist Franz Oppenheimer (1864–1943), were translated into Hebrew in a pamphlet published by the Jewish National Fund in 1914 and quoted enthusiastically that same year by the writer Yosef Hayim Brenner.[15] Forty years later, this motif reappears in the poem of Nathan Alterman discussed above. After enumerating the maladies and strengths of Diaspora Jewry, the poet of Jewish independence and glorifier of Israel's army alludes to Jacob's wrestling with the angel at the Jabbok River before entering the Land. The Jewish people has just established its state in the course of a cruel and bloody struggle, and he voices the wish that the outcome of the ancient match will leave its stamp on the way Jacob's descendants, too, wage their wars.

> But may this resurgent nation
> Limp a bit on its thigh,
> Even when the land gives it a new body.
> Let there still be noticeable, even on parade,
> The blemish that the angel made.[16]

Notes

Introduction

1. See Hegel 1967, 103–11; Taylor 1979, 83–95.

2. Tocqueville 1988, 287.

3. On the importance of loyalty for moral behavior, see Daskal 1977, 29–38; Oldenquist 1982, 173–93.

4. Niebuhr 1935, 206.

5. Cohen 1972, 423.

6. Ibid., 441–45.

7. Bellah 1985, 262.

8. Cf. Kemp 1988, 187–97; Walzer 1983; MacIntyre 1981, 216–22.

9. Nietzsche 1949, 19.

10. Kolakowski 1972, 31.

11. Walzer 1987, 71–90.

12. See Habermas 1989, 373.

13. Cf. Kelly 1988, 369–80. On the issue of tradition-criticism, cf. also Bernstein 1986.

14. Buber 1953, 142.

15. Buber 1954, 223.

16. For a critical view of Foucault's concept of power, as expressed in his historical studies, see Habermas 1987, 266–93.

17. See Funkenstein 1995, 346.

18. See Eagleton 1983, 146–47.

19. Nora 1983, 6.

20. Nietzsche 1949, 28–29, 36, 49, 51.

21. Niebuhr 1968, 85–100: "Do the State and the Nation Belong to God or Devil?"

22. Funkenstein 1995, 345–46.

23. Funkenstein 1992a, 209.

24. Tal 1987, 52–53.

25. See Liebman 1989, 51–60.

26. See Walzer, 1989, 34–37, 126–28.

27. Liebman 1989, 57–58.

28. Tamir 1992, 95–98.

29. Ibid., 95.

30. Ibid., 79.

31. See, e.g., Anderson 1983, 1. See also Ginossar and Bar-eli 1996.

32. Shils 1983, 14.

33. Talmon 1968, 6.

34. On the influence of Russian literature and culture on the Jewish intelligentsia in Russia, see Segal 1989, 1–16. See also remarks by the historian Michael Confino, London 1993. See also Confino 1993, 341–48: "Tefisat hamahapekha shel Berl Katznelson" (Berl Katznelson's concept of revolution).

35. Gadamer 1989, 273ff., 337ff.

36. Buber 1948, 147.

37. Rosenzweig 1965, 90.

38. Scholem 1989, 59–60 (letter to Franz Rosenzweig, 26 Dec. 1926).

39. Elazari-Vulcani 1950, 35–36.

Chapter 1. Power, Freedom, and Political Independence in Jewish Thought

1. See Don Yehiya and Susser 1986.

2. See ch. 7 for a discussion of Dubnow's position.

3. Graetz 1936.

4. An allusion to Jesus' saying "Render unto Caesar that which is Caesar's and to God that which is God's" (Matthew 22:21).

5. Buber 1956, 88–89.

6. See Elazar and Cohen 1985, 5–6.

7. Shlomo Pines, "Gilgulim shel hamunah herut" (The changing concept of freedom) in Yovel and Mendes-Flohr 1984, 247–65.

8. Josephus 1965, 9:21.

9. See Tosefta, Sota 14:4: "They cast off the yoke of the rule of heaven and set over themselves the yoke of the rule of flesh and blood"; Cf. Mishna, Avot 3:5; Mekhilta, Yitro, ed. Horowitz-Rabin, 203. Ibid., 150; in these sources, the concept of freedom is thus linked to liberation from human domination, on one hand, and the acceptance of the yoke of Torah, i.e., of "the kingdom of heaven," on the other.

10. Josephus relates that Judah the Galilean, the founder of the Zealots, "incited his countrymen to revolt, upbraiding them as cowards for consenting to pay tribute to the Romans and tolerating mortal masters, after having God for their lord" (Josephus 1961, 2:367–69.

11. Cf. the words of Jesus in Matthew 11:18. On the recasting of the notion of freedom in Pauline Christianity, see Pines (n7, above). Under Paul's influence, Christianity turned the Jewish concept of freedom into something completely internal: the place of political liberation was taken by liberation from the yoke of the Torah and the cmmandments.

12. See Schirman 1955, 521.

13. See Elon 1973, 1:51–59.

14. Weinfeld 1964, 662–65.

15. Lam 3:30; Isa 50:6. The image of the servant of the Lord, suffering for the sake of the redemption of humankind as a whole, became central in both Christian and Jewish thinking.

16. Moshe Greenberg 1986; Weinfeld 1964.

17. On Maimonides' attitude to war, see Blidstein 1983; Reuven Kimelman, "Hilkhot milhama umigbeloteha" (The laws and limitations of war), in Gafni and Ravitzky 1993, 233–54; Yosef Ahituv, "Milhemot yisrael ukedushat hahayim" (Israel's wars and the sanctity of life), in Gafni and Ravitzky 1993, 255–76.

18. Based on the demands of Halakha, Shlomo Zevin concludes that there is no legitimacy to "optional wars," either for Jews today or for the descendants of Noah at any time, and that the shedding of blood in such a war is plain murder. See Zevin 1979, 17.

19. On attitudes toward war in Western culture in general and in Christianity in particular, see "Peace, ethics of" in Wiener 1973, vol. 3.

20. See "Gihad," in Eliade 1987, 15–63; Sivan 1995, 9–12.

21. Yeshayahu Leibowitz, "Milhama ugevura beyisrael ba'avar uvahove" (War and heroism in Israel, past and present), in Leibowitz 1982, 133, 175.

22. Jacob's words to Joseph, "I will give you one portion more than your brothers, which I wrested from the Amorites with my sword and bow" (Gen 48:21), are interpreted by Rabbi Yehuda as follows: "'With my sword and bow'—with [the performance of] sacred precepts and good deeds" (Genesis Rabba 97:6); similarly, earlier, in Targum Onkelos. On this, Yosef Heinemann comments: "It is clear that the Sages rejected the simple interpretation of these words both on theological grounds and out of patriotic and educational motives, at a time when they were developing a position that negated warfare as a means of achieving the salvation and redemption of Israel." See Heinemann 1974, 154. See also Kook 1963a, 75.

23. Rosenzweig 1987, 247.

24. James, "The Moral Equivalent of War," in James 1968, 660–71; James 1960, 356–57.

25. See Rabbi Hayim Volozhiner's commentary *Ruah hayim* (The breath of life) on the Mishna, Avot 1:4: "Study [of Torah] is referred to as war . . . and the student may not accept his teacher's words when he has a problem with them. And sometimes the student is right."

26. Feierberg 1973, 157.

27. The midrash makes the following comment on the "blessing" (in fact, a curse) given by Jacob to Simeon and Levi, "Their weapons [*mekheroteihem*] are tools of lawlessness" (Gen 49:5): "These weapons you hold are stolen. To whom are they suited? To *mekheroteihem*—to Esau, who sold [*makhar*] his birthright" (Genesis Rabba 98:5). Cf. Rashi's comment on Num 31:8.

28. Kook 1963, 14.

29. Halevi 1964, 78.

30. Nietzsche 1967, 33–35.

31. Nietzsche 1997, fragment 205, pp. 124–25.

32. Kant 1964, 99.

33. See Baer 1988.

34. Luz 1988, 212.

35. Horowitz 3:25a. See also Ravitzky 1996, 227–28.

36. Emanuel Rackman, "Violence and the Value of Life in Jewish Tradition," in Baron and Wise 1977, 33–34.

37. Walzer 2000, introduction, xxii.

38. On Jewish "passivity" in the Diaspora, see Funkenstein 1982; Schorsch 1977.

39. Baer 1941, 129–30.

40. Moses Mendelssohn, *Gesammelte Schriften* (Collected works) (Leipzig: Brockhaus, 1843–45), 5:494, as translated in Halpern 1961, 67.

41. See Ravitzky 1996, 11.

42. See Isaiah Berlin, "The Originality of Machiavelli," in Berlin 1979, 47.

43. Scholem 1974, 129; Bosak 1956, 440–43.

Chapter 2. Shame, Guilt, and Suffering in Jewish Culture until Modern Times

1. On guilt and shame as important mechanisms of cultural socialization, see Piers and Singer 1971.

2. Geertz 1973, 401. For a comprehensive philosophical analysis of shame, see Rotenstreich 1965, 55–86.

3. Translator's note: The same Hebrew word, *kavod,* can mean either "honor," a term with primarily social connotations, or "dignity," which refers to an inner value, largely independent of one's position in society. In modern Hebrew, we may specify that "dignity" is meant by using the term *kevod ha-adam* (the *kavod* of the individual qua human being) or *kavod atzmi* (*kavod* for oneself, self-respect). See further discussion of this point toward the end of the present chapter.

4. Nietzsche 1997, 124.

5. "For the longest time these Greeks used their gods precisely so as to ward off the 'bad conscience,' so as to be able to rejoice in their freedom of soul — the very opposite of the use to which Christianity put its God. . . . In this way the gods served in those days to justify man to a certain extent even in his wickedness; they served as the originators of evil — in those days they took upon themselves, not the punishment but, what is *nobler,* the guilt." Nietzsche 1969, 93–94. A different perspective on the nature of guilt in Greek tragedy is offered by Bernard Williams. In Williams' view, the Greek equivalent of "shame" (*aidos*) includes certain aspects of guilt as the latter is understood in our culture (Williams 1993, 90–91).

6. Jaeger 1945, 1: 7–9.

7. Plato, Protagoras in Plato 1924, 1:143.

8. Friedrich Nietzsche, *Thus Spoke Zarathustra,* in Nietzsche 1971, 170.

9. Cf. Bowra 1957, 32–53.

10. Aristotle 1966, 89, 104.

11. See Leo Strauss, "Progress or Return?" in Strauss 1989, 249–50.

12. There are also cultures known to us today in which the prevailing ethos ascribes little importance to guilt but decisive importance to shame and honor, e.g., the Japanese and Muslim Arab cultures. For different opinions concerning the role of honor in Arab culture, see Levi 1991. See especially, in that article, the remarks of Matti Peled: "This motif occupies a position of unparalleled depth in the Arab frame of reference. There is, among the Arabs, no forgiveness for humiliation except in death. This extends from offenses to family honor to offenses to the honor of the tribe, the nation, or the faith. These can never be forgiven. For [the Arabs], there is nothing worse than a public affront, until this very day." On the other hand, self-incrimination, which is the opposite of self-criticism, is quite rare in this culture.

13. On the different meanings assigned to honor in the Jewish and Greek ethoses, see Luzzato 1948, 53, 97–98; Luzzato 1976, 53–54. In his poem "Derekh eretz" (Proper conduct), Luzzato contrasts the Greek pursuit of honor with the biblical commandment to honor one's parents. On this contrast, see also Nietzsche 1971, 57.

14. Cohen 1972, 265.

15. See Schimmel 1992, 43–52.

16. This point is made by Steven Schwarzschild, who believes Maimonides, in his *Commentary to the Mishna* (Avot 4:4), abandons the Aristotelian golden mean in his discussion of the virtue of humility. In Jewish ethics, humility is an absolute virtue. See Schwarzschild 1990, 141.

17. Cohen 1972, 426. Cf. Kaufmann 1969, 8:494.

18. See Ben Halpern, "Ethical Issues in Extreme Situations: Some Current Paradigms from Jewish History" (unpub. MS).

19. "Why sob, Sister Ruhama? / . . . The disgrace is not yours but your tormentors.' " Yehuda Leib Gordon, "Ahoti Ruhama" (Sister Ruhama), in Gordon 1964, 11–12.

20. See Nietzsche 1997, 124.

21. Johan Huizinga, "Chivalric Ideas in the Middle Ages," in Huizinga 1960, 197. For Nietzsche, the Jews' powerlessness gave them a venomous hatred for the chivalric value system, which was based on physical prowess and vigor in the context of war, hunting and adventure. Nietzsche 1969, para. 7, pp. 33–34.

22. Burckhardt 1944, 263.

23. Huizinga 1960, 206.

24. Cohen 1972, 283.

25. Lessing 1930, 12–15.

26. Simon 1966, 313.

27. On Kant's notion of human dignity, see Haezrahi 1961, 180–86.

28. Berger 1984, 149–58

29. Cited in Haezrahi 1961, 229.

30. Beyond the antisemitic stereotypes implicit in his play "The Merchant of Venice," Shakespeare shows keen insight into the feelings of the Jew Shylock. His demand for the "pound of flesh" owed him flows not only from a desire to avenge his disgrace as the representative of a scorned race but from a desire for equality and solidarity between Jew

and Christian, which naturally had no chance of being realized under medieval conditions. See Act II, Scene 1.

31. Cited in Brandes 1970, 9–10.

32. On the rejection of the traditional concept of suffering and martyrdom in modern Jewish thought, see Schwarzschild 1970, 287–314; Baron 1964, 96–100. The view that there is no meaning to suffering in exile is the central motif in Bialik's poem "Igeret ketana: min hagola le'ehai betzion" (A brief letter: from the diaspora to my brethren in Zion), Bialik 1954, 8–9.

33. Ahad Ha'am, "Hatzi nehama" (Partial consolation), Ahad Ha'am 1953, 70–71.

34. Ahad Ha'am, "Shalosh madregot" (Three steps), ibid., 150.

35. See Goffman 1963.

36. Berlin 1952, 31–33.

37. Piekarz 1990, 443.

38. Ibid., 336.

39. Berlin 1980, 268.

40. Otto Weininger (1880–1903) was an Austrian philosopher and apostate Jew who committed suicide at the age of twenty-three. His thinking is an outstanding example of Jewish self-hatred. In his philosophy, he identifies the duality of good and evil with that of male and female. In his view, Judaism symbolizes the inferiority of the feminine to the healthy masculinity of the gentiles. See Kurzweil 1958, 112–28, and Lessing 1930. A well-known example of a generation ago is the eponymous hero of Philip Roth's novel *Portnoy's Complaint*.

41. The German-Jewish writer Friedrich Torberg, who, in his 1948 book, describes the bitter awakening that brought him back to Judaism, provides an example. See Torberg 1962. Cf.Shaked 1992.

42. Max Nordau, speech to the First Zionist Congress (1897), in Hertzberg 1959, 239.

Chapter 3. The Shame of Exile and the Zionist Recovery of Jewish Dignity

1. Brenner 1955–67, 3:46. See also his story "Hu amar la" (He said to her), which stresses the ugliness of the character of the father murdered by the rioters and at the same time defends his behavior on moral grounds.

2. Leo Pinsker, *Auto-Emancipation,* in Hertzberg 1959, 190, 192. On Zionism's aspiration to restore Jewish honor, see Almog 1987, 23–37.

3. See Shavit 1996, 76–84.

4. Luz 1988, 163–70.

5. Yosef Hayim Brenner, "Min hamish'ol" (From the path) (1911), Brenner, 1955–67, 3:80.

6. There was undoubtedly a close connection between the negation of the Diaspora and the elevation of "masculine" values in Zionist thinking. Such values included activism in conquest and combat, as opposed to exilic passivity. Cf. Boyarin 1998. In their relation to the land, too, which was sometimes described in erotic terms, the settlers saw themselves as playing a masculine role and the land a feminine one.

7. Brenner, "Ha'arakhat atzmenu" (Self-Evaluation), in Brenner 1955–67, 3:57–78.

8. Brenner 1955–67, 2:106; Gershom Scholem, too, attributed to messianism "the

basic weakness of Jewish history" and "the terrible price" it paid for it. See Ben Ezer 1974, 265–66, 269.

9. The image of the Jewish people as a lamb among seventy wolves appears in Rabbinic literature as a symbol of Israel's persecution by the other nations but also as a sign of the miracle of its survival. The reappearance of this image in modern Hebrew literature deserves investigation in its own right; there is hardly a writer or poet in the period of the revival who does not make use of this image. Berdyczewski is apparently the first writer to reject the image outright. See also below.

10. Cahan 1912, 54; Heine 1925, 13.

11. Gordon 1957a, 216–17, 256.

12. Kaufmann 1970, 118, 128. As an example, Kaufmann quotes Yehuda Leib Gordon to the effect that the enlightened person is "one who acknowledges the truth," i.e., one who accepts certain antisemitic accusations. This is also the point of departure of Brenner's "self-evaluation."

13. Dubnow 1961, 171–72. His remarks here are reminiscent of the passionate debate over the "passivity" of the Jews during the Holocaust.

14. Brenner 1955–67, 3:74–77.

15. Hazaz 1963a, 189.

16. Hazaz 1963, 157.

17. Greenberg 1930, 3; Greenberg 1936, 162.

18. See Mintz 1982–83, 278–300.

19. Shazar 1971, 189–91.

20. Iviansky 1991, 224–26.

21. Ibid., 232.

22. Kovner 1988, 51. See also Gutman 1977, 7–27.

23. See Laor 1984, 50–52.

24. Simon Rawidowicz, "The Concept of Galut," in Rawidowicz 1988, 97, 113.

25. Halpern 1960, 27–34.

26. Greenberg 1936, 155.

27. Abba Ahimeir was a prolific journalist who opposed concessions of any kind to either the Arabs or the British.

28. Ahimeir 1966, 109.

29. "Not in the hour of heroism but persistently, in everyday actions and everyday life." Brenner, "Min hametzar" (In dire straits), in Brenner 1955–67, 1:252.

30. Ahad Ha'am 1950, 163.

31. Ahad Ha'am 1973, 45–47.

32. Ahad Ha'am 1950, 20. This article was first published in 1891.

33. A group of intellectuals, founded in 1925 and centered in Jerusalem, that favored compromise with the Arabs.

34. See the discussion of the "remnant of Israel" in ch. 4, below.

35. Berdyczewski 1909, 27–31.

36. Berdyczewski 1899a, 82.

37. See, e.g., the debate over the lessons of the first- and second-century Jewish rebellions against Rome. Eldad 1982; Harkabi 1983.

38. Ahimeir 1966, 272–73.

39. Ibid., 248.

40. See Porat 1989.

41. Tabenkin 1967–85, 2:38. This was said in 1937.

42. Kaufmann 1961, 2:400.

43. There is an extensive literature on the Massada myth. See, e.g., Alter 1973; Zerubavel 1991, 42–67; Kedar 1982 (original article in *Ha'aretz,* 22 Apr. 1972); Ben-Yehuda
1995; Talmon 1976, 82–90; Lewis 1976; Liebman and Don Yehiya 1984.

44. On the Zionist gamble, see ch. 4, below.

45. Lavi 1949, 45–46.

46. Quoting Nahman Ben-Yehuda; see *Ha'aretz,* 25 Mar. 1997. On whether the mass
suicide was in accordance with Halakha, see Goren 1982, 391–404; Neria, 1992, 198–
99.

47. Oz 1975.

48. Tabenkin 1967–85, 4:38.

49. Cf. the discussion of this question in the Babylonian Talmud, Baba Batra, end of
ch. 3.

50. Rothenstein 1948, 98–100.

51. Arendt 1978, 176–82.

52. Levi 1988, 103.

53. Bettelheim 1967, 157.

54. Frankl 1978, 34. See also Levi, 1988, above, 117.

55. Hehalutz halohem 1984, 102. See also Schweid 1994, 205–41.

56. Ibid., 65. Cf. also Abba Kovner's remark: "In utter despair, when all is going
against you, you cannot be reconciled; there is a dream beyond your own life. Whether it
is addressed to the Holy One, blessed be He, or to the future of your people, its meaning is
the same. There is something to which you will eventually have to give an accounting,"
Kovner 1988, 50.

57. "Yizkor" (The memorial prayer) in Zerubavel 1966, 179–203; See also the statement made by Abba Kovner during the ghetto revolt: "A light will shine upon us when, in
this bleeding darkness, we are given to realize once again that we are masters over death.
Then shall our lives have meaning." — in Korchak-Marla 1946, 56; and Nathan Alterman's verse, "My brethren! Perhaps once in a thousand years our death has a meaning! /
My brethren, this time it may not be in vain!" — in Alterman 1956, 91.

58. Sharon 1946.

59. An extreme example of blaming the victim is provided by the writer Yehoshua Bar-
Yosef, who rejects "moralistic" attempts to heap blame and shame upon the murderers
alone. In fact, the fault is entirely that of the murdered for not having developed a
sufficiently realistic, predatory mentality. Bar-Yosef bases his opinion on "moral" arguments drawn from the realm of biology: "Throughout the animal world, it is the predatory killer that is in the right, that is entitled to live, while its prey is in the wrong and is
sentenced to death." See the interview with Bar-Yosef in *Proza* 51–53 (Feb. 1982): 124.

60. Alterman 1989, 23, 70, 93. See also Laor's comments there, 134–35. See also Beit-
Tzvi 1977, 426–61. The author cites many reasons for the Jews' attitude toward their
own humiliation. Cf. Gutman 1977, 14–15.

61. Hehalutz halohem 1984, 217–19.

62. See Levi 1988, 62–63. See also Lieblich 1991, 162–66. On the ambivalence of the Yishuv toward the fate of Diaspora Jewry under the Nazis, which combined feelings of shame and guilt, see Weitz 1988, 74–85; Weitz 1986, 40–41, 55.

63. Dinur 1958, 18, 59.

64. Kovner 1988, 51.

Chapter 4. "The Remnant of Israel"

1. There were 25,000 Jews in Palestine on the eve of the first Zionist immigration (1882). Twenty-five years later, the figure had doubled. By then, however, settlement had become a more viable option.

2. For formulations and philosophical rationales of the notion of the wager, see Pascal 1961, 155–62; James 1956, 1–31.

3. James 1956, 1–31.

4. Buber 1993, 112.

5. Cf. Bergman 1967, 374–75. See also interview with Bergman in Ben Ezer 1974, 98–99.

6. Buber 1960, 103.

7. Buber 1968, 186.

8. See also Amos 5:15: "Perhaps the Lord, the God of Hosts, will be gracious to the remnant of Joseph"; Joel 2:13–14: "Rend your hearts rather than your garments, and turn back to the Lord your God. . . . Who knows but He may turn and relent and leave a blessing behind . . . ?"

9. Buber 1960, 104–5.

10. Shlomo Ibn Verga, *Shevet Yehuda* (The scepter of Judah), 32:122, as quoted in Bergman 1970, 57–58.

11. See Werblowsky 1964, 104–18.

12. Bergman 1970, 41–42.

13. Buber 1993, 137–50.

14. E.g., on the importance of Jewish messianic hopes for humanity, see Mumford 1951, 139: "The binding force of an ethical system based on purpose has been dramatically confirmed in the history of the Jews. By holding to these purposes, the Jews kept together as a people under conditions that would have ground any less hopeful nation out of existence: that itself would constitute a pragmatic justification of purpose. But these goal-seeking people have done more than hold together, while their conquerors and opperssors, given to ephemeral satisfactions and immediate aims, vanished. Today the Jews have performed the incredible feat of returning as a unified political group to their native home in Palestine. Thus a collective purpose, working over an almost cosmic stretch of time, has brought its own fulfillment."

15. Rosenzweig 1972, 404–5.

16. Ibid., 404.

17. Rawidowicz 1974, 221.

18. Weiner 1984, 103–16.

19. Schwarzschild 1970, 290–93; Twersky 1980, 347–50.

20. Maimonides 1985, 102.

21. See Friedmann 1967; Whitfield 1986, 385–407.

22. See Alter 1968, 346–53.

23. Shapira (Avraham) 1994, 121–23.

24. Neumann 1988, 163.

25. Neumann 1988, 164.

26. Amos Oz said of the pioneers that "they were people who, at a young age, took enormous, existential, life decisions. . . . They had to decide what to be (yeshiva students, Communists, [immigrants] to America, etc.), but they decided to undertake this adventure, to [come to] the Land of Israel. And the Land of Israel then was not some kind of stock in which you put a little money, and if it went up it went up, if it went down it went down. You had to put your whole life into it. To give up everything." See Shavit 1990.

27. Brenner 1955–67, 1:215.

28. Brinker 1990, 187–88.

29. Brenner 1955–67, 3:99.

30. Brinker 1990, 200.

31. Brinker 1990, 288.

32. Brenner 1955–67, 3:70.

33. Brinker 1990, 186.

34. The motif of stubborn loyalty to the Hebrew heritage appears clearly in Brenner's famous article in *Hame'orer* (Jan. 1906). See Brenner 1955–67, 2:128.

35. Brenner 1955 , 2:406.

36. Cited in Hoffman 1989, 166.

37. Brenner 1955–67, 3:478.

38. Shoham 1986, 25.

39. For a discussion of the Massada myth, see ch. 3, above.

40. Livneh 1966–67, 396.

41. Vitkin 1961, 23–31.

42. Beilinson 1949, 423.

43. Ibid., 373.

44. Syrkin 1921.

45. Katznelson 1945–50, 4:19.Cf: 5:175, 247.

46. Oppenheim 1982, 190–91. In his view, "the pioneer's sense of destiny is sometimes expressed in apocalyptical, eschatological terms borrowed from the sphere of religion."

47. Buber 1962, 14.

48. Eshed 1978, 69.

49. Appelfeld 1979, 104.

50. Shalev 1992, 192–98.

51. Berdyczewski 1900b, 95–96: Avar vehove (Past and present).

52. Bialik 1939, 289.

53. Gordon 1953, 357. On the nature of the distinction, see 330.

54. Ibid., 340.

55. Ibid., 159.

56. Tabenkin 1967–85, 2:422: "Hagola hayehudit nokhah hamilhama hamitkarevet" (The Jewish diaspora faces the coming war) (Dec. 1938).

57. Katznelson 1929–32, 2:316.

58. Katznelson 1945–50, 9:260.

59. Katznelson 1929–30, 2:367.

60. Katznelson, 1945–50, 11:107.

61. Sereni 1970, 263.

62. Eshed 1978, 319–20.

63. The importance of the timing of redemption is the main subject in Bialik's story "Hamelekh David bame'ara" (King David in the cave), in Bialik 1954, 292–95.

64. Remarks of David Ben-Gurion, in Erez 1962, 579.

65. Ben-Gurion 1946, 142.

66. Scholem 1989, 76.

67. See Frischman 1912, 149–62.

68. Rosenzweig 1935, 282.

69. Rosenzweig 1972, 324.

70. Rawidowicz 1948, 109–25; 1945, 82–83. See also 1988, 65–95: The End and the Endless.

71. Rawidowicz 1948, 110, 112.

72. Karni 1988. See also Neusner 1998, 121–28.

73. Kurzweil 1970, 255. On the ideological argument about Israel versus the Diaspora, see Gorny 1990.

74. Katznelson 1945–50, 9:117–18.

75. See Laor 1983.

76. Shapira 1992, 424–26.

77. Ben-Gurion 1946, 2:211.

78. Katznelson 1945–50, 9:59.

79. Reply given by Moshe Sharett (Shertok) in the name of the Zionist Executive to the debate in the Twenty-first Zionist Congress, 1939. Cited in Heller 1985, 270–71.

80. Simon 1947.

81. Ilan 1977, 104–5.

82. At the end of 1940, Ben-Gurion announced that "our strength is in not having any choice." Ben-Gurion 1946, vol. 4, pt. 2, pp. 111, 150.

83. Alterman 1957, 155.

84. Gal 1986, 147.

85. See Inbar 1989, 22–37.

86. Kundera 1995, 192–93.

87. Shaked 1993.

88. Herman 1977, 97.

89. Bar-Tana 1984, 307.

90. Bartov 1988.

91. Megged 1990.

Chapter 5. The Wager in Greenberg's The Ways of the River

1. The title comes from a phrase in Gen 36:37 and I Chr 1:48, thought to refer to a place, Rehovot-on-the-River (Euphrates) but literally meaning "the ways / roads of / at the river." For Greenberg, it is a metaphor for the grand sweep of Jewish history. The

book was first published in 1951. All my citations from this book are taken from: Uri Tzvi Greenberg, *Rehovot hanahar* (The Ways of the River), Jerusalem and Tel Aviv: Schocken, 1954. The numbers in parentheses refer to the page numbers.

2. Miron 1992, 125–26.

3. Neher 1987, 878–79. Cf. also Neher 1977, 144–45.

4. On the inadequacy of traditional models for dealing with the Holocaust, see Steven T. Katz, "Holocaust: Jewish Theological Responses," in Eliade 1987.

5. See Huppert 1978.

6. Greenberg is here referring to the well-known saying of Rabbi Nahman of Bratslav, "Nothing is as whole as a broken heart," in Nahman ben-Simha of Bratslav, *Sefer likutei moharan* (Gleanings from our master Rabbi Nahman), Tanina, para. 24 (Jerusalem: Bratslav Yeshiva, 1962, among other editions).

7. Greenberg 1963, 11–14.

8. Greenberg 1957, 1.

9. Yeivin 1975, 36–87.

10. Kurzweil 1966, 80–88.

11. On this, see Debi-Guri 1980.

12. Soloveitchik 1966, 333–43.

13. At a party in his honor marking the publication of *Rehovot hanahar,* Greenberg said: "There should have been an earthquake in our hearts; by all rights, we should have come to a new Sinai revelation, more awesome and terrifying than the first. . . . We must take stock: either/or. Either we say this Western world is basically good, except that it does not tolerate the existence of a Jewish nation, and so we must adapt to the elements of its culture as well as the framework of its religion and the codex of its laws; that is, the trampled, slaughtered Jewish nation should be done away with, and we should all be baptized . . . or we muster all our strength and mental powers to carry on, not in the physical Europe or even the spiritual one, but here, in the territory of Abraham and the Bible, in both its physical and its spiritual dimensions. . . . We hate summations, because every summation points to a reality requiring a decision. It is making decisions that we wish to avoid. . . . We can no longer take the easy, middle path, so familiar and always so miserable. . . . There is no returning to this path." See "Uri Tzvi Greenberg one lime-varkhav" (Uri Tzvi Greenberg answers his well-wishers), *Ha'aretz* (15 Jan. 1951).

14. On these implications, see below, ch. 10.

15. See Greenberg 1979, 141–43.

16. Brinker 1990, 103.

Chapter 6. Messianism and Realism

1. There is a voluminous literature on the affinity of Zionism to Jewish messianism. I would mention only two recent publications: Almog 1987, and Kolatt 1984. See also Hertzberg 1959, introduction.

2. Scholem 1971, 35–36; Ben Ezer 1974, 269. On Scholem's approach to messianism and its place in Zionism, see Biale 1979, 174–77.

3. Katz 1982, 1987.

4. Weber 1991, 139.

5. See White 1982, 113–37.

6. Dinur 1939, vol. 1, bk. 1, p. 14.

7. Klausner 1897, 544.

8. Gordon 1953, 84.

9. Gordon 1957, 33.

10. Gordon 1953, 84–85.

11. The site, in the far north of Israel, of one of the earliest armed clashes between Jews and Arabs. In 1920, a small number of Jewish workers were attacked there by a large band of Arab marauders and, in the course of the ensuing battle, most were killed.

12. Katznelson 1929–32, 1:211.

13. Brenner 1955–67, 2:175.

14. Ben-Gurion 1946, 1:221.

15. Dinur 1950, 1:12–90.

16. Ibid., 12, 75.

17. The Bloc of the Faithful, a religious movement devoted to Jewish settlement of the areas seized in the Six-Day War.

18. See Aviner 1983a, 2:191–95.

19. See Re'uveni 1985, 66–75. To my knowledge, this important article was the first to raise the subject and to highlight its importance for Zionist history.

20. Hanokh 1927, 30–31.

21. Herzl 1956, 22.

22. Greenberg 1930, 4. Beitar, near Jerusalem, was the last stronghold of Bar Kokhba's revolt against Rome. Yohanan of Gush Halav was one of the last leaders of the Zealots, who revolted in the previous century.

23. Yeivin 1951.

24. See Schnitzer 1986, 91–95. The essay deals with the debate over the territories occupied in 1967. Schnitzer writes: "Mysticism deals rationality a heavy blow, today, not in some legendary time past" (p. 95).

25. Eldad 1991.

26. Nietzsche 1949, 23–25.

27. Katznelson 1945–50, 6:121.

28. Ben-Gurion 1946, 2:211–12.

29. Ibid., 242–43.

30. Ibid., 222.

31. Ibid., 79.

Chapter 7. Criticism of the Idea of Sovereignty in Non-Zionist Thought

1. See Sabine 1963, 398–414.

2. According to the United Nations constitution this right is not unlimited when the conduct of the internal affairs concern basic human rights

3. Talmon 1977, 295.

4. According to B.T. Ketubot 111b, God adjured the Jews not to return en masse to the Land of Israel and not to "force the End." At the same time, He adjured the gentiles not to oppress the Jews.

5. Hirsch 1969, 54. The book was first published in 1836.

6. Ibid., 60.

7. Breuer 1959, 68.

8. Amalek is the first and most treacherous of the peoples who attacked the Israelites as they made their way to the promised land, hence the archetype of all Israel's would-be annihilators. Amalek was descended from Jacob's brother Esau (Gen 36:16), a figure later vested with a similar symbolic import.

9. Hirsch 1966, 2:190–95.

10. On Breuer's stand on the issues of nationality and Zionism, see Horowitz 1987, 109–32; Kurzweil 1976, 117–30; Schweid 1991, 117–39; Breuer 1974 (henceforth, *Concepts*); Goldman 1989, 66–67.

11. Breuer 1982b, 35–36. See also Breuer 1934, 324–25.

12. Breuer 1982a, 26.

13. Ibid., 26–30, 233.

14. Breuer 1982b, 248.

15. Ibid., 102–3.

16. Breuer 1974, 91.

17. Breuer 1982b, 312.

18. Ibid., 310–11.

19. Breuer 1982a, 54; Breuer 1982b, 276.

20. Breuer 1959, 17.

21. Breuer 1974, 86.

22. Ibid., 105.

23. Breuer 1982a, 230.

24. Ibid., 234–35.

25. Goldman 1989, 67.

26. Breuer 1982b, 374–76; Schweid 1991, 138–39.

27. Breuer 1934, 48.

28. Many scholars and thinkers, e.g., his disciple Rabbi David Cohen ("the Nazirite"), have pointed out the importance of prophecy in the teachings of Rav Kook. On views of Kook's that were close to those of the Orthodox pacifists, such as Tamares and Zeitlin, see ch. 12, below. On the prophetic element in Hillel Zeitlin's thought, see Bar-Sela 1991, 109–24; Bar-Sela, Hamifne.

29. On Hillel Zeitlin, see articles by Bar-Sela 1991. Some of my quotes are taken from these articles.

30. Zeitlin 1983, 36. This work was originally written in Yiddish and published at the beginning of the twentieth century.

31. Zeitlin 1906.

32. Zeitlin 1983, 89–90.

33. Zeitlin 1930, 42–43.

34. Zeitlin 1979, 76.

35. Bar-Sela, Hamifne.

36. On Tamares and his thought, see Luz 1992.

37. Letter to Rabbi Tzvi Yehuda Kook, 28 Av 5681 (1921). The letter is in the collection of the Genazim Institute.

38. Tamares 1920, 18.

39. Tamares 1922–23, 174.

40. Tamares 1923, 8.

41. Tamares 1920, 39.

42. Tamares 1913, 194.

43. Tamares 1920, 41.

44. Tamares 1912, 122.

45. Zeitlin 1920.

46. Tamares 1922–23, 176.

47. Tamares 1911, 29.

48. Tamares 1922–23, 224.

49. Tamares 1922, 18.

50. Letter to Ya'akov Klatzkin, Passover, 1925. The letter is in the possession of the Tamares family.

51. Tamares 1920, 16.

52. Ibid., 81.

53. Ibid., 79.

54. Cf. Boyarin 1994, 84–86.

55. On Cohen's concept of exile, see Ben-Shlomo 1982, 502–5.

56. Cohen 1972, 234.

57. Ibid., 234.

58. Ibid., 360.

59. Scholem 1976a, 581–82.

60. Zweig 1922, 316–18.

61. Ibid., 331–32.

62. Buber 1983, 35.

63. On Rosenzweig's attitude toward Zionism, see Luz 1984, 472–89.

64. Fleischman 1956, 151–53, 171–79. Altmann 1958, 204–5; Funkenstein 1992b, 117–35; Moses 1992.

65. Rosenzweig 1972, 333.

66. Rosenzweig 1935, 53.

67. Ibid., 476.

68. Ibid., 201.

69. Rosenzweig 1972, 404.

70. Ibid., 300.

71. Ibid., 299.

72. Ibid., 333.

73. Ibid., 329.

74. Rosenzweig 1935, 326.

75. Ibid., 335–36. See also Güdemann 1897.

76. Rosenzweig 1972, 330.

77. Ibid., 330–31.

78. Ibid., 332.

079. Rotenstreich 1968, 233.

80. Glatzer 1961, 33–34.

81. Rosenzweig 1935, 150.

82. Ibid., 199.

83. Rosenzweig 1972, 413; Rosenzweig 1935, 670–71.

84. Rosenzweig 1972, 335.

85. Dubnow 1961, 81. This book was originally published in Russia in 1897–1902. In the Hebrew edition, Dubnow made many changes and softened his polemic against Zionism.

86. Ibid., 98–99.

87. Ibid., 126.

88. Ibid., 123.

89. Ibid., 82.

90. Ibid., 87.

91. Ibid., 97.

92. Ibid., 130.

93. Frischman 1912, esp. 155–62.

Chapter 8. Sovereignty and Jewish Commitment after the Holocaust

1. Fackenheim 1972, 8–9.

2. Ibid., 88.

3. Ibid., 84–85.

4. Fackenheim 1959.

5. Fackenheim 1967; Fackenheim 1972, 67–98.

6. Steven T. Katz, "Holocaust, the Jewish Theological Responses," in Eliade 1987; Katz 1983, 205–7.

7. Fackenheim 1972, 94.

8. Ibid., 87.

9. Ibid., 84.

10. Ibid., 76.

11. Ibid., 87.

12. Cf. Wyschograd 1971, 286–94.

13. See Lichtenberg-Ettinger 1990, 31. Cf. Gould 1985, 3–25 (interview with Jabès). Similar views are expressed by the American-Jewish literary critic Harold Bloom. He sees the writings of Freud, Kafka, and Gershom Scholem as having inherited the mantle of the classical texts — the Bible, the Talmud, etc. — in that they provide models of authentic identity for the secular Jew living outside the State of Israel. See Bloom 1983, 7–19.

14. On Steiner as a critic of Western culture, see Wyschograd 1994, 151–79.

15. For a comprehensive, critical summary of Steiner's views on Zionism, see Krantz 1988, 22–72.

16. Steiner 1967, 140–54. See also Steiner 1969, 13–21.

17. Steiner 1967, 153. Many critics have pointed out a remarkable similarity between Steiner's formulations in this article and statements made by Hitler in Steiner's provocative novel *The Portage to San Cristobal of A. H.* (London: Faber & Faber, 1981). In his last speech to the Jews, Hitler stresses that his racial doctrines are based on Jewish and

even Zionist sources. Hitler's ambivalence reflects that of Steiner himself. See Krantz 1988, 37–38.

18. Steiner 1969, 17.

19. Steiner 1967, 152–53.

20. Ibid., 151.

21. Steiner 1969, 17.

22. Ibid., 152. Similar ideas were expressed in 1989 by the French-Jewish philosopher Bernard Henri Levy: "Zionism carries the risk that Judaism will be reduced to the idea of rootedness, the sense of place, territoriality.... There would be a severe amputation from the body of the Jewish message if it were to be detached from the suspicion that nourished Judaism for thousands of years, the suspicion of notions of rootedness, of nature, of soil.... All Frenchmen I meet have a home, a plot of land. I have none.... For me, cosmopolitanism is not a curse but an opportunity for good.... The greatness of the Jewish people lay in the fact that it related to places as way-stations.... Land has a value only if [that value] does not contradict the values of justice, of law." Tocker 1989.

23. Steiner 1967, 154.

24. Steiner 1970, 8 (a letter in response to Robert Alter's attack on his contribution to the Israeli-American dialogue published in *Congress Bi-Weekly*, 24 Feb. 1969. See Alter 1970: 47–57.

25. Steiner 1970, 6.

26. See Yona Hadari's interview with him, *Yediot aharonot*, 17 Feb. 1989.

27. Steiner 1985, 8–25.

28. Steiner 1985, 9.

29. Ibid., 11–12, 13.

30. Ibid., 13.

31. Ibid., 19. An allusion to 2 Corinthians 3:6: "What is written kills, but the Spirit gives life."

32. Steiner 1985, 18–19, 20.

33. Ibid., 24.

34. Steiner 1969, 17.

35. Bloom 1983, 7.

36. Works germane to our discussion include Greenberg 1981a, 1988a, 1988b (esp. the chapters on Yom Hashoa and Yom Ha'atzma'ut), and 1981b, 47–63 (Hebrew abridgement of 1981a). On Greenberg's theology and ethics, see Katz 1993, 59–60; Ellis 1990, 19–28; Wyschograd, 1977.

37. Katz 1993, 69.

38. Greenberg 1988a, 1.

39. Greenberg 1981b, 49.

40. Greenberg 1981a, 16.

41. Greenberg 1988b, 320–22.

42. Greenberg 1981a, 25–26.

43. Greenberg 1988b, 396.

44. Greenberg 1988a, 27.

45. Greenberg 1981a, 25–26.

46. Greenberg 1988a, 6.

47. Ibid., 6.

48. Ibid., 6, 23.

49. On Diaspora Jews' demands that Israelis be more moral than other peoples, see Bellow 1976, 26 (*contra* George Steiner), 128 (*contra* Jean-Paul Sartre).

50. Greenberg 1988a, 7.

51. Ibid.

52. Ibid.

Chapter 9. Sovereignty and Power in Zionist Debate during the Mandate Period

1. Walzer 1977, 21–22. For more discussion of the complexity of the relation between means and ends in war, see Holmes 1989, 146–82; Popper 1962, 286–87.

2. Kant 1965, 41–42.

3. See Melzer 1975, 168–75.

4. Arendt 1970, 4–5.

5. Melzer 1975.

6. Rotenstreich 1963, 112.

7. Melzer 1975, 91.

8. Buber 1983, 3. I have paraphrased the editor.

9. On political theology, see Uriel Tal, "Lehavharat hamusag teologia politit" (Toward a clarification of the concept of political theology), in Yovel and Mendes-Flohr 1984, 195–218.

10. Buber 1948b, 11.

11. Buber 1958, 13.

12. Simon 1982, 65.

13. Tillich 1966, 303–8.

14. Martin Buber, "Hebrew Humanism" (1941), in Buber 1963, 246. Cf. Gordon 1953, 259–60, 405. As I have shown in ch. 7, Hillel Zeitlin held similar views.

15. Buber 1983, 270.

16. Martin Buber, "The National Home and National Policy in Palestine," in Buber 1983, 86. Buber's position seems to me close to that of Jaspers. See Jaspers 1963, 44.

17. Susser 1981, 124–25.

18. Martin Buber, "The Validity and Limitation of the Political Principle"(1947), in Buber 1954, 217.

19. Martin Buber, "Hebrew Humanism," in Buber 1963, 247.

20. See also Weltsch 1950. The book deals with the law of the minimum — the minimum amount of "nature" needed by "the spirit" — as a restraining force in politics: minimal safety and security, a minimal standard of living. On this book, see Bergman 1967, esp. 365–67: "Barukh Felix Weltsch kefilosof" (Barukh Felix Weltsch as a philosopher).

21. Martin Buber, "And If Not Now, When?" (1932), in Buber 1983, 105; "The National Home and National Policy in Palestine" (1929), in Buber 1983, 86.

22. Martin Buber, "Nationalism" (1921), in Buber 1983, 53.

23. Ibid.
24. Ibid., 56.
25. See Dotan 1980, 210.
26. Gorny 1987, 198.
27. Gorny 1987, 192.
28. Ibid., 198.
29. Cohen 1972, 362.
30. Buber 1954, 218.
31. Buber 1963, 260.
32. Buber 1954, 218.
33. Martin Buber, "Our Pseudo-Samsons," in Buber 1983, 133.
34. Martin Buber, "No More Declarations" (address to the Sixteenth Zionist Congress, Basel, 1929), in Buber 1983, 79–80.
35. Martin Buber, "And If Not Now, When?" in Buber 1983, 104.
36. Magnes 1930, 32.
37. Bentwich 1954, 180.
38. Arthur Goren 1982, 5.
39. Ruppin 1968, 3:149.
40. Arthur Goren 1982, 234.
41. Buber 1983, 12.
42. Gorny 1987, 301.
43. Buber 1983, 125.
44. Martin Buber, "Al habegida" (On treason) (1938), in Buber 1983, 129.
45. In reply to Ehud Ben Ezer's question as to whether the Zionist movement had missed opportunities for peace, Gershom Scholem wrote, "Looking back today [1970] as a member of Brit Shalom I doubt whether much would have been different then had we done one thing rather than another. See Ben Ezer 1974, 271.
46. See his letter to Zweig in Buber 1983, 37; see also his response to the writer Rabindranath Tagore, who had expressed to him a fear that the return of the Jewish people to national independence would harm its character, in Buber 1965, 204.
47. Nedava, 1980, 184.
48. Ze'ev Jabotinsky, "Kir habarzel" (The iron wall), in Nedava 1980, 233ff.
49. Gorny 1987, 171.
50. A symbolic contribution to the Zionist cause, solicited from Jews all over the world. The name was derived from the unit of value levied from the biblical Israelites for the building of the sanctuary in the wilderness (Ex 30:13).
51. Nedava 1980, 233.
52. Gorny 1987, 170.
53. Jabotinsky 1949, 98–99.
54. Huizinga 1970, 58, 64.
55. Ze'ev Jabotinsky, "Ra'yon Beitar" (The idea of Beitar), in Nedava 1980, 167–73.
56. Ze'ev Jabotinsky, "Al hamilitarizm" (On militarism), in Nedava 1980, 134–38.
57. Ze'ev Jabotinsky, "Al ha'ah" (At the hearth), in Nedava 1980, 138–45.
58. Talmon 1968, 27.
59. Berl Katznelson, "Be'ikvot siha al hagola" (Following a discussion of the Dias-

pora), in Katznelson 1945–50, 12:226–27. On Jabotinsky's alienation of Jewish culture, see now Stanislawsky 2001.

60. Shavit 1978, 112–13; Gorny 1987, 237–38.

61. Greenberg 1936, 163–64.

62. Ibid., 162.

63. Huppert 1979, 97–103.

64. Greenberg 1930, 4.

65. Ibid., 10.

66. Greenberg 1936, 112.

67. Ibid., 162.

68. Ibid., 166.

69. Yeivin 1938, 56.

70. Eldad 1981, 22–23.

71. Eldad 1959.

72. Ibid.

73. Eldad 1950.

74. Ibid.

75. Eldad 1970, 8.

76. Yisrael Eldad, "Devarim peshutim al musar hayahadut" (Simple words about Jewish morality), *Sulam* 10 (Shevat 5714 [Jan. 1954]): 10–13; repr. in Eldad 1981, 166.

77. Eldad 1952, 5–10.

78. Yisrael Eldad, "Musaram shel kovshei kena'an," in Eldad 1981, 18–19.

79. Eldad 1957, 9–14.

80. Eldad 1952.

81. Shashar 1990, 108–10.

82. For a comprehensive overview of the Young Hebrews (also known as the Young Canaanite) movement and the ideology of Yonatan Ratosh, see Diamond 1986.

83. "Masa hapetiha" (The opening vision), in Ratosh 1982, 161.

84. Ibid., 193.

85. "Haholkhi bahoshekh" (Walking in darkness), in Ratosh 1977, 130.

86. Shapira 1988b, 149–58; see also Shapira 1992, various locations.

87. Shapira 1988b, 149–58.

88. Scholem 1976, 41. Cf. also the debate over "mysticism and realism" in ch. 6.

89. Gorny 1987, 67.

90. Gordon 1953, 419.

91. Aharonowitz 1970, 147.

92. Halpern 1961, 24.

93. "The 'socialist-constructivist' worldview, which originated with the Second Aliya, was by nature opposed to violence as a social or political practice. It was understood that the way the labor movement would achieve hegemony in the Yishuv and in the Zionist movement would be through building, not violent class struggle or armed political terror." See Gorny 1976, 183.

94. Cf. Arendt, 1970, 4–5.

95. Laskov 1983, 177.

96. Ibid., 183, quoted from David Gordon 1959. Similar ideas were expressed by

Shlomo Lavi: "Yes, our culture, our education, abhors violence—not out of excessive delicacy, heaven forbid, but from the knowledge that we shall pay a price for violence, and it is out of necessity that we have allowed our self-defense to be conducted with force of arms. From this arises a good deal of ambivalence in our lives." See Lavi, *Ketavim* 1944, 1:35.

97. Gorny 1987, 169.

98. Berl Katznelson, "Likrat hayamim haba'im" (Looking toward the coming days), in Katznelson 1929–32, 2:7.

99. Shmuel Yavnieli, in Katznelson 1929–32, 1:159.

100. Gordon 1953, 405–6.

101. Mordekhai Kushnir, "Devarim shelo be'itam" (Untimely remarks), in Katznelson 1929–32, 1:164–68.

102. Brenner 1955–67, 2:323. The image of the Jewish people as a lamb among seventy wolves appears in the Rabbinic literature as a symbol of the persecution of the Jews by the nations of the world but also as a sign of the miracle of their survival. Berdyczewski was apparently the first in a long list of writers and poets to explicitly reject this image.

103. Brenner, "Avoda o tzeva'iyut?" (Work or militarism), in Brenner 1955–67, 180; and in Katznelson 1929–32, 1:183.

104. Katznelson 1929–32, 1:184.

105. Tabenkin 1942. Cf. Kafkafi 1986, 26–27, 108; Shapira 1984, 113.

106. Gorny 1987, 183.

107. The elite strike force of the Hagana, the Yishuv's underground army.

108. Sadeh 1946, 11.

109. Ibid., 84–85. Cf. also remarks made by Moshe Sharett in 1942: "We are on the edge of a spiritual abyss in this country, and we know we must bring a million Jews here, while protecting the life of every Jew, and particularly every young Jew; may he not meet his maker or his gods through rifle fire, and may he pray for the day when he can throw [his weapons] down." Cited in Gorny 1987, 379.

110. See David Shimoni's poem "Night Dew," written during the 1936–38 Arab Revolt, in Shimoni 1948.

111. The use of the term "Palestinian" to refer exclusively to the country's Arab population is a recent coinage and the subject of some controversy.

112. Gorny 1987, 214.

113. Beilinson 1929.

114. On David Ben-Gurion's approach to the Arab problem in the 1930s, after the failure of his talks with the Arab leaders about the possibility of an agreement, see Tevet 1985, 89–90.

Chapter 10. Reacting to Arab Terror

1. Ahad Ha'am 1953, 462. The Aramaic *yeitei velo ahminei* is used.

2. Ahad Ha'am 1944, 186–87.

3. For the discussion of rabbinic opinions on this affair, see Zion 1999.

4. Ya'akov Shavit 1983, introduction; Shapira 1992, 319–51.

5. Former editor of the German Zionist organ *Jüdische Rundschau.*

6. Cited by Ya'akov Shavit 1983, 21.

7. See Radler-Feldman and Petrazil 1939, 93. This is an anthology of protests against Jewish terror drawn from various quarters of the Yishuv, both religious and nonreligious.

8. Ben-Gurion 1946, 1:31. These remarks were made in 1936.

9. Ibid., 12.

10. A term designating the legal status of Jews in certain areas of Germany before the Emancipation.

11. On this disappointment, see Berl Katznelson's statement, "Being the apple of the Jewish people's eye, they [Diaspora Jewry] want us to be all virtuous. The Diaspora Jew is permitted to do business on the Sabbath and to eat forbidden food, but he wants to see us as Sabbath-observers and upholders of the commandments. He himself can be a coward, but we must be brave. He has heard there are defenders here, heroes, horsemen, victors, those who terrify the Arabs, and, lo and behold, this sudden disappointment! May we not disappoint his idealizations?" Katznelson 1945–50, 8:32.

12. Greenberg 1936, 163–64.

13. In Jewish tradition, the archetype of all who seek to exterminate the Jewish people.

14. Greenberg 1936, 165–67: Kad sha'ata matya (When the time comes). See also Yeivin 1938, 86–89. In Yeivin's words, "it is evident that if there is anything utterly foreign to Judaism in all its forms, it is this pseudo-pacifism of 'abhorring vengeance.'"

15. Katznelson 1945–50, 8:215. These remarks were made in August 1936.

16. Ibid., 217.

17. Ibid., 221. Cf. Shlonsky 1988:273 (orig. pub. 1936): "Many thought that in our case—not only because we are, as it were, the chosen people (and what people is not chosen, not right in its own eyes?) but mainly because we are a people schooled in tribulation—there was less likelihood of such madness or such baseness than in the case of any other people—many thought this and were proven wrong. All signs point to the fact that, by the law of action and reaction, the Jew, when he reaches his homeland, is capable of yearning for this phony shine . . . precisely because we suffered from [it] in the Diaspora and especially because we lacked [it]."

18. Katznelson 1945–50, 9:65–66. These remarks were made in 1936.

19. Sadeh 1946, 86–88.

20. Ibid., 11.

21. Schatzberger 1985, 40–41, 102.

22. Don Yehiya 1993, 155–90; Eliash 1984, 193–209.

23. Shapira 1981, 46–48. Indeed, many traditionalists refused to believe that Jews would be capable of shedding innocent blood .See: Hen 1938, 411–17.

24. Radler-Feldman and Petrazil 1939, 71.

25. Cf. Ex 20: 25.

26. Don Yehiya 1993, 165, 186. For more on Rabbi Amiel, see ch. 12, below.

27. Schatzberger 1985, 103.

28. Eliash 1984, 200.

29. Don Yehiya 1993, 172–73.

30. Ibid., 188–89.

31. Shapira 1992, 223.

32. On the emergence of a retaliation policy in the first years of Israel's independence, see Morris 1996a, 200–207, 447–48.

33. On the Kibiyeh operation, see Morris 1996a, 255–91.

34. See Teveth 1994. Cf. also the 1953 documents in the state archives published in *Ha'aretz,* 19 Apr. 1996.

35. Quoted by Morris 1996a, 291.

36. Deir Yassin was an Arab village near Jerusalem where the Stern Gang had perpetrated a massacre of civilians.

37. See Melman 1997.

38. Morris 1996b, 33–46.

39. Yeshayahu Leibowitz, "After Kibiyeh," in Leibowitz 1992, 185–90.

40. See Yeshayahu Leibowitz in the "Responses" section of *Beterem,* 15 Jan. 1954, 21.

41. Yisraeli 1953–54: 113; republished in expanded form as Yisraeli 1991, 3:253–89.

42. Eldad 1954, 10–13; repr. in Eldad 1980, 163–71.

43. Etzioni 1954, 10.

44. Kahan Commission 1983, 56–57.

45. Cf. High Court Justice Menahem Elon's reasons for ruling against the participation of Kach in the 1984 Knesset elections: "The makeup of the Kach list and its objectives are blatantly contrary to the world of Judaism, its laws and sentiments, the nation's past and its yearnings. They are totally opposed to the basic principles of human morality and the morality of the [Jewish] people, to Israel's Proclamation of Independence, to the underpinnings of the modern, enlightened democracies. They are meant to import into the Hebrew state ideas and actions espoused by the world's most corrupt nations." Cited in Ravitzky 1985, 29. Ravitzky notes that such condemnation came from all across the political spectrum.

46. See *Ha'aretz,* 14 Feb. 1990.

47. Marcus 1988.

48. Karni 1988a

49. See *Ha'aretz,* 15 Feb. 1988.

50. Ahad Ha'am (1953, 159–64) generally uses the term *musar le'umi* (national morality) but sometimes speaks of the moral outlook or doctrines of Judaism, as opposed to those of Christianity.

51. Mishna, Avot, II, 6.

52. Levinas 1990, 138.

53. Ibid., 224.

54. Ibid., 21–22.

55. Moses Maimonides, *Mishne Torah,* Laws of Repentance 2:10, Laws of Forbidden Congress 19:17, Laws of the Poor 10:2, Laws of Slaves 9:8. The following translation of the latter passage is from Maimonides, 1972, 177.

56. Laws of Slaves 9:8.

57. Rosenberg 1983, 81. In extending morality beyond the bounds of Halakha in relation to gentiles, Maimonides also employs the concept of *darkei shalom* (ways of peace). He does not mean this in the sense of mere pragmatism for the sake of Jewish interests but rather as a principle with universal moral significance. Cf. Laws of Kings 10:12. He cites the verse "His mercies are over all His works" (Ps 145:9) to rule out any

possibility of a narrow, utilitarian interpretation. Cf. Wurzburger 1977–78, 80–86. On this verse was grounded the authority of the Sages to make innovative halakhic rulings based on "ways of peace," particularly in relation to non-Jews. On the question of the relation between Halakha and morality, see ch. 11, below.

58. Gadamer 1976, 18–43.

59. What Maimonides derives from the principle of "beyond the call of duty" is derived by Luzzato from the principle of "compassion" (*hemla*), which is the most basic moral sentiment. In fact, it bursts the bounds of law to encompass all human beings and not only the Jewish people.

60. The Yiddish word *mensh* is most appropriate here.

61. See DeNicola 1983, 149–64.

62. Williams 1973, 97–99.

63. See Habermas 1988, 326.

64. See Schweid 1979, 315–24.

65. Elazari-Vulkani, 1950, 41–46: Hateologia hale'umit (The theology of the nation).

66. See the conclusion of his essay "Ha'arakhat atzmenu bishloshet hakrakhim" (Our self-image in three volumes), Brenner 1955–67, 3:78. Cf. also Schwadron 1930. Schwadron here takes issue with Judah Magnes's book *Kekhol hagoyim?* (Like all the nations?), which was published that year.

67. Schweid 1976, 164; Schweid 1990, 277.

68. Gavison 1995, 676.

69. See also Talmon 1977, 395–96.

70. Scholem 1976, 294–95.

Chapter 11. Halakha and Morality in Religious Zionism after the Six-Day War

1. Schwartz 1996, 198ff.

2. On Kook and Amiel, see ch. 7.

3. Cf. Holtzer 1999.

4. Cf. Aminah 1940, 195.

5. See Leibowitz 1976, 412.

6. Yaron 1973, 37–44.

7. There is extensive literature on religious messianism (as exemplified by the Bloc of the Faithful) in the Zionist movement. Cf. Tal 1977, 1–40; Tal 1984, 137–57; Ravitzky 1996. Aran 1991.

8. Tzvi Yehuda Kook 1983, 44. A contrary halakhic perspective is to be found in remarks by Rabbi Sha'ul Yisraeli, Oz Veshalom 1978, 4–5. Cf. Rabbi Hayim David Halevi, Oz Veshalom 1978, 7–9.

9. Tzvi Yehuda Kook 1983, 227. Cf. Bazak 1995.

10. Tzvi Yehuda Kook 1978, 142–43, 146.

11. Tzvi Yehuda Kook 1983, 1:97.

12. Tzvi Yehuda Kook 1978, 144.

13. Tzvi Yehuda Kook 1983, 1:202, 97.

14. Ibid., 218.

15. Melamed 1974, 64–65. Written after the Yom Kippur War.

16. Aviner 1982a, 16.

17. Ibid., 11.

18. Ariel 1975, 147.

19. Neria 1974, 21–22.

20. Waldman 1983a, 24–25; cf. Waldman 1982, 4–5.

21. Waldman 1983b.

22. Levinger 1969; cf.Levinger 1981, 8–11, 15; and his remarks in "Yisrael veyisham'el" 1986, 528.

23. Melamed 1988, 10–11. Melamed is the principal of the Bet-el yeshiva. The prevalence of such paternalism among the religious settlers in Judea, Samaria, and Gaza can be seen in the leaflet they distributed among the Arabs, explaining how bad it would be for them if the Jews left. The leaflet was published in *Ha'aretz,* 1 Mar. 1988.

24. Cf. Lehrer 1983, 76.

25. Uriel Simon 1977, 8.

26. Aviner 1983a, 30–32; repr. in Aviner 1983b, vol. 2 .

27. Aviner 1983b, vol. 2.

28. Levinger 1981, 8–11, 15.

29. Aviner 1983a.

30. Cf. Zohar 1996, 18.

31. Aviner 1982b.

32. Yashar 1976, 142–44.

33. Rosen 1988, 3.

34. Rahat 1988. The article deals with a rabbinical conference on responses to the Intifada.

35. Blum 1985, 152.

36. Quoted in Uriel Simon 1977, 9.

37. Dov Lior, in the symposium "Milhama umusar" (War and morality), *Tehumin* 4 (1983): 186.

38. Eliahu Zayini, "Al Hamusar bishe'at milhama" (On morality in wartime), in Blum n.d., 31.

39. Segal 1982, 7. This issue includes a number of halakhic discussions of the treatment of the conquered population. Segal has since changed his views and left Gush Emunim.

40. See Ahituv 1993, esp. 268–70. On the affinity between the views of Sha'ul Yisraeli (on whom other rabbis relied) and those of Meir Cahane, see Rosner 1986.

41. Ariel 1984, 28–32. On this issue, see also *Lenokhah* 1985. Shragai 1994, 1995a, 1995b. Yisraeli's statements lent authority to extremist thinkers close to Cahanism. In his view, the slaying of an Arab under conditions of war and terrorism was to be seen as a religious duty, or at least not a sin and certainly not a mortal sin, because it was not forbidden by the Torah (Shragai 1994). By contrast, Rabbi Yoel Ben-Nun told Shragai that rabbis who interpret the Halakha in this way "are egregiously ignorant of the halakhic sources."

42. Goren 1983–86, 1:14–25.

43. Ibid., 3:64.

44. Leibowitz 1976, 412.

45. See Ross 1962, 55–61.

46. See Sagi 1996, 30–48. Sagi terms the dominant model among the Orthodox "halakhic formalism": "This model, which stresses the closed-mindedness of the Halakha, was chosen, consciously or unconsciously, following the recent failure of religious Zionism to cope with what was going on around it, with the whole value system of modern politics and society" (47).

47. On dialectical theology, see Harvey 1966, 127–63.

48. Avraham Kook, "Musar veyir'at elohim" (Morality and the fear of God), in Kook 1964, vol. 3, foreword and 19–34.

49. Luz 1988, 380–83.

50. Cf. Soloveitchik 1994, 74. Soloveitchik sees this growth as the main change in Orthodoxy in the last generation.

51. Ahituv 1995, 13–21. The article includes a wide range of material about *da'at Torah* ("the Torah viewpoint") and *emunat hakhamim* ("trust in the sages"). Cf., further, Urbach 1985, 283–93.

52. Cf. Hartman 1985, 98–103.

53. Statman and Sagi 1993, 237–48.

54. Goldman 1963, 59. This article was published in installments in nos. 20–22 of *De'ot* and again in Goldman 1997, 265–305.

55. Goldman 1997, 301. Cf. Ravitzky 1989, 96–100. Ravitzky cites examples showing that the metahalakhic considerations employed by arbiters of Halakha sometimes contradict the formal law, so that the role of the halakhic framework is not clear-cut.

56. Goldman 1997, 298–305.

57. Ibid., 361–71.

58. Guttmann 1970, 19–26. (The article was translated from German.)

59. On Ernst Simon, see my article Luz 1983b, 613–44.

60. See Kimmerling 1990.

61. See Liebman 1981a, 63–78.

62. Be'er 1988. Be'er's book is an important autobiographical document of the crisis experienced by many religious Zionists in Israel as a result of their encounter with power.

63. Friedman and Rubin 1995.

64. See Liebman 1983, 236.

65. Sheleg 1990.

66. Ibid. Avraham Sagi draws similar conclusions. For him, "the religious Zionist is trapped today in a schizophrenic reality; on the one hand, his thinking has been shaped by a one-dimensional religious Zionism that recognizes but one source of norms [the Torah]. On the other, in his economic, social, professional, and cognitive life he needs other sources of norms." Thus arises a split between the world of action and that of the spirit, and the question is whether the modern Jew's value system can be based on more than one source. See Sagi 1997.

Chapter 12. Persecuted or Persecutor?

1. Don Yehiya 1988, 1:167–88.

2. Liebman 1981b, 101–4; Liebman, 1983, 9–10.

3. Liebman 1983, 9–10.

4. Eldad 1982, 6–7.

5. Cf. Jaffee 1991, 223–38.

6. Interview from 1966 with Avineri, in Ben Ezer 1974, 54.

7. Gershon Shaked holds that "until the War of Independence, guilt feelings toward the Arabs were repressed. It was precisely victory in the War of Independence and the Sinai Campaign that aroused guilt feelings. . . . The majority has become a minority and the minority a majority, and the one who had been the threatening outsider has become a resident alien. The Arab outsiders have become Jews in our midst, and the historical experience of the Jewish people obliges us not to treat them as Jews were treated in the past." See Hadari-Ramage 1994, 661.

8. A collection of dialogues among kibbutz members who had fought in the Six-Day War, which appeared shortly afterward; edited by Avraham Shapira.

9. Ben Ezer 1968, 1976, 1977, 1978. A distinction similar to Ben Ezer's is made in Shaked 1983, 74–77; 1992b, 129–30.

10. Tammuz 1973, 55–59. See also Guri 1992: "After 1948, things changed. Many of us, at one time or another, reflect on the story 'Hirbet Hiz'a' [about a destroyed Arab village]. Henceforth, in addition to feeling 'besieged and in the right,' there is the feeling of guilt and regret. This is not infrequently reflected in [our] prose and theater."

11. Oren 1981, 46. See also Almog 1997, 303–16.

12. Oren 1981, 45.

13. Tuchman 1982, 186. The Jewish psychologist Erik Erikson writes in a similar vein that "the triumph of the Israeli soldiery is markedly subdued, balanced by a certain sadness over the necessity to re-enter historical actuality by way of military methods not invented by Jews, and yet superbly used by them" (cited in Halpern 1970, 70). On Israeli guilt feelings, see also Zweig 1969, 243–44.

14. Megged 1985, 135.

15. Bar-Yosef 1984, 114.

16. Fuchs 1989. On the political use of the Holocaust by the Palestinians, see Wieseltier 1988.

17. See Harkaby 1967, 37.

18. The reference is mainly to a debate triggered by Benny Morris' book *The Birth of the Palestinian Refugee Problem 1947–1949* (Morris 1987).

19. See Gershon Shaked's debate with the American-Jewish novelist Cynthia Ozick, who took some Hebrew writers to task for aiding and abetting Arab efforts to delegitimize Zionism. In his view, this fiction plays such an important role within Israeli society that we cannot be concerned with whether or not it serves Arab propaganda. Shaked 1993b.

20. Statman 1991, 159.

21. Ibid., 156–57.

22. Buber 1983, 271.

23. Cf. Haezrahi 1965, 57–63.

24. At a ceremony in Hawaii marking the fiftieth anniversary of the bombing of Pearl Harbor, President George Bush apologized in the name of the American people for the way the U.S. government had treated American citizens of Japanese descent during the

Second World War. The Japanese parliament, however, decided it had nothing to apologize for. See Marcus 1991. Of course, one must take into consideration that the concepts of shame and guilt are understood differently in each culture.

25. Cited by Halpern 1970.

26. Ben Halpern, "Ethical Issues in Extreme Situations," unpub. MS.

27. Kleinman 1978, 27–29. Cf. Shabtai 1991.

28. Halpern 1967, 270.

29. Ibid.

Chapter 13. Challenging the Zionist Ethos

1. Nash 1980, 162–63.

2. Ibid.

3. Ibid.

4. Frieschman 1912, 157.

5. Berdyczewski 1952, 375.

6. On Berdyczewski's views, see Luz 1988, 163–72.

7. Berdyczewski 1899a, 18–23, 89–95.

8. On the conflict between "Yavne" to "Jerusalem," cf. ch. 3.

9. Berdyczewski 1952, 382–83: Beirur devarim (A clarification).

10. Kurzweil 1961, 229–32.

11. Schweid 1970, 172. Cf. Rahel 1954, 62.

12. Kook 1941, 53.

13. Kook 1984, 2:234–36: Ahdut usheni'ut (Unity and duality).

14. Kook 1963a, 159.

15. Bialik 1935, 1:140.

16. See esp. the articles by Dan Miron and Yeshurun Keshet in Barzel 1978; Shaked 1984.

17. Shaked 1988, 49.

18. Miron 1957, 14–18.

19. Hazaz 1963, 181–82: Drabkin.

20. Shaked 1984, 13.

21. Hazaz 1950, 107.

22. See, e.g., "Ofek natui" (Extended horizon), in Hazaz 1968, 124–25.

23. Hazaz 1963, 155–58.

24. Hazaz 1968, 125.

25. Hazaz 1950, 70.

26. Hazaz 1968, 125.

27. Said by Matushka in the story "Gematriot" (Ciphers), Hazaz 1930, and cited in Shaked 1984, 51.

28. Keshet, in Barzel 1978, 185.

29. On the influence of Canaanism on Palestinian Jewish youth during the years immediately preceding the establishment of the State of Israel, see Shavit 1984, 139–41. On the roots of Canaanite thinking among young people of the period of the Second and Third Aliyot, see Elboim-Dror 1996, 123–27. This Canaanite mentality was shared by "most younger groups in the new Palestinian community, except for the religious youth" (125).

30. Shaked 1988, 3:235, 239.

31. Tzvi Luz 1970, 97–110; Elboim-Dror 1996, 126–28. Ziva Shamir points out that although most of the generalizations made about the literature of the generation of the War of Independence are questionable, a valid one is that there is hardly any mention in this literature of the Jewish heritage that weighed so heavily on the previous generation. "Classical Jewish subjects . . . disappeared completely." See Shamir 1988.

32. Megged 1950, 353, 354–57.

33. Miron 1962, 314–21. Cf. Schweid 1962, 219.

34. Shapira 1992, 474–75.

35. Shimoni 1948, 312–16.

36. Ben Ezer 1986, 11.

37. Oren 1983a, 149–50.

38. Tammuz 1978a.

39. Ibid.

40. Tammuz 1978b, 105.

41. Porat 1976, 481–88.

42. Oz 1981, 39ff.; Schwartz 1995.

43. Oz 1982b, 189.

44. Oz 1983a, 225–26.

45. Ibid., 177.

46. Ibid., 155.

47. Oren 1983b, 1983c.

48. Holtzman 1991.

49. Oz 1983b, 239–40.

50. Oz 1982a.

51. Oz 1987, 73.

52. Ibid., 140.

53. Ibid., 183–84.

54. Ibid., 95.

55. Oz 1990.

56. Oz 1991, 184.

57. Ibid., 183.

58. Ibid., 185.

59. Ibid., 10.

60. Ibid., 264.

61. Cf. Rotenstreich 1966; Simon 1947, 9–11. See also, Oren, 1986. On trends in the development of Israeli drama, see Ofrat 1980, last chapter.

62. Buber 1948a, 158–59.

63. As early as 1929, Bialik pointed out that the main mistake of Zionist education, and the reason it might fail, was its narrow tendentiousness . See Bialik, "Tzimtzum veharhava bakeren hakayemet" (The narrowing and broadening of the [perspective of the] Jewish National Fund), in Bialik 1935, 1:138–41. On the crippling effects of hidebound ideology, see Shabtai 1985. See also Calderon 1980, 431–37.

64. See Elboim-Dror 1986, 1:382; See also Ya'akov Fichman's critique of education in the 1930s in Graetz 1988, 48–51: "The complete removal of intellectual elements from the new educational program has diminished the stature of the Hebrew school, deprived

our children of confidence in their thinking, [and] left them [intellectually] ill-equipped," so that they are incapable of grasping anything requiring thought. Fichman saw a direct connection between this anti-intellectualism and the inability to make the Jewish source-texts appealing to the students.

65. Shapira 1984, 63.

66. Ezrahi 1983, 221–22.

67. Scholem 1975, 135–36.

68. Ibid., 221.

69. Ibid., 41–42.

70. Ibid., 584.

71. The literature on Post-Zionism is extensive. A good summary can be found in Silberstein 1998. On the argument among historians over questions raised by scholars of Zionism in the last decade, see *History and Memory* 1 (1995). For a summary of Post-Zionist research up to 1996, see *Teoria uvikoret* 8 (1996), and Ginossar and Bar'eli 1996.

72. Talmon 1968, 19.

73. Talmon 1977, 12.

74. Talmon 1968, 4.

75. Gershom Scholem, cited in Ben Ezer 1974, 294. On guilt feelings in the Hebrew literature toward the Palestinians, see ch. 12, above.

76. Margalit 1986, 253–58.

77. Arendt 1978, 176–91. In the early fifties, Simon expressed his trepidations again in a series of articles in *Ha'aretz*. Part of this series was reprinted as "Sparta o atuna?" (Sparta or Athens?), in Simon 1982, 49–69.

78. Horovitz 1977, 59. See also Shlomo Avineri, "Subjugation of the Means to the State's Ends?" in Ben Ezer 1974, 65.

79. Horovitz 1977, 61.

80. Dan Horovitz and Moshe Lissak, "Demokratia uvitahon le'umi besikhsukh mitmashekh" (Democracy and national security in a protracted conflict), *Yahadut Zmanenu* 4 (1988): 64.

81. Ibid., 63.

82. Kimmerling 1993, 124. The thesis that the army is the sole common denominator of the Israeli people was first proposed by Yeshayahu Leibowitz. He maintained that, when Israelis lost Judaism as a way of life without losing their Jewish consciousness, their nationhood no longer had any content other than "statism" (*mamlakhtiut*), the main element of which was military power. See Leibowitz 1982, 194, 222–23.

83. Kimmerling 1993, 125.

84. Ibid., 131.

85. Ben-Eliezer 1995.

86. Ben-Eliezer 1994, 51–65.

87. Kimmerling 1993, 135.

88. Almog 1997, 303–16, 388–89. See also Almog 1995; Peri 1995, 1996, 94–112.

89. See Rotenstreich 1980, 33–35.

90. See Rotenstreich 1978, 140–43.

91. See Cohen 2001, 131–50.

92. Rotenstreich 1978, 143.

93. This is the conclusion arrived at by Peri 1996.

Conclusion

1. Simon 1966, 317–18.
2. Alterman 1957, 136–57.
3. Ibid., 110.
4. Ibid., 144, 146.
5. Ibid., 137. Shalev 1992, 205, points out that victory as loss is a subject treated in the best of the classical Zionist literature. See also Kurzweil 1966, 166–69.
6. Alterman 1957, 117.
7. Ibid., 155.
8. Ibid., 153.
9. Alterman 1961, 2:494–502.
10. Alterman 1957, 143.
11. Ibid., 149.
12. Ibid., 152.
13. Ibid., 119.
14. Heine 1982, 285.
15. Brenner 1955–67, 2:350.
16. Alterman 1957, 146.

References

Ahad Ha'am. 1944. Megilat hasetarim (The scroll of secrets). In *Magen vekeshet: Yalkut itim le'ish tzava ivri* (Shield and bow: A periodic anthology for the Hebrew soldier). Tel Aviv: Hava'ad Ha'artzi Lema'an Hahayal Hayehudi.

———. 1953. *Kol kitvei Ahad Ha'am* (Collected works of Ahad Ha'am). Tel Aviv: Dvir.

———. 1973. *Ten Essays on Zionism and Judaism*. New York: Arno.

Aharonowitz, Yosef. 1970. *Ha'am veha'aretz* (The people and the land). Tel Aviv: Tarbut Vehinukh.

Ahimeir, Abba. 1966. *Hatzionut hamehapkhanit* (Revolutionary Zionism). Tel Aviv: Hava'ad Lehotza'at Kitvei Ahimeir.

Ahituv, Yosef. 1993. Milhemot yisrael ukedushat hahayim (Israel's wars and the sanctity of life). In Gafni and Ravitzky 1993.

———. 1995. Hakham adif minavi (Better a sage than a prophet). *Gilyon Ne'emanei Torah Va'avoda*, Kislev 5755 (Nov.).

Almog, Oz. 1995. Hahoker hamithashben (The scholar who settles accounts). Letter in *Ha'aretz*, 17 Nov.

———. 1997. *Hatzabar: Dyokan* (The Sabra: A portrait). Tel Aviv: Am Oved.

Almog, Shmuel. 1987. *Zionism and History*. New York: St. Martin's.

Alter, Robert. 1968. Yisrael veha'intelektualim (Israel and the intellectuals). *Ha'uma* 23.

———. 1970. Zionism for the 70s. *Commentary* 49:2 (Feb.).

———. 1973. The Massada Complex. *Commentary* 56:1 (July).

Alterman, Nathan. 1956. *Simhat ani'im* (The joy of the poor). Tel Aviv: Mahbarot Lesifrut.

——. 1957. *Ir hayona* (City of the dove). Tel Aviv: Mahbarot Lesifrut.

——. 1961. *Ketavim* (Writings). Tel Aviv: Hakibbutz Hame'uhad.

——. 1989. *Al shtei haderakhim* (On both paths), ed. Dan Laor. Tel Aviv: Hakibbutz Hame'uhad.

Altman, Alexander. 1958. Franz Rosenzweig on History. In *Between East and West,* ed. Alexander Altman. London: East and West Library.

Amiel, Moshe Avigdor. 1934. *Hayesodot ha'ideologi'im shel hamizrahi* (The ideological foundations of the Mizrahi [party]). Warsaw: Hahistadrut Hamizrahit.

——. 1942. *Linevukhei hatekufa* (To the perplexed of our day). Jerusalem: Mosad Harav Kook, 1943.

——. 1964. *Derashot el ami* (Sermons to my people). 3 vols. Tel Aviv: Va'ad Lehotza'at Sifrei Rav Amiel.

Aminah, Nehemiah. 1940. Yahasim (relations). In *Sefer hehalutz* (The book of the pioneer), ed. Moshe Bassok. Jerusalem: Jewish Agency.

Amitzur, Ilan. 1977. Haminimaks ve'ormat hahistoria (The Minimax and the cunning of history). In *Medina'i be'itot mashber: Darko shel Chaim Weizmann batenua hatzionit* (A statesman in times of crisis: Chaim Weizmann's conduct in the Zionist movement), ed. Yosef Gorny and Gedalia Yogev. Tel Aviv: Tel Aviv University Press.

Anderson, Benedict. 1983. *Imagined Communities.* London: New Left Books.

Appelfeld, Aharon. 1979. *Masot beguf rishon* (Essays in the first person). Jerusalem: Zionist Library.

Aran, Gideon. 1991. Jewish Zionist Fundamentalism: The Bloc of the Faithful in Israel (Gush Emunim). In *Fundamentalism Observed,* ed. Martin Marty and Scott Appelby. Chicago: University of Chicago Press.

Arendt, Hannah. 1970. *On Violence.* New York: Harcourt, Brace, and World.

——. 1978. *The Jew as Pariah.* New York: Grove.

Ariel, Israel. 1984. Devarim kehavayatam (Things as they are). *Tzefia* 1 (Av 5744 [July]).

Ariel, Ya'akov. 1975. Hebetim hilkhati'im shel be'ayat hanesiga mishithei eretz israel. (Halakhic perspectives of the problem of withdrawl from areas of Eretz Israel). *Morasha* 9 (winter).

Aristotle. 1966. *The Nichomachean Ethics of Aristotle,* trans. and ed. David Ross. London: Oxford University Press.

Aviner, Shlomo. 1982a. *Artzi* 1.

——. 1982b. Leromem et haru'ah (To lift the spirits). *Nekuda* 48 (Oct.).

——. 1983a. Hare'alizm hameshihi (Messianic realism). *Artzi* 4.

——. 1983b. *Am kelavi* (A people like a lion). Jerusalem: n.p.

Baer, Yitzhak. 1941. Ha'erekh hahinukhi shel hahistoria hayisra'elit (The educational value of Jewish history). *Gilyonot* 12.

——. 1988. *Galut,* trans. Robert Warshaw. Lanham: University Press of America.

Baron, Salo W. 1964. *History and Jewish Historians.* Philadelphia: Jewish Publication Society.

Baron, Salo W., and G. S. Wise, eds. 1977. *Violence and Defense in the Jewish Experience.* Philadelphia: Jewish Publication Society.

Bar-Sela, Shraga. 1991. Yahaduto hanevu'it-meshihit shel Hillel Zeitlin (Hillel Zeitlin's prophetic, messianic Judaism). *Da'at* 26.

———. N.d. Hamifne ha'aharon bitefisato hale'umit shel Hillel Zeitlin (The latest turn-about in Hillel Zeitlin's nationalist thinking). Unpub. MS.

Bar-Tana, Or-Tzion. 1984. Anatomia shel hamelankholia hayehudit: He'arot nosafot al hayehudi ha'aharon (The anatomy of Jewish melancholy: Further comments on the last Jew). *Akhshav* 49.

Bartov, Hanokh. 1988. Ani ba'al menaya be'eretz yisrael va'ani do'eg (I'm a stockholder in the Land of Israel and I'm worried). *Iton 77* (Nov.–Dec.).

Bar-Yosef, Yehoshua. 1984. *More derekh lepatriotim nevokhim* (A guide for confused patriots). Tel Aviv: Hadar.

Barzel, Hillel, ed. 1978. *Hayim Hazaz: Mivhar ma'amarim al yetzirato* (Hayim Hazaz: Selected essays on his work). Tel Aviv: Am Oved.

Bassok, Moshe. 1939. *Sefer hehalutz* (The book of the pioneer). Jerusalem: Jewish Agency.

Bazak, Amnon, ed. 1995. *"Vehai bahem" : Mivhan arakhim: Iyun bishe'elat kedushat hahayim ushelemut ha'aretz* ("And live by them": A test of values: An inquiry into the question of the sanctity of life and the integrity of the Land of Israel). Jerusalem: Meimad.

Be'er, Hayim. 1988. Kol hator nishma be'artzenu (The voice of the turtledove is heard in our land). Interview on the occasion of the publication of his novel *Et hazamir* (The time of the nightingale). *Devar Hashavua,* 8 Jan.

Beilinson, Moshe. 1929. Haderekh aruka (There's a long way to long). *Davar,* 1 Jan.

———. 1949. *Baderekh le'atzma'ut* (On the road to independence). Tel Aviv: Davar.

Beit-Tzvi, Shabtai. 1977. *Hatzionut hapost-ugandit bemashber hashoa* (Post-Uganda Zionism during the Holocaust crisis. Tel Aviv: Bronfman.

Bellah, Robert, et al. 1985. *Habits of the Heart.* Berkeley: University of California Press.

Bellow, Saul. 1976. *To Jerusalem and Back: A Personal Account.* New York: Viking.

Ben-Eliezer, Uri. 1994. Uma bemadim umilhama: Yisra'el bishnoteha harishonot (A nation in uniform and war: Israel in its first years). *Zmanim* 49 (summer).

———. 1995. *Derekh hakavenet: Hivatzruto shel hamilitarizm hayisra'eli 1936–1956* (Through the gunsight: The emergence of Israeli militarism 1935–56). Tel Aviv: Dvir.

Ben Ezer, Ehud. 1968. Portzim unetzurim (Breaking through and besieged). *Keshet.*

———. 1976. The Arab Question in Israeli Literature. *Shdemot 6.*

———. 1977. War and Siege in Israeli Literature (1948–1967). *Jerusalem Quarterly* 2 (winter).

———. 1978. War and Siege in Hebrew Literature after 1967. *Jerusalem Quarterly* 9 (fall).

———. 1986. *Ein sha'ananim betzion* (Unease in Zion). Tel Aviv: Am Oved.

Ben Ezer, Ehud, ed. 1974. *Unease in Zion.* New York: Quadrangle.

Ben-Gurion, David. 1946. *Bama'arakha* (In the fray). 4 vols. Tel Aviv: Mapai.

Ben-Shlomo, Yosef. 1971. Filosofiat hadat utefisat hayahadut shel Cohen (Cohen's philosophy of religion and concept of Judaism). Afterword to Hermann Cohen, *Dat utevuna mimekorot hayahadut* (Religion and reason from the sources of Judaism), trans. T. Vislavsky. Jerusalem: Mossad Bialik.

Bentwich, Norman. 1954. *For Zion's Sake: A Biography of Judah L. Magnes.* London: East and West Library.

Ben-Yehuda, Nahman. 1995. *The Massada Myth: Collective Memory and Mythmaking in Israel.* Madison: University of Wisconsin Press.

Berdyczewski, Mikha Yosef. 1899a. *Nemushot* (Stragglers). Warsaw: Tze'irim.

——. 1899b. *Al em haderekh* (At the crossroads). Warsaw: Tze'irim.

——. 1899c. *Mibayit umihutz* (Within and without). Piotrkov: Belbatovsky.

——. 1900a. *Osef ma'amarot* (Collected essays). Warsaw: Tze'irim.

——. 1900b. *Arakhim* (Values). Warsaw: Tze'irim.

——. 1902. *Din u-dvarim* (Criticism). Berlin: Tze'irim.

——. 1909. *Miyamin umismol* (Right and left). Breslau: Tze'irim.

——. 1952. *Ma'amarim* (Articles). Tel Aviv: Dvir.

——. 1982. *Amarot* (Statements), trans. Yosef Even. Jerusalem: Dvir.

Berger, Peter. 1984. On the Obsolescence of the Concept of Honor. In *Liberalism and Its Critics,* ed. Michael Sandel. Oxford: Blackwell.

Bergman, Shmuel Hugo. 1967. *Anashim uderakhim* (People and paths). Jerusalem: Mosad Bialik.

——. 1970. *The Quality of Faith.* Jerusalem: World Zionist Organization.

Berlin, Isaiah. 1952. Jewish Slavery and Emancipation. In *Hebrew University Garland,* ed. Norman Bentwich. London: Constellation.

——. 1979. *Against the Current.* London: Hogarth.

——. 1980. *Against the Current.* New York: Viking.

Bernstein, Richard G. 1986. What Is the Difference That Makes a Difference? Gadamer, Habermas, and Rorty. In *Hermeneutics and Modern Philosophy,* ed. Brice R. Wachterhauser. Albany: State University of New York Press.

Bettelheim, Bruno. 1967. *The Informed Heart.* New York: Free Press.

Biale, David. 1979. *Gershom Scholem: Kabbalah and Counterhistory.* Cambridge: Harvard University Press.

——. 1987. *Power and Powerlessness in Jewish History.* New York: Schocken.

Bialik, Hayim Nahman. 1935. *Devarim shebe'al pe* (Addresses). 2 vols. Tel Aviv: Dvir.

——. 1939. Koho shel hehalutz (The strength of the pioneer). In Bassok 1939.

——. 1954. *Kol kitvei Hayim Nahman Bialik* (Collected works of Hayim Nahman Bialik). Tel Aviv: Dvir.

Blidstein, Jacob. 1983. *Ekronot medini'im bemishnat harambam* (Political principles in Maimonides' teaching). Ramat Gan: Bar-Ilan University Press.

Bloom, Harold. 1983. Jewish Culture and Jewish Memory. *Dialectical Anthropology* 8.

Blum, Eli, ed. N.d. *Arakhim bemivhan: Milhama umusar bire'i hayahadut* (A test of values: War and morality from the perspective of Judaism). Alon Shvut, Israel: Yeshivat Har Etzion.

Bosak, M. 1956. Mickiewicz, Frank, vekibush Eretz Yisrael (Mickewicz, Frank, and the conquest of the Land of Israel). *Molad* 13.

Bowra, Morris. 1957. *The Greek Experience.* New York: New American Library.

Boyarin, Daniel. 1998. *Unheroic Conduct.* Berkeley: University of California Press.

Boyarin, Daniel, and Jonathan Boyarin. 1994. Ein moledet leyisrael: Al hamakom shel hayehudim (Israel has no homeland: On the place of the Jews). *Teoria uvikoret* 5.

Brandes, George. 1970. *Ferdinand Lassalle.* Westport, Conn.: Greenwood.

Brenner, Yosef Hayim. 1955–67. *Kol kitvei Y. H. Brenner* (Collected works of Y. H. Brenner). Tel Aviv: Hakibbutz Hame'uhad.

Breuer, Isaac. 1934. *Der neue Kusari* (The new Kuzari). Frankfurt a. M.: Rabbiner Hirsch Gesellschaft.

———. 1974. *Concepts of Judaism,* ed. and intro. Jacob Levinger. Jerusalem: Israel Universities Press.

———. 1982a. *Moria,* 2d ed. Jerusalem: Mosad Harav Kook,

———. 1982b. *Nahaliel,* 2d ed. Jerusalem: Mosad Harav Kook.

Breuer, Mordekhai. 1959. Hagalut bemishnatam shel harav Shimshon Refael Hirsch vedoktor Yitzhak Breuer (Exile in the teachings of Rabbi Samson Raphael Hirsch and Dr. Isaac Breuer). In *Galut* (Exile), ed. Mordekhai Breuer. Jerusalem: Hug Amana.

Brinker, Menahem. 1990. *Ad hasimta hateverianit* (As far as the Tiberias alley). Tel Aviv: Am Oved.

Buber, Martin. 1948a. *Israel and the World.* New York: Schocken.

———. 1948b. *Hassidism.* New York: Philosophical Library.

———. 1953. *The Eclipse of God.* London: Gollancz.

———. 1954. *Pointing the Way.* New York: Harper.

———. 1956. *Koenigtum Gottes* (The kingdom of God). Heidelberg: Lambert Schneider.

———. 1958. *Paths in Utopia.* Boston: Beacon Press.

———. 1960, *The Prophetic Faith.* New York: Harper.

———. 1961. *Am ve'olam* (People and world). Jerusalem: Zionist Library.

———. 1962. *Penei adam* (The human countenance). Jerusalem: Mosad Bialik.

———. 1965. *Nachlese.* Heidelberg: Lambert Schneider.

———. 1967. *On Judaism,* ed. Nahum N. Glatzer. New York: Schocken.

———. 1968. *On the Bible,* ed. Nahum N. Glatzer. New York: Schocken.

———. 1983. *A Land of Two Peoples,* ed. Paul Mendes-Flohr. New York: Oxford University Press.

———. 1993. Darki el hahasidut (My way to Hasidism). In *Tikva lesha'a zu* (Hope for this hour). Tel Aviv: Am Oved.

Burckhardt, Jacob. 1944. *The Civilization of the Renaissance in Italy.* London: Allen and Unwin.

Cahan, Ya'akov. 1912. Hamahapekha ha'ivrit (The Hebrew revolution). In *Ha'ivri hahadash.* Warsaw: Ha'ivri Hahadash.

Calderon, Nissim. 1980. Ad ha-17 lemai 1977: Al *Zikhron devarim* ve-Eretz Yisra'el ha'ovedet (Up to May 17, 1977: On *Past Continuous* and the Palestinian-Jewish labor movement). *Siman kria* 10.

Cohen, Hermann. 1972. *Religion of Reason out of the Sources of Judaism,* trans. Simon Kaplan. New York: Ungar.

Cohen, Stuart. 2001. Hamashma'ut hahevratit shel hasherut hatzeva'i beyisrael: Mabat mehudash" (The Social Meaning of Military Service in Israel: A Reappraisal). *Tarbut demokratit* 4–5.

Confino, Michael. 1993. *Mi-Senkt Peterburg le-Leningrad* (From St. Petersburg to Leningrad). Tel Aviv: Am Oved.

———. 1993. Interview with Michael Confino, by Yaron London. *Shiv'a yamim* (supplement to *Yediot Aharonot*), 21 May.

Daskal, Marcello. 1977. Ne'emanut relevantit (Relevant loyalty). In *Hatzodek vehabilti tzodek* (Right and wrong). Tel Aviv: Mif'alim Universitai'im Lehotza'a Leor.

Debi-Guri, Lillian. 1980. Galut uge'ula beshirat Uri Tzvi Greenberg (Exile and redemption in the poetry of Uri Tzvi Greenberg). *Bikoret Ufarshanut* 15.

DeNicola, Daniel R. 1983. Supererogation: Artistry in Conduct. In *Foundations of Ethics,* ed. Leroy S. Rouner. South Bend, Ind.: University of Notre Dame Press.

Diamond, Games S. 1976. *Homeland or Holy Land? The "Canaanite" Critique of Israel.* Bloomington: Indiana University Press.

Dinur, Ben Zion. 1939. *Sefer hatzionut* (The book of Zionism). Tel Aviv: Mosad Bialik.

——. 1950. *Shivat tzion* (The return to Zion). Jerusalem: Mosad Bialik.

——-. 1958. *Zakhor: Devarim al hasho'a ve'al likha* (Remember: Observations on the Holocaust and its lessons). Jerusalem: Yad Vashem.

Don Yehiya, Eliezer. 1983. Dat veteror politi bayahadut hadatit ufe'ulot hagemul bitekufat "hame'ora'ot" (Religion and political terrorism among Orthodox Jewry and retaliation during the period of the Arab Revolt). *Hatzionut* 17.

Don Yehiya, Eliezer, and Bernard Susser. 1986. *Reztifut utemurot behagut hamedinit hayehudit* (Continuity and change in Jewish political thought). Ramat Gan: Bar-Ilan University Press.

——. 1988. Mamlakhtiut vesho'a (Statism and Holocaust). In *Bishvilei hatehia* (Along the paths of rebirth). Ramat-Gan: Bar-Ilan University Press.

Dotan, Shmuel. 1980. *Pulmus hahaluka bitekufat hamandat* (The partition debate during the Mandate period). Jerusalem: Yad Ben-Tzvi.

Dubnow, Simon. 1961. *Nationalism and History.* Cleveland: World.

Eagleton, Terry. 1983. *Literary Theory.* Minneapolis: University of Minnesota.

Elazar, Daniel. 1981. *Kinship and Consent: The Jewish Political Tradition and Its Contemporary Uses.* Ramat-Gan: Turtledove.

Elazar, Daniel J., and Stuart A. Cohen. 1985. *The Jewish Polity.* Bloomington: Indiana University Press.

Elazari-Vulcani, Yitzhak. 1950. *Sefirot* (Spheres). Tel Aviv: Twersky.

Elboim-Dror, Rahel. 1986. *Hahinukh ha'ivri be'Eretz Yisrael* (Hebrew education in the Land of Israel). Jerusalem: Yad Ben-Tzvi.

——. 1996. Hu holekh uva mikirbenu, hu ba ha'ivri hahadash (Emerging from amongst us is the new Hebrew). *Alpayim* 12.

Eldad, Yisrael. 1950. Kotev hamahapekha ha'ivrit (The focus of the Hebrew revolution). *Sulam* (Tshrei 5710 [Sept.] 12).

——. 1952. Yesodot ideologi'im ufoliti'im lamahapekha ha'ivrit (Ideological and political foundations of the Hebrew revolution). *Sulam* (Tevet 5712 [Dec.]).

——. 1954. Devarim peshutim al musar hayahadut (Simple words about Judaic morality). *Sulam* (Shevat 5714 [Jan.]).

——. 1957. Tahalikh hage'ula mimeromei sulam histori (The process of redemption [as seen from] the top of a historical ladder). *Sulam* (Tammuz 5717 [July]).

——. 1959. Al demokratia vetzionut (On democracy and Zionism). *Sulam* (Tishrei 5720 [Sept.]).

——. 1970. *The Jewish Revolution,* trans. H. Schmorak. New York: Shengold.

——. 1980. *Hegionot Yisrael* (Reflections on Israel). Tel Aviv: Hamidrasha Hale'umit.

———. 1981. *Hegionot Yehuda* (Reflections on Judah). Tel Aviv: Hamidrasha Hale'umit.

———. 1982. *Pulmus hahurban velekahav* (The debate over the destruction [of the Temple] and its lessons). Jerusalem: Van Leer Institute.

———. 1991. Harpatkanut lesugeha (The varieties of adventurism). *Yediot aharonot,* 12 July.

Eliade, Mircea, ed. 1987. *Encyclopedia of Religion.* New York: Macmillan.

Eliash, Shulamit. 1984. The Response of the Jewish Community to Arab Terror, 1936–1939: The Religious Position. *Bar-Ilan Studies in History* 2.

Ellis, Mark H. 1990. *Beyond Innocence and Redemption.* San Francisco: Harper and Row.

Elon, Menahem. 1973. *Hamishpat ha'ivri* (Hebrew law). Jerusalem: Magnes.

Erez, Y., ed. 1962. *Yalkut ha'ahdut* (The Ahdut anthology). Tel Aviv: Am Oved.

Eshed, Ya'akov. 1978. *Heshbon shel zekhut* (The reckoning of a right). Tel Aviv: Hakibbutz Hame'uhad.

Etzioni, Amitai. 1954. Al Kibiyeh (On Kibiyeh). *Beterem,* 15 Jan.

Ezrahi, Yaron. 1983. Metahim shebein hazon medini lemada'i (Tensions between political and scientific visions). In *Ha'omnam kashe lihyot yisraeli?* (Is it really difficult to be an Israeli?), ed. Alouf Hareven. Jerusalem: Van Leer Institute.

Fackenheim, Emil. 1959. Jewish Existence and the Living God. *Commentary* 38 (Aug.).

———. 1967. Jewish Values in the Post-Holocaust Future. *Judaism* 16.

———. 1972. *God's Presence in History.* New York: Harper.

Feierberg, Mordekhai Ze'ev. 1973. *"Whither?" and Other Stories.* Philadelphia: Jewish Publication Society.

Fleischman, Ya'akov. 1956. Franz Rosenzweig kimevaker hatzionut (Franz Rosenzweig as a critic of Zionism). In *Diyunei Beit Hillel al Franz Rosenzweig bimlot esrim vehamesh shanim liftirato* (The Beit Hillel symposium on Franz Rosenzweig on the 25th anniversary of his death). Jerusalem: Magnes.

Frankl, Viktor E. 1978. *The Unheard Cry for Meaning.* New York: Simon and Schuster.

Friedman, Menahem, and Nisan Rubin. 1995. Yadeinu lo shafkhu et hadam? (Didn't our hands shed this blood?). *Ha'aretz,* 18 Nov.

Friedmann, Georges. 1967. *The End of the Jewish People?* Garden City: Doubleday.

Frischman, David. 1912. Al hayehudim (Concerning the Jews). *He'atid* (Berlin) 4.

Fuchs, Sarit. 1989. Haradat hagilgul bedramat hasho'a (Role-reversal anxiety in the drama of the Holocaust). *Iton 77* (Mar.).

Funkenstein, Amos. 1982. *Hapasiviut kesimana shel yahadut hagola: Mitos umetziut* (Passivity as the hallmark of Diaspora Jewry: Myth and reality). Tel Aviv: Keren Aran.

———. 1992a. Historia, historia shekeneged, vesiper (History, counterhistory, and narrative). *Alpayim* 4.

———. 1992b. An Escape from History: Rosenzweig on the Destiny of Judaism. *History and Memory* 2.

———. 1995. Toldot Yisra'el bein hahohim (The history of Israel among the thornbushes). *Tzion* 60.

Gadamer, Hans-Georg. 1976. On the Scope and Function of Hermeneutical Reflection. In *Philosophical Hermeneutics.* Berkeley: University of California Press.

———. 1989. *Truth and Method.* New York: Crossroad.

Gafni, Yeshayahu, and Aviezer Ravitzky, eds. 1993. *Kedushat hahayim veheruf hanefesh* (The sanctity of life and self-sacrifice). Jerusalem: Zalman Shazar Center.

Gal, Reuven. 1986. *A Portrait of the Israeli Soldier.* Westport, Conn.: Greenwood.

Gavison, Ruth. 1995. Medina yehudit vedemokratit: Zehut politit, ideologia, umishpat (A Jewish and democratic state: Political identity, ideology, and law). *Iyunei mishpat* 19.

Geertz, Clifford. 1973. *The Interpretation of Cultures.* New York: Basic Books.

Ginossar, Pinhas, and Avi Bar'eli, eds. 1996. *Tsionut: pulmus ben zmanenu* (Zionism: a contemporary polemic). Sde Boker: Ben-Gurion Heritage Center.

Glatzer, Nahum N., ed. 1961. *Franz Rosenzweig: His Life and Thought.* New York: Schocken.

Goffman, Erving. 1963. *Stigma.* Englewood Cliffs, N.J.: Prentice-Hall.

Goldman, Eliezer. 1963. Hamusar, hadat, vehahalakha (Morality, religion, and the Halakha). *De'ot* 21.

———. 1989. Responses to Modernity in Orthodox Jewish Thought. *Studies in Contemporary Jewry* 3.

———. 1997. *Mehkarim ve'iyunim* (Studies and investigations). Jerusalem: Magnes.

Gordon, Aharon David. 1953. *Ha'uma veha'avoda* (The nation and labor). Jerusalem: Zionist Library.

———. 1957a. *Mikhtavim ureshimot* (Letters and notes). Tel Aviv: Zionist Library.

———. 1957b. *Ha'adam vehateva* (Man and nature). Tel Aviv: Am Oved.

Gordon, David. 1959. Yosef Trumpeldor, hayotzer harishon shel tzava ivri (Yosef Trumpeldor, the first to create a Hebrew army). *Ha'olam* 22 (10 Mar.).

Gordon, Yehuda Leib. 1964. *Shirei higayon, meshalim, veshirei alila* (Reflective poems, parables, and narrative poems). Tel Aviv: Schocken.

Goren, Arthur, ed. 1982. *Dissenter in Zion.* Cambridge: Harvard University Press.

Goren, Shlomo. 1982. Gevurat Metzada le'or hahalakha (The heroism of Massada in light of Halakha). In *Torat hashabat vehamo'ed* (The doctrines of the Sabbath and festivals). Jerusalem: Tzioni.

———. 1983–86. *Meshiv milhama* (Fighting back). Jerusalem: Ha'idra Raba.

Gorny, Yosef. 1975. *Ahdut Ha'avoda hahistorit* (The historical Ahdut Ha'avoda). Tel Aviv: Am Oved.

———. 1976. *Shutafut uma'avak* (Cooperation and struggle). Tel Aviv: Hakibbutz Hame'uhad.

———. 1987. *Zionism and the Arabs, 1882–1948: A Study of Ideology.* Oxford: Clarendon.

———. 1990. *Behipus ahar hazehut hale'umit* (In search of national identity). Tel Aviv: Am Oved.

Gould, Eric, ed. 1985. *The Sin of the Book: Edmond Jabès.* Lincoln: University of Nebraska Press.

Graetz, Heinrich. 1936. *Die Konstruktion der Juedischen Geschichte.* Berlin: Schocken.

Graetz, Nurit. 1988. *Sifrut ve'ideologia bishnot hasheloshim* (Literature and ideology in the Thirties). Tel Aviv: Open University.

Greenberg, Irving. 1981a. *The Third Great Cycle in Jewish History.* New York: National Jewish Resource Center.

———. 1981b. Otzma ufolitika: Idan shelishi betoldot yisrael (Power and politics: A third era in Jewish history). *Gesher* 27.

———. 1988a. *The Ethics of Jewish Power.* New York: Clal.

———. 1988b. *The Jewish Way.* New York: Summit.

Greenberg, Moshe. 1986. *Hasegula vehako'ah* (Chosenness and power). Oranim: Haifa University.

Greenberg, Uri Tzvi. 1930. *Ezor magen une'um ben hadam* (A protective belt and the speech of the bloody son). Jerusalem: Sadan.

———. 1936. *Sefer hakitrug veha'emuna* (The book of accusation and faith). Jerusalem: Sadan.

———. 1954. *Rehovot hanahar* (The ways of the river). Jerusalem and Tel Aviv: Schocken.

———. 1957. Mishirat habote bekoah hakissuf (From the poetry of one moved by longing to speak out). *Sulam* 4, July.

———. 1963. Devarim betekes kabalat pras Miriam Talpier (Address at the Miriam Talpier Prize award ceremony). *Gazit* 21:1–4.

———. 1979. Moledet hadevai al admat haslavim (The morbid homeland on Slavic soil) (1923). *Siman Kria* 10.

Guedemann, Moritz. 1897. *National Judentum.* Leipzig and Vienna: Breitenstein.

Guri, Hayim. 1992. Ani, anahnu vehi (I, we, and she). *Davar,* 6 Mar.

Gutman, Yisrael. 1977. "Kiddush hashem" ve-"kiddush hahayim" ("Sanctification of God's name" and "sanctification of life"). *Yalkut Moreshet* 24.

Guttmann, Julius. 1970. Binyan Eretz Yisrael vehayahadut (Judaism and the upbuilding of the Land of Israel). *Petahim* 2 (1 Adar 5730 [Mar.]).

Habermas, Jürgen. 1987. *The Philosophical Discourse of Modernity,* trans. Fredrick G. Lawrence. Cambridge: Polity Press.

Habermas, Jürgen. 1988. Ethics, Politics, and History: An Interview with Jürgen Habermas. *Philosophy and Social Criticism* 14: 3–4.

———. 1989. Die Grenzen des Neu Historismus. *Die Neue Gesellschaft* 35.

Hadari-Ramage, Yona, ed. 1994. *Osim hoshvim* (Reconsidering). Ramat Ef'al: Yad Tabenkin.

Haezrahi, Pepita. 1961. *The Price of Morality.* London: Allen and Unwin.

———. 1965. Hape'ula ha'ahara'it (The responsible act). In *Me'asef ledivrei sifrut* (A literary anthology). Jerusalem: Agudat Hasofrim.

Halevi, Judah. 1964. *The Kuzari.* New York: Schocken.

Halpern, Ben. 1960. Herzl's Historic Gift: The Sense of Sovereignty. *Herzl Yearbook* 3.

———. 1961. *The Idea of the Jewish State.* Cambridge: Harvard University Press.

———. 1967. Hirhurim al hatzharat Balfour (Second thoughts about the Balfour Declaration). *Molad,* n.s. 1.

———. 1970. Militancy and Passive Resistance. *Midstream* 16:3.

Hanokh, Gershon. 1927. Al dorshei hahazon (On the interpreters of the vision). *Hapoel Hatza'ir* 20.

Harkaby, Yeshoshafat. 1967. *Emdat Yisrael besikhsukh Yisrael-Arav* (Israel's position in the Arab-Israeli conflict). Tel Aviv: Dvir.

———. 1983. *The Bar Kokhba Syndrome: Risk and Realism in International Politics.* Chappaqua, N.Y.: Rossel.

Hartman, David. 1985. *A Living Covenant.* New York: Free Press.

Harvey, Van A. 1966. *The Historian and the Believer.* New York: Macmillan.

Hazaz, Hayim. 1930. Gematriot (Ciphers). *Davar* magazine supp., 28 Aug.

———. 1950. *Beketz hayamim* (At the end of days). Tel Aviv: Am Oved.

———. 1963. *Avanim rot-hot* (Boiling stones). Tel Aviv: Am Oved.

———. 1963a. *Sippurim nivharim* (Selected stories). Tel Aviv: Dvir.

———. 1968. *Hagurat mazalot* (A band of constellations). Tel Aviv: Am Oved.

Hehalutz halohem, iton hamahteret bekrakov, ogust-oktober 1943 (The fighting pioneer, journal of the Cracow underground, August–October 1943). 1984. Lohamei Hageta'ot, Israel: Ghetto Fighters House.

Hegel, Georg W. F. 1967. *The Philosophy of Right,* trans. T. M. Knox. Oxford: Clarendon Press.

Heine, Heinrich. 1925. *Confessio Judaica,* ed. H. Bieber. Berlin: Welt.

———. 1982. *The Complete Poems of Heinrich Heine,* trans. Hal Draper. Oxford: Oxford University Press.

Heinemann, Yosef. 1974. *Agadot vetoldoteihen* (Rabbinic narratives and their history). Jerusalem: Keter.

Heller, Yosef, ed. 1985. *Bema'avak limedina* (Struggling for a state). Jerusalem: Zalman Shazar Center.

———. 1989. *Lehi: Ideologia ufolitika* (Lehi: Ideology and politics). Jerusalem: Zalman Shazar Center.

Hen, Avraham. 1938. Lo tirtzah (Thou shalt not murder). *Sinai,* Tishrei-Heshvan 5698 (Sept.–Oct.).

Holtzer, Elli. 1999. Le'umiyut umusar: Hashkafot al hashimush bekoah bizramim ideologi'im bekerev tzionim dati'im (Nationalism and morality: Perspectives on the use of force among religious-Zionist ideological groups). Ph.D. diss., Hebrew University of Jerusalem.

Herman, Simon N. 1977. In the Shadow of the Holocaust. *Jerusalem Quarterly* 3.

Hertzberg, Arthur, ed. 1959. *The Zionist Idea.* Philadelphia: Jewish Publication Society.

Herzl, Theodor. 1956. *The Diaries of Theodor Herzl.* New York: Dial.

Hirsch, Samson Raphael. 1966. *Bema'agelei shana* (In the cycle of a year). Bnei Brak: Netzah.

———. 1969. *The Nineteen Letters on Judaism.* Jerusalem: Feldheim.

Hoffman, Haya. 1989. Ha-"af-al-pi-khen" habreneri beshirat Lamdan (The Brennerian "nevertheless" in Lamdan's poetry). In *Hasifrut ha'ivrit utenuat ha'avoda* (Hebrew literature and the labor movement), ed. Pinhas Ginossar. Beersheba: Ben-Gurion University Press.

Holmes, Robert L. 1989. Can War Be Morally Justified? In *On War and Morality.* Princeton: Princeton University Press.

Holtzman, Avner. 1991. Fima mekhake lenes (Fima waits for a miracle). *Ha'aretz,* 15 Feb.

Horovitz, Dan. 1977. Is Israel a Garrison State? *Jerusalem Quarterly* 4 (summer).

Horowitz, Rivka. 1987. Yitzhak Breuer, Franz Rosenzweig, ve-Ra'ya Kook. In *Torah im derekh eretz* (Torah with secular culture), ed. Mordekhai Breuer. Ramat-Gan: Bar-Ilan University Press.

Horowitz, Yeshaya. N.d. *Shnei luhot habrit* (The two tablets of the covenant). Jerusalem: n.p.

Huizinga, Johan. 1960. *Men and Ideas*. New York: Meridian.

———. 1970. *The Waning of the Middle Ages*. London: Edward Arnold.

Huppert, Shmuel. 1978. Galut uge'ula: Tefisatan vederekh itzuvan beshirato shel Uri Tzvi Greenberg (Exile and redemption: How they are understood and cast in the poetry of Uri Tzvi Greenberg). Ph.D. diss., Hebrew University of Jerusalem.

———. 1979. Hagalut beshirato ha'eretz-yisraelit shel Uri Tzvi Greenberg (Exile in the Land of Israel poetry of Uri Tzvi Greenberg). *Hasifrut* 29.

Inbar, Ephraim. 1989. The "Unavoidable War" Debate in Israel. *Journal of Strategic Studies* 12:1.

Iviansky, Ze'ev. 1991. *Al hitnagdut umered* (On resistance and rebellion). Tel Aviv: Yair.

Jabotinsky, Ze'ev. 1949. *Ketavim tzioni'im rishonim* (First Zionist writings). Jerusalem: Ari Jabotinsky.

Jaeger, Werner. 1945. *Paideia: The Ideals of Greek Culture*. Oxford: Blackwell.

Jaffee, Martin S. 1991. The Victim Community in Myth and History. *Journal of Ecumenical Studies* 28.

James, William. 1956. *The Will to Believe and Other Essays in Popular Philosophy*. New York: Dover.

———. 1960. *The Varieties of Religious Experience*. New York: Collins, 1960.

———. 1968. *The Writings of William James*, ed. James. J. McDermott. New York: Random House.

Jaspers, Karl. 1963. *The Future of Mankind*. Chicago: University of Chicago Press.

Josephus, Flavius. 1961. *The Jewish War*. London: Heinemann.

———. 1965. *Jewish Antiquities*, trans. H. St. J. Thackeray. London: Heinemann.

Kafkafi, Eyal. 1986. Temurot ba'ideologia shel Hakibbutz Hame'uhad 1944–54 (The changing ideology of Hakibbutz Hame'uhad 1944–54). Ph.D. diss., Tel Aviv University.

Kahan Commission. 1983. *The Beirut Massacre: The Complete Kahan Commission Report*. Princeton: Karz-Cohl.

Kant, Immanuel. 1964. *Critique of Judgment*. New York: Hafner.

———. 1965. *The Metaphysical Elements of Justice*, trans. John Ladd. New York: Bobbs Merrill.

Karni, Yoav. 1988a. Bein yehudei America (Among the American Jews). *Ha'aretz*, 12 and 19 Feb.

———. 1988b. Ha'aretz hamuvtahat shel Neusner (Neusner's promised land). *Ha'aretz*, 4 Mar.

Katz, Jacob. 1982. Israel and the Messiah. *Commentary* (Jan.).

———. 1987. Is Messianism Good for the Jews? *Commentary* (Apr.).

Katz, Steven T. 1983. *Post-Holocaust Dialogues*. New York: New York University Press.

———. 1993. Irving Greenberg. In *Interpreters of Judaism in the Late Twentieth Century*. Washington: B'nai B'rith.

Katznelson, Berl, ed. 1929–32. *Yalkut Ahdut Ha'avoda* (An Ahdut Ha'avoda anthology). 2 vols. Tel Aviv: Ahdut.

———.1945–50. *Kitvei Berl Katznelson* (The writings of Berl Katznelson). 12 vols. Tel Aviv: Mapai.

Kaufmann, Yehezkel. 1961. *Gola venekhar* (Exile and alienation). Tel Aviv: Dvir.

———. 1969. *Toldot ha'emuna hayisra'elit* (History of the Israelite religion). Tel Aviv: Mosad Bialik.

———. 1970. The Ruin of the Soul. In *Zionism Reconsidered,* ed. Michael Selzer. New York: Macmillan.

Kedar, Binyamin Ze'ev. 1982. Massada: The Myth and the Complex. *Jerusalem Quarterly* (summer).

Kelly, Michael. 1988. The Gadamer-Habermas Debate Revisited. *Philosophy and Social Criticism* 14.

Kemp, Thomas Peter. 1988. Towards a Narrative of Ethics. *Philosophy and Social Criticism* 14.

Kimmerling, Baruch. 1990. Hakesher hahonek shel hatzionut (Zionism's choking knot). *Ha'aretz,* 29 Apr.

———. 1993. Militarizm bahevra hayisra'elit (Militarism in Israeli society). *Teoria uvikoret* 4 (fall).

Klausner, Yosef. 1897. Yissud hatenua hahadasha beyisrael (The founding of the new movement in Israel). *Hashiloah* 2.

Kleinman, Aharon. 1978. Hirbet Hiz'a vezikhronot lo ne'imim (Hirbet Hiz'a and unpleasant memories). *Proza* (Sept.).

Kolakowski, Leszek. 1972. *The Presence of Myth.* Chicago: University of Chicago Press.

Kolatt, Israel. 1984. Tzionut umeshihiut (Zionism and messianism). In *Meshihiut ve'eskatologia* (Messianism and eschatology), ed. Tzvi Baras. Jerusalem: Zalman Shazar Center.

Kook, Avraham. 1941. *Hazon hage'ula* (The vision of redemption). Jerusalem: Ha'aguda Lehotza'at Sifrei Hara'ya.

———. 1962. *Igrot hare'iya* (Letters of Rabbi Avraham Yitzhak Hacohen). Jerusalem: Mosad Harav Kook.

———. 1963a. *Orot* (Lights). Jerusalem: Mosad Harav Kook.

———. 1963b. *Olat hare'iya* (Rav Kook's burnt offering). Jerusalem: Mosad Harav Kook.

———. 1964. *Orot hakodesh* (The holy lights). 3 vols. Jerusalem: Mosad Harav Kook.

———. 1984. *Ma'amarei hare'iya Kook* (Essays of Rabbi Avraham Yitzhak Hacohen Kook). Jerusalem and TelAviv: n.p.

Kook, Tzvi Yehuda. 1978. Kedushat am hakodesh al admat hakodesh (The holiness of the holy people on holy soil). In *Hatzionut hadatit vehamedina* (Religious Zionism and the state), ed. Yosef and Avraham Tirosh. Jerusalem: World Zionist Organization.

———. 1983. *Mitokh hatora hago'elet* (From the redemptive teachings). Jerusalem: Makhon Tzemah Tzvi.

Korchak-Marla, Rozhka. 1946. *Lehavot ba'efer* (Flames in the ashes). Merhavia, Israel: Sifriat Poalim.

Kovner, Abba. 1988. *Mishelo ve'alav* (Of and about him). Tel Aviv: Moreshet.

Krantz, Fredrick. 1988. George Steiner's Negative Zionism. *Zionist Ideas* 17.

Kundera, Milan. 1995. The Unloved Child of the Family. In *Testaments Betrayed,* trans. Linda Asher. New York: Harper Collins.

Kurzweil, Baruch. 1958. Sin'at atzmo basifrut hayehudit (Self-hatred in Jewish literature). *Molad* 16.

———. 1961. *Bialik ve-Tchernichowsky: Mehkarim beshiratam* (Bialik and Tchernichowsky: Studies in their poetry). Jerusalem: Schocken.

———. 1966. *Bein hehazon levein ha'absurdi* (Between vision and the absurd). Jerusalem:
Schocken.

———. 1970. *Bema'avak al erkei hayahadut* (Struggling over the values of Judaism).
Jerusalem: Schocken.

———. 1976. *Lenokhah hamevukha haruhanit shel dorenu* (Facing the intellectual confusion of our generation). Ramat-Gan: Bar-Ilan University Press.

Laor, Dan. 1984. *Hashofar vehaherev* (The ram's horn and the sword). Tel Aviv: Hakibbutz Hame'uhad.

Laskov, Shulamit. 1983. Ha'ish Yosef Trumpeldor (Yosef Trumpeldor the man). In *Hayishuv ba'et hahadasha: Tsiunei derekh* (The Yishuv in modern times: Milestones), ed. S.
Stampler. Tel Aviv: Ministry of Defense.

Lavi, Shlomo. 1942. One Day. In *Palestine Stories,* ed. and trans. I. M. Lask. Jerusalem:
Tarshish, 211–12.

———. 1944. *Ketavim* (Writings). Tel Aviv: Am Oved.

———. 1949. *Banim: Kovetz zikaron livnei Ein-Harod* (Sons: An anthology in memory of
the sons of Ein-Harod). Ein-Harod, Israel: Kibbutz Ein-Harod.

Lehman-Wilzig, Samuel N., and B. Susser, eds. 1981. *Comparative Jewish Politics: Public
life in Israel and the Diaspora.* Ramat Gan: Bar-Ilan University Press.

Lehrer, Shim'on. 1983. Hakoah kimeyased zekhut (On might making right). *Artzi* 4.

Leibowitz, Yeshaya. 1976. *Yahadut, am yehudi, medinat Yisrael* (Judaism, the Jewish
people, the State of Israel). Tel Aviv and Jerusalem: Schocken.

———. 1982. *Emuna, historia, va'arakhim* (War, history, and values). Jerusalem: Akademon.

———. 1992. *Judaism, Human Values, and the Jewish State.* Cambridge: Harvard University Press. *Lenokhah hahaslama beyahas la'aravim* (Confronting the escalation in relations with the Arabs). 1985. Tel Aviv: Hakibbutz Hadati.

Lessing, Theodor. 1930. *Der Jüdische Selbsthasse* (Jewish self-hatred). Berlin: Judische
Verlag.

Levi, Gideon. 1991. Lemi yesh yoter kavod? (Who gets more respect?). *Ha'aretz,* 1 Mar.

Levi, Primo. 1988. *The Drowned and the Saved.* London: Michael Joseph.

Levi, Ze'ev. 1984. *Hermenoitika* (Hermeneutics). Tel Aviv: Sifriat Poalim.

Levinas, Emmanuel. 1990. *Difficult Freedom,* trans. Sean Hand. Baltimore: Johns Hopkins University Press.

Levinger, Moshe. 1969. Shulhan meruba (A square table). *Ma'ariv,* 4 Apr.

———. 1981. Anahnu veha'aravim (We and the Arabs). *Nekuda* 36 (Nov.).

Levy, Bernard Henri. 1989. Lehe'asot mimedinat-miklat limekor metzuka (A country of
refuge becoming a source of distress): Interview with Bernard Henri Levy. By Yoav
Tocker. *Ha'aretz,* 19 Apr.

Lewis, Bernard. 1976. *History Remembered, Recovered, Invented.* Princeton: Princeton
University Press.

Lichtenberg-Ettinger, Brakha. 1990. Hakshavat hamedaber hi hazikaron: Keta'im mis-ihot im Edmond Jabès (It is the speaker's listening that constitutes memory: Excerpts from conversations with Edmond Jabès). *Studio* (Dec.).

Lieblich, Amia. 1991. Sofiut hahayim vehashpa'oteha hapsikhologiot (The finitude of life and its psychological effects). In *Hahayim: mahut va'erekh* (Life: Essence and value), ed. L. Mazor. Jerusalem: Magnes.

Liebman, Charles. 1983. *Attitudes Toward Jewish-Gentile Relations in the Jewish Tradition and Contemporary Israel.* Cape Town: University of Cape Town.

Liebman, Charles, and Eliezer Don Yehiya. 1984. *Civil Religion in Israel.* Berkeley: University of California Press.

Liebman, Yeshayahu (Charles). 1981a. Hamarkiv hadati bale'umanut hayisraelit (The religious element in Israeli nationalism). *Gesher* 113.

——. 1981b. Mitos hasho'a bahevra hayisraelit (The myth of the Holocaust in Israeli society). *Tefutzot Yisrael* 19 (winter).

——. 1983. Hahitpat-hut haneomasortit bekerev yehudim ortodoksim beyisrael (Neo-traditionalism among Orthodox Jews in Israel). *Megamot* 27.

——. 1989. Hamusag medinat yisra'el utefisato bahevra hayisra'elit (The concept of the State of Israel and how it is understood in Israeli society). *Medina, memshal veyahasim beinle'umi'im* 30.

Livneh, Eliezer. 1966–67. Takhlita shel yisrael (Israel's purpose). *Moznayim* 24.

Luz, Ehud. 1983a. Tzionut umeshihiut behaguto shel Franz Rosenzweig (Zionism and messianism in the thought of Franz Rosenzweig). *Mehkerei Yerushalayim Bemah-shevet Yisrael* 2.

——. 1983b. Hatemimut hasheniya (The second naïveté) *Mehkerei Yerushalayim Bemahshevet Yisrael* 2.

——. 1988. *Parallels Meet,* trans. Len Schramm. Philadelphia: Jewish Publication Society.

——. 1992. *Patzifizm leor hatora: Mivhar ketavav shel Aharon Shmuel Tamares* (Pacifism in light of the Torah: Selected writings of Aharon Shmuel Tamares). Jerusalem: Dinur Center.

Luz, Tzvi. 1970. *Metzi'ut ve'adam basifrut ha'eretz-yisra'elit* (Reality and man in the literature of the Land of Israel). Tel Aviv: Dvir.

Luzzato, Shmuel David. 1948. *Yalkut Shadal* (A Luzzato anthology). Jerusalem: Schocken.

——. 1976. *Mivhar ketavim* (Selected works). Jerusalem: Mosad Bialik.

MacIntyre, Alisdair. 1981. *After Virtue.* South Bend, Ind.: University of Notre Dame Press.

Magnes, Judah L. 1930. *Like All the Nations?* Jerusalem: Herod's Gate.

Maimonides, Moses. 1972. *A Maimonides Reader,* ed. Isadore Twersky. New York: Behrman House.

——. 1985. The Epistle to Yemen, trans. Abraham Halkin. In *Crisis and Leadership: Epistles of Maimonides,* ed. David Hartman. Philadelphia: Jewish Publication Society.

Marcus, Yoel. 1988. Leil ha'alot ha'arukot (The night of the long clubs). *Ha'aretz,* 26 Jan.

——. 1991. Keta'im al olam akum (Random thoughts on a lopsided world). *Ha'aretz,* 1 Dec.

Margalit, Avishai. 1986. Zekhuyot historiot (Historic rights). *Iyun* 35.

Megged, Aharon. 1985. Shisha yamim ve'od shisha (Six days and six more). In *Le'ahar hara'ash* (The earthquake zone). Tel Aviv: Hakibbutz Hame'uhad.

——. 1990. Lihyot yehudi (To be a Jew). *Davar*, 19 Sept.

Megged, Matti. 1950. Adam bemilhama (Man at war). In *Yevul: Kovetz likhvodo shel A. Shlonski* (Harvest: An anthology in honor of A. Shlonsky), ed. Yaakov Fichman. Merhavia, Israel: Sifriat Po'alim.

Melamed, Zalman. 1974. Mikhtav letalmid (Letter to a student). *Morasha* 7 (winter).

——. 1988. Shlav nosaf bemahalakh hage'ula (Another phase in the process of redemption). *Nekuda* 119 (Mar.).

Melman, Yosef. 1997. Hasheker hamuskam shel Kibiyeh: Keta'im miprotokol yeshivat hamemshala be'inyan hape'ula (The falsification of the Kibiyeh [incident]: Excerpts from the protocol of a cabinet meeting concerning the operation). *Ha'aretz,* 18 Apr.

Melzer, Yehuda. 1975. *Concepts of Just War.* Leiden: Sijthoff.

Mintz, Alan. 1982–83. The Russian Pogroms in Hebrew Literature and the Subversion of the Martyrological Ideal. *AJS Review* 18.

Miron, Dan. 1957. Hayim Hazaz ben hashishim (Hayim Hazaz at sixty). *Gazit* 15:11–12.

——. 1962. *Arba panim basifrut ha'ivrit bat yameinu* (Four aspects of contemporary Hebrew literature). Jerusalem: Schocken.

——. 1992. *Mul ha'ah hashotek* (Facing the silent brother). Tel Aviv: Open University.

Morris, Benny. 1987. *The Birth of the Palestinian Refugee Problem, 1947–1949.* Cambridge: Cambridge University Press.

——. 1996a. *Milhemot hagvul shel yisrael, 1949–1956* (Israel's border wars, 1949–1956). Tel Aviv: Am Oved.

——. 1996b. Ha'itonut hayisraelit beparashat Kibiyeh, October–November 1953 (The Kibiyeh affair in the Israeli press, October–November 1953). *Teoria uvikoret* 8.

Moses, Stephane. 1992. *System and Revelation.* Detroit: Wayne State University Press.

Mumford, Lewis. 1951. *The Conduct of Life.* New York: Harcourt Brace.

Nash, Stanley. 1980. Aliyot umordot batenua lema'an ha'ivriut" (Ups and downs in the Hebraist movement). In *Peles: Mehkarim bevikoret hasifrut ha'ivrit* (Balance: Studies in the criticism of Hebrew literature), ed. Nurit Guvrin. Tel-Aviv: Tel-Aviv University Press.

Nedava, Yosef, ed. 1981. *Ze'ev Jabotinsky: Ha'ish umishnato* (Ze'ev Jabotinsky: The man and his teachings). Tel Aviv: Israel Ministry of Defense.

Neher, André. 1977. *Uvekhol zot* (Nonetheless). Jerusalem: Reuven Mass.

——. 1987. Silence. In *Contemporary Jewish Religious Thought,* ed. Arthur A. Cohen and Paul Mendes-Flohr. New York: Free Press.

Neria, Moshe T. 1992. Hit'abdut anshei Metzada behalakha (The suicide of the people of Massada in Halakha). In *Tznif melukha* (The royal turban). Kfar Haro'e, Israel: Hai Ro'i.

——. 1974. Milhemet yerah ha'eitanim (The September war). *Morasha* 7.

Neumann, Micha. 1988. Hayahasim bein Karl Gustav Jung ve-Erich Neumann (The relations between Karl Gustav Jung and Erich Neumann). *Sihot* 3.

Neusner, Jacob. 1998. Is America the Promised Land for the Jews? In *Zionism: The Sequel,* ed. Carol Diament. New York: Hadassah.

Niebuhr, Reinhold. 1935. *An Interpretation of Christian Ethics.* New York: Harper.
——. 1968. *Faith and Politics.* New York: Braziller.
Nietzsche, Friedrich. 1949. *The Use and Abuse of History.* New York: Liberal Arts Press.
——. 1967, *The Genealogy of Morals,* trans. Walter Kaufmann. New York: Vintage.
——. 1971. *The Portable Nietzsche,* trans. Walter Kaufmann. London: Chatto and Windus.
——. 1997. *Daybreak: Thoughts on the Prejudices of Morality.* Cambridge: Cambridge University Press.
Nora, Pierre. 1983. Introduction: Between Memory and History. In *Realms of Memory,* trans. Arthur Goldhammer, vol. 1. New York: Columbia University Press.
Ofrat, Gid'on. 1980. *Adama, adam, dam* (Soil, man, blood). Tel Aviv: Tcherikover.
Oldenquist, A. 1982. Loyalties. *Journal of Philosophy* 79:4.
Oppenheim, Yisrael. 1982. *Tenuat hehalutz bepolin 1917–1929* (The pioneer movement in Poland, 1917–1929). Jerusalem: Magnes.
Oren, Yosef. 1981. *Shevavim* (Splinters). Tel Aviv: Yahdav.
——. 1983a. *Hitpak-hut basiporet hayisraelit* (Sobriety in Israeli literature). Rishon Letzion, Israel: Yahad.
——. 1983b. Hebet geneti al hamatzav hayisraeli (A genetic look at the Israeli condition). *Ha'aretz* literary supp., 25 Feb.
——. 1983c. Yumrat hamered keneged hagalut (The presumption of the revolt against exile). *Ha'aretz,* 4 Mar.
——. 1986. Preida midemut hatzabar (Taking leave of the Sabra image). *Ma'ariv* literary supp., 3 and 10 Oct.
Oz, Amos. 1975. *Devar hashavua,* 18 Apr.
——. 1981. The Way of the Wind. In *Where the Jackals Howl.* New York: Harcourt Brace Jovanovich.
——. 1982a. Eikh lahazor le'eretz yisrael: Rav siah (How to return to the Land of Israel: a roundtable discussion). *Proza* 51–53 (Feb.).
——. 1982b. *Menuha nekhona* (A perfect peace). Tel Aviv: Am Oved.
——. 1983a. *A Perfect Peace,* trans. Hillel Halkin. San Diego: Harcourt Brace Jovanovich.
——. 1983b. *In the Land of Israel.* San Diego: Harcourt Brace Jovanovich.
——. 1987. *Black Box,* trans. Nicholas de Lange. San Diego: Harcourt Brace Jovanovich.
——. 1990. Mumhe leromantika (Expert in romance). Interview with Amos Oz, by Ari Shavit. *Ha'aretz* magazine. 13 July.
——. 1991. *Fima.* San Diego: Harcourt Brace Jovanovich.
Oz Veshalom. 1978. *"Af sha'al": Mitzva min hatora?* ("Not one step further": A precept of the Torah?). Jerusalem: Oz Veshalom.
Pascal, Blaise. 1961. *The Pensées,* trans. J. M. Cohen. Baltimore: Penguin.
Peri, Yoram. 1995. Ha'omnam anu militaristim? (Are we really militarists?). *Ha'aretz,* 22 Nov.
——. 1996. Ha'omnam hahevra hayisraelit militaristit? (Is Israeli society really militaristic?). *Zmanim* 56 (summer).
Piekarz, Mendel. 1990. *Hasidut polin: Megamot ra'yoniot bein shtei hamilhamot uvige-*

zerot tash-tashah (Polish Hasidism: Intellectual tendencies between the two wars and during the Holocaust). Jerusalem: Mosad Bialik.

Piers, Gerhard, and Milton B. Singer. 1971. *Shame and Guilt: A Psychoanalytic and Cultural Study.* New York: Norton.

Plato. 1924. *The Dialogues of Plato,* trans. B. Jowett, 3d ed. London: Oxford University Press.

Popper, Karl. 1962. *The Open Society and Its Enemies.* London: Routledge.

Porat, Tzefira. 1976. Hagolem mitzion (The golem from Zion). *Molad* 7.

Porat, Yehoshua. 1989. *Shelah ve'et beyado* (Shelah, pen in hand). Tel Aviv: Mahbarot Lesifrut.

Radler-Feldman, Yehoshua, and Ya'akov Petrazil, eds. 1939. *Neged hateror* (Against terror). Jerusalem: n.p.

Rahel (Bloubstein). 1954. Kan al pnei ha'adama (Here on earth). In *Shirat rahel* (The poetry of Rahel). Tel Aviv: Davar.

Rahat, Moshe. 1988. Report. *Ma'ariv,* 4 Mar.

Ratosh, Yonathan. 1977. Shirei herev (Poems of the sword). Tel-Aviv: Hadar.

———. 1982. Reshit hayamim (The earliest days). Tel-Aviv: Hadar.

Ravitzky, Aviezer. 1985. *Hakahana'ut ketofa'a toda'atit ufolitit* (Cahanism as a cognitive and political phenomenon). Jerusalem: Sifriat Shazar.

———. 1989. *Judaic Sources of Human Rights.* Tel Aviv: Tel Aviv University Press.

———. 1996. *Messianism, Zionism and Jewish Religious Radicalism,* trans. Michael Swirsky and Jonathan Chipman. Chicago: University of Chicago Press.

Rawidowicz, Simon. 1945. Kiyum lelo tenai (Unconditional existence). *Metzuda* (London) 3–4.

———. 1948. Sof ve'ein sof (The end and the endless). *Metzuda* (London) 5.

———. 1974. Israel: The Ever-Dying People. In *Studies in Jewish Thought.* Philadelphia: Jewish Publication Society.

———. 1988. *Israel: The Ever-Dying People.* Philadelphia: Jewish Publication Society.

Re'uveni, Ya'akov. 1985. Re'alizm utevuna medinit: Behina mehudeshet shel vikuah yashan (Realism and political wisdom: A re-examination of an old argument). *Gesher* 112.

Rosen, Israel. 1988. Bein ya'akov le'esav. (Between Jacob and Esau). *Nekuda* 118 (Feb.).

Rosenberg, Shalom. 1983. Vehalakhta biderakhav (You shall walk in His ways). In *Pilosofia yisraelit* (Israeli philosophy), ed. Moshe Halamish. Tel Aviv: Papyrus.

Rosenzweig, Franz. 1935. *Briefe* (Letters). Berlin: Schocken.

———. 1965. *On Jewish Learning.* New York: Schocken.

———. 1972. *The Star of Redemption,* trans. William W. Hallo. Boston: Beacon Press.

———. 1987. *Mivhar igrot vekit'ei yoman* (Selected letters and diary entries), ed. R. Horwitz. Jerusalem: Mosad Bialik.

Rosner, Shlomo. 1986. Ke'ev rav (Great pain/the pain of a rabbi). *Emda* 8 (Tevet 5746 [Dec.]).

Ross, Ya'akov. 1962. Dat umusar: Leva'yat hanituk bein dat umusar (Religion and morality: On the problem of the separation of religion from morality). *De'ot* 19.

Rotenstreich, Nathan. 1963. *Otzma udemuta* (Power and its image). Jerusalem: Mosad Bialik.

——. 1965. On Shame. *Review of Metaphysics* 19.

——. 1966. *Bein am limedinato* (Between a people and its state). Tel Aviv: Hakibbutz Hame'uhad.

——. 1968. *Jewish Philosophy in Modern Times.* New York: Holt, Rinehart and Winston.

——. 1978. *Iyunim batzionut bazman haze* (Studies in Zionism today). Jerusalem: Zionist Library.

——. 1980. *Essays on Zionism and the Contemporary Jewish Condition.* New York: Herzl Press.

Rothenstein, Shmuel. 1948. *Toldot Rabbi Menahem Zemba* (A biography of Rabbi Menahem Zemba). Tel Aviv: Netzah.

Ruppin, Arthur. 1968. *Pirkei hayai* (Chapters of my life). Tel Aviv: Am Oved.

Sabine, George H. 1963. *A History of Political Theory.* London: Harrap.

Sadeh, Yitzhak. 1946. *Misaviv lamedura* (Around the campfire). Tel Aviv: Ahdut Ha'avoda.

Sagi, Avraham. 1996. Halakha, musar, aharayut, vetzionut datit (Halakha, morality, responsibility, and religious Zionism). *Gilion Ne'emanei Torah Va'avoda,* Nisan 5756 (Apr.).

——. 1997. Hatzionut hadatit bein petihut lisegirut (Religious Zionism between open- and close-mindedness). *Netivot Shalom,* Tishrei 5757 (Sept.).

Schatzberger, Hilda. 1985. *Meri umasoret* (Revolt and tradition). Ramat Gan: Bar-Ilan University Press.

Schimmel, Solomon. 1992. *The Seven Deadly Sins: Jewish, Christian and Classical Reflections on Human Nature.* New York: Free Press.

Schirman, Hayim. 1955. *Hashira ha'ivrit bisefarad uveprovans* (Hebrew poetry in Spain and Provence). Jerusalem: Mosad Bialik.

Schnitzer, Shmuel. 1986. Al tzionut vesikhletanut (On Zionism and rationality). In *Avnei yesod* (Foundation stones). Tel Aviv: Sifriat Ma'ariv.

Scholem, Gershom. 1971. *The Messianic Idea in Judaism.* New York: Schocken.

——. 1974. *Mehkarim umekorot letoldot hashabta'ut vegilguleha* (Studies and sources in the history of Sabbateanism in its various forms). Jerusalem: Mosad Bialik.

——. 1975. *Devarim bego* (For good reason), ed. Avraham Shapira. Tel Aviv: Am Oved.

——. 1976. *On Jews and Judaism in Crisis: Selected Essays,* ed. Werner J. Dannhauser. New York: Schocken.

——. 1989. *Od davar* (One more thing). Tel Aviv: Am Oved.

Schorsch, Ismar. 1977. *On the History of the Political Judgment of the Jew.* New York: Leo Baeck Institute.

Schwadron (Sharon), Avraham. 1930. Kimetukanim shebagoyim? (Like the most civilized of the gentiles?). *Moznayim,* 13 Nisan 5690 (Apr.).

Schwartz, Dov. 1996. *Emuna al parashat derakhim: Bein ra'yon lema'ase batzionut hadatit* (Faith at a crossroads: Between theory and practice in religious Zionism). Tel Aviv: Am Oved.

Schwartz, Yigal. 1995. Mi-"makom aher" le-"Dolly City" (From "Elsewhere" to "Dolly City"). *Ha'aretz,* 16 June.

Schwarzschild, Steven. 1970. On the Theology of Jewish Survival. In *Judaism and Ethics,* ed. Daniel Jeremy Silver. New York: Ktav.

——. 1990. *The Pursuit of the Ideal*, ed. M. Kellner. Albany: State University of New York Press.

Schweid, Eliezer. 1962. *Shalosh ashmorot* (Three watches). Tel Aviv: Am Oved.

——. 1970. *Hayahid: Olamo shel A. D. Gordon* (The individual: The world of A. D. Gordon). Tel Aviv: Am Oved.

——. 1976. *Emunat am yisrael vetarbuto* (The faith and culture of the Jewish people). Jerusalem: Zack.

——. 1979. Hayahas hadu-erki lera'yon am segula behagut zmanenu (Ambivalence toward the chosen-people idea in contemporary thought). *Moznayim* 48.

——. 1990. Dat umusar bemisgeret ha'aharayut hamamlakhtit shel am yisrael (Religion and morality in the framework of the sovereign responsibility of the Jewish people). In *Behevlei masoret utemura: Asufat ma'amarim lezikhro shel Arye Lang* (Tradition and change: Articles in memory of Arye Lang), ed. Menahem Kehana. Rehovot: Kivunim.

——. 1991. Medinat hatorah bemishnato shel Yitzhak Breuer (The Torah state in the thought of Isaac Breuer). In *Hashiva mihadash* (Rethinking). Jerusalem: Akademon.

——. 1994. The Existential and Moral Dilemma of Armed Resistance in the Ghetto: Shimshon Dranger's Realistic-Idealistic Thought. In *Wrestling Until Daybreak*. Jerusalem: Jerusalem Center for Public Affairs.

Segal, Dmitri. 1989. Hasifrut vehatarbut harusit vesugiat hivatzruta shel tenuat hashihrur heyehudit (Russian literature and culture and the issue of the emergence of the Jewish liberation movement). In *Hasifrut ha'ivrit utenuat ha'avoda* (Hebrew literature and the labor movement), ed. Pinhas Ginossar. Beersheba: Ben-Gurion University Press.

Segal, Yedidya. 1982. Akhen, lekhu lahalakha (Yes, refer to the Halakha). *Nekuda* 47 (Sept.).

Shabtai, Ya'akov. 1985. *Past Continuous*. New York: Schocken.

——. 1991. Hare'ayon ha'aharon (The last interview), *Yediot aharonot*, 2 Aug.

Shaked, Gershon. 1983. *Ein makom aher* (There is no other place). Tel Aviv: Hakibbutz Hame'uhad.

——. 1984. Za'akat hamahapekha (The cry of revolution). In *Hayim Hazaz: Ha'ish vitzirato* (Hayim Hazaz: The man and his work), ed. D. Laor. Jerusalem: Mosad Bialik.

——. 1988. *Hasiporet ha'ivrit 1880–1980* (Hebrew fiction, 1880–1980). Tel Aviv: Keter.

——. 1992a. Galut beli ge'ula, shoa beli tekuma (Exile without redemption, holocaust without rebirth). *Davar*, 29 Nov.

——. 1992b. Or vetzel, ahdut veribui (Light and shadow, unity and multiplicity). *Alpayim* 4.

——. 1993a. Bein hakotel limetzada (Between the Western Wall and Massada). *Yediot Aharonot*, 23 July.

——. 1993b. Bein sin'at liberalim le'ahavat eretz yisrael (Between the hatred of liberals and the love of the Land of Israel). *Yediot Aharonot*, 15 Jan.

Shalev, Mordekhai. 1992. Mi mefahed misimhat ani'im? (Who's afraid of the joy of the poor?). *Alpayim* 5.

Shamir, Ziva. 1988. Dor hama'avak le'atzma'ut umeshorerav (The generation of the struggle for independence and its poets). *Iton 77* 100 (May).

Shapira, Anita. 1981. Bein havlaga leteror: Hakinus hayishuvi be-ogust 1938 (Between restraint and terror: The all-Yishuv conference of August, 1938). *Hatzionut 6.*

———. 1988a. *Halikha al kav ha'ofek* (Walking along the horizon). Tel Aviv: Am Oved.

———. 1988b. Tzionut umeshihiut medinit (Zionism and political messianism). In *Temurot bahistoria hayehudit hahadasha: Kovetz lezikhro shel Shmuel Ettinger* (Change in modern Jewish history: An anthology in memory of Shmuel Ettinger), ed. Shmuel Almog et al. Jerusalem: Zalman Shazar Center.

———. 1992. *Herev hayona* (The sword of the dove). Tel Aviv: Am Oved.

Shapira, Avraham, ed. 1994. *Retzifut umered: Gershom Scholem be'omer uvesiah* (Continuity and rebellion: Gershom Scholem in speech and discussion). Tel Aviv: Am Oved.

Shapira, Yonatan. 1984. *Ilit lelo mamshikhim* (An elite without heirs). Tel Aviv: Sifriat Po'alim.

Sharon, Avraham. 1946. Vekhi kan betuhim anu? (And are we safe here?). *Davar* (2 Shvat 5706).

Shashar, Michael. 1990. Yamin usmol batzionut (Right and left in Zionism). Interview. *Kivunim,* n.s. 1.

Shavit, Uzi. 1996. *Ba'alot hashahar: Shirat hahaskala: Mifgash im hamoderniut* (At dawn: The poetry of the Haskala: Encounter with modernity). Tel Aviv: Hakibbutz Hame'uhad.

Shavit, Ya'akov, ed. 1978. The attitude of the Revisionist movement to the Arab national movement. *Forum* 30–31.

———. 1983. *Havlaga o teguva?* (Restraint or response?). Ramat Gan: Bar-Ilan University Press.

———. 1984. *Me'ivri ad kena'ani* (From Hebrew to Canaanite). Tel Aviv: Hadar.

Shazar (Rubashov), Zalman. 1971. *Orei dorot* (The lights of generations). Jerusalem: Mosad Bialik.

Sheleg, Yair. 1990. Hafundamentalizm lo ya'avor (Fundamentalism is not a passing thing). *Ha'aretz,* 7 Dec.

Shils, Edward. 1983. *Tradition.* Chicago: University of Chicago Press.

Shimoni (Shimonovitz), David. 1948. *Sefer ha'idiliot* (The book of idylls). Tel Aviv: Massada.

Shlonsky, Avraham. 1988. Lo tirtzah (Thou shalt not murder). In *Sifrut ve'ideologia bishnot hashloshim* (Literature and ideology in the 1930s), ed. Nurit Graetz. Tel Aviv: Open University.

Shoham, Uri. 1986. Oved etzot bein niputz elim levein kedusha hadasha (al M*ikan umikan* levrener) (Unable to decide between iconoclasm and a new holiness [on Brenner's *From here and there*]). In *Gibor dorenu ba'aretz* (The hero of our generation in the Land [of Israel]). Tel Aviv: Papyrus.

Shragai, Nadav. 1994. Report in *Ha'aretz,* 28 Oct.

———. 1995a. Report in *Ha'aretz,* 15 Mar.

———. 1995b. Report in *Ha'aretz,* 25 Mar.

Silberstein, Laurence. 1998. *The Post-Zionism Debate.* New York: Routledge.

Simon, Akiva Ernst. 1947. *Hamashber batzionut uvahinukh* (The crisis in Zionism and education). Tel Aviv: Bita'on.

———. 1966. The Jews as God's witnesses. *Judaism* 15.

———. 1982. *Ha'im od yehudim anahnu?* (Are we still Jews?). Tel Aviv: Sifriat Po'alim.

Simon, Uriel. 1977. Dat, musar, ufolitka (Religion, morality, and politics). *Bitefutzot Hagola* 81–82.

Sivan, Emanuel. 1995. Jihad: Mitos vehistoria (Jihad: Myth and history). *Alpayim* 11.

Soloveitchik, Hayim. 1994. Rupture and Reconstruction: The Transformation of Contemporary Orthodoxy. *Tradition* 28.

Soloveitchik, Yosef Dov. 1966. Kol dodi dofek (The sound of my beloved, knocking). In *Besod hayahid vehayahad* (Individual and communal discourse). Jerusalem: Orot.

Stanislawsky, Michael. 2001. *Zionism and the Fin du Siècle: Cosmopolitanism and Nationalism from Nordau to Jabotinsky*. Berkeley: University of California Press.

Statman, Daniel. 1991. *Dilemot musariot* (Moral dilemmas). Jerusalem: Magnes.

Statman, Daniel, and Avraham Sagi. 1993. *Dat umusar* (Religion and morality). Jerusalem: Mosad Bialik.

Steiner, George. 1967. A Kind of Survivor. In *Language and Silence*. New York: Atheneum.

———. 1969. From Without. *Congress Bi-Weekly*, 24 Feb.

———. 1970. The Unique and the Universal. *Commentary* 49:2 (May).

———. 1985. Our Homeland: The Text. *Salmagundi* 66.

Strauss, Leo. 1989. *The Rebirth of Classical Political Rationalism*. Chicago: University of Chicago Press.

Susser, Bernard. 1981. *Existence and Utopia*. Rutherford, N.J.: Fairleigh Dickinson University Press.

Syrkin, Nahman. 1921. Klaya (Annihilation). *Kuntres* 4, Aug.

Tabenkin, Yitzhak. 1942. Beit hasefer vehamilhama (The school and the war). *Mibifnim*, Nov.

———. 1967–85. *Devarim* (Talks). 7 vols. Tel Aviv: Hakibbutz Hame'uhad.

Tal, Uriel. 1977. The Land and the State of Israel in Israeli Religious Life. *Proceedings of the Rabbinical Assembly*.

———. 1984. Totalitarian Democratic Hermeneutics and Politics in Modern Jewish Religious Nationalism. In *Totalitarian Democracy and After: An International Colloquium in Memory of Jacob Talmon*, editor not stated. Jerusalem: Magnes.

———. 1987. *Mitos utevuna beyahadut yameinu* (Myth and reason in contemporary Judaism). Tel Aviv: Sifriat Poalim.

Talmon, J. L. 1968. *Israel among the Nations*. New York: College of the City of New York.

———. 1976. Reflections of an Historian in Jerusalem. *Encounter* (May).

———. 1977. Be'idan ha'alimut (In the age of violence). Tel Aviv: Am Oved.

Tamares, Aharon Shmuel. 1911. *Sefer ha'emuna hatehora vehadat hahamonit* (The book of pure faith and popular religion). Odessa: Halperin.

———. 1912. *Musar hatora vehayahadut* (The morality of the Torah and Judaism). Vilna: Garber.

———. 1913. Lishe'elot hayahadut (On questions of Judaism). In *He'atid* (Journal). Berlin.

———. 1920. *Kneset yisrael umilhemot hagoyim* (The assembly of Israel and the wars of the gentiles). Warsaw: Hamol , 1920.

——. 1922. Al hatehiyot: Hazut kasha (Concerning revivals: A bleak prospect). *She'ar yashuv* 3–4, ed. H. Y. Bonin, Lodz.

——. 1922–23. Hishtahrerut hamahshava ha'ivrit (The liberation of Hebrew thought), *Kolot* 6–8, ed. Y. E. Steinman, Warsaw.

——. 1923. "Kuntres ma'alot hatora" (A tract on the virtues of the Torah). Introduction to *Yad Aharon* (The hand of Aaron). Piotrkov.

Tamir, Yael. 1992. *Liberal Nationalism.* Princeton: Princeton University Press.

Tammuz, Benjamin. 1973. Second Encounter with the Angel. *Jewish Quarterly* 21:1–2.

——. 1978a. Demamat hakinor magia el kitza (The silence of the violin comes to an end). *Ha'aretz* Sabbath supp., 14 Apr.

——. 1978b. *Requiem lena'aman* (Requiem for Na'aman). Tel Aviv: Zmora-Bitan.

Taylor, Charles. 1979. *Hegel and Modern Society.* Cambridge: Cambridge University Press.

Teveth, Shabtai. 1985. *Ben-Gurion va'arviei yisrael* (Ben-Gurion and the Israeli Arabs). Jerusalem and Tel Aviv: Schocken.

——. 1994. Pe'ulat kibiyeh (The Kibiyeh operation). *Ha'aretz,* 16 Sept.

Tillich, Paul. 1966. Critique and Justification of Utopia. In *Utopias and Utopian Thought,* ed. Frank E. Manuel. Boston: Houghton Mifflin.

Tocqueville, Alexis de. 1988. *Democracy in America.* New York: Harper and Row.

Torberg, Friedrich. 1962. *Hier bin Ich, mein Vater.* Munich: Langen and Miller.

Tuchman, Barbara. 1982. Israel's Sword. In *Practicing History.* New York: Ballantine.

Twersky, Isadore. 1980. Survival, Normalcy, Modernity. In *Zionism in Transition,* ed. Moshe Davis. New York: Herzl Press.

Urbach, Ephraim. 1985. Shilton hatora o derekh hatora? (The rule of Torah or the way of Tora?). In *Al tzionut veyahadut* (On Zionism and Judaism). Jerusalem: Zionist Library.

Vitkin, Yosef. 1961. *Ketavim* (Writings). Tel Aviv: Am Oved.

Waldman, Eliezer. 1982. Oz ligmor et hamelakha (The strength to finish the job). *Nekuda* 46 (Aug.).

——. 1983a. Interview. *Artzi* 3.

——. 1983b. Hama'avak al hashalom (The struggle for peace). *Artzi* 3.

Walzer, Michael. 1977. *Just and Unjust Wars.* New York: Basic Books.

——. 1983. *Spheres of Justice.* Oxford: Robertson.

——. 1987. *Interpretation and Social Criticism.* Cambridge: Harvard University Press.

——. 1989. What Kind of State Is a Jewish State? *Tikkun,* July–Aug.

——. 2000. *The Jewish Political Tradition,* ed. Michael Walzer et al. New Haven: Yale University Press.

Weber, Max. 1991. *From Max Weber.* London: Routledge.

Weiner, Eugene E. 1984. The Death Taint and Uncommon Vitality: The Case of the Ever-Dying Jewish People. In *Voices from Israel,* ed. E. Levine. New York: Herzl Press.

Weinfeld, Moshe. 1964. "Am kadosh" ve-"goi kadosh": Ye'ud ruhani le'umat ye'ud medini ("Holy people" and "holy nation": Cultural versus political destiny). *Molad* 21.

Weitz, Yehiam. 1986. Efo hayinu uma asinu? (Where have we been and what have we done?). *Politika* 8.

——. 1988. Hebetim beyahas hayishuv el sho'at yehudei eropa, 1941–1943 (Aspects of the attitude of the Yishuv to the Holocaust of European Jewry, 1941–1943). In

Nekudot tatzpit: Tarbut vehevra be'eretz yisrael (Vantage points: Culture and society in the Land of Israel), ed. Nurit Graetz. Tel Aviv: Ha'universita Hapetuha.

Weltsch, Felix. 1950. *Teva, musar, umediniut* (Nature, morality, and policy). Jerusalem: Mosad Bialik.

Werblowsky, R. Zwi. 1964. Faith, hope, and trust: A study in the concept of *bitahon*. *Papers of the Institute of Jewish Studies*. Jerusalem: Magnes.

White, Hayden. 1982. The Politics of Historical Interpretation: Discipline and Desublimation. *Critical Inquiry* 9.

Whitfield, Stephen J. 1986. The End of Jewish History. In *Religion, Ideology, and Nationalism in Europe and America*, ed. H. Ben Israel et al. Jerusalem: Historical Society of Israel and Zalman Shazar Center.

Wiener, Philip P., ed. 1973. *A Dictionary of the History of Ideas*. New York: Scribner's.

Wieseltier, Leon. 1988. Palestinian Perversion of the Holocaust. *New York Times*, 12 June.

Williams, Bernard. 1973. A Critique of Utilitarianism. In *Utilitarianism: For and Against*, ed. J. J. C. Smart and Bernard Williams. Cambridge: Cambridge University Press.

———. 1993. *Shame and Necessity*. Berkeley: University of California Press.

Wurzburger, Walter S. 1977–78. Darkhei shalom (in English). *Gesher (Annual of the students organization in Yeshiva University, New York)* 6.

Wyschograd, Edith. 1994. The Mind of a Critical Moralist: Steiner as a Jew. In *Reading George Steiner*, ed. N. A. Scott and R. A. Sharp. Baltimore: Johns Hopkins University Press.

Wyschograd, Michael. 1971. Faith and the Holocaust. *Judaism* 20.

———. 1977. Auschwitz: Beginning of a New Era. *Tradition* (fall).

Yaron (Singer), Tzvi. 1973. Dat umusar beyisrael uvatefutzot (Religion and morality in Israel and the Diaspora). *Bitefutzot hagola* 64.

Yashar, (Penname) 1976. Ahiv ani berama'ut" (I am his brother in deception). *Morasha* 11 (summer),

Yeivin, Yehoshua Heschel. 1938. *Uri Tzvi Greenberg: Meshorer umehokek* (Uri Tzvi Greenberg: Poet and lawgiver). Jerusalem: Sadan.

———. 1951. Mamashuto shel habilti-mamashi ke'ekron-yesod shel tenuat hashihrur hayisraeli (The reality of the unreal as a basic principle of the Israeli liberation movement). *Sulam* (June).

———. 1975. Hazikaron vehakosef beshirat Uri Tzvi Greenberg (Memory and longing in the poetry of Uri Tzvi Greenberg). In *Uri Tzvi Greenberg: Mivhar ma'amarei bikoret al yetzirato* (Uri Tzvi Greenberg: Selected criticism of his work), ed. Yehuda Friedlander. Tel Aviv: Am Oved.

Yisrael veyishma'el: Hayelkhu yahdav? (Israel and Ishmael: Shall they walk together?). 1986. Symposium. *Tehumin* 7.

Yisraeli, Sha'ul. 1953–54. Pe'ulat Kibiyeh le'or hahalakha (The Kibiyeh operation in the light of Halakha). *Hatorah vehamedina* 6.

———. 1991. Pe'ulot tagmul le'or hahalakha (Retaliation in the light of Halakha). In *Betzomet hatora vehamedina* (At the crossroads of Torah and state), ed. Yehuda Shaviv. Jerusalem: Makhon Tzomet. (Republication of Yisraeli 1953–54 in expanded form).

Yovel, Yirmiahu, and Paul Mendes-Flohr, eds. 1984. *Bein iyun lema'ase: Mehkarim likhvod Nathan Rotenstreich bimlot lo shiv'im shana* (Between theory and practice: Studies in honor of Nathan Rotenstreich on his seventieth birthday). Jerusalem: Magnes.

Zeitlin, Hillel. 1906. Kinyenei haruah: Mahshavot shelo be'itan (Acquisitions of the spirit: Untimely thoughts). *Hazman* 45.

———. 1920. A bikhl vegn yidisher kultur (A booklet about Jewish culture). *Der moment* 182.

———. 1930. *Vos ikh hob yetst tsu zogn dem yidishn folk* (What I now have to tell the Jewish people). Warsaw: Atzma'ut.

———. 1979. Lahalutz lemor (Speaking to the pioneer). In *Sifran shel yehidim* (The book of a few). Jerusalem: Mosad Harav Kook.

———. 1983. *Alef-beit shel yahadut* (An alphabet of Judaism). Jerusalem: Mosad Harav Kook.

Zevin, Shlomo. 1979. Le'or hahalakha (In light of the Halakha). Jerusalem: Beit Hillel.

Zerubavel, Ya'akov. 1966. *Bimei milhama umahapekha* (In times of war and revolution). Tel Aviv: Y. L. Peretz.

Zerubavel, Yael. 1991. Mot hazikaron vezikhron hamavet: Metzada vehashoa kemetaforot historiot (The death of memory and the memory of death: Massada and the Holocaust as historical metaphors). *Alpayim* 10.

Zion, Noam. 1999. *Hakana'i: Gibor le'umi o okher yisrael?* (The zealot: National hero or subversive?). Jerusalem: Shalom Hartman Institute.

Zohar, Noam. 1996. Halakha, politika, vehidush hatora (Halakha, politics, and the renewal of the Torah). *Gilyon Ne'emanei Tora Va'avoda,* Nisan 5756 (Apr.).

Zweig, Ferdynand. 1969. *Israel: The Sword and the Harp.* London: Heinemann.

Zweig, Stefan. 1922. *Jeremiah,* trans. Eden and Cedar Paul. New York: Seltzer.

Index